DEVELOPMENT AND SECURITY
IN SOUTHEAST ASIA

The International Political Economy of New Regionalisms Series

The *International Political Economy of New Regionalisms Series* presents innovative analyses of a range of novel regional relations and institutions. Going beyond established, formal interstate economic organizations, this essential series provides informed interdisciplinary and international research and debate about myriad heterogeneous intermediate level interactions.

Reflective of its cosmopolitan and creative orientation, this series is developed by an international editorial team of established and emerging scholars in both the South and North. It reinforces ongoing networks of analysts in both academia and think-tanks as well as international agencies concerned with micro-, meso- and macro-level regionalisms.

Development and Security in Southeast Asia

Volume I: The Environment

Edited by

DAVID B. DEWITT
York University, Canada
CAROLINA G. HERNANDEZ
University of the Philippines, Philippines

ASHGATE

Published by
Ashgate Publishing Limited
Gower House
Croft Road
Aldershot
Hants GU11 3HR
England

Ashgate Publishing Company
Suite 420
101 Cherry Street
Burlington, VT 05401-4405
USA

Ashgate website: http://www.ashgate.com

British Library Cataloguing in Publication Data
Development and security in Southeast Asia : the
    environment. - (The international political economy of new
    regionalisms)
    1. Security, International 2. Asia, Southeastern - Economic
    conditions 3. Asia, Southeastern - Economic policy
    I. Dewitt, David B. (David Brian), 1948- II. Hernandez,
    Carolina G
    338.9'59

Library of Congress Control Number: 2001091161

ISBN 0 7546 1767 X

Printed and bound in Great Britain by Antony Rowe Ltd.,
Chippenham, Wiltshire

Contents

VOLUME II: THE PEOPLE

PART I: INTRODUCTION

PART II: CASE STUDIES

VOLUME III: GLOBALIZATION

PART I: INTRODUCTION

PART II: REGIONAL CASE STUDIES

List of Figures

List of Tables

List of Contributors

EDITORS

David B. Dewitt is Professor of Political Science and since 1988, Director of the Centre for International and Security Studies, York University, Toronto.

Carolina G. Hernandez is President, Institute for Strategic and Development Studies, Inc. (ISDS) and Professor, Department of Political Science, University of the Philippines, Diliman, Quezon City.

AUTHORS

Wiku Adisasmito is Senior Vice President at the Agency Planning and Secretariat Division, Indonesian Bank Restructuring Agency and Faculty Member at the Health Policy and Administration Department of Faculty of Public Health, University of Indonesia.

Pia C. Bennagen is Lecturer at the Department of Political Science, University of the Philippines and Executive Director, Pulse Asia, Inc.

Jennifer Clapp is Associate Professor in the International Development and Environmental and Resource Studies Programs at Trent University, Canada.

Eliseo M. Cubol is Research Fellow, Institute for Strategic and Development Studies, Inc. (ISDS), and Ph.D. student in Public and Urban Policy, New School University, New York City.

Peter Dauvergne is Senior Lecturer at the University of Sydney and is the founding and current editor of the journal *Global Environmental Politics*, published by the MIT Press.

Francisco Magno is Associate Professor of Political Science and Director of the Social Development Research Center at De La Salle University, Manila.

Agus P. Sari is President Director of *Pelangi*, an Indonesian environmental think tank and concurrently a member of the Indonesian Interdepartmental National Local Environmental Initiatives, the Scientific Steering Committee of the Institutional Dimension of Global Environmental Change (IDGEC), and Steering Committee member of the Clean Air Initiative of the World Bank, the Asian Development Bank, and others.

Mary Young is a graduate student affiliate with the York University-University of Toronto Joint Center for Asian Pacific Studies (JCAPS) and a Ph.D. student in the Department of Political Science, York University.

Acknowledgements

It is a pleasure to acknowledge the institutions that provided the support so essential to undertaking a somewhat unusual multifaceted research program. The Canadian International Development Agency (CIDA) reached beyond its traditional focus when it agreed to explore in what ways the expanded discourse on security in the post-cold war world might be relevant to their primary mandate of development. In cooperation with the Ottawa-based International Development Research Centre (IDRC), funding was received to bring together experts from throughout Southeast Asia (SEA) and from Canada to undertake some exploratory work. We are most thankful to Ann Bernard, then of IDRC, and Norm Macdonnell of CIDA, who shepherded us through the early stages and provided guidance and advice along the way.

CIDA generously agreed to fund the program, and we are grateful to the Asia Branch and to Jean-Marc Metevier, then Vice-President Asia and to Susan Davies, then Regional Director, for their support. Brian Hunter, Senior Economist did much more than serve as our principal contact and project manager. He offered sustained intellectual support, took an individual interest in each and every researcher, and never failed to challenge and to provoke. Indeed, had either of us encountered economists like Brian when we were students it is quite likely that we would now be in his, rather than our profession.

The Canadian embassies in Manila and in Jakarta provided in-country support throughout the program. We are particularly thankful to Ambassador Stephen Heeney and Mr Stewart Henderson, both in Manila during the start and early part of the Development and Security in Southeast Asia (DSSEA) Program, and to Ambassador Gary Smith, then in Jakarta, for their assistance. We would be remiss if we did not acknowledge the intellectual encouragement offered by General Jose T. Almonte, ret., then National Security Adviser to Philippine President Fidel V. Ramos, who insisted that we were exploring questions that to him, were fundamental to a better understanding of the challenges facing the nations of SEA. Since leaving government many of his public statements continue to reflect his unique sense of obligation to humanist values, the obligation of government to its people, and the necessity for the peoples of SEA to forge a new consensus in its common fight against poverty and injustice.

Three research centers carried the bulk of the administrative and organizational responsibilities for the DSSEA program. Our colleagues at the Centre for International and Strategic Studies (CSIS) in Jakarta, especially Hadi Soesastro and Clara Joewono who managed all the field research, conferences, and echo seminars which took place in Indonesia. Hadi served both as the Chair of the Task Force on Globalization for the DSSEA program and as the Indonesia country coordinator. A man of remarkable intellect and kindness, it is always a pleasure and honor to work with him. Clara provides all of us with a model of humility, modesty, and graciousness even in the face of extremely trying and, at times, dangerous circumstances. She is a remarkable stabilizing force, and has an exceptional knowledge of the politics of Indonesia and, more generally, SEA. It is a pleasure to acknowledge, with thanks, our good friend and colleague, Jusuf Wanandi, who ensured that CSIS Jakarta was always available to assist us throughout the life of the program.

The Institute of Strategic and Development Studies, Inc. (ISDS), Manila, served not only as the coordinating center for all the Philippine-based DSSEA activities, but also took on the primary responsibility for the *DSSEA Update*, a publication which emerged as an unanticipated major aspect of our program. It is a pleasure to acknowledge the devotion and extraordinary efforts that Crisline Torres, Josefina Manuel, Maria Ela Atienza, and Rowena Layador have brought to this program. Their unflagging support and commitment made the complications and challenges of running a multiyear, international program manageable, even during the most trying political circumstances. We also wish to note the important help received in the final stages of preparing the manuscript for publication: Myla Tugade who did the layout, Dona Dolina who assisted with transforming the materials into the Ashgate format, and Amado Mendoza, Jr. and Ruth Lusterio-Rico who assisted the final editing of the second and third volumes, respectively.

The Centre for International and Security Studies (CISS), York University (Toronto) assumed the lead role in handling all the administrative and financial details of the program, from negotiating the contracts first with CIDA and IDRC and then with each of the researchers, through to providing the accounting and preparing the annual reports. Heather Chestnutt and Joan Broussard not only managed all these technical details with their characteristic combination of efficiency, effectiveness, and accuracy, but also monitored the quality of the DSSEA activities, provided advice to the program co-directors, and often served as the first lifeline to the researchers as they each faced what often would seem as unique challenges in undertaking field work. Without fail Joan and Heather would solve whatever problems occurred and thereby ensured that each scholar was able to pursue his or her research unencumbered by administrative or other problems. Their skills and knowledge make directing this complex research and outreach program much easier and more pleasant than it otherwise would have been.

Our final thanks must go to those colleagues who provided the intellectual guidance and strength of this program. Paul Evans, now of the University of British Columbia, but formerly a colleague at York University, was a principal motivator behind launching this effort, and together with us and Amitav Acharya engaged CIDA and the IDRC in the initial ideas of linking development with security. Tim Shaw of Dalhousie University not only was a participant in the pilot study, but also convinced us that we should transform a difficult and eclectic set of research papers into a somewhat more coherent book project. We thank him for his unfailing encouragement and his personal commitment to these volumes. And of course, the last word goes to our colleagues, those whose chapters you are about to read and to those many scholars, policy makers, and members of non-government organizations who joined us in this endeavor. The authors of the following chapters are a remarkable group of scholars, some senior and with deserved international reputations, others just starting off on what we are certain will be important careers. This was an unusual program that each of them agreed to join, and we are thankful and appreciative of their contributions. We also must point out the special roles played by Jennifer Clapp, Peter Dauvergne, Hadi Soesastro, and Jorge V. Tigno, each of whom served as principal guide to their colleagues on their respective task forces. Without their participation, our task as co-directors would have been much more difficult and far less pleasant. We thank them.

David B. Dewitt and Carolina G. Hernandez
Toronto and Manila

List of Abbreviations

ADB	Asian Development Bank
AFTA	ASEAN Free Trade Area
APEC	Asia Pacific Economic Cooperation
ASEAN	Association of Southeast Asian Nations
BAN	Basel Action Network
BAPEDAL	Environmental Impact Management Agency – Indonesia
BAPPENAS	National Development Planning Agency – Indonesia
BIMAS	Indonesian National Rice Intensification Program
BMC	Benguet Mining Corporation
BOD	Biological Oxygen Demand
BOT	Build-Operate-Transfer
BPS	Badan Pusat Statistik or Indonesian Central Bureau of Statistics
BULOG	Indonesian Food Logistics Agency
CADC	Certificate of Ancestral Domain Claim
CEPA	Consolidated Electric Power Asia
DECS	Department of Education, Culture and Sports
DENR	Department of Environment and Natural Resources – Philippines
DILG	Department of Interior and Local Government
DND	Department of National Defense
DoE	Department of Energy
DOH	Department of Health
DOTC	Department of Transportation and Communications
DTI	Department of Trade and Industry
ECC	Environmental Clearance Certificate
EIA	Environmental Impact Assessment
EMB	Environmental Management Bureau
EP	Exploration Permit
ESCAP	Economic and Social Commission for Asia and the Pacific
EU	European Union
FAO	Food and Agriculture Organization
FCCC	Framework Convention on Climate Change
FDI	Foreign Direct Investment
FTAA	Financial or Technical Assistance Agreement
GATT	General Agreement on Tariffs and Trade
GI	Government of Indonesia
G-77	Group of 77
HYVs	High-yielding Varieties
IPCC	Intergovernmental Panel on Climate Change
IPM	Integrated Pest Management

IRR	Implementing Rules and Regulations
IRRI	International Rice Research Institute
ISI	Import-Substitution Industrialization
ITPC	Indonesian Trade Promotion Center
KLH	Ministry of Population and Environment – Indonesia
LGU	Local Government Unit
MGB	Mines and Geo-sciences Bureau
MNC	Multinational Corporation
MOA	Memorandum of Agreement
MPSA	Mineral Production Sharing Agreement
NAPOCOR	National Power Corporation – Philippines
NEDA	National Economic and Development Authority
NGOs	Non-Governmental Organizations
NIE	Newly Industrialized Economy
NIPAS	National Integrated Protected Areas System
NWLGQ	Northwestern Luzon Growth Quadrangle
OECD	Organization for Economic Cooperation and Development
PAN	Pesticides Action Network
PEC	Pangasinan Electric Corporation
PMRB	Provincial Mining Regulatory Board
PNP	Philippine National Police
PROKASIH	Proyek Kali Bersih
PROPER	Program for Pollution Control, Evaluation, and Rating
PRRP	Pasig River Rehabilitation Program
SCFTPP	Sual Coal-Fired Thermal Power Plant
SEA	Southeast Asia
SME	Small- and Medium-sized Enterprises
STE	State Trading Enterprises
TVI	Toronto Ventures Pacific, Inc.
UK	United Kingdom
UN	United Nations
UNCTC	United Nations Centre for Transnational Corporations
UNEP	United Nations Environment Programme
UNESCAP	United Nations Economic and Social Commission for Asia and the Pacific
US	United States
USAID	United States Agency for International Development
WALHI	Wahana Lingkungan Hidup Indonesia
WB	World Bank
WMC	Western Mining Corporation
WMO	World Meteorological Organization
WTO	World Trade Organization

Map Showing Location
of Study Area

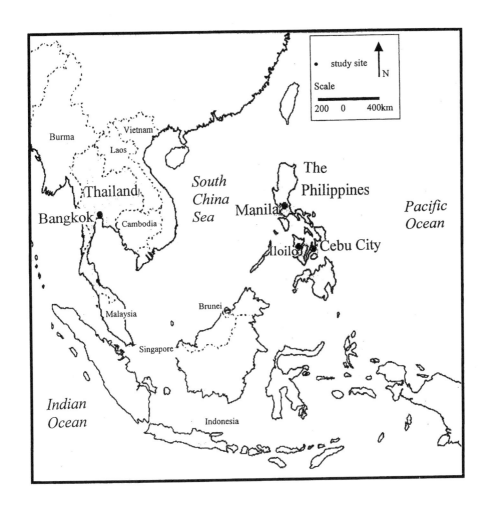

PART I
INTRODUCTION

Chapter 1

Defining the Problem and Managing the Uncertainty

David B. Dewitt and Carolina G. Hernandez

Introduction

Development and Security in Southeast Asia (DSSEA) has as its core the question of the relationship between government and civil society in their efforts to define and to pursue security, broadly defined. Thus, the DSSEA research program at the outset posits a tension between how government and its instruments understand and pursue security and how people and the communities that they comprise understand and seek their own particular security interests. It is based on the premise that the process of development is, essentially, a partnership between official agencies, the private sector, and people, and that the issue of security is found across levels of social, economic, and political organization and is intimately entwined with the challenges posed by the dynamics of (mis)managing development. Moreover, our approach to development and security explicitly acknowledges the potential importance of the tensions between local and external factors across levels of authority, production, and distribution.

Governance, whether in terms of an explicit 'social contract' or implicitly as the control, management, and allocation of public resources (including goods and services) and, in some cases, intruding into and distorting the relationship between the public and the private, is at the heart of the overarching challenges linking development with security in SEA. A subset of this focus is the underlying realization of the importance of human resource development. Consequently, the concept of social capital runs throughout all the specific projects pursued within this research program and reported in these three volumes.

The DSSEA program is concerned with the attainment of three goals: (1) identifying and understanding the linkages between security and development through conducting case studies across levels of state-society relations, as well as comparatively within the region; (2) developing enhanced theoretical and conceptual understanding of these complex linkages both to further our knowledge and to improve our abilities to develop practical instruments in support of improved human well being; and (3) using the acquired knowledge and information for empowerment and change. This volume, along with the accompanying other two, reports the results of empirical research conducted primarily in Indonesia and the Philippines by scholars from these two countries and Canada.

The three volumes represent research organized around the complementary themes of environment and resources, globalization, and people and communities, with each connected through the common concern on the linkages between the dynamics of development and the challenges to security.[1] The approach is based on two underlying assumptions: (1) that the model of development on which the rapid economic expansion of SEA has been articulated is not sustainable because it involves dynamics of social and political inequality bound to cause its demise over the long term; and (2) that the language of security provides the best vocabulary through which these problems can be delineated, debated, and resolved. Supporting these two assumptions are the ideas of human security and social capital, the former, while acknowledging the primacy of the state, focuses on the well being of the individual and her community, and the latter referring to the extent to which community-based organizations and civil society more generally are engaged participants in forms of local and national political and economic decision-making.[2]

Defining the Problem

In the post-cold war era, the concepts of both development and security have been transformed to meet new strategic realities. Development has long been recognized as a non-linear process often accompanied by unintended consequences; it also is no longer presumed to be either benign or necessarily a public good. On the other hand, development is increasingly argued to be inherently linked with freedom, as 'a process of expanding the real freedoms that people [ought to] enjoy'.[3] Within this broader understanding, the economic, social, and political are entwined into a composite which provides the foundation for such personal and community freedom and, hence, also enhanced security.

Security no longer is defined simply as defense of one's national territory by armed forces against military threat. Neither threat nor risk to the state or its people come only from military forces or groups prepared to engage in violence but also from many other factors which cross boundaries, penetrate society, and challenge the capacity of the state to regulate entry and exit. Further, security is more than protecting the state or even the governing regime as important as both of those may be. Today, security also is viewed as a descriptor of community and individual life; that the authorities have a responsibility to ensure personal safety and well being, just as the integrity of communities and their sense of their own future needs confirmation. The question of agency – the instruments responsible for the security of people and institutions – therefore, likely involves more than only the military and the police, and as such also becomes entwined with the concerns about the agents for development.[4]

Neither development nor security as policies can be achieved through unilateral means. Both are dependent on a mix of short-, medium-, and long-term factors located in the interstices between the individual, the society, the state, and the inter-state systems. Yet relatively little is understood about the linkages, never mind casual relations, which bind these two core components of national expression. The DSSEA program addresses aspects of these linkages. Most concretely, our interest is to locate the strong and weak links between some of the complex dynamics of development and the challenges of security. We situate this effort initially within the paradigm of the nation-state, but explicitly acknowledge that many non-state and sub-state actors, as well as the attendant social forces, may turn out to be the defining variables in this exercise. Indeed, as it turns out almost all of the case studies in this project explore the linkages between government, the private sector, and civil society.

Non-military threats to security seem to be crowding the policy agenda of nations throughout the world. Particularly after the attacks against the United States on 11 September 2001, the rise of terrorism, whether domestic or international, has hugged the headlines of national and international media and assumed the status of a major security concern in countries the world over. The alarming global spread of the devastating disease acquired immunodeficiency syndrome (AIDS) threatens the security of individuals as well as entire nations. The rate of ecological damage rapid economic development creates is wreaking havoc of immense proportions with devastating consequences for our collective futures whether in terms of biodiversity or simply making less land either habitable or productive. Non-renewable resources have been exploited to the point of making them a focal point of international competition and even war, while individuals and their communities become increasingly vulnerable and insecure to the globalized forces of extraction, production, and distribution. Access to and management of 'strategic resources' including water continues to command bilateral and multilateral attention. Disputes over fish stocks have brought allies and partners to the point of diplomatic brinkmanship, while communities at home suffer from resulting massive unemployment and its consequent social dislocation.

Markedly different from the Western concept of security based essentially and primarily on the state's military and defense capability, East Asian concepts view security in a comprehensive, multidimensional, and holistic manner. The five non-communist states of Indonesia, Malaysia, the Philippines, Singapore, and Thailand which together formed the original core of the Association of Southeast Asian Nations (ASEAN), have viewed security in these terms since the Association's founding in August 1967.[5] Believing that a nation's security begins from within, Indonesia stressed the primacy of domestic security by solving internal sources of security threats such as communist insurgency, ethnic tensions, economic malaise, and social divisions within its far-flung archipelago, creating in the process a condition of national resilience.[6] According to the Indonesian view, one subsequently and implicitly supported by the rest in ASEAN, when all the states in the region achieve national resilience, there would be no security problems they could export to their neighbors. The result would be a community of confident and secure nation-states, resilient to extra-regional threats, and hence, better able to promote and to sustain regional stability and security.[7]

The Malaysian concept of comprehensive security emphasized non-military sources of security threats. It was seen as 'inseparable from political stability, economic success, and social harmony'.[8] As with national resilience, security threats were seen as originating primarily from within the state. This conception was in large measure due to the presence of domestic insurgencies and the problems engendered by the task of nation building in multiethnic societies with great disparities in wealth and income among their constituent ethnic communities. While the inter-ethnic violence of 30 years ago has not reappeared, the 1997 Asian financial crisis and the controversy surrounding Prime Minister Mahathir Mohamed's continuing efforts to retain political dominance have introduced a level of domestic tension and unease not witnessed for a number of decades. The vulnerability of developing states and their governments to the fortunes of 'performance legitimacy' can be seen throughout the region, though Malaysia, as well as Thailand and Singapore, has been sufficiently resilient to withstand the havoc experienced in Indonesia.

Singapore developed a similar notion of security. Viewed in terms of 'total defense', it is also multidimensional, holistic, comprehensive, and begins from within. The Philippines and Thailand also adopted similar conceptions of security making for an ASEAN-wide acceptance of comprehensive security in SEA by the 1980s, though this is now under severe strain since the expansion to the ASEAN-10 coming almost simultaneously with the shock of the 1997-98 Asian financial meltdown.

While security in the cold war era focused an external threats to states and relied primarily on military means, including the establishment of a network of bilateral and multilateral military alliances focused on nuclear deterrence, a new concept of security mechanism launched by former Canadian Secretary of State for External Affairs, Joe Clark, emphasized an evolving inclusive regionalism and multilateralism as a complement to bilateralism, mutual reassurance instead of nuclear deterrence, and the use of both military and non-military means to promote security in recognition of the multifaceted nature of threats to security. Cooperative security as the notion came to be known, is a complementary mechanism to comprehensive security in dealing with a post-cold war environment increasingly challenged by non-military threats to the security of individuals, communities, societies, and nation-states as well as the international system.[9]

This Canadian contribution has been complemented by the more recent articulation of human security. Initially given wide attention as a result of the United Nations Development Programme (UNDP) *Report on Human Development*,[10] it was adapted by then Canadian Foreign Minister Lloyd Axworthy to frame Canada's articulation of how, when, where, and why Canada and like-minded countries should be prepared to intervene to protect and make safe individuals and communities from the ravages of war, whether domestic or international, the threats to their safety and well being from systemic challenges, as well as to enhance their security in the face of man-made or natural calamities. In Axworthy's language, 'human security entails taking preventive measures to reduce vulnerability and minimize risk, and taking remedial action where prevention fails'.[11] One of the critical aspects of this approach is the acknowledgement that security not only is multifaceted but that it is both a process and an objective which calls on responsible actions by both governments and others. In this construction, security is no longer a state-centric phenomenon; nor can it be achieved merely by employing the traditional instruments of the state. Indeed, in many situations it is its very reliance on the state and its dominance in defining the meaning of security that renders people, communities, and other states insecure.[12]

Most of the regimes in Southeast Asia (SEA) are – or were until recently – authoritarian; their legitimacy has been sustained either by force or by remarkable levels of economic development. Failure, as dramatically witnessed by the 1997 financial crisis and the ensuing upheaval in Indonesia, severe economic downturn in Thailand and South Korea along with the tensions experienced by Malaysia and the Philippines, has eroded support, even among elites, and challenged the foundations of some governing regimes. The stark alteration in the economic well being of these countries and the capacity of the governments to distribute, even minimally, the benefits that previously accrued through economic expansion, has shaken their political and social structures. Though the general resilience of the political, military, and economic classes to such pressures has been notable in spite of the precipitous decline of specific families, the inter-ethnic domestic tensions released have threatened the security of the state as well as many of its communities. Moreover, the precarious raw materials and resource-based economic system, laid vulnerable to the financial upheavals combined with the impact of the globalization of production and marketing which affects commodity pricing, has exacerbated the already uncertain situation faced by poorly educated workers and migrant labor, creating both domestic and cross-border tensions.

Sustainable development is not possible in an unstable domestic environment. Ironically, however, economic development has unleashed a set of dynamics generating social, economic, and political change, including increasing popular participation in the economy and in the society, increasing access to education and information, increasing mobility of peoples, along with the rise of a middle class. If the experiences of Taiwan and South Korea in Northeast Asia and more recently Thailand and the Philippines in SEA are relevant in this discussion, demands for greater political participation, liberalization, and democratization are likely to occur in other parts of Eastern Asia. Resistance on the part of governing elites to accommodate these demands, whether dramatically as in Indonesia or more cautiously in Malaysia, can lead to political instability of the sort that undermines sustainable development and domestic security itself. In this context, sustainable development also encompasses the creation of domestic and inter-state institutions that have the specialized knowledge and skills to regulate, to manage, and to facilitate stable political pluralism, economic development, and social equity. Thus, sustainable development is more than merely attaching specific conditions to economic change; it is also the evolution of a responsible civil society in which there exists a consensus concerning the benefits that accrue from institutionalizing good governance, resource management, and social equity. It provides an approach to achieving 'development as freedom' enunciated so passionately by Amartya Sen.

Since well before the UN-sponsored World Commission on Environment and Development (Brundtland Commission) published their 1987 report, *Our Common Future*, scholars, journalists, and non-governmental organizations had been raising serious concerns over the relationship between economic development, environmental consequences, and security. However, it was the Brundtland report that finally gave political meaning to the range of implications that were becoming ever more apparent, thereby moving ecology from the esoteric to center stage. The core concept around which the analysis and recommendations evolved was sustainable development, defined as the ability 'to ensure that [development] meets the needs of the present without compromising the ability of future generations to meet their own needs'. For this to be achieved, policy, behavior, and analysis among all sectors of society – government, industry, individuals – would have to come to terms with the implications of the nature of the 'interlocking crises' to be faced.[13]

Although some wrote on the probable connections between economic development, environmental degradation, and politics, few explored these linkages with any scientific rigor, and fewer with questions of security explicitly in mind.[14] While the ending of the cold was has not had a marked affect on the realities of this complex set of issues – if anything the 'facts on the ground' may be worse – it has led to an increased awareness of and concern with development and security. The 1992 Earth Summit and its adoption of *Agenda 21* gives some indication that political leaders are becoming more aware of the core significance of the environmental-economic-political linkages for their own countries if not the globe, although this does not mean that a consensus has been achieved concerning appropriate action.[15] Indeed, recent environmental summits in Kyoto and The Hague have underlined the extent to which state and private sector interests continue to coalesce in ways which impede significant progress on global environmental norms and regulations. Undoubtedly, while much of this has to do with the domestic politics of participating countries, it also is a reflection of the pervasive impact of the forces of globalization and the uncertainties attendant among the public, the private sector, and governments about how to address this market phenomenon which, in so many ways, impacts upon environmental and ecological issues.

The linkage between sustainable development and the environment is relatively well-known and has formed the basis of much discussion since the Brundtland Commission, as well as efforts at encouraging both standards and policy since the United Nations 1992 Conference on Environment and Development (UNCED). Over the last few years, the relationship between sustainable development (or aspects of it) and security has become a focus for research, for it encapsulates the tensions between the demands for economic growth, political stability, and individual and collective rights. Depending upon the context and the mix of choices, some scholars have pointed to the causal linkages between environmental degradation – often caused by resource depletion, improperly managed industrial development, and human displacement – and conflict. The scale of conflict can vary from interpersonal violence to challenges to governmental authority, from internal disturbances to regime repression, from revolution to interstate violence. Unsustainable and mismanaged economic activities which degrade the environment, aggravate human relations, and exacerbate intra-state as well as inter-state relations can lead to social upheaval, challenging the security of the individual, of the community, of the country, and potentially of the region.

Both problems and opportunities abound. Over the three decades prior to the 1997 financial crisis, SEA had been the locus of remarkable economic development. The stability of governing regimes was tied to performance legitimacy. The costs, however, were profound, including depletion of scarce resources, deterioration of marine and land environments, population migrations, and inadequately controlled rapid urbanization. Domestic as well as territorial problems, including current secessionist efforts, can be linked to policies fostering specific forms of economic growth in a vacuum of political representation, a fundamental political unwillingness to redress the inequitable redistribution of economic benefits, and the presence of an emerging and demanding civil society. Due to accompanying environmental scarcities and degradation, already difficult domestic situations carried the potential to exacerbate points of tension with neighboring states.[16]

What was evident from both the research literature as well as the regular and reputable journalistic accounts well before the 1997 financial crisis was a sense that the then current economic developments, especially those viewed as evidence of the mismanagement of development, could compromise if not severely undermine the security of these states, where security is understood as being 'essentially concerned with the maintenance of society's basic values; and with the institutions, such as legitimate political or legal system, which enable a country to sustain and defend the values its nationals regard as central to its independent existence'.[17] As the decade of the 1990s evolved, it also became clear that the growing insecurity of individuals and their communities could be ignored only at the peril of governing institutions. The previous decades of development strategies, as inequitable and incomplete as they might have been, had created sufficient awareness and heightened expectations that the authorities no longer could assume their citizens' compliance, especially as their own performance-based legitimacy was under threat.

The economy and the environment are separate but intertwined – and in some cases, integrated – systems. Though the causal relations are complex, and even more so when linking them to politics and to security, it is evident that to separate them in an arbitrary manner, as if decisions about one can be taken in isolation and with impunity concerning the others, is both wrong and foolhardy. 'Threats to the peace and security of nations and regions [and individuals] from environmental breakdown are potentially greater than any foreseeable military threat from conventional arms'.[18]

There are no significant parts of the globe which have not suffered from environmental degradation, though not all are affected equally nor are all equally culpable. Nevertheless, almost without exception the causes are political and economic choices, at times made from afar and even with the best of intentions given the available options. The results are a combination of resource depletion, uneven distribution of benefits, displacement, debt, and often political instability, conflict, and violence, as well as the intensification of 'poor governance'.[19] SEA is repository of all these factors.

Local political, economic, and commercial decisions have environmental consequences that, as with acid rain and deforestation, have not only regional but global ecological impact. As MacNeill notes, 'If nations are to stop depleting their basic stocks of ecological capital, governments will need to reform those public policies that now actively encourage the infamous *de's*: *de*forestation, *de*sertification, *de*struction of habitat and species, *de*cline of air and water quality'.[20] In many places, these second-order phenomena aggravate already contentious resource-based contexts, where two or more countries draw on the same river system, fish from the same sea, or claim under-sea and under-seabed rights from the same location at a time when each has increased needs driven by, among other things, demography, development, and rapid unplanned and unmanaged urbanization.[21] Much the same occurs with agricultural and grazing lands as well as with timber stands and mineral and ore deposits, though these usually are less state boundary questions initially and more likely to be tribal, clan, and other sub-state boundary problems.

Hence, for the DSSEA program, development makes sense only when understood in terms of sustainable development, a comprehensive concept with ecological, economic, social, and political dimensions. To be sustainable, economic development must be sensitive to its excessive demands on natural resources and its negative impact on the physical environment. Development, broadly defined, must also take into account the social dimension which includes the competing requirements of economic development and the preservation of social structures and cultural norms and values without which the survival of communities would be at risk. These include rights to ancestral lands without access to which tribal communities are likely to perish, and the capacity of both rural and urban dwellers to maintain their primary identities seriously diminished. The fruits of economic development need to be shared more equitably within the state's regions and peoples as well as across regions beyond the nation-state. The alternative would be economic deprivation for the powerless, a phenomenon that has often led to social tension and division within the society, and ultimately insecurity, conflict, and violence.

There is also a political dimension to sustainable development. Erosion of the ecological balance, uneven distribution of the economic pie, neglect or destruction of the rights of peoples, and other negative outcomes of the (mis)management of development results in eventual political decay, contributing to social tension and political turmoil that ties up the resources of the state as it reacts defensively to such challenges, dissipating state resources, fraying the social fabric, undermining the political legitimacy of ruling elites, and leading to violence. That this is at least partially a snapshot of what became the Asian financial crisis, the mirror image of the Asian economic miracle, is generally conceded. What remains in dispute are the appropriate responses more immediately as well as over the longer term.

The emergence of human rights, democratization, and the environment, in addition to economic development and market reforms, as issues in contemporary international relations that challenge the traditions of the inviolability of the sovereign state raises their potentials for engendering tensions and conflict between and among states. Examples within SEA are all too plentiful, not least of course the recent conflict and intervention in East Timor or the earlier hesitant involvement of ASEAN in the putative coup in Cambodia. The diplomatic tensions between the Philippines and Singapore in the mid-1990s must be seen not only in terms of uneven economic development within ASEAN but also in terms of divergences in their conceptions about human rights and democracy, about which Singapore ardently advocates a set of Asian values distinct from those in the West.[22] The protracted multilateral disputes around, in, and under the South China Sea are more than an issue of Chinese-ASEAN relations or bilateral security and defense politics. It is a set of issues that range from classic questions of boundary legitimacy to fundamental concerns about access to and control over the management of fish, mineral, and energy resources, and all the economic, social, and political factors linked with these productive and extractive sectors. Forest fires in Indonesia continue to undermine sustainable development and create threats to the well being of individuals both at home and abroad, thereby creating political demands which require governmental response with the potential for exacerbating relations between states in both bilateral as well as regional terms. Even the seemingly benign decision to allow Taiwanese entrepreneurs to introduce a non-Asian snail into Vietnam for commercial harvesting and sales is evolving into a serious threat to Vietnam's capacity to produce sufficient rice to feed its people. How that will play into the emerging regional interdependencies and competition, including the Mekong River project, remains uncertain but is at least instructive concerning the unintended consequences of economically driven decisions. Furthermore, both these examples (forest fires and snails), depending upon how they are handled, could undermine movement towards democratic and market reforms in various states in the region. Thus, understanding the complex linkages between the processes of development and their implications for the security of individuals at various levels of governance is an urgent imperative of our time, particularly where state-society relations remain biased in favor of the state.

DSSEA: The Research Program

The research was organized around three task force themes – environment, globalization, and people – that had been identified as principal factors in the development-security nexus. Our preference to understand these phenomena at least partially through human security and social capital concepts as a means to balance the privileged position of the state in both the security and development literature informed the selection of specific research projects, with the results of each task force presented in three volumes. The most significant findings and their policy implications are stated in each volume's overview chapter immediately following this one.

The program involved two additional activities beyond the conventional empirical research: echo seminars and a broader outreach effort. Echo seminars were designed to engage member of civil society (including other researchers), and the private sector, as well as local and national officials and politicians. The purpose was both to inform them of our work and to involve them, when possible, as participants. These meetings took place both in capital cities as well as in regional centers in the Philippines and Indonesia, at times drawing in excess of 150 local experts to a single session. Although the impact of these meetings on this initial research phase is difficult to measure, it is evident that the discussions and the ensuing contacts among interested parties has heightened awareness of the issues, stimulated opportunities for more intensive collaboration on future research, and in some locales invigorated policy development and political action. These meetings also made clear the extent to which, in both Indonesia and the Philippines, local activists and researchers have intensive knowledge and intuitive understanding of the security-development linkages, and a strong desire to have a role in policy formulation. Equally clear is the absence of positive dialogue between civil society and both the government and the private sector. The solitudes are striking given the profound long-term consequences and the fact that to address the security-development nexus requires involvement of all the principal stakeholders. Further outreach was undertaken through the regular publication and wide distribution of the *DSSEA Update*, designed to inform the various participants in the program, to engage the wider governmental audience throughout SEA and within ASEAN, and to encourage as well as to facilitate the involvement of civil society.

While both the *DSSEA Update* and our echo seminars were very well received, our three-year program confirmed what conventional wisdom has long asserted: that the differences in perceptions as well as policy preferences and priorities between researchers from universities and the institutions of civil society in Manila and Jakarta and the elites from the political and private sector are striking; and even more so from non-governmental experts and locals from provincial arenas. Although echo seminars often provided very positive encounters between researchers, activists, private sector representatives and government officials, our research tended to confirm the embedded nature of the dilemma: that development as defined by some combination of government policy and private sector interests undermined security as defined by individuals and their communities.

Much of the discourse of disagreement revolved around the different points of departure and of purpose: a government-defined security of national well being and the capacity to deal with threat focused on the harnessing of state capacity, whether in terms of military security or economic security, in support of regime stability. This became increasingly evident in the shadow of the 1997 financial crisis, where domestic political, communal, and economic matters and the importance of regional interstate political and economic relations highlighted the inside/outside duality of managing national security. Security was threatened both by domestic instabilities and by external factors at times beyond the control of the government. On the other hand, locally-defined security was premised on the capacity individuals, families, and communities to ensure well being, to be free of fear and of want, and to find ways to better manage the personal and inter-communal consequences of the intervention of government and the private sector in their daily lives. Whether the issue was the availability of food at fair and constant prices or protection from environmental degradation or the challenges introduced through the phenomenon of globalization, locals understood the multi-layered nature of security even as they were alienated from the process. Their extraordinary vulnerability was exacerbated and highlighted by the incapacity of the government to address the national-level security challenges in the wake of the 1997 financial crisis.

The DSSEA Research Program, begun before the financial crisis, found itself caught up in the spiral of events precipitated by the financial meltdown throughout much of SEA. Though requiring some adjustment by a number of the researchers, what the crisis did offer was a sudden opportunity for fieldwork that could track the local and regional impacts of the ensuing events. The chapters offered in these three volumes present insights into how different sectors of society weathered not only the chronic challenges of development and their impact on facets of security, but how the unanticipated acute changes were managed. To what extent were the local-through-national forces of security able to respond? How did this dramatic economic dislocation that posed fundamental challenges to the political integrity of the governing regimes affect the processes of development, and to what extent did any of this heighten insecurity? How resilient were the political, social, and economic forces that underpin much of the development ethos and are the building blocks of government policy and are reflected in the criteria of performance legitimacy? Do we now know something new about the linkages between development and security because this research program was able, by chance, to factor in the crash of 1997?

Managing the Uncertainty

Even before the 1997 financial crisis, it was evident to scholars and practitioners alike the SEA was in the midst of some profound transformations in state-society relations. Although still struggling with the extremes of wealth and poverty while encumbered by the twin scourges of authoritarian politics and corruption, civil society was increasingly a force for social, economic, and political change, at times challenging but also often in partnership with government and the private sector. Moreover, the forces of globalization along with the actions of regional and global organizations, especially financial institutions, had an ever growing impact on the range of policy options available, while introducing new issues around productive competitiveness and market vulnerability. For most of SEA, this period of economic growth, although not equitably distributed, did usher in a period of heightened expectations and confirmed the model of 'performance legitimacy' as one of the templates by which regime success was assessed.

Yet even at this time the uncertainty of what dramatic economic change could bring was evident in the inability of most governments to address the social dislocations and political discord fostered by the all too often mismanagement of development strategies. From the individual to community through to the state levels, the basic issue should have been how to manage the uncertain outcomes brought forth by the actions of interventionist governments, the role of medium-and large-scale private enterprise, the pervasive results of globalization, and the profound impact of the international financial markets on local conditions. As challenging as all these would have been in more cohesive, well off and structurally-integrated societies, when imposed upon polities which were divided by ethnicity, religion, language, loyalties, and wealth differentials, and already under stress from profound environmentally induced dislocations, the only certainty was insecurity.

The research reported in these three volumes attests to the intimate relationship between the process of development and the perceived sense of well being and security, whether of the individual or the nation. Further, this scholarship identifies the importance of governments recognizing that in their pursuit of wealth (especially if it is linked with more equitable distribution of well being), power, and political stability, taking seriously their obligations to view civil society as partners in development is essential for overall security and even to regime survival, unless the preference is a return to authoritarian or totalitarian rule. To ensure that security is a positive outcome of economic development requires that other aspects of development, including social and political freedoms, were strengthened. Our research testifies to the centrality of this assertion. Whether in land management, agricultural production or resource practices, or the challenges faced by labor in response to the changing nature of globalized competition, development cannot occur solely as an economic phenomenon blind to the issue of its two-sided impact on the individual, the community, or the nation. The improvement of economic well being, as Amartya Sen declared, is not the sole criterion of development; it need not nor should it occur at the cost of individual or community security. Indeed, it should be synonymous with enhancing the security of the nation and its government through the process of empowering citizens and ensuring their well being.

The chapters in these three volumes report on original research undertaken in an effort to better understand the intricate relationship between the human desire for security and, concomitantly, its expression through seeking an improved standard of living. Too often we uncovered examples where the pursuit of economic change as the dominant and clearly too narrow expression of development policies compromised the desire for security. The overview chapters that begin each of these volumes offer a number of insights and policy recommendations which attempt, in a very modest way, to address this tension between the dynamics of development and the desire for security. Though we began this project with an overriding sense of wanting to explore how development intersected with inter-state security, what has emerged from this research is a profound refocusing on the sub-state levels of security as the engine of change. From this perspective, inter-state and regional security can only be strengthened when each national community is secure in its place and its sense of a welcome future. Ironically, this harkens back to the earliest thinking within ASEAN when the ideas of comprehensive security and national resilience as the guides for national development strategies provided a rationale also for arguing the need for each country to pursue these twin goals and, out of that would emerge a secure, stable, and increasingly prosperous region. In some interesting and unanticipated ways, this research project tends to confirm that early intuitive position. Although it is too early to suggest that regional security in fact would be a natural derivative of successful country-by-country development (in the fuller Amartya Sen terms), it is likely that it would allow the dynamics of cooperative security arrangements to emerge as an effective approach to the management of inter-state and inter-regional relations.[23]

Notes

1   The two project co-directors authored a draft paper which set out the assumptions and the conceptual direction of the project. This was revised and published as Acharya, A., Dewitt, D. B., and Hernandez, C. G. (1995), 'Sustainable Development and Security in Southeast Asia: A Concept Paper', *CANCAPS Papier Number 6*, August. Much of the conceptual discussion in this chapter is drawn from this paper though informed by the results of the ensuing research program. In this regard it is a pleasure to acknowledge the ongoing

contributions to our thinking by our academic colleagues in the DSSEA program, and to Brian Hunter, Senior Economist, Asia Pacific Branch, Canadian International Development Agency, who, while supporting our work, actively confronted and challenged us throughout this effort.

2 This language is partially paraphrased from an undated Fall 1999 discussion brief, *Development, Security, and Post-Crisis Reconstruction in Southeast Asia*, prepared by Pierre Lizee as he responded to our request for DSSEA researchers to reflect on this project.

3 Sen, A. (1999), *Development as Freedom*, Alfred A. Knopf, New York, pp.3.

4 Amartya Sen explores these issues in much detail. See his *Development as Freedom*.

5 These five were joined by the admission of Brunei Darussalam in 1984 and then in 1995 Vietnam was admitted and in 1997 Laos and Myanmar, followed in 1998 by Cambodia. See Acharya, A. (2001), *Constructing a Security Community in Southeast Asia*, Routledge, London.

6 While useful as political rhetoric and ideological orthodoxy in Indonesia's and ASEAN's formative years of nation-building and regional consolidation, comprehensive security and resilience clearly fell to the forces of revisionism, fundamentalism, corruption, mismanagement of development, and economic inequities most recently and cruelly seen both in the East Timor struggle and the protracted domestic violence and ongoing expressions of secessionism or autonomy. Nevertheless, in principle these ideas of comprehensive security and national resilience so widely shared among the original five ASEAN partners afford a clear and well-reasoned statement about the inherent linkages between economic progress, well being, governance, regional cooperation, and security.

7 We are not offering any judgement on the validity of these assertions, nor on any causal connections these might have with the political, social, or economic realities which are the histories of the countries and communities of contemporary Southeast Asia. Rather, the point here is to identify the security-relevant doctrines and ideologies which have been articulated and employed by the leaders of these countries as they faced the challenges of nation-building and regime survival.

8 Malaysian Prime Minister Mahathir Mohamad as cited in Acharya, *Constructing a Security Community in Southeast Asia*, 2001, pp.4.

9 For an overview of these ideas see Dewitt, D. B. (1994), 'Common, Comprehensive, and Cooperative Security in Asia Pacific', *The Pacific Review*, vol. 7, no.1.

10 United Nations Development Program (UNDP) (1994), *Human Development Report 1994*, Oxford University Press, New York.

11 Department of Foreign Affairs and International Trade (1999), *Human Security: Safety for People in a Changing World*, Government of Canada, April, pp.5.

12 For a most interesting statement on human security, see Almonte, J. T. (2000), *A Human Agenda for ASEAN*, remarks drawn from his presentation at the 'Inaugural Meeting of the ASEAN People's Assembly', Batam Island, Indonesia, 24-26 November 2000, distributed as *PacNet 1*, 5 January 2001, CISIS/Pacific Forum, Honolulu.

13 The World Commission on Environment and Development (1987), *Our Common Future*, Oxford University Press, Oxford, chapter 1.

14 *Ibid.*, chapter 11, did address aspects of the relationship between development, peace, conflict, and security. A more recent statement by the principal author of the Brundtland Report is MacNeill, J. (1989), 'Strategies for Sustainable Economic Development', *Scientific American* 261, September; also in still more developed form, see MacNeill, J., Winsemius, P., and Yakushiji, T. (1991), *Beyond Interdependence: The Meshing of the World's Economy and the Earth's Ecology*, Oxford University Press, New York. See also Holmberg, J., Bass, S., and Timberlake, L. (1991), *Defending the Future: A Guide to Sustainable Development*, International Institute for Environment and Development,

16 Development and Security in Southeast Asia

London. Among the earlier pieces which challenged the cold war definition of security, see Ullman, R. H. (1983), 'Redefining Security', *World Politics*, vol.8, no.1; and Mathews J. T. (1989), 'Redefining National Security', *Foreign Affairs*, vol.68, no.2, Spring. An important contribution to this literature was an article which provided the first public report of a large and ongoing research program exploring the causal connections between environment and conflict; see Homer-Dixon, T. (1991), 'On the Threshold: Environmental Changes as Causes of Acute Conflict', *International Security*, vol.16, no.2, Fall.

15 For a view which clearly challenges the now orthodox view of sustainable development as expressed in *Our Common Future* as well as *Agenda 21*, see Crovitz, L. G. (1994), *The Asian Manager: Asian Imperatives and Western Perspectives in Sustainable Development*, a paper presented at the 'Asian Institute of Management Conference', Manila, Philippines, 17 February 1994.

16 For relatively early statements which foreshadowed much of this, see Lonergan, S. (1994), *Environmental Change and Regional Security in Southeast Asia*, Project Report No. PR 659, Directorate of Strategic Analysis, Ottawa, March; and Myers, N. (1993), *Ultimate Security: The Environmental Basis of Political Stability*, W. W. Norton, New York; and MacNeill, et. al., (1991), 'Environmental refugees' has become a significant factor of both cross-border and internal tensions and conflict in many parts of Eastern Asia, both north and south.

17 Harris, S. (1994), 'Enhancing Security: Non-Military Means and Measures II', in B. Nagara and K.S. Balakrishnan (eds), *The Making of A Security Community in the Asia-Pacific*, ISIS Malaysia, Kuala Lumpur, pp.191.

18 MacNeill, J. (1991), 'Strategies for Sustainable Economic Development', chapter 10.

19 See a superbly focussed discussion on this issue by Jones, S. 'Promoting Human Rights', in Nagara and Balakrishnan (eds), *The Making of a Security Community*, 1994, pp.344-46.

20 MacNeill, et. al., *Beyond Interdependence: The Meshing of the World's Economy and the Earth's Ecology*, 1991, pp.23.

21 There is a growing literature, some anecdotal but much increasingly scientific, which describes and begins the difficult process of explaining the causal relationships between environment, ecology, economic development, land tenure, social construction, displacement, violence, etc. In addition to the previous citations, see for example, Homer-Dixon, T. F. (1999), *Environment, Scarcity, and Violence*, Princeton University Press, Princeton, N.J.; Kaplan, R. (1994), 'The Coming Anarchy', *The Atlantic*, February; Homer-Dixon, T. F., Boutwell, J. H. and Rathjens, G. W. (1993), 'Environmental Change and Violent Conflict', *Scientific American*, February; Homer-Dixon, T. F. (1994), 'Across the Threshold: Empirical Evidence on Environmental Scarcities as Causes of Violent Conflict', *International Security*, Summer; Homer-Dixon, T. F. (1994), 'The Ingenuity Gap: Can Poor Countries Adapt to Resource Scarcity?', University of Toronto ms., April; Ruckelshaus, W. D. (1989), 'Toward a Sustainable World', *Scientific American* 261, September; and Westing, A.H. (ed.) (1986), *Global Resources and International Conflict: Environmental Factors in Strategic Policy and Action*, Oxford University Press, New York. On the important issue of maritime environments, see, for example, Townsend-Gault, I. (1994), 'Testing the Waters: Making Progress in the South China Sea', *Harvard International Review*, Spring; and his *Ocean Diplomacy, International Law, and the South China Sea*, preliminary draft paper presented at the 'Eighth Asia Pacific Roundtable', Kuala Lumpur, June 1994; and 'Part IV: SLOCs and Maritime Security', in Nagara and Balakrishnan (eds) (1994), *The Making of a Security Community*.

22 Hernandez, C. G. (1995), *ASEAN Perspectives on Human Rights and Democracy in International Relations: Divergencies, Commonalities, Problems, and Prospects*, Center for Integrative and Development Studies, University of the Philippines, Quezon City.

23 One can consider the difficulties which the expanded ASEAN-10 now faces as evidence of what continued national asymmetries coupled with substantial domestic underdevelopment and insecurity within a number of Southeast Asian countries can do to any efforts to create an improved sense of security or consolidate a more effective regional mechanism to manage uncertainty.

References

Acharya, A. (2001), *Constructing a Security Community in Southeast Asia*, Routledge, London.

Acharya, A., Dewitt, D. B., and Hernandez, C. G. (1995), 'Sustainable Development and Security in Southeast Asia: A Concept Paper', *CANCAPS Papier Number 6*, August.

Almonte, J. T. (2000), *A Human Agenda for ASEAN*, paper presented at the 'Inaugural Meeting of the ASEAN People's Assembly', Batam Island, Indonesia, 24-26 November 2000, distributed as *PacNet 1*, 5 January 2001, CSIS/Pacific Forum, Honolulu.

Crovitz, L. G. (1994), *The Asian Manager: Asian Imperatives and Western Perspectives in Sustainable Development*, paper presented at the 'Asian Institute of Management Conference', Manila, Philippines, 17 February 1994.

Department of Foreign Affairs and International Trade (1999), *Human Security: Safety for People in a Changing World*, Department of Foreign Affairs and International Trade, Government of Canada, April, pp.5.

Dewitt, D. B. (1994), 'Common, Comprehensive, and Cooperative Security in Asia Pacific', *The Pacific Review*, vol. 7, no. 1.

Harris, S. (1994), 'Enhancing Security: Non-Military Means and Measures II', in B. Nagara and K.S. Balakrishnan (eds), *The Making of A Security Community in the Asia-Pacific*, ISIS Malaysia, Kuala Lumpur, pp. 191.

Hernandez, C. G. (1995), *ASEAN Perspectives on Human Rights and Democracy in International Relations: Divergencies, Commonalities, Problems, and Prospects*, Center for Integrative and Development Studies, University of the Philippines, Quezon City.

Holmberg, J., Bass, S., and Timberlake, L. (1991), *Defending the Future: A Guide to Sustainable Development*, International Institute for Environment and Development, London.

Homer-Dixon, T. F. (1999a), *Environment, Scarcity, and Violence*, Princeton University Press, Princeton, N.J.

Homer-Dixon, T. F. (1994b), 'Across the Threshold: Empirical Evidence on Environmental Scarcities as Causes of Violent Conflict', *International Security*, Summer.

Homer-Dixon, T.F. (1994c), *The Ingenuity Gap: Can Poor Countries Adapt to Resource Scarcity?*, University of Toronto ms., April.

Homer-Dixon, T. F. (1991d), 'On the Threshold: Environmental Changes as Causes of Acute Conflict', *International Security*, vol. 16, no. 2, Fall.

Homer-Dixon, T. F., Boutwell, J. H. and Rathjens, G. W. (1993), 'Environmental Change and Violent Conflict', *Scientific American*, February.

Jones, S. 'Promoting Human Rights', in B. Nagara and K.S. Balakrishnan (eds), *The Making of A Security Community in the Asia-Pacific*, ISIS Malaysia, Kuala Lumpur, pp.344-46.

Lonergan, S. (1994), *Environmental Change and Regional Security in Southeast Asia*, Project Report No. PR 659, Directorate of Strategic Analysis, Ottawa, March.

MacNeill, J. (1989), 'Strategies for Sustainable Economic Development', *Scientific American*, no. 261, September.

MacNeill, J., Winsemius, P., and Yakushiji, T. (1991), *Beyond Interdependence: The Meshing of the World's Economy and the Earth's Ecology*, Oxford University Press, New York.

Mathews J. T. (1989), 'Redefining National Security', *Foreign Affairs*, vol. 68, no. 2, Spring.

Myers, N. (1993), *Ultimate Security: The Environmental Basis of Political Stability*, W.W. Norton, New York.

Ruckelshaus, W. D. (1989), 'Toward a Sustainable World', *Scientific American*, no. 261, September.

Sen, A. (1999), *Development as Freedom*, Alfred A. Knopf, New York, pp.3.

The World Commission on Environment and Development (1987), *Our Common Future*, Oxford University Press, Oxford.

Townsend-Gault, I. (1994a), *Ocean Diplomacy, International Law, and the South China Sea*, preliminary draft paper presented at the 'Eighth Asia Pacific Roundtable', Kuala Lumpur, June 1994.

Townsend-Gault, I. (1994b), 'Part IV: SLOCs and Maritime Security', in B. Nagara and K.S. Balakrishnan (eds), *The Making of A Security Community in the Asia-Pacific*, ISIS Malaysia, Kuala Lumpur.

Ullman, R. H. (1983), 'Redefining Security', *World Politics*, vol. 8, no. 1.

United Nations Development Programme (UNDP) (1994), *Human Development Report 1994*, Oxford University Press, New York.

Westing, A. H. (ed.) (1986), *Global Resources and International Conflict: Environmental Factors in Strategic Policy and Action*, Oxford University Press, New York.

Chapter 2

Environment, Development, and Security in Southeast Asia: Exploring the Linkages

Jennifer Clapp and Peter Dauvergne

Decades of rapid economic growth with few environmental safeguards has left Southeast Asia (SEA) one of the most polluted and degraded regions in the world. The mega-cities of Manila, Jakarta, and Bangkok are congested, dirty, and unhealthy. The United Nations Environment Programme (UNEP) ranked Bangkok as the second and Jakarta as the third most polluted cities in the world in the mid-1990s. Vehicle lead emissions are well above the standards of the World Health Organization (WHO). Many of the poor do not have access to clean drinking water nor adequate sewage systems. Industrial and toxic waste is often disposed of improperly. Industrial agriculture has polluted lands with chemicals, as well as contributed to a loss of genetic diversity. Loggers have degraded much of Southeast Asia's old-growth forests, contributing to a tropical Asia-Oceania suffering the highest rate of forest loss in the developing world during 1990-95. Countries like the Philippines, once largely blanketed in lush tropical forests, suffer from severe soil erosion as less than 20 per cent of the country now contains forests.

These environmental problems directly threaten state and, more so, human security in SEA. Studies have found that lead in Manila may be affecting some children's IQ scores by four or more points, potentially threatening the intellectual capital of an entire generation of Filipinos. Deforestation has lowered agricultural productivity and undermined the ability of indigenous peoples to survive in outlying areas. Degradation of forest and agricultural land, sometimes combined with droughts, has triggered food shortages and malnutrition. Environmental problems even have the potential to trigger regional security crises among states, as was demonstrated after Indonesia's 1997 fires smothered the region in a smoky haze, generating angry reactions from Malaysia and Singapore.

We can find, then, examples of environmental problems escalating to the point of triggering conflicts among states. Yet environmental degradation poses the greatest threat to state security by undermining human security that, in turn, can trigger social and economic instability. Human security, defined broadly as the adequate provision of basic human needs from the individual to the global level, relies on the natural environment. In other words, environmental problems undermine human security when they challenge basic human needs in an absolute and relative sense. Previously the search for security in the global arena focused mainly on sovereign states as the key actors, in terms of posing threats and in providing security. A broader conception of security that includes the environment as a potential threat both above and below the state level leads to the view that states are not the only actors involved in ensuring security. Local communities, non-governmental organizations (NGOs), and international organizations are increasingly taking a greater role in dealing with environmental threats to security. Such an approach to development and security is especially relevant to SEA where severe environmental problems now threaten human welfare, and where broader understandings of security are more common than in many parts of the world.

Southeast Asia's environmental problems have their roots in economic and political activities, yet they pose daunting threats to future human survival. The need to attain truly 'sustainable development' has never been more urgent as it is a vital ingredient in the pursuit of security in the region. States in the region have increasingly recognized the need to promote sustainable development through the adoption of environmental regulations. But while they have taken some positive steps, states are not adequately protecting the environment. The environmental 'externalities' of industrialization and rapid economic growth in SEA threaten the environmental security of individuals and local communities. Understanding these changes below the state level is becoming increasingly critical for understanding security within the region. Analyzing, for example, the relationship between environmental changes and community cooperation or conflicts (such as ethnic or class violence) is vital to understanding the stability of particular regions. Looking above the state level, we see that regional and global organizations are now more aware of the security threats of environmental degradation and are making some attempts to address them. A broad conceptualization of security beyond the state level, then, needs to be embraced to effectively analyze and improve the linkages between the environment, development, and security in SEA.

The Environment, Development, and Security Team of the Development and Security in Southeast Asia (DSSEA) program based its work on such an approach. Our purpose in analyzing environmental threats to human security in this way was two-fold. First, we aimed to identify problems that deprive people of their basic needs before these problems escalate into crises in order to propose preventative actions. Second, we identified situations already in crisis, in order to propose policies and actions to ameliorate the crisis. Both of these sets of goals proved vital in examining the connections between the environment, development, and security in SEA. The chapters of the team members draw on extensive field research, especially in the Philippines and Indonesia. They cover a wide range of environmental problems, including mining, forestry, water, food, energy projects, industrial pollution, hazardous waste, and global warming. Together, this research adds significantly to the empirical and theoretical understanding of the linkages between development, environmental change, and security. They also propose policy options to help governments, aid agencies, and international organizations better address the ways that environmental degradation contributes to community and human insecurity.

This chapter provides an overview of the main themes that both informed and emerged from the Environment Team's research. These themes fall into three main categories. They are: (1) the linkage between the concepts of environment, development, and security, (2) the restructuring of state-society relations, and (3) global economic pressures. These three main themes, each with their own sub-themes, are what connect the Environment Team's chapters, and also informed the policy recommendations made by each of the authors. The following three sections of this chapter outline these main themes and the final section provides a summary of the main policy recommendations arising from the work of the Environment Team.

Environment, Development, and Security Linkages

Each of the chapters examines the environment, development, and security linkages for a particular case, with some important cross cutting themes. These include the overlap of human security and development, the environmental crisis as a 'slow-motion' security threat, the differing perceptions of such 'slow-motion' threats, and the different uses of the environment and security linkage by different actors.

Human Security, Human Development, and the Environment

All of the researchers took, as their starting point, a broad understanding of the linkages between human security, human development, and the environment.

The past decade has seen the broadening of the concept of security beyond military threats, as well as the expansion of the actors beyond the state. Threats to security are seen to come from a variety of sources, not only those linked to military conflict, but also degradation of the natural environment, economic instability, and political persecution. These sources of insecurity threaten not only states, but also individuals, communities, regions, and indeed the planet as a whole. This broader view of security, sometimes referred to as 'human' or 'global' security, is now increasingly being accepted by academics in security studies, as well as by governmental and non-governmental actors.

As the scope of security studies has broadened, so have the conceptions of development. Once seen primarily in terms of economic growth, over the past few decades, development has come to mean much more than just expanding a country's Gross Domestic Product (GDP). Development is now widely seen to involve improving not only a state's economy, but also human and international well being, often referred to as 'human development'. This view of development includes improvements in the provision of basic human needs, such as access to sustainable livelihoods, environmental quality, health, food, shelter, human rights, and gender equity.

As the concepts of security and development have broadened, it has become apparent that the concerns and analysis of these two areas of study, once largely viewed separately, overlap considerably. The environment is one of the most important areas where human security and human development intersect. While environmental degradation is a source of insecurity for individuals, states, and the planet, environmental protection is an essential ingredient to promote both economic and human development.

Environmental Degradation: A 'Slow-Motion' Security Crisis

The environmental problems analyzed by the Environment Team represent both short- and long-term threats to environmental and human security. Yet, while these problems are of utmost importance and directly threaten human security, their slow development has meant that even when they reach crisis proportions governments and societies do not always recognize the urgency of the situation, often because people have become accustomed to it. This phenomenon is sometimes referred to as a 'slow-motion' crisis, in this case a slow-motion security threat, which can lead to complacency about the problem, despite its seriousness.

Perceptions about the seriousness of slow-motion environmental security crises vary widely, depending on who is most affected. For example, people of different genders, ages, or locations may perceive the problems differently. Communities and individuals facing the direct effects of environmental and human insecurity are more likely than governments to see the situation as a 'crisis' requiring action. Similarly, women are often the first to feel the impact of environmental degradation on their families and communities, and thus are likely to be aware of environmental problems before others take notice. Government officials often discount calls by local communities and environmental activists for immediate action if they do not perceive the situation as potentially erupting into a 'state' security threat.

So, while environmental destruction may threaten peoples' lives and livelihoods, the fact that it occurs over an extended period of time can lead to minimal state action to deal with the situation, even when communities are demanding that action be taken. As a result, environmental problems may become more severe than they would have otherwise. When states finally recognize the problem as serious enough to take action, it is often too late to repair, and little more is done than damage control.

Different Uses of the Environment-Security Linkage

The chapters in this volume were sensitive to the fact that various actors may link environment and security in very different ways in order to rationalize action. In an attempt to enhance their security, communities may refer to this linkage as a way to get states or other actors to ameliorate environmental problems more quickly than they would otherwise. But, while local communities make such calls, governments may not always be so receptive to making the link between environment and security. States in SEA often ignore or resist evidence that environmental degradation is contributing to community insecurity, even when it leads to violence and protests. This is sometimes due to the strong connections between government and business, and the fact that states in many cases still overwhelm civil society.

Some governments, on the other hand, may argue that environmental problems are a security threat as a way of justifying policies and programs that increase their control over local communities, especially ones that are seen as a threat to state stability. This approach to environment and security by the state is not unknown in SEA. Although in practical terms it is useful to encourage governments to accept the links between environmental degradation and security (and perhaps encourage governments to reallocate military funds for environmental protection), this must be pursued with great care as it could inadvertently bolster the tools of suppression in the authoritarian and semi-authoritarian countries of SEA. Thus, it is important to examine carefully the way governments in SEA link environment and security and be aware of the implications.

Restructuring State-Society Relations

The restructuring of state-society relations as well as the importance of non-state and global actors in reducing insecurities is an important theme of the Environment Team. This restructuring of state-society relations has been spurred by a weakening or changing state capacity, the decentralization of activity to enhance security including the development of social capital, as well as the growing importance of regional and international institutions in dealing with environmental insecurities.

Changing Capacity of the State

Globalization and global economic competition has, in many instances, weakened the capacity of states to provide security and development. The Asian financial crisis that began in July 1997 has severely undermined the implementation and enforcement of environmental regulations in SEA, indicated by the sharp drops in how much governments are spending on environmental activities. This decrease in capacity is partly due to forces outside of the control of Southeast Asian states; yet it is also partly a deliberate move by these states to ride out the current economic turmoil. The chapters in this volume all refer, in some way, to the weaknesses of the state in coping with particular environmental problems.

Policymakers are increasingly interested in voluntary initiatives to improve the environmental performance of firms most associated with pollution generation and degradation. Such initiatives can be seen either to supplement state efforts, or to supplant them. There is also greater recognition of the need for both global and local environmental governance in order to bolster efforts at the state level. This recognition follows from the increasingly visible weaknesses of states in dealing with environmental issues alone.

Among Southeast Asian states, there has been an increasing awareness of the environmental consequences of rapid economic development, particularly over the past two decades. Policymakers have responded with a variety of government initiatives, although the quality and breadth of these programs have not been even. Differing historical, political, and socioeconomic situations in the region partially account for these differences. Nonetheless, most Southeast Asian countries had created environmental ministries and enacted environmental laws and regulations by the late 1970s. Yet, despite adequate regulations and administrative structures, enforcement has generally been poor, although some countries, such as Singapore, have been more successful than others in protecting the environment.

Enhanced Role of Civil Society and the Potential of Social Capital

As state capacity and willingness to protect the environment declines, there has been a greater reliance in SEA on non-state actors to perform this function. At the national and local levels, NGOs and local webs of social capital have become increasingly important. Social capital is generally understood in our research to be the social glue that binds together networks of community cooperation and creates layers of social trust. It involves social connections that facilitate the development of trust, cooperation, identification, and norms of interaction. This is often crucial to enable decisive and effective action to promote economic growth and protect the environment. In other words, it is necessary to empower civil society. Forms of social capital include churches, neighborhoods, trade unions, voluntary associations, families, and companies embedded in a local setting. Building and maintaining social capital is, in our view, essential for effective community participation, well being, and environmental security. Although the extent of social capital in particular areas is frequently unclear, most authors in our team see opportunities to enhance social capital in local communities with the eventual goal of reducing insecurity linked to environmental problems.

Partly in response to the state's inability to manage and protect the environment, thousands of environment and development NGOs and community groups have emerged in SEA over the last few decades. These range from large nation-wide environmental advocacy groups to local community initiatives. Most Southeast Asian countries now have a substantial number of such groups, although some, such as the Philippines have far more than others.

Many of the groups in the Philippines are linked to the Green Forum, a coalition of several hundred such organizations established in 1989. This umbrella organization links a diverse group of NGOs and church organizations that promote aspects of sustainable development. Malaysia also has numerous NGOs aimed at environmental protection, such as *Sabat Alam* Malaysia, the Environmental Protection Society of Malaysia, and the Consumers' Association of Penang. While many of these groups began as conservation organizations, they have gradually become more radical in recent years. Thailand also has a healthy NGO sector concerned with development and the environment. One prominent organization is the Project for Ecological Recovery (PER), which has been involved in protests against logging and dam construction. The environmental NGO movement was not well established in Indonesia before the 1980s and at present, although many are emerging in the wake of Soeharto's resignation in 1998, relatively few powerful ones exist. One important organization set up in 1980s is the Indonesian Environmental Forum *Badan Pengendalian Dampak Lingkungan* (WALHI) which links over 150 NGOs with environmental and development concerns.

In all of these countries, these non-governmental groups are a crucial source of innovative ideas and dedicated energy to improve environmental management.

Nevertheless, there is a need to guard against overly relying on NGOs and local communities without giving them adequate support.

Role of International Actors and Regional Institutions

Just as reliance has increased on non-state actors 'below' the state level to address environmental problems, there has been growing support for environmental initiatives undertaken by non-state actors 'above' the state, or at the international level. The weakness of states to deal effectively with environmental problems, particularly those with global consequences, shows the necessity of international cooperation. Global agreements and treaties, international organizations, NGOs with worldwide reach, and transnational corporations can all play important roles in attempts to enhance environmental security.

State and non-state actors are now cooperating more at the regional level. Since the early 1980s, members of the Association of Southeast Asian Nations (ASEAN) have worked through ASEAN to promote environmental cooperation through treaties as well as other projects and initiatives. Over the past decade, ASEAN has also worked closely with other countries and organizations, such as Canada, Australia, the United States (US), the European Community, and the UNDP on joint projects aimed at environmental improvement in SEA. Another regional institution for cooperation in SEA is the Asian Development Bank (ADB) which has started to incorporate environmental provisions into its loans, and is working to forge links with regional and local NGOs for the implementation of the projects it funds. In addition, there are a number of regional NGOs working on environmental issues, such as the Asian Pacific Peoples' Environmental Network (APPEN) formed in 1983, with approximately 300 member-NGOs. This organization seeks to collect and distribute environmental information to member-NGOs in the region, and to act as a global advocate.

At the global level, a number of inter-governmental and NGOs undertake activities that also have important implications for the security of the Southeast Asian region. Global economic organizations such as the World Bank (WB) and the World Trade Organization (WTO) are increasingly incorporating environmental provisions into their operations. This has resulted in a growing number of development projects that aim to enhance environmental protection, and to incorporate environmental concerns into specific trade measures. Southeast Asian countries have also signed and/or ratified most of the major international environmental treaties, such as the ones on ozone layer protection, global warming, trade in endangered species, and the hazardous waste trade. Global environmental activist groups with specific campaigns or local chapters in the Southeast Asian region, such as Greenpeace, Friends of the Earth, and the Third World Network, have also influenced the debate and decisions surrounding environmental protection.

Global Economic Pressures

Economic globalization, specifically the growing internationalization of trade, foreign direct investment, and finance has important implications for the quality of the environment in SEA. This region's economic growth is tied, in large part, to its global economic relationships. However, there have been increasing concerns over the ways in which Southeast Asia's trade, investment, and finance relationships with the rest of the world can lead to environmental harm. At the same time, there is also discussion about the ways of making these relationships more compatible with environmental protection in the region. The relationship between economic globalization and environmental quality was made in all of the research conducted by the Environment Team.

International Trade and the Environment

The chapters in this volume relate, either directly or indirectly, to the current debates over trade and the environment as well as their implications for SEA. These debates are often heated and difficult to resolve. For simplicity, it is possible to break them into three broad camps: pro-trade, anti-trade, and trade-environment compatibility.

Pro-trade writers argue that trade and open markets promote economic growth, which they see as an essential ingredient for effective environmental management. In their view, trade benefits all participants regardless of environmental standards. They also claim that tariff and non-tariff barriers are bad for the environment as they distort markets and lead to economic losses.

Anti-trade writers maintain that trade can directly harm the environment by ignoring the environmental costs of extraction and production. They argue that trade can also harm the environment as products are transported over long distances, thereby wasting resources and contributing to pollution through oil spills and transportation fumes. Finally, the anti-trade advocates stipulate that trade can harm the environment by encouraging governments and firms to compete in the international market by lowering environmental standards. They state that this competition can create pollution havens, as some governments encourage polluters to locate in particular areas which leads some companies to lower environmental standards in certain countries – usually poor, perhaps authoritarian ones – while maintaining higher standards in rich countries.

A third school of thought sits in the middle of the first two, arguing that anti- and pro-trade arguments are simplistic, one-sided, and even potentially dangerous to the world's economy and environment. These writers argue that trade and the environment should not be seen in conflict, but rather as mutually compatible. In other words, a healthy environment is critical for efficient trade and trade is essential for effective and lasting environmental management. In their view, international trade is not seen as more harmful to the environment than regional or local trade, since each kind of trade involves a mixture of benefits and problems. This is an important distinction from the anti-trade school that sees international trade as particularly detrimental.

These debates are increasingly important in SEA since trade liberalization has been a major theme of global trade relations through the WTO, as well as regional agreements such as the Asia-Pacific Economic Cooperation (APEC) and ASEAN.

Foreign Investors

Foreign and multinational investors can have as great, if not greater, environmental effects as trade. Most of the team members' chapters include an analysis of the role of foreign investors in SEA and the controversial debates surrounding their influence on the environment. Foreign investors can improve environmental conditions, for example, by bringing newer and cleaner production technologies. They generally bring substantial revenue as well, provide vital funds for governments and the private sector to protect the environment. First World foreign investors may also be more susceptible than local companies in the Asia Pacific to pressures for environmental reforms, perhaps because they have high public profiles or perhaps because their operations are more transparent.

But at the same time, foreign investors, including ones from the First World, may also pressure host governments to lower environmental standards, perhaps creating pollution havens, or simply creating double standards where firms take environmental concerns into account more in the developed than in the developing worlds. The advanced technology of foreign firms may also increase production, especially of natural resources and agricultural products. This has occurred, for example, as foreign loggers bring chainsaws and bulldozers to extract huge volumes of commercial logs from the region's old-growth forests. Foreign companies are also more able than small local firms to pack up and leave after environmental resources are depleted and may, therefore, care less about the long-term environmental and community security of the region within which they are working. Highly secretive and complex corporate groups of companies in the Asia Pacific make it exceptionally difficult for environmental NGOs and state environmental officials to monitor and pressure these corporations. Many of the conglomerates have tight political ties, providing them with protection from pressures for environmental reforms.

The Asian Financial Crisis: Environmental Implications

The team's research is informed by the broader context of the Asian financial crisis. The financial crisis has both aggravated existing environmental problems as well as created opportunities to improve environmental management. There is also less money available for environmental protection, although it is not yet clear whether governments have cut environmental budgets disproportionately. Early evidence shows that urban air pollution appears to have decreased as the number of industrial plants and vehicles operating fell. Logging in the region, which is well over theoretically sustainable levels, also declined in the first year of the crisis as demand in Japan and South Korea fell. On the other hand, despite the decline in overall production, water pollution seems worse as more firms simply dump untreated waste to lower costs. Governments in the region are less able and willing to enforce these environmental rules since they do not want to drive firms out of business. The decline in water quality has especially grave implications for the poor, many of whom do not have access to safe drinking water.

The long-term environmental implications of the crisis may well be worse than the short-term ones. The crisis has generated powerful incentives for governments and firms to expand export-oriented agriculture, plantations, fishing, mining, and once demand resurges, forestry projects. Many of the costs of these operations are felt locally, while the profits are often in foreign currencies. Indonesia is already planning to build massive plantations, especially for palm oil, which may threaten huge areas of natural forests. The government has also announced plans to rapidly expand fish-product exports. The long-term picture for industrial pollution is equally bleak. Once production resumes to previous levels, the large numbers of old vehicles, outdated factory technologies, and a general corporate reluctance to invest in cleaner technologies could lead to even worse air pollution than if no crisis had occurred. The quality of water is likely to be even worse than that of the air as more dumping of untreated waste has offset the lower production levels.

Policy Recommendations

Each of the chapters in this volume lists policy recommendations arising from the particular issue examined. There are also broader policy recommendations that arise from the three main themes that connect these chapters. Some of the main policy implications are as follows:

1. **Environmental issues need to be a priority for both security and development reasons.**
   Local communities and individuals most affected by environmental problems, including women and indigenous peoples, generally recognize this. States and international agencies, however, need to internalize this link between environment, development, and security much further into policies and programs.
2. **State capacity needs to be enhanced to deal with environmental threats to human security.**
   This must not simply translate into better environmental legislation, but also into better enforcement and monitoring. This will involve recognizing that state command-and-control techniques alone are not enough. There is also a need for pressure and participation from the global community and local communities to enhance state capacity.
3. **Support for NGO and community activities needs to be enhanced.**
   This is the case in both countries like the Philippines with a relatively vibrant civil society as well as countries like Indonesia with a nascent NGO community. NGOs, states, international actors, and local communities need to develop more cooperative relationships. It is especially important to support the development and maintenance of social capital, both vertically as well as horizontally. Finally,

international supporters must ensure that NGOs are not used merely as 'cheap labor'.

4. **There is a need to recognize the environmental and security implications of global economic linkages.**
The Asian financial crisis brought this point home in a dramatic way. Both the negative and positive effects of these linkages need to be recognized, such as the transfer of environmental technology, and international pressure for environmental standards on both domestic and foreign investors.

5. **Environmental projects and budgets need external support in the face of economic crisis in the region.**
At this point it is unclear whether environmental budgets have absorbed disproportionate cuts. Nevertheless, overall funds available for environmental protection have certainly fallen. Donors and NGOs also need to recognize that in the long-term the crisis could lead to significantly worse environmental conditions, perhaps even triggering an environmental crisis that in turn could trigger community insecurity throughout the region.

6. **International agencies, donors, and NGOs need to recognize that the underlying meaning of environmental language within SEA can differ within and between countries.**
Most states now use language such as sustainable development, environmental protection, and biodiversity conservation. Some are now starting to use terms like environmental security. This may not translate, however, into the outcomes expected by outsiders, such as using the goals of conservation to increase controls over outlying and dissident groups. Outsiders must therefore scrutinize programs with labels like 'community forestry'.

7. **Environmental reforms face particularly great obstacles in areas where valuable natural resources remain – such as minerals, fish, and timber – and where corporate interests are tightly linked to the political and bureaucratic worlds.**
State officials in these areas, both at the national and local levels, tend to resist linking environmental degradation with security or insecurity, largely because this kind of linkage could potentially threaten their personal income or the income of their political grouping. These state-business linkages tend to weaken as the value of the natural resource declines, leading to the rather paradoxical finding that environmental management tends to improve only after the environment is already destroyed. It does mean, however, that greater opportunities exist in degraded areas to work on rebuilding the environmental security of local communities, such as through reforestation projects. This now appears to be occurring in some areas of the Philippines, where efforts are underway to alleviate some of the community and environmental insecurity generated by the mismanagement of the Marcos years.

8. **It is useful to work to convince governments in the region to accept that environmental degradation creates insecurity, perhaps encouraging these states to channel funds allocated for security to environmental protection.**
Empirical studies such as the ones conducted by the Environment Team add weight to this argument.

9. **These studies further suggest that decentralization will not automatically improve management and enhance community security.**
There are certainly many examples of decentralization improving management by integrating communities and local groups. But in some cases it has triggered greater insecurity as local elites fight over control and rewards, as disgruntled groups resist environmental programs (such as reforestation), or as NGOs and communities struggle at cross-purposes. Decentralization is most effective in settings with strong social capital and civil societies as well as one with effective state and international support.

10. **Environmental and community security in Indonesia needs to be carefully monitored in the wake of the financial crisis.**
Soeharto's resignation in 1998, along with the repercussions of the Asian financial crisis, has created great potential for change in Indonesia. Most optimistically, this could create a more active civil society, perhaps similar to the post-Marcos period in the Philippines, where future governments manage the environment more effectively and with greater concern for community security. On the pessimistic side, however, Indonesia could disintegrate into chaos. Nonetheless, regardless of the direction in which Indonesia heads, the country will need significant external support to maintain environmental and community security.

11. **Enhancing environmental and community security will require building and maintaining social capital, through such means as education, training, and associational arrangements.**
This may involve providing financial or technical support for community, non-governmental, or voluntary associations working on community development.

PART II
CASE STUDIES

Chapter 3

Hazardous Waste and Human Security in Southeast Asia: Local–Global Linkages and Responses

Jennifer Clapp

The presence of hazardous wastes, both locally-generated and imported is a serious and growing problem in the rapidly-industrializing countries of Southeast Asia (SEA). In the current era of economic globalization, competition for foreign direct investment (FDI), and the means to earn foreign exchange have led to the attraction of highly-polluting multinational corporations (MNCs), the importation of hazardous wastes from more industrialized countries as well as growth in highly-polluting domestic export industries. While these trends have emerged over the past few decades, there has been little regulation on the handling of hazardous wastes in the region, leading to a serious environmental problem. Human security has been threatened directly and indirectly by this growing problem of exposure to hazardous wastes. The direct effects have been a compromise in the health of those exposed to the wastes, and diminished environmental quality. The indirect effect has been a decline in the ability of contaminated lands and waterways to provide sustainable livelihoods.

This chapter seeks to examine the causes, the human security threat, and responses to the hazardous waste problem as it has manifested itself in SEA over the past few decades. It argues that the problem of hazardous wastes is a 'slow-motion' human security threat that, if not addressed in the coming years, could explode into a major health and environmental crisis in the region with the potential to contribute to conflict between polluting firms and affected citizens. However, addressing the problem is not merely one of improving government regulation. The emergence of the hazardous waste problem is intricately linked to relationships of local, national, and regional economies to the global economy and, therefore, action must be taken at all levels if the human security threat is to be alleviated. Needed is coordinated action, not only to deal with existing waste problems, but also to prevent future problems through improved regulation, monitoring, enforcement, and perhaps most importantly, the installation of cleaner production technologies in the region. The extent to which social capital has been organized around hazardous waste issues is vital in understanding the success and/or failures of these efforts. Social capital is the depth at which actors at different levels interact and coordinate their efforts towards a specific goal. Some action has already been undertaken by governments, non-governmental organizations (NGOs), regional and international organizations, as well as by the private sector to deal with the hazardous waste problem. This action is sometimes, but not always, successful. Clearly there is room for further development of social capital around this specific issue, which in turn will help enhance human security in the region.

The chapter is structured as follows. It first draws the linkages between human security and hazardous waste in SEA. Second, the scope of the problem outlines and identifies the key sources, from the local to the global levels, which have contributed to the hazardous waste problem in SEA. The third section of the chapter outlines and assesses the actions to address the hazardous waste issue which have or have not been taken by various actors at different levels of governance (state, NGO, regional and global institutions, private firms) and the impact of these policies on the waste crisis in SEA. Special attention is paid to policies implemented in the Philippines and Indonesia by different actors and the extent to which social capital has developed thus far around the hazardous waste issue in those countries.

Human Security and Hazardous Waste in SEA

This chapter is concerned with the environmental and human security threats posed by hazardous wastes in the rapidly industrializing countries of SEA and the efforts to reduce those threats. Before outlining the linkages between hazardous waste and human security, it is important first to explain what human security and its linkages to the environment and society mean.

Human security, for the purposes of this chapter, is defined as human well being and the attainment of basic needs such as access to sustainable livelihoods, health, food, shelter, and human rights. This definition of human security overlaps significantly with current popular broader definitions of 'human development'. Environmental quality is seen to be integral to the provision of basic human needs, and thus, is key in the search for human security and human development. That is, human security and development are threatened by environmental problems when the latter pose fundamental challenges to basic human needs in both an absolute as well as a relative sense. Most studies on environment and security focus almost exclusively on situations of violent conflict that have arisen due to a shrinking natural resource base.[1]

While natural resource depletion is a serious concern for human security, threats are also presented by problems of pollution generation and disposal. Environmental problems arising from industrialization can pose both long-term and immediate threats to human security. Thus, in the quest for improving human security, it is important to focus not just on immediate violent crises arising from diminished environmental quality, but also to be aware of the longer-term, or 'silent' threats to human security that prolonged exposure to toxic pollutants can bring.

The growing presence of hazardous waste in Southeast Asian countries poses a significant human security threat. While there is a dearth of hard statistics on the levels of hazardous waste being generated (due to a lack of sampling and a lack of firm disclosure of the amount and types of wastes generated), estimates place the growth in the generation of this waste in Thailand, Indonesia, and the Philippines to be in the area of 4 to 10 times that for the 1975-88 period.[2] This growth in the generation of hazardous waste not surprisingly coincided with rapid industrial growth in these countries. World Bank (WB) estimates for Asia suggest that in Indonesia, the Philippines, and Thailand toxic wastes and water-based pollutants are 'growing three to five times faster than the underlying economies'. And in Bangladesh, Indonesia, the Philippines, and Pakistan, growth in seven of the dirtiest industrial subsectors has been stronger than in the six cleanest industrial subsectors.[3] The amounts of pollutants generated are staggering. For example, about 2.2 million tons of hazardous wastes are generated per year in West Java and *Daerah Khusus Ibukota* (DKI) Jakarta alone.[4] Lindsay estimates that some countries in SEA may produce as much or more hazardous waste per square kilometer than the United States (US).[5]

This growth in the generation of hazardous waste has been a serious problem in the region because its disposal was virtually unregulated in most Southeast Asian countries before the mid-1990s. Though there is now some regulation in place, its enforcement is still weak, and in most Southeast Asian countries, there are still very few places to properly dispose of hazardous waste. Much of this waste was and still is dumped in rivers, stored on industrial sites, or dumped in landfills along with other solid wastes. Some of it even makes its way to agricultural areas through irrigation water and wind. This lack of regulation and waste-treatment facilities has led to a growing number of hazardous environmental incidents, such as the recent discovery of 41 drums of toxic potassium cyanide dumped by a small chemical trading firm on Pangkor Island in Malaysia. An official of the Malaysian International Development Authority remarked that this incident was just the tip of the iceberg.[6] In Thailand's Klong Toey port, a toxic fire caused by the explosion of abandoned and imported wastes and chemicals in 1991 generated deadly gasses which clouded a nearby shanty town and killed at least five people. After the explosion, the wastes were transported to a nearby village and simply buried, leaving its residents to deal with the long-term effects.[7]

This expanding mountain of relatively unregulated hazardous wastes poses serious threats to human and environmental security in Southeast Asian countries. Situations of community unrest have erupted over the waste crisis. These incidents may not be as widely reported as other environmental crises, but they represent a ticking time bomb. The generation of these wastes is generally associated with industrial growth which is fuelled by income from FDIs and exports, but it has come with an environmental cost which may over the long run negate these benefits altogether. The advocates of industrialization have swept the problem of hazardous wastes under the rug. Consequently, it has been a relatively 'invisible' problem, except for those exposed to the waste. However, if not addressed, the problem of hazardous waste could explode into a major health and environmental security threat in the coming years.

The accumulation and unsafe handling of hazardous wastes in SEA poses a threat to human security in both direct and indirect ways. The direct impacts are its effects on human health due to exposure to these wastes. Occupational exposure appears to be on the rise as more and more people are employed in hazardous industries. There has been a rise, for example, in work-related poisoning by toxic chemicals in Thailand, a problem which no doubt also affects other Southeast Asian developing countries.[8] Exposure also occurs downstream from where wastes have been disposed of in environmentally-unsound ways. The lack of zoning laws in Asia is a serious problem, as industrial firms are often adjacent to densely populated communities.[9] This type of exposure generally affects the poor and children in particular. Especially vulnerable are poor urban communities located along rivers which are used as dumpsites for hazardous waste-producing factories.[10] Such exposure has serious health impacts. Diseases related to over-exposure to heavy metals and chemicals appear to be on the rise. The exact effects of long-term exposure to toxic wastes are not known, but these substances have been associated with the growing incidence of cancer, genetic damage, and endocrine disruption which affects reproductive systems.[11] High population densities and the tropical climate in Southeast Asian countries only compound these effects. Thus, the fundamental basic need of health is threatened by increased exposure to the toxins in hazardous waste.

Indirect economic impacts of hazardous waste exposure are also felt through the loss or reduction of livelihoods. At the individual and community levels, the weakened physical capacity of those with health problems related to waste exposure and the reduced capacity of the earth's resources to provide livelihoods can pose serious economic consequences: polluted rivers and bays do not produce as much fish, poisoned soil cannot produce high quality food, and ill people cannot work as hard or as long as healthy people. Again, the poor are the most vulnerable to these types of threats as they are frequently the ones relying directly on the land and waterways for the provision of their livelihoods.

These indirect economic impacts are also felt at the state level. Health problems and reduced incomes for its citizens lead to an increased economic burden on the state resulting in higher costs and lower productivity. Environmentally-associated health and economic problems cost governments billions of dollars a year in large Asian cities.[12] In addition, clean-up costs of hazardous waste dumps can be exorbitant and may fall on the state if other means to clean up are not negotiated with polluting firms.

In addition to the slow-motion threat, the generation and indiscriminate disposal of toxic waste also poses the potential threat of a serious accident, such as the disaster at Bhopal, India, in 1984. In this well-known accident over 3,000 people died as a result of exposure to toxic gases that leaked from a Union Carbide pesticide plant. Such potential 'time bombs' need to be diffused before they get out of hand as they could cause conflicts over economic losses or serious health effects. The WB notes that 'the evidence of community unrest arising from industrial pollution is not well documented, but press reports and anecdotal accounts seem to be increasing'.[13] Unfortunately, thus far governments have not moved to address the situation until disaster has already struck. All of these effects add up to a serious environmental and human security threat in SEA that cannot be ignored.

Affected local communities and environmental non-governmental organizations have been aware of the problem for years, and have attempted to address the situation through legal action and protests. Their efforts have often been unsuccessful, however, as the industries responsible have been largely able to avoid legal sanctions. States in the region have just begun to recognize the importance of these issues and the environmental and economic consequences of not acting to alleviate the crisis.[14] An increase in hazardous waste regulations placed on industry has helped to give a boost to efforts by non-governmental and community groups in recent years. Social capital on this issue is slowly solidifying, but still has a far way to go to eliminate the security threat posed by hazardous waste. Before looking further into the efforts being undertaken to address the problem, it is important to take a closer look at the various sources of the hazardous waste problem in SEA, from the local to the global levels.

Local to Global Dimensions of the Toxic Waste Crisis

In many ways the hazardous waste crisis appears to be local in nature, as the effects are primarily felt locally. However, the waste crisis is far from being just a local crisis. Global factors are closely intertwined with the local in terms of hazardous waste-generation and the contamination of local spaces in SEA. It is, therefore, important to analyze the sources of this waste. These sources include: (1) the generation of wastes by locally-owned firms, especially the large number of small-and medium-sized enterprises (SMEs) in the region; (2) MNCs and their affiliates in hazardous industries operating in the region; and (3) imports of toxic wastes from other countries. The types of waste problems posed by each of these key sources in the Southeast Asian region are discussed below.

Locally-Owned Firms and Hazardous Wastes

Data on the generation of hazardous wastes by locally-owned firms, particularly SMEs, is extremely sparse. It can be said, however, that the main domestic industries responsible for toxic emissions in SEA include leather tanning, pesticides, chemicals, metal plating, electronic industries, and textile dyeing. The prevalence of these industries varies by country. Most of the wastes generated by locally-owned firms in these industries are indiscriminately dumped into rivers, mixed with domestic solid waste and disposed of in landfills, or stored on site. The lack of facilities to treat hazardous waste has only compounded this problem.

Most locally-owned firms in SEA are SMEs. Locally-owned and operated SMEs are responsible for some of the hazardous waste-generation and improper disposal in SEA, particularly those in the leather tanning, textile-dyeing, and metal-plating industries. But at the same time, much of the waste generated by small-and medium-sized local firms is tied to global economic relationships (for example export industries, such as computer chips, electro-plating, and textile-dyeing) as they are increasingly integrated into the global economy. There are differing views on the extent to which SMEs contribute to the toxic waste crisis in developing countries. Some argue that SMEs have an incentive to keep their own backyards clean since work and living quarters are close in many cases. Others argue that these firms are more polluting than large firms as they lack funds to install cleaner production technologies and to properly dispose of the hazardous wastes that they generate. Locally-owned firms may also be more polluting because incentives to be more 'clean' are lower where land ownership and rights are not clearly delineated, as is the case in much of SEA.[15] In addition, the small size of SMEs, and the fact that they are often dispersed, may make it easier for them to evade government regulations.

In assessing the role of SMEs in the toxic waste crisis, it is important to determine the share of manufacturing output produced by SMEs and the amount of waste generated per unit of output compared to larger firms.[16] In some parts of Asia, such as India and China, SMEs make up 60-70 per cent of manufacturing output, and thus, their contribution to the toxic waste crisis is significant. But in other Asian countries, such as those in SEA, the share of SMEs in total output is much lower. For example, small-and medium-sized firms make up 18 per cent of output in Indonesia and about 13 per cent in the Philippines.[17] An illustration of this is the leather-tanning industry in Indonesia that is comprised of some 540 enterprises. But the vast majority, 470 firms, are small enterprises that make up only 12 per cent of the total output. The WB notes that 'although [SMEs] are not the major polluters in most subsectors, they often pollute more per unit of output than large firms operating in the same sector...'.[18] But while SMEs may pollute more per unit of manufacturing output than large firms, they do so in relatively small amounts due to the much smaller percentage of output compared to large firms. It appears that SMEs, then, are not the most significant source of toxic waste in the region, but they do contribute to the problem.

There are a variety of reasons for pollution problems in locally-owned firms, large and small, in SEA. Many locally-owned firms in SEA, large and small, do not have any policies on pollution control. This is in contrast to most MNCs and their affiliates currently operating in the region which do at least have policies related to pollution control. For example, a joint report by the UN Economic and Social Commission for Asia and the Pacific (UNESCAP) and the UN Centre for Transnational Corporations (UNCTC) indicated that only half of the locally-owned firms they surveyed in the Asian semiconductor industry had an environmental policy at all. The report stated that where such policies existed, they were usually based on local laws, themselves often weak and not enforced.[19] Compliance levels with local laws among locally-owned firms is in many cases extremely low. For example, in the leather-tanning industry in Indonesia, compliance with pollution discharge regulations in the early 1990s was only two per cent.[20] This poor performance reflects the fact that locally-owned firms often lack monitoring equipment and have poor training with respect to environmental concerns. Health risks to workers in locally-owned firms are also high, due to the inadequate availability of safety equipment and a lack of adequate emergency procedures.[21]

These problems are compounded by a lack of industrial zoning policies in most Southeast Asian countries. Industrial firms of all sizes, especially smaller firms, are often located near residential areas. Poor urban communities are often most affected, with large shanty towns located near industrial areas. The lack of separation between residential and industrial areas only increases the exposure of urban populations to toxins from hazardous wastes and industrial effluents, particularly along rivers where toxic waste is often discharged by local manufacturing firms.

One of the largest problems faced by local firms with respect to environmental policies and procedures is their lack of financial resources with which to develop or operate elaborate pollution control policies or technologies.[22] SMEs in particular often do not have the funds to hire environmental consultants to help them improve their environmental performance, and find it especially difficult to take advantage of economies of scale relating to the adoption of environmentally-sound technologies.

MNCs and MNC Affiliate Firms

While local firms pose a problem with hazardous waste, they are only part of the problem. MNCs and subsidiary corporations, mainly large firms, operating in SEA also generate large amounts of hazardous wastes. Since the mid-1980s there has been remarkable growth in inward investment into the developing countries in SEA by MNCs. The majority of this investment has come from firms in Japan, though North American-and European-based firms are also key investors in the region. The recent drive toward economic liberalization in the region has reinforced these broad trends of FDI particularly in Thailand, China, and Indonesia.[23]

Following the trend of MNCs in general, those which have set up shop in the developing countries in SEA have been concentrated in environmentally-sensitive sectors, and for this reason they have had a significant environmental impact.[24] According to a study on the environment and MNCs in the Asia Pacific region undertaken in the late 1980s by ESCAP and UNCTC, there appears to be little systematic evidence of 'pollution havens' or 'industry flight' for industry as a whole into SEA in the 1980s.[25] However, this same study shows that there is evidence in the region that some MNC firms in the *most hazardous* industries have relocated to developing countries in Asia, and that MNCs operating there do tend to practice 'double standards'.[26]

There has been heavy FDI into the developing countries in SEA over the past decade in the chemicals, pesticides, petroleum, crude oil, mining, electronics, and other heavy and toxic industries.[27] Those countries which have received especially large amounts of FDI in these hazardous industries relative to total FDI in manufacturing in the 1980s include Singapore, the Philippines, Thailand, and Indonesia. The increase in FDI in the chemicals sector in many of these countries increased significantly throughout the 1980s. For example, FDI stock in the chemicals sector over the 1980-89 period increased by a factor of 11 in Singapore, and by a factor of 9.4 in Thailand.[28] For some countries, particularly Singapore and Thailand, the amount of FDI in the electronic machinery industry as a share of total FDI in manufacturing was over 30 per cent in 1989. At the same time, the increase in FDI stock over 1980-89 in that sector in these two countries was 5.5 and 13.3 times, respectively.[29]

A second ESCAP/UNCTC study published in 1990 noted that because of the inadequacy of information on environmental practice provided by transnational firms in the Asia Pacific region, these firms have been able to relocate potentially-hazardous industrial facilities without making those hazards known to the local population.[30]

Most MNCs in the region withhold information regarding management practices, pollution problems, and the types of hazardous substances and waste that they produce.[31]   By refusing to disclose this information, these firms can give the impression that their activities are clean and safe. This lack of information makes it difficult to provide systematic statistical evidence of global firms' environmental performance. It also makes it extremely difficult to trace environmental problems to specific firms. Certain hazardous activities undertaken by MNCs operating in SEA, however, particularly those that have been difficult to hide, have attracted attention over the past few decades. Three trends in particular have been apparent in SEA. These are the relocation of some hazardous industrial processes to developing countries in the region, the practice of 'double standards' between home firms and those affiliates located in developing countries, and the sale of outdated and hazardous industrial technologies to local firms in developing countries. Each of these is discussed briefly below.

Japanese multinational firms, as the principal investors in the region, have drawn a number of complaints for transferring hazardous industries to the rest of Asia over the past few decades. It appears that both push and pull factors have been involved in this migration of Japanese hazardous industry. Most analyses of Japanese FDI into SEA point to the desire on the part of Japanese firms to take advantage of lower labor costs, to gain closer access to raw materials, and to secure export markets for Japanese products.[32]   But it appears that environmental concern and regulation within Japan have also been a key reason why its firms in some hazardous industries have set up shop in the developing countries in the region.[33]   Following the toxic scandals in Japan in the 1960s and 1970s linked to its own industrialization, such as the case of mercury pollution at Minimata, Japanese firms seem to have been particularly keen to move highly hazardous processes to other countries in the region. Some have argued that this migration of hazardous industry away from Japan has in fact occurred with the assistance of the Japanese government.[34]   Low environmental costs in the developing countries in the Asia Pacific region only increased the attractiveness of these countries to Japanese firms seeking to relocate hazardous production processes abroad.

A number of studies have documented individual cases of hazardous and toxic industry migration from Japan to developing countries in SEA and illustrate this trend. One clear example of this was the relocation in 1977 of an iron-sintering plant, the most polluting and highly hazardous segment of Kawasaki Steel Company's production, from Japan to the island of Mindanao in the Philippines.[35]   The iron-sintering process releases many toxic chemicals such as cyanide and phenol, while other air pollutants are also emitted. Chiba, the Japanese city which previously was home to this plant, had suffered the effects of these pollutants through high rates of asthma and a number of deaths which were directly attributed to the plant.[36]   The fact that the raw iron ore which was processed at the new plant in Mindanao came not from the Philippines, but rather was imported from Brazil and Australia, and that the other stages of the firm's steel production were still carried out in Japan, provides a strong indication that environmental and health considerations were an incentive for moving this part of the production process to the Philippines.

Other cases of Japanese FDI have been blamed for transferring hazards to the developing countries in Asia. For example, in 1982 the Japanese multinational firm Mitsubishi relocated its 'rare earth' plant to Papan, Malaysia. This plant, which produced compounds used for the production of color television screens, was seen to be too dangerous to locate in Japan because of the radioactive wastes that it produced.[37] In Papan, these wastes were dumped in plastic bags behind the plant, and led to serious health problems among employees. Legal action taken against Mitsubishi by members of the community dragged on into the 1990s.[38] In another incident, in the mid-1970s the Japanese multinational Nihon Kagaku relocated a chromium plant to South Korea following protests over pollution and illness at the firm's Japanese plant.[39] Japanese textile firms have also invested heavily in Thailand over the past few decades and have been known to dispose of untreated toxic dyes directly into rivers and streams.[40] Other hazardous processes carried out by Japanese MNCs in Asia, such as the production of polyvinyl chloride and pesticides, have also raised complaints.[41]

Global chemical giants based not only in Japan but also in the US and Europe are also now making further inroads into Asia in the 1990s, which is seen to be the 'rising star' of the industry.[42] This movement is in part to meet the rising demand for chemicals in the region. But it seems that environmental concerns are on the minds of some chemical company executives. Dr. M. Schnieder, chief executive of Bayer, for example, has pointed out that his firm's growing investments in Asia are linked to higher labor, tax, *and environmental* regulations in Europe.[43] Moreover, not all Southeast Asian countries have an expanding domestic demand for chemicals. Singapore, for example, has very little domestic demand, but has a significant chemicals industry dominated by MNCs which produce mainly for export to other countries.[44] Thailand, Malaysia, Indonesia, and Singapore are seen to be key areas in which the chemicals industry is expanding with heavy involvement of FDI in the 1990s. Environmental activists have argued, for example, that global firms in the chlorine industry are seeking to relocate to SEA just as demand in North America and Europe is declining with the rising concern over the environmental and health effects of that chemical.[45]

A second trend in the developing countries in the region is that a number of MNCs that have located there, particularly those involved in the most hazardous industries, are operating on double standards. In addition to differential environmental practices, MNCs have not always followed the same health and safety standards as in their home plants in similar industries, and they have also in some cases sought to reduce their liabilities in host countries. According to several studies undertaken by the UNESCAP and UNCTC in the late 1980s, over half of the transnational firms surveyed in the Asia Pacific region followed standards which were lower than those to which they adhered in developed countries.[46] In many cases, this was because they only attempted to meet local standards, which were by and large much weaker than at home, rather than adopting industry-wide or home-country standards. Only a quarter of multinational firms in the pesticide industry operating in Thailand, for example, adopted global environmental standards. While careful not to blame MNCs as the primary cause of environmental problems in the region, a UNESCAP/UNCTC study noted, 'It would appear that transnational corporations (TNCs) have indulged in various lapses in environmental practice in several developing countries in Asia and the Pacific'.[47]

Double standards employed by MNCs in the region often result in practices which are known to be environmentally damaging. The impact of these differential standards is felt most acutely in hazardous industries. Most MNCs in the region, for example, do not properly manage the hazardous wastes that they generate. This is largely because there is a serious lack of hazardous waste-treatment facilities in the region and a lack of legislation that requires the proper disposal and treatment of hazardous wastes. Hong Kong, Malaysia, Indonesia, and the Philippines, to name but a few countries in the region experiencing high rates of FDI in hazardous industries, still have extremely weak environmental regulations and do not require hazardous wastes to be disposed of separately from other solid wastes.[48] While MNCs may not be required by law to manage their hazardous wastes properly, the question remains as to whether they should make use of the technologies available to them in their home countries to do so. The use of double standards among MNCs only discourages the transfer of more environmentally sound technologies and practices to developing countries in the region.[49]

A third trend related to MNCs and environmental hazards in the region is the growing incidence of the sale of entire 'used' manufacturing plants from industrialized countries to poorer countries, including those in SEA. Many of these sales involve the transfer of outdated technologies which are no longer wanted in the North because they are either judged to be inefficient, or involve hazardous processes which rich industrialized countries are seeking to replace to meet rising environmental standards on industry at home. Most of these outdated plants and other equipment which are sold to developing countries are in the manufacturing and chemical industries. According to one of the partners of an international plant and property-consulting firm which handles such sales, much of the outdated technology has made its way to Asia, particularly China, the Indian subcontinent, and SEA.[50] There is a high demand in the these countries for this equipment, as it is seen as an affordable way to speed up industrialization. Indonesia, for example, has been the recipient of second-hand chloralkalai technology in the past decade, which is much less expensive to purchase than newer, cleaner technologies.[51] Highly-polluting medical waste incinerators which could not be sold legally in the US or Canada have recently been peddled by a Canadian firm in the Philippines, Indonesia, and Thailand.[52]

Imports of Toxic Waste

SEA has been the recipient of imported toxic wastes since the mid-1980s. Southeast Asian countries received wastes that were destined for both disposal and recycling from more industrialized countries. As mentioned above, the toxic wastes that burned in the fire at the Klong Toey port in Bangkok, Thailand in 1991, for example, were imported from other countries. These wastes had been piling up at the Klong Toey port from the late 1970s and were only discovered in the late 1980s. The wastes were falsely labeled and shipped to non-existent firms in Thailand. Because they were impossible to deliver, they were abandoned at the port and ended up sitting on the docks for years in open containers. Most of the containers came from unidentified shippers in Singapore, though some were also reported to have originated in the US, Japan, Germany, and Taiwan.[53] The Philippines and Indonesia were also targeted by waste traders when the now infamous waste ship, the Khian Sea, sailed through in 1988 with its load of toxic waste which originated in the US. After being rejected by a number of other developing countries around the world, the ship was also denied entry to ports in the Philippines and Indonesia. These wastes eventually 'disappeared' somewhere in the region, presumably dumped at sea.[54] When the practice of toxic waste exports to Third World countries was brought to international attention in the late 1980s, many developing countries took action to halt it. The Philippines banned the import of toxic wastes in 1988, and Indonesia threatened to sue in international court anyone found importing hazardous wastes.[55]

The 1989 Basel Convention on the Transboundary Movement of Hazardous Wastes sought to regulate the hazardous waste trade in such a way that stopped unwanted imports into developing countries. The convention was soon criticized for not being effective in that regard.[56] The convention's requirement of prior informed consent from waste-recipient countries for wastes exported for final disposal has only encouraged imports of waste destined for recycling operations through subterfuge. Wastes sent to Third World countries for recycling were not labeled as 'wastes' but rather products for 'further use' and thus, were able to easily circumvent informed consent rules and national toxic waste import bans. Southeast Asian countries began to receive large amounts of hazardous wastes for supposed recycling. Plastics, metal scraps, and lead are the key hazardous waste imports sent to SEA for this purpose. But, not all of these wastes are recycled in an environmentally sound way, and much of it is in fact dumped in landfills. Even for toxic wastes legitimately recycled, hazardous by-products are produced which must then be disposed of. Thus, the recycling of hazardous waste and the disposal of by-products can pose a serious health and environmental risk for those involved in this process. During 1990-93, the Philippines received some 65,000 tons of toxic waste from Organization for Economic Cooperation and Development (OECD) countries destined for recycling operations.[57] And there were no less than 84 proposed waste-exporting schemes targeting SEA as a whole between 1990 and 1993, all of which were to be recycled.[58]

The used plastics trade has had a devastating impact on the health of recycling plant workers and the environment in a number of less-industrialized countries. SEA has been a particularly popular destination for such wastes. Indonesia was the recipient of some 100,000-150,000 tons of plastic wastes from the US and Germany every year in the early 1990s. Only 60 per cent of this plastic could in fact be recycled. The rest, a quarter of which was hazardous, was dumped into landfills. The plants that carried out the recycling of the remaining plastic operated under extremely unsafe conditions. These plants employed mainly women and children, many of whom did not wear protective clothing. The workers sorted and melted down the plastics, a great deal of which still contained residues from their previous contents, such as toxic cleaners, pesticides, and fertilizers.[59] The devastating health and environmental effects of imported plastic waste led the government of Indonesia to ban its import in 1993. The Philippines faces similar problems with plastic-waste imports. In 1991 alone, the US shipped over six million kilograms of plastic wastes to the Philippines.[60]

The highly dangerous reclamation of lead from used lead-acid car batteries imported from industrialized countries is also a thriving business in SEA. Used car batteries are exported to the region from the US, Australia, Japan, Canada, and the United Kingdom (UK). These countries have an efficient system of used battery collection, but many lead recycling plants have been closed down in these countries due to the high cost of implementing environmental and health precautions for workers. The destination of these used batteries are recycling operations in Indonesia, the Philippines, and Thailand where such precautions are not taken. Their recycling costs are as a result much lower. According to environmental groups, a lack of protective clothing, insanitary conditions, and poor ventilation are typical in these lead-recycling firms. Most of the workers in these plants suffer from severe lead poisoning, and some have lost their lives due to lead contamination. The pollution emitted from these recycling plants also affects neighboring communities and wildlife through the contamination of the air, soil, and water from lead fumes and discharges.[61]

The Philippines, for example, imported some 76,000 tons of batteries between 1991 and 1996. The main sources of these batteries were Saudi Arabia, Singapore, and Australia, with some also coming from Canada, Japan, New Zealand, the UK, Germany, and the US.[62] Many of the batteries which make their way to the Philippines from Singapore are transported from elsewhere, with Singapore acting as a transshipment center. For example, Philippine Recyclers, Inc. (PRI), located near Manila, recycled 24,000 tons of car batteries per year in the early 1990s.[63] PRI is an affiliate of US-based company, Ramcar Batteries. Greenpeace studies at PRI have shown that levels of lead in and around this plant are extremely high, and that elevated levels of lead in the blood of children and workers have led to a host of health problems.[64] Indonesia also has a number of lead-acid battery recycling plants and imports batteries from Australia and the UK in particular.[65] The largest of these plants, *PT Indo Era Multa Logam* (IMLI), located south of Surabaya, processes some 60,000 tons of lead-acid batteries each year, almost all of which are imported.[66] The Indonesian government has attempted to control these processors since the early 1990s, leading to the closure of several plants.

Political Responses to the Waste Crisis: Social Capital and the Reduction of Hazards

Social capital plays a vital role in the provision of human and environmental security, particularly in developing societies. While not a new concept, social capital has become popular in the development literature in recent years, and is used broadly to refer to the extent to which actors at different levels are able to work with one another towards a social goal.[67] Networks of association, mutual trust, and norms of reciprocity are all key to understanding this ability to coordinate efforts among different actors toward common goals. High levels of cooperation and coordination of efforts among governments, NGOs, international organizations, and business toward a specific goal can lead to significant advances toward achieving that goal. This is seen to represent a high degree of 'social capital'. Social capital, thus, plays an important role in determining the success and/or failure of efforts to alleviate human and environmental insecurities.

A number of political responses to the growing problem of hazardous wastes in SEA have emerged in recent years and these have contributed to the development of social capital around this issue. These responses have come from a variety of actors, from NGOs and local community groups, national governments, regional and international organizations, as well from the business community. The extent to which these different groups of actors are willing to cooperate and coordinate with one another to mitigate the hazardous waste threat is key to understanding actions that have or have not taken place to date on this issue. In this section the responses of governments, NGOs, regional and international organizations and law, as well as private industry to the problem of wastes generated within SEA, both by local firms and multinational firms located in the region will be discussed first. This will be followed by a discussion of the responses of these actors to the problem of waste imports.

Responses to Wastes Generated in SEA

National governments in SEA are only beginning to regulate hazardous waste disposal. As mentioned above, before the early 1990s most countries in the region had no laws on their books regarding waste generation, disposal, or treatment, and most did not have any facilities to treat or safely dispose of hazardous wastes generated by industry. This began to change in the early 1990s as the problem became increasingly apparent. Government responses with particular reference to both Indonesia and the Philippines are discussed more fully below.

In Indonesia, the government ministry principally responsible for environmental strategy and policy is the state Ministry for Population and Environment, or KLH. In 1990, the KLH set up an environmental impact management agency, *Badan Pengendalian Dampak Lingkungan* (BAPEDAL), which is the main agency responsible for pollution control and enforcement, and thus, is most directly responsible for regulations regarding hazardous wastes.[68] However, BAPEDAL is a small agency with less than 100 professional staff.[69] The agency is based in Jakarta and monitoring and enforcement is carried out at the provincial level. BAPEDAL, the Environment Ministry, and other relevant ministries began to draft regulations relating to hazardous wastes in 1993 since before this time there were no laws specifically dealing with it. The new regulations, unveiled in 1994, relate to the collection, transport, labeling, storage, licensing and permits, treatment plant location, and Environmental Impact Assessment (EIA) requirements as well as penalties for not abiding by these laws.[70] However, the ability of the government to regulate hazardous wastes is seriously hampered by the lack of treatment facilities. Indonesia's first hazardous waste treatment facility was built only in 1994 and coincided with the introduction of the new regulations regarding the handling of hazardous waste.

Prior to the drafting of the new hazardous waste regulations, the government of Indonesia set up an innovative program that attempts to reduce industrial effluent dumped in waterways using voluntary agreements and public pressure. The *Proyek Kali Bersih* (PROKASIH), or 'clean streams' program, is an attempt to reduce industrial effluents that are dumped in waterways. The PROKASIH program, initiated by the KLH in 1989, is overseen by BAPEDAL and is implemented at the provincial level. Under this program, major polluters are asked to sign statements obliging them to reduce their effluents into the rivers by 50 per cent in an agreed time frame. The initial focus was to reduce the pollution loads in the 24 most highly polluted rivers in the program's first two years. NGOs have been encouraged by the government to participate in monitoring and enforcement, and to help get local communities involved to apply pressure on those firms that do not comply with their promise to reduce pollution. The media has also been encouraged to report on the firms' performance.

There are PROKASIH teams to monitor progress in each of the 11 provinces, and some 2000 firms had signed agreements by 1994. Non-governmental groups have been active in participating in this program, and the cooperation between government and NGOs on this issue has resulted in some reduction of pollution loads of the highly polluted rivers. While this high degree of social capital around the PROKASIH program has led to some successes, it is not perfect. Problems that have arisen include the weak capacity of the government to monitor actual discharges by firms, the firms' own weak desire to control pollution, as well as the difficulties of tracking large numbers of smaller firms involved in toxic industries.[71]

Another public pressure campaign, known as *Program Penilaian Peringkat Kinerja Perusahaan* (PROPER), is currently being implemented in Indonesia as part of the PROKASIH program. The PROPER program involves the public disclosure of data on firms' industrial pollution emissions. The WB helped the government to develop this new program in 1995 that ranks firms on their emissions and releases findings. Firms are put into one of five categories: gold for excellent, green for very good, blue for adequate, red for being in violation of regulations, and black for the worst polluters. The government reported that no firms were ranked in the gold category in the first set of rankings. At first the government only released names of those firms that did well, and threatened to release names of those who were in the red and black categories. Firms reportedly responded by asking how they could improve their ratings. The government plans to expand this disclosure technique to hazardous wastes specifically.[72] While this program has brought some initial response from firms to improve their environmental performance, some issues have arisen which must be addressed. The program has been much more successful in wealthier, better-educated communities than in poor uneducated communities, a fact that raised concerns that poorer communities may become pollution havens in the country. Thus, the degree of social capital around this issue varies by community and some firms have been more willing to participate than others.

In the Philippines, earlier and stricter legislation has been put in place regarding toxic waste management than in Indonesia. The 'Toxic Substances and Hazardous and

Nuclear Wastes Control Act of 1990' was the first of that country's laws specifically dedicated to hazardous waste regulation. The act gives the government stronger powers to control waste imports and authorizes the Philippine Department of Environment and Natural Resources (DENR) to adopt new hazardous waste-management regulations.[73] Regulations subsequently adopted in 1992, which stress that waste prevention and minimization is the preferred method of waste management, cover responsibilities of those who generate, transport, treat, store, recycle, or dispose of hazardous waste.[74] These regulations include strict rules regarding the management, treatment, and disposal of hazardous wastes. In 1996, the DENR also set up a pilot program similar to the PROPER program in Indonesia that rates firms based on their emissions and makes the information available to the public. The program, called EcoWatch, was set up with assistance from the World Bank. Firms' ratings are made available to the public through a computer located at the DENR office.[75] Following a successful pilot, this program was adopted as a permanent program by the Philippine government in July 1998.[76]

Community pressure appears to be a large factor in getting firms to comply with regulations and voluntary reductions in emissions, as is seen by the PROPER and PROKASIH programs in Indonesia and the recent adoption of the EcoWatch system in the Philippines.[77] NGO networks are an extremely important part of organizing such community pressure, and when they link up with other levels of authority working towards the same goals, in this case the government and global environmental law support groups, their impact can be significant. Hundreds of NGOs in both Indonesia and the Philippines are involved in helping communities fight for compensation when polluted and when health and/or livelihoods are threatened. To give one specific example, *Wahana Lingkungan Hidup Indonesia* (WALHI), the umbrella organization for environmental NGOs in Indonesia was instrumental in helping a small village near *Semerang* on the north coast of Java to fight the release of industrial effluent into the waterways. The discharge polluted fish ponds and rice paddies, and made the local water supply unpotable. The village sought help from NGOs to seek compensation and put an end to the pollution. WALHI launched a successful consumer boycott of the upstream firms, and the Indonesian legal aid society filed a suit against them. BAPEDAL stepped in to oversee negotiations between the firms and the village, as these firms had previously signed agreements under the PROKASIH program. The outcome was a compensation award to the villagers, development funds for the village, and waste water treatment facilities were to be immediately installed.[78]

But, not all cases turn out to be this successful. In North Aceh, Indonesia, for example, only one of eight villages that sought to sue firms for polluting the local water supply was able to file suit because of the high costs of filing a claim. Other law suits regarding industrial pollution are still pending.[79] Here the lack of government response to reduce the costs of filing a legal claim reduced the effectiveness of NGOs' efforts, even though in theory the government supported the goal of reducing hazardous waste exposure. Thus, while collaboration between NGOs and the government can bring significant change, it must take place in a context that does not place costly obstructions on those seeking change.

The Philippines also has a rich network of environmental NGOs, many of which are linked to the Green Forum, a coalition of several hundred NGOs in the Philippines that was established in 1989. This umbrella organization links a diverse group of NGOs and church organizations that promote the similar goal of sustainable development. It is not yet clear what the participation of these NGOs will be in the government's new EcoWatch program. As it is based on the Indonesian PROPER model, there will likely be active encouragement by the government for NGOs to become involved in the monitoring and enforcement of the scheme, as well as in helping individual communities to sue firms which are in contravention of the government's environmental regulations.

Some private firms are now responding to public pressure regarding the waste crisis by improving their environmental management. In addition to participation by a number of firms in the PROPER and EcoWatch programs in Indonesia and the Philippines, many larger firms and those with global connections are interested in becoming certified under the new global environmental management standard, ISO 14001. Certification under this standard, which calls for firms to establish a management system which takes environmental concerns into account, is predicted by many to become a *de facto* condition for selling goods on global markets. Among the requirements of the standard are the development of firm-level environmental policy and a commitment to the prevention of pollution. But while the standard does force firms to establish environmental management systems, it has already been criticized as being weak, only calling for firms to meet existing environmental regulations in the countries in which they are operating.[80] At the same time, locally-owned firms in SEA are finding it very expensive to obtain this certification.

While some firms are attempting to improve their environmental management, others are seeking to benefit from the hazardous pollution problems in the region. Environmental clean-up firms that are going global see the rapidly industrializing countries of SEA to be a promising market. Recently tightened domestic hazardous waste regulations in the region have been good news for the global environment industry, as it has meant a growing market for cleaning up after hazardous industries. The Asian environmental services market has been growing at a rate of 16-20 per cent annually and in 1993 was worth US$47 billion, not far behind the US$68 billion value of environmental services in the US and US$58 billion value in Europe that same year.[81] Although it is important to clean up existing hazardous wastes which have been improperly disposed of, some have been critical of the drive to clean up Asia's hazardous wastes which has deflected attention from the need to adopt clean production processes which would avoid the generation of such wastes in the first place.[82]

There appears to be a high level of social capital currently emerging around forcing firms in SEA, whether local or foreign, to comply with state-level regulations on the disposal of hazardous wastes. Governments and NGOs are working together with international organizations such as the WB to put in place a mechanism for effective community pressure on firms to clean up their practices. In cases where firms have responded positively, there seems to be a high level of social capital, especially where firms are moving toward voluntary improvements in environmental management systems and implementation of ISO 14000 type standards. While levels of social capital around the hazardous waste crisis may be relatively higher than they have been in the past, there is room for it to increase. Some problems have emerged. These have centered on governments' lack of support in certain cases of community pressure on firms, and on firms that have attempted to profit from hazardous pollution clean up, rather than adopting clean production technologies.

Responses to Waste Imports

The import of hazardous wastes has elicited a somewhat different set of political responses, which have focused on the issue of banning the import and export of hazardous wastes through national legislation and the Basel Convention. The Indonesian government ratified the Basel Convention in July 1993. It also banned the import of plastic wastes as mentioned above, and banned the import of all hazardous waste in 1994. This latter ban, however, was amended less than a year later to in fact allow the import of hazardous wastes for recycling which were seen to be an important source of raw materials for the country.[83] The Philippines was one of the first countries in the region to ban the import of toxic wastes in 1988 and it ratified the Basel Convention in October of 1993. But in 1994, the Philippine government also decided to let in wastes for recycling. As a result, the problem of waste imports destined for recycling operations has continued to plague both the Philippines and Indonesia.[84]

The practice of environmentally unsound disposal of Northern-generated toxic wastes in the Third World was in fact widely acknowledged in SEA in the early 1990s. In late 1993, the Association of Southeast Asian Nations (ASEAN) agreed to begin to draft regional waste trade conventions banning the importation of waste for disposal and recycling from industrialized countries.[85] These efforts arose from concerns by these countries that the Basel Convention was not providing sufficient protection from toxic waste imports for disposal and recycling. The annual ASEAN communiqué urged governments to ban waste imports for any purpose, and indicated that efforts had begun to draft a Regional Convention Prohibiting the Importation and Transboundary Movement into the ASEAN Region of Hazardous Waste. This announcement followed strong lobby efforts by a coalition of environmental activists in the region. But a regional agreement has not yet been reached. These efforts were no doubt hampered by the fact that both Indonesia and the Philippines amended their waste bans in 1994 to allow imports of wastes destined for recycling operations.

While some Northern industrialized countries have firmly denied that the practice of toxic waste dumping and recycling in SEA and other parts of the developing world is environmentally unsound, this view has been overshadowed by the overwhelming empirical data, gathered largely by non-governmental environmental groups, to the contrary. At the March 1994 conference of parties to the Basel Convention held in Geneva, a decision was adopted which effectively bans the toxic waste trade for both disposal and recycling between the OECD countries and non-OECD countries within the context of the Basel Convention. This decision was made on the grounds that such disposal and recycling was, according to evidence to date, highly unlikely to be carried out in an 'environmentally-sound manner' in non-OECD countries.[86] This evidence along with the resolve of most developing countries and environmental groups to halt these practices were largely behind the ban decision. The ban applies to wastes exported for disposal (effective immediately) as well as that destined for recycling (effective 31 December 1997). The Basel Convention was formally amended to this effect in September 1995 at the Third Conference of Parties, and this amendment will come into force once the necessary 63 ratifications are made. The commitment to the 1995 Basel Convention amendment was reaffirmed by parties to the Convention at the Fourth Conference of Parties held in Kuala Lumpur in early 1998.

Both national and international NGOs played important roles in the rejection of the waste trade by the signatories to the Basel Convention. Together these national and international groups provided vital data to the international community on the environmentally unsound disposal and recycling of imported waste that ultimately swayed the parties to the Convention to adopt the ban amendment. Indeed, this successful cooperation by NGOs prompted the establishment of the Basel Action Network (BAN) in the late 1990s. BAN is a network of NGOs from around the world that seeks to lobby governments to ratify the Basel Convention and its amendment and to report on toxic waste trade incidents. The Indonesian environmental umbrella organization WALHI is a participant in this network.[87] WALHI has recently used this network to gain global support for its efforts to protest the importation of soil contaminated with heavy metals by the Indonesian government.[88]

But while NGOs have been successful in networking and influencing the outcome of the Basel amendment, it is not clear that Southeast Asian governments are working in collaboration with them toward this goal. Publicly these governments have been supportive of the ban. For example, the Indonesian Environment Minister said that the developing countries had 'for a long time suffered from the consequences of being used as a dumping ground for toxic and hazardous waste from industrialized countries'.[89] But while a number of Southeast Asian countries pledged their support for the Basel ban at the 1998 meeting of the parties in Kuala Lumpur, including China, Malaysia, Indonesia, and Singapore, none of these countries has yet ratified the amendment.

Reflecting this lack of government action, toxic waste imports are still making their way into SEA in the late 1990s. In 1998, PVC plastic-waste imports from the Netherlands entered the Philippines,[90] while imported waste problems continue to plague Indonesia. For example, some 250 containers of imported hazardous wastes that were shipped to Tanjung Priok Harbor in Jakarta in 1992 are still in the country. The waste containers sat in the harbor for a number of years. The Dutch government took back around 75 containers, but the origin and the owners of the remaining wastes could not be determined.[91] As of early 1998, 116 shipping containers were still stored at the harbor. The wastes are a mixture of plastics – some recyclable, some not – and hazardous waste.[92] Japan is also reported to be exporting toxic ships to be scrapped in the Philippines and Vietnam. During 1993-97, some 380,000 tons of ships were exported to the Philippines and 650,000 tons to Vietnam by Japanese companies.[93] Mercury-contaminated waste was also shipped to the Cambodian port city of

Sihanoukville by a Taiwanese firm in late 1998. The importation of the waste sparked a mass exodus from the city in which several people died. This waste caused a global reaction by NGOs that tracked the waste to Formosa Plastics that took back the waste and attempted to ship it to the US. The waste was then returned to Taiwan.[94] The continuation of toxic waste imports into SEA is blamed by environmental groups on their respective government's inability to stop this practice.

While the degree of social capital at the international level among international NGOs, developing-country governments, and international organizations is high and has resulted in the ban on wastes within the Basel Convention, social capital on a practical level, that is, action on the part of governments and their cooperation with domestic and international NGOs to stop waste imports, has been extremely weak. The result is tough international legislation that Southeast Asian governments have chosen not to adopt at the domestic level, at least for the moment.

Policy Recommendations for Hazardous Pollution Prevention in SEA

This chapter had attempted to show that the growing problem of hazardous waste generation and imports in SEA pose a mounting human and environmental security threat. The problem is linked to economic processes from the global to the local level. Actions to mitigate the security threat posed by the hazardous waste crisis must come from a variety of actors at the local, national, and global levels. The extent to which social capital exists around this issue, in other words, the extent to which these various actors at different levels are willing and able to cooperate with one another towards the goal of reducing the human and environmental security threat posed by hazardous waste, plays a key role in determining whether such actions are successful. It is clear that relying on government regulations alone to deal with this problem is not adequate. Pressure by affected communities, NGOs, and international legislation is essential. Cooperation among all of these actors, and including private businesses, seems to enhance the chances of reducing the waste threat even further.

Some positive steps in this regard have taken place, as previously discussed. These include the WB-assisted PROPER and EcoWatch programs of the Indonesian and Philippine governments, respectively, which operate on the premise that community pressure through the public disclosure of firms' pollution levels is vital to improving the latter's performance. Recent investments in hazardous waste treatment facilities have also been seen as important in removing the threat of exposure to these wastes through waterways and municipal landfills. The involvement of NGOs and community groups in the governments' efforts, particularly the PROPER and EcoWatch programs, has been vital to their success. The growing interest of firms in SEA to adopt environmental management systems such as the ISO 14001 standard, is seen to be a sign that firms are now coming on side in the drive to reduce the threats posed by hazardous waste. And the achievement of the Basel ban amendment at the international level also has been an important step in the struggle to stop the export of hazardous wastes to the region. All of these developments in recent years have created opportunities for cooperation and collaboration among different actors, and in some cases have resulted in a high degree of social capital that has been able to effect some positive change.

But these changes, while important, have been modest thus far, and there is room for much improvement. In the meantime, the actors working towards mitigating the hazardous waste crisis are facing some serious challenges that can be addressed by appropriate policies. Some of these policies have already been identified above; others have only recently emerged. These are outlined below.

1. **Better co-operation and collaboration between governments and NGOs regarding hazardous waste pollution in the region is needed.**
   What is crucial is that government provides a context within which NGOs can help communities to fight for their environmental rights. And it is important that NGOs are not simply 'used' by governments to do their work for them as a revenue-saving exercise. The cooperation between NGOs and government must be one with mutual trust and reciprocity, and not simply a business transaction. Ensuring that all communities receive equal support from governments and NGOs is also vital, as the creation of 'pollution havens' both among and within these countries is a real possibility.

2. **Governments as well as local communities and NGOs should encourage firms to adopt clean production practices.**
   There is a focus by some firms in the region on benefiting from cleaning up hazardous wastes rather than preventing their generation in the first place. The emphasis on building hazardous waste disposal facilities, while important, addresses only part of the problem, and one of the biggest challenges facing SEA, and the world, in the next century is the move to truly 'clean' production processes which do not generate hazardous wastes. There seems to be an emerging consensus, at least in academic circles, that the best way to deal with the mounting environmental and human security threat posed by hazardous waste is not so much to clean up existing mess, but rather to prevent them from occurring in the first place. This means a role for governments not just in forcing firms to comply with existing government regulations, but giving firms incentives to get them to go beyond regulation toward the adoption of clean production technologies that do not create hazardous wastes or which drastically reduce them. These incentives can come not just from government, but also from community pressure. While this may sound radical, it is in fact the most sensible strategy, as it is cheaper and more effective to prevent pollution than to clean it up. Since most industrial growth (85 per cent) in Indonesia, for example, will be new growth by the year 2010,[95] it is extremely important that the goal of clean production be met.

3. **Governments could do more to stand behind their words when it comes to international efforts to halt the waste trade.**
   Though most Southeast Asian governments have denounced the trade and have supported the amendment to the Basel Convention which bans this trade, none have ratified the ban amendment, and the Philippine and Indonesian governments in particular have continued to allow the importation of toxic wastes into their

countries for the purposes of recycling, even though this is in direct contravention of the Basel ban amendment. While social capital among environmental activists and developing-country governments was high in the negotiation of the Basel Convention and its amendment, it appears that governments have been less willing to cooperate with NGOs domestically than they have been at the international level. Bringing the efforts to halt this trade home, and cooperating with NGOs, both domestic and international that are seeking to end the trade is a key ingredient to ending waste imports to the region.

4. **There is an urgent need for action at all levels – local communities, governments, and international aid agencies – to address the environmental impacts of the recent economic crisis in the region.**
The outlook for the goal of reducing hazardous waste generation since the recent economic crisis is not good. A recent study on industrial pollution in Indonesia during the first year of the crisis showed that while it declined by 18 per cent, at the same time pollution intensity in industrial effluents increased by 15 per cent.[96] It is likely that similar results would hold for most hazardous waste-generating industries. So while one might have expected reduced industrial output to result in less waste generation, in fact it resulted in more. Why? The increase in waste generation during the financial crisis was likely to be due to reduced government ability, financially and physically, to monitor and enforce environmental regulations during the time of crisis. NGO ability to monitor firms' performance and relay this information to affected communities also was probably diminished due to financial constraints. Thus, relatively unwatched, those firms still in production were not attempting to comply with environmental regulations, presumably because there were short-term cost advantages to not complying. This sort of outcome demonstrates that the industry component of social capital is tenuous, and that it is only when firms have the financial luxury to adopt voluntary environmental measures for the longer term that they actually do so. The financial crisis also no doubt strained relations between governments and NGOs which cooperated in the past on exposing polluting firms, as it is clear that reducing the hazardous waste threat fell from the government's top list of priorities given its dwindling resources, while it no doubt still remained high on the list of concerns of environmental groups. And it is likely that attempts to import toxic wastes by some recycling firms increased during the crisis because, despite the risks, it was seen as a cheap source of raw materials, and because governments were doing little to stop it. Whether the nascent social capital that was beginning to emerge around these issues in the early 1990s can be re-established before a dramatic rise in hazardous waste exposure occurs in the region remains to be seen. In the meantime, human and environmental insecurities arising from toxic waste in SEA remain.

Notes

1   See, for example, Homer-Dixon, T. F. (1994), 'Environmental Scarcities and Violent Conflict: Evidence from Cases', *International Security*, vol.19, no.1; Barber, C. (1997), 'The Case of Indonesia', *Project on Environmental Scarcities, State Capacity and Civil Violence*, American Academy of Arts and Sciences, Cambridge, MA.

2   Brandon, C. and Ramankutty, R. (1993), *Toward an Environmental Strategy for Asia*, World Bank Discussion Paper No. 224, World Bank, Washington, DC, pp.66.

3   Brandon, C. (1996), 'Reversing Pollution Trends in Asia', *The Environment Industry: The Washington Meeting*, OECD, Paris, pp.186.

4   World Bank (1999), *Indonesia: From Crisis to Opportunity*, World Bank Report, July, pp.77.

5   Lindsay, J. (1993), 'Overlaps and Tradeoffs: Coordinating Policies for Sustainable Development in Asia and the Pacific', *The Journal of Developing Areas*, vol.28, October, pp.28.

6   Jayasankaran, S. (1995), 'Waste Not, Want Not: Malaysia needs a waste-treatment facility fast', *Far Eastern Economic Review*, 13 April, pp.61.

7   'Three Regions Move to Ban Waste Trade', *Toxic Trade Update*, vol.6, no.4, 1993.

8   Brandon and Ramankutty (1993), *Toward an Environmental Strategy for Asia*, pp.66, 72.

9   Nelson, D. (1997), 'Toxic Waste: Hazardous to Asia's Health', *Asia Pacific Issues: Analysis from the East-West Center*, no.34, pp.3.

10 Brandon (1996), *'Reversing Pollution Trend in Asia'*, pp.188.

11 See, for example, Colborne, T., Dumanoski, D. and Myers, J. P. (1996), *Our Stolen Future*, Dutton, New York.

12 Brandon (1996), *'Reversing Pollution Trend in Asia'*, pp.186.

13 World Bank (1999), *Indonesia: From Crisis to Opportunity*, pp.201-2.

14 'ADB Warns of Grim Economic Future unless Region Protects Environment', *International Environment Reporter*, vol.18, no.10, pp.367.

15 Kent, L. (1991), *The Relationship Between Small Enterprises and Environmental Degradation in the Developing World (With Special Emphasis on Asia)*, Development Alternatives, Inc., Washington, DC, pp.10.

16 *Ibid.*, pp.13-22.

17 Brandon and Ramankutty (1993), *Toward an Environmental Strategy for Asia*, pp.74.

18 *Ibid.*, pp.72.

19 ESCAP/UNCTC (1990), *Environmental Aspects of Transnational Corporation Activities in Pollution-Intensive Industries In Selected Asian and Pacific Developing Countries* UN/ESCAP, Bangkok, pp.69-70.

20 Brandon and Ramankutty (1993), *Toward an Environmental Strategy for Asia*, pp.69.

21 ESCAP/UNCTC (1990), *Environmental Aspects of Transnational Corporation Activities in Pollution-Intensive Industries In Selected Asian and Pacific Developing Countries*, pp.71-2.

22 O'Connor, David (1994), *Managing the Environment with Rapid Industrialization: Lessons from the East Asian Experience*, OECD, Paris, pp.167-72.

23 Dixon, C. (1995), 'Origins, Sustainability and Lessons from Thailand's Economic Growth', *Contemporary Southeast Asia*, vol.17, no.1, June, pp.48-9; UNCTAD Division on TNCs and Investment (1995), *World Investment Report 1995: Transnational Corporations and Competitiveness*, New York, UN, pp.58.

24 ESCAP/UNCTC (1990), *Environmental Aspects of Transnational Corporation Activities in Pollution-Intensive Industries In Selected Asian and Pacific Developing Countries*, pp.4.

25 ESCAP/UNCTC (1998), *Transnational Corporations and Environmental Management in Selected Asian and Pacific Developing Countries*, UN/ESCAP, Bangkok, pp.10-11.

26 *Ibid.*, pp.5.

27 ESCAP/UNCTC (1990), *Environmental Aspects of Transnational Corporation Activities in Pollution-Intensive Industries In Selected Asian and Pacific Developing Countries*, pp.28-39.

28 UNCTC (1992), *World Investment Directory 1992*, Asia and the Pacific, vol.1, UN, New York.

29 *Ibid.*

30 ESCAP/UNCTC (1990), *Environmental Aspects of Transnational Corporation Activities in Pollution-Intensive Industries In Selected Asian and Pacific Developing Countries*, pp.58; see also Fowler, R. (1995), 'International Environmental Standards for Transnational Corporations', *Environmental Law*, vol.25, no.1, pp.15.

31 *Ibid.*, pp.63-4.

32 The extent to which these various factors dominate and the way that they play themselves out in the region is the subject of some debate. See, for example, Cummings, B. (1984), 'The Origins and Development of the Northeast Asian Political Economy: Industrial Sectors, Product Cycles and Political Consequences', *International Organization*, vol.38, no.1; and Bernard, M. and Ravenhill, J. (1995), 'Beyond Product Cycles and Flying Geese: Regionalization, Hierarchy, and the Industrialization of East Asia', *World Politics*, vol.47, January; Bello, W. (1993), 'Trouble in Paradise: The Tension of Economic Integration in the Asia-Pacific', *World Policy Journal*; Hisahiko, O. (1993), 'Southeast Asia in Japan's National Strategy', *Japan Echo*, vol.20; Bello, W. and Rosenfeld, S. (1990), 'Dragons in Distress: The Crisis of the NICs', *World Policy Journal*.

33 Bello (1993), *'Trouble in Paradise: The Tension of Economic Integration in the Asia-Pacific'*, pp.33; Maull (1991); McDowell, M. (1989), 'Development and the Environment in ASEAN', *Pacific Affairs*, vol.62, no.3, pp.326-7.

34 Nishikawa, J. (1982), 'The Strategy of Japanese Multinationals and Southeast Asia', in Consumer's Association of Penang (ed.), *Development and the Environmental Crisis: A Malaysian Case*, CAP, Penang, pp.252.

35 Ofreneo, Rene (1993), 'Japan and the Environmental Degradation of the Philippines', in M. Howard (ed.), *Asia's Environmental Crisis*, Westview, Boulder, pp.214-6.

36 Nishikawa (1982), *'The Strategy of Japanese Multinationals and Southeast Asia'*, pp.256; and *Ibid.*, pp.215.

37 Castleman, B. (1987), 'Workplace Health Standards and Multinational Corporations in Developing Countries', in C. Pearson (ed.), *Multinational Corporations, the Environment, and the Third World*, Duke University Press, Durham, pp.164; Karliner, J. (1994), 'The Environmental Industry', *The Ecologist*, vol.24, no.2, pp.61; *Toxic Trade Update*, vol.6, no.1, 1993, pp.31.

38 Ichihara, M. and Harding, A. (1995), 'Human Rights, the Environment and Radioactive Waste: A Study of the Asian Rare Earth Case in Malaysia', *Review of European Community and International Environmental Law*, vol.4, no.1, pp.1-14.

39 Castleman (1987), *Workplace Health Standards and Multinational Corporations in Developing Countries*, pp.163.

40 Nishikawa (1982), *'The Strategy of Japanese Multinationals and Southeast Asia'*, pp.258; McDowell (1989), *'Development and the Environment in ASEAN'*, pp.327.

41 Castleman (1987), *Workplace Health Standards and Multinational Corporations in Developing Countries*, pp.157.
42 Wood, A. (1995), 'Asia/Pacific: Rising Star on the Chemical Stage', *Chemical Week*, 15 February, pp.36.
43 Abrahams, P. (1994), 'The Dye is Cast by Growth and Costs', *Financial Times*, 13 May.
44 Wood, *'Asia/Pacific: Rising Star on the Chemical Stage'*, 1995, pp.36; Ng Weng Hoong (1995), 'Singapore's Catchphrase: Add Value', *Chemical Week*, 15 February, pp.40.
45 Bruno, K. and Greer, J. (1993), 'Chlorine Chemistry Expansion: The Environmental Mistake of the 21st Century', *Toxic Trade Update*, vol.6, no.2.
46 ESCAP/UNCTC, *Environmental Aspects of Transnational Corporation Activities in Pollution-Intensive Industries In Selected Asian and Pacific Developing Countries*, 1990, pp.61.
47 *Ibid.*, pp.4.
48 Kaji, G. (1994), 'Challenges to the East Asian Environment', *The Pacific Review*, vol.7, no.2, pp.212.
49 ESCAP/UNCTC (1990), *Environmental Aspects of Transnational Corporation Activities in Pollution-Intensive Industries In Selected Asian and Pacific Developing Countries*, pp.69.
50 Taylor, A. (1996), 'Third World looks to First World Cast-offs', *Financial Times*, 16 January, pp.5.
51 Anderson, I. (1992), 'Dangerous Technology Dumped on Third World', *New Scientist*, vol.133, 7 March, pp.9.
52 Nelson (1997), *'Toxic Waste: Hazardous to Asia's Health'*, pp.5.
53 Usher, A. D. (1988), 'Thailand Becomes a Waste Dump', *The Nation*, 26 June, reprinted in Third World Network, *Toxic Terror*, Third World Network, Penang, Malaysia, 1991, pp.64.
54 Greenpeace (1990), *The International Trade in Wastes: A Greenpeace Inventory*, pp.21-5; Moyers, B. and the Center for Investigative Reporting (1991), *Global Dumping Ground*, Lutterworth Press, Cambridge, MA, pp.14-27.
55 *Ibid.*, pp.181-9.
56 For analysis, see Kummer, K. (1992), 'The International Regulation of Transboundary Traffic in Hazardous Wastes: The 1989 Basel Convention', *International and Comparative Law Quarterly*, vol.41, no.3, July; Clapp, J. (1994), 'The Toxic Waste Trade with Less Industrialized Countries: Economic Linkages and Political Alliances', *Third World Quarterly*, vol.15, no.3.
57 'Philippines Changes Position on Waste Imports', *Toxic Trade Update*, vol.7, no.1, 1994, pp.18.
58 Greenpeace (1994), *Database of Known Hazardous Waste Exports from OECD to non-OECD Countries 1989-March 1994*, Greenpeace International, Amsterdam, pp.II-4.
59 Bokerman, I. and Vorfelder, J. (1993), *Plastics Waste to Indonesia: The Invasion of the Little Green Dots,* Greenpeace, Hamburg, Germany.
60 Greenpeace (1994), *The Waste Invasion of Asia,* Greenpeace, Sydney, Australia, pp.20-2.
61 Cobbing, M. (1991), *Lead, Astray: The Poisonous Lead Battery Waste Trade*, Greenpeace International, Amsterdam; Moyers and CIR, *Global Dumping Ground*, 1991, pp.52-61.
62 Greenpeace (1996), 'Philippines Fails to Halt Toxic Waste Imports', *International Toxics Investigator*, vol.8, no.4, pp.12.
63 Wallace, C. (1994), 'Asians Vie for Toxic Trade as Danes seek Ban on Waste from West', *Vancouver Sun*, 24 March, pp.A17.
64 Greenpeace (1996), *'Philippines Fails to Halt Toxic Waste Imports'*, pp.13.

65 Cobbing (1991), *Lead, Astray: The Poisonous Lead Battery Waste Trade*, pp.4-5.

66 *Ibid.*, pp.9.

67 See, for example, Brown, L. D. and Ashman, D. (1996), 'Participation, Social Capital and Intersectoral Problem Solving: African and Asian Cases', *World Development*, vol.24, no.9, pp.1467-8; Putnam, R. (1995), 'Bowling Alone: America's Declining Social Capital', *Journal of Democracy*, vol. 6, no.1, pp.67; Hyden, G. (1995), 'Civil Society, Social Capital, and Development: Dissection of a Complex Discourse', *Studies in Comparative International Development*, vol.32, no.1.

68 Spitalnik, E. (1992), *Hazardous Waste Management Legislation in Asia*, (mimeo) paper presented at 'International Chemical Regulation Briefing', Washington, DC, 12-13 November 1992, pp.15.

69 World Bank (1999), *Indonesia: From Crisis to Opportunity,* pp.130.

70 Warren, C. and Elston, K. (1994), 'Environmental Regulation in Indonesia,' *Asia Paper No.3*, University of Western Australia Press, Nedlands, pp.61.

71 World Bank (1999), *Indonesia: From Crisis to Opportunity,* p.133.

72 'World Bank Endorses Disclosure of Emissions Data as Enforcement Technique', *International Environment Reporter*, vol.19, no.18, 4 September 1996, pp.774-5.

73 Spitalnik (1992), *Hazardous Waste Management Legislation in Asia*, pp.19.

74 *Ibid.*, pp.20.

75 Sandique, R. (1996), 'Rating System for 2000 Industries in Manila Set', *Manila Standard*, 9 December; 'Computer to List Firms Polluting Environment', *Philippine Daily Inquirer*, 29 April 1997.

76 Press Release, 'Implementation of Industrial Ecowatch System', DENR, Government of the Philippines, 9 July 1998.

77 Pargal, S. and Wheeler, D. (1996), 'Informal Regulation of Industrial Pollution in Developing Countries: Evidence from Indonesia', *Journal of Political Economy*, vol.104, no.6; Hettige, H., Huq, M., Pargal, S. and Wheeler, D. (1996), 'Determinants of Pollution Abatement in Developing Countries: Evidence from South and Southeast Asia', *World Development*, vol.24, no.12.

78 World Bank, *Solar Home Systems Project: Staff Appraisal Report, Indonesia*, pp.202.

79 See, for example, 'Public Interest Environmental Law in Indonesia: Courage, Skill and Networking', Environmental Law Alliance Worldwide homepage: *http://www.igc.apc.org/elaw/update_summer_95.html.*

80 Clapp, J. (1998), 'The Privatization of Global Environmental Governance: ISO 14000 and the Developing World', *Global Governance*, vol.4, no.3; Roht-Arriaza, N. (1997), 'Environmental Management Systems and Environmental Protection: Can ISO 14001 be Useful Within the Context of APEC?', *Journal of Environment and Development*, vol.6, no.3.

81 Lucus, A. (1995), 'Chemical Companies Play the Environmental Market', *Chemical Week*, 18 January, pp.32.

82 Karliner (1994), *'The Environmental Industry'*.

83 'Environmentalists push for legislation on strict liability for toxic waste importers', *International Environment Reporter*, vol.19, no.5, March 1996, pp.179.

84 'Philippines Changes Position on Waste Imports', 1994, pp.18.

85 'Three Regions Move to Ban Waste Trade', 1993, pp. 4-6; 'South Pacific Forum to Negotiate a Regional Waste Trade Ban', and 'Southeast Asian Activists Call for a Regional Waste Trade Ban', *Toxic Trade Update*, vol.6, no.3, 1993, pp.4 and 5, respectively.

86 See Clapp (1994), *'The Toxic Waste Trade with Less Industrialized Countries: Economic Linkages and Political Alliances'*, 1994, pp. 512-5.

87   See the Basel Action Network web-site: *www.ban.org*
88   BAN Action Alert, BAN Electronic Newsletter, 26 July 1999.
89   Quoted in Ng, E. (1998), 'Asia Pushes for Ban on Toxic Waste Exports', *Agence France Press*, 26 February.
90   Greenpeace Press Release, 'Dutch PVC Waste Still Exported to Asia Despite International Agreement', 4 February 1998.
91   'Environmentalists to Push for Legislation on Strict Liability for Toxic Waste Importers', *International Environment Reporter*, 6 March 1996, pp.179.
92   Kalmirah, J. (1998), 'Global Dumping Lays Waste to Scavengers' Livelihood', *Basel Action News*, vol.1, no.1.
93   'Shipbreaking in Southeast Asia', Basel Action News, *http: www.ban.org/ban_news/ shipbreaking_in_sea.html*, 23 August 1998.
94   Reuters (1999), 'Taiwan to bury mercury-laced waste at home', *TAIPEI*, 5 August.
95   Brandon and Ramankutty (1993), *Toward an Environmental Strategy for Asia*, pp.75.
96   Afsah, S. (1998), 'Impact of Financial Crisis on Industrial Growth and Environmental Performance in Indonesia', World Bank New Ideas in Pollution Reduction web-site: *www.worldbank.org/nipr/work/shakeb/index.htm,* July.

References

Abrahams, P. (1994), 'The Dye is Cast by Growth and Costs', *Financial Times*, 13 May.
Anderson, I. (1992), 'Dangerous Technology Dumped on Third World', *New Scientist*, vol. 133, no. 7, March, pp. 9.
Barber, C. (1997), 'The Case of Indonesia', *Project on Environmental Scarcities, State Capacity and Civil Violence*, American Academy of Arts and Sciences, Cambridge, MA.
Bernard, M. and Ravenhill, J. (1995), 'Beyond Product Cycles and Flying Geese: Regionalization, Hierarchy, and the Industrialization of East Asia', *World Politics*, vol. 47, January.
Brandon, C. (1996), 'Reversing Pollution Trends in Asia', *The Environment Industry: The Washington Meeting*, OECD, Paris, pp. 186.
Brandon, C. and Ramankutty, R. (1993), *Toward an Environmental Strategy for Asia*, World Bank Discussion Paper No. 224, World Bank, Washington, DC, pp. 66.
Brown, L. D. and Ashman, D. (1996), 'Participation, Social Capital and Intersectoral Problem Solving: African and Asian Cases', *World Development*, vol. 24, no. 9, pp. 1467-8.
Bruno, K. and Greer, J. (1993), 'Chlorine Chemistry Expansion: The Environmental Mistake of the 21st Century', *Toxic Trade Update*, vol. 6, no. 2.
Castleman, B. (1987), 'Workplace Health Standards and Multinational Corporations in Developing Countries', in C. Pearson (ed.), *Multinational Corporations, the Environment, and the Third World*, Duke University Press, Durham, pp. 164.
Clapp, J. (1998a), 'The Privatization of Global Environmental Governance: ISO 14000 and the Developing World', *Global Governance*, vol. 4, no. 3.
Clapp, J. (1994b), 'The Toxic Waste Trade with Less Industrialized Countries: Economic Linkages and Political Alliances', *Third World Quarterly*, vol. 15, no. 3.
Cobbing, M. (1991), *Lead, Astray: The Poisonous Lead Battery Waste Trade,* Greenpeace International, Amsterdam.
Colborne, T., Dumanoski, D. and Myers, J. P. (1996), *Our Stolen Future*, Dutton, New York.
Cummings, B. (1984), 'The Origins and Development of the Northeast Asian Political Economy: Industrial Sectors, Product Cycles and Political Consequences', *International Organization*, vol. 38, no. 1.

Dixon, C. (1995), 'Origins, Sustainability and Lessons from Thailand's Economic Growth', *Contemporary Southeast Asia*, vol. 17, no. 1, June, pp. 48-9.

'Environmentalists push for legislation on strict liability for toxic waste importers' (1996), *International Environment Reporter*, vol. 19, no. 5, March, pp. 179.

ESCAP/UNCTC (1990a), *Environmental Aspects of Transnational Corporation Activities in Pollution-Intensive Industries In Selected Asian and Pacific Developing Countries* UN/ESCAP, Bangkok, pp. 69-70.

ESCAP/UNCTC (1998b), *Transnational Corporations and Environmental Management in Selected Asian and Pacific Developing Countries,* UN/ESCAP, Bangkok, pp. 10-1.

Fowler, R. (1995), 'International Environmental Standards for Transnational Corporations', *Environmental Law*, vol. 25, no. 1, pp. 15.

Greenpeace (1994a), *Database of Known Hazardous Waste Exports from OECD to non-OECD Countries 1989-March 1994*, Greenpeace International, Amsterdam, pp. II-4.

Greenpeace (1994b), *The Waste Invasion of Asia*, Greenpeace, Sydney, Australia, pp. 20-2.

Greenpeace (1996c), 'Philippines Fails to Halt Toxic Waste Imports', *International Toxics Investigator*, vol. 8, no. 4, pp. 12.

Hettige, H., Huq, M., Pargal, S. and Wheeler, D. (1996), 'Determinants of Pollution Abatement in Developing Countries: Evidence from South and Southeast Asia', *World Development*, vol. 24, no. 12.

Hisahiko, O. (1993), 'Southeast Asia in Japan's National Strategy', *Japan Echo*, vol. 20.

Homer-Dixon, T. F. (1994), 'Environmental Scarcities and Violent Conflict: Evidence from Cases', *International Security*, vol. 19, no. 1.

Hyden, G. (1995), 'Civil Society, Social Capital, and Development: Dissection of a Complex Discourse', *Studies in Comparative International Development*, vol. 32, no. 1.

Ichihara, M. and Harding, A. (1995), 'Human Rights, the Environment and Radioactive Waste: A Study of the Asian Rare Earth Case in Malaysia', *Review of European Community and International Environmental Law*, vol. 4, no. 1, pp. 1-14.

Jayasankaran, S. (1995), 'Waste Not, Want Not: Malaysia needs a waste-treatment facility fast', *Far Eastern Economic Review*, 13 April, pp. 61.

Kaji, G. (1994), 'Challenges to the East Asian Environment', *The Pacific Review*, vol. 7, no. 2, pp. 212.

Kalmirah, J. (1998), 'Global Dumping Lays Waste to Scavengers' Livelihood', *Basel Action News*, vol. 1, no. 1.

Karliner, J. (1994), 'The Environmental Industry', *The Ecologist*, vol. 24, no. 2, pp. 61.

Kent, L. (1991), *The Relationship Between Small Enterprises and Environmental Degradation in the Developing World (With Special Emphasis on Asia)*, Development Alternatives, Inc., Washington, DC, pp. 10.

Kummer, K. (1992), 'The International Regulation of Transboundary Traffic in Hazardous Wastes: The 1989 Basel Convention', *International and Comparative Law Quarterly*, vol. 41, no. 3, July.

Lindsay, J. (1993), 'Overlaps and Tradeoffs: Coordinating Policies for Sustainable Development in Asia and the Pacific', *The Journal of Developing Areas*, vol. 28, October, pp. 28.

Lucus, A. (1995), 'Chemical Companies Play the Environmental Market', *Chemical Week*, 18 January, pp. 32.

McDowell, M. (1989), 'Development and the Environment in ASEAN', *Pacific Affairs*, vol. 62, no. 3, pp. 326-7.

Moyers, B. and the Center for Investigative Reporting (1991), *Global Dumping Ground*, Lutterworth Press, Cambridge, MA, pp. 14-27.

Nelson, D. (1997), 'Toxic Waste: Hazardous to Asia's Health', *Asia Pacific Issues: Analysis from the East-West Center*, no. 34, pp. 3.

Ng Weng Hoong (1995), 'Singapore's Catchphrase: Add Value', *Chemical Week*, 15 February, pp. 40.

Nishikawa, J. (1982), 'The Strategy of Japanese Multinationals and Southeast Asia', in Consumer's Association of Penang (ed.), *Development and the Environmental Crisis: A Malaysian Case*, CAP, Penang, pp. 252.

O'Connor, David (1994), *Managing the Environment with Rapid Industrialization: Lessons from the East Asian Experience*, OECD, Paris, pp. 167-72.

Ofreneo, Rene (1993), 'Japan and the Environmental Degradation of the Philippines', in M. Howard (ed.), *Asia's Environmental Crisis*, Westview, Boulder, pp. 214-6.

Pargal, S. and Wheeler, D. (1996), 'Informal Regulation of Industrial Pollution in Developing Countries: Evidence from Indonesia', *Journal of Political Economy*, vol. 104, no. 6.

'Philippines Changes Position on Waste Imports', *Toxic Trade Update*, vol. 7, no. 1, 1994, pp. 18.

Putnam, R. (1995), 'Bowling Alone: America's Declining Social Capital', *Journal of Democracy*, vol. 6, no. 1, pp. 67.

Roht-Arriaza, N. (1997), 'Environmental Management Systems and Environmental Protection: Can ISO 14001 be Useful Within the Context of APEC?', *Journal of Environment and Development*, vol. 6, no. 3.

Sandique, R. (1996), 'Rating System for 2000 Industries in Manila Set', *Manila Standard*, 9 December.

'Southeast Asian Activists Call for a Regional Waste Trade Ban', *Toxic Trade Update*, vol. 6, no.3, 1993, pp. 5.

'South Pacific Forum to Negotiate a Regional Waste Trade Ban', *Toxic Trade Update*, vol. 6, no.3, 1993, pp. 4.

Spitalnik, E. (1992), *Hazardous Waste Management Legislation in Asia*, (mimeo) paper presented at 'International Chemical Regulation Briefing', Washington, DC, 12-13 November 1992, pp. 15.

Taylor, A. (1996), 'Third World looks to First World Cast-offs', *Financial Times*, 16 January, pp. 5.

'Three Regions Move to Ban Waste Trade', *Toxic Trade Update*, vol. 6, no. 4, 1993, pp. 4-6.

UNCTAD Division on TNCs and Investment (1995), *World Investment Report 1995: Transnational Corporations and Competitiveness*, New York, UN, pp. 58.

UNCTC (1992), *World Investment Directory 1992*, Asia and the Pacific, vol. 1, UN, New York.

Usher, A. D. (1988), 'Thailand Becomes a Waste Dump', *The Nation*, 26 June, reprinted in Third World Network, *Toxic Terror*, Third World Network, Penang, Malaysia, 1991, pp. 64.

Wallace, C. (1994), 'Asians Vie for Toxic Trade as Danes seek Ban on Waste from West', *Vancouver Sun*, 24 March, pp. A17.

Warren, C. and Elston, K. (1994), 'Environmental Regulation in Indonesia', *Asia Paper No. 3*, University of Western Australia Press, Nedlands, pp. 6.

Wood, A. (1995), 'Asia/Pacific: Rising Star on the Chemical Stage', *Chemical Week*, 15 February, pp. 36.

'World Bank Endorses Disclosure of Emissions Data as Enforcement Technique', *International Environment Reporter*, vol. 19, no. 18, 4 September 1996, pp. 774-5.

World Bank (1999a), *Indonesia: From Crisis to Opportunity*, World Bank Report, July.

World Bank (1996b), *Solar Home Systems Project: Staff Appraisal Report, Indonesia*, Indonesia Policy and Operations Division, Country Department III, East Asia and Pacific Regional Office, The World Bank, Washington, DC. pp. 77.

Chapter 4

Communities in Turmoil: Comparing State Responses to Environmental Insecurity in Southeast Asian Forests

Peter Dauvergne[1]

This chapter explores the links between commercial forest management and community insecurity in Southeast Asia (SEA), focusing in particular on the roles and responses of the states of the Philippines, Indonesia, and Malaysia (Sarawak). It argues that state-business domination of lucrative timber operations in Indonesia and Sarawak leaves little scope for innovative and far-reaching responses to alleviate community anger at forest management practices or tackle forest degradation and concomitant environmental insecurity. Tight controls on the press, political opposition, non-governmental organizations (NGOs), communities, and associational groups further impeded environmental reform in the authoritarian state of New Order Indonesia (1965/67-98) and the Malaysian semi-authoritarian state where Sarawak belongs. This suggests that as long as state-business alliances in Indonesia and Sarawak maintain a strong financial interest in timber production, as long as timber continues to hold significant commercial value, and as long as the state dominates civil society, even if forest management practices contribute to sporadic violence (such as the Dayak-Madurese ethnic clashes in East Kalimantan), resistance (such as from the Penan of Sarawak), or regional tensions (such as over the 1997 forest fires in Kalimantan and Sumatra), state leaders are unlikely to implement major environmental reforms. In this context, NGOs, communities, environment agencies within the state, and international organizations are likely to continue to have peripheral influence. These also impede the development of social capital that underpins networks of community cooperation and layers of social trust, essential components for effective community participation, well being, and environmental security. Even more unsettling, instead of reacting to community anger and conflicts with genuine reforms, state leaders in Indonesia and Sarawak have made a self-serving conceptual link between security and forest management, using the language and policies of conservation to justify greater controls over dissident and outlying groups – what Nancy Peluso labels 'coercing conservation'.[2]

The situation in the Philippines was similar to Sarawak and Indonesia during the regime of Ferdinand Marcos (1965-86). Now, however, it is fundamentally different. There is little commercial timber left, eroding corporate influence and state resistance to reforms. Moreover, since 1986, under Presidents Corazon Aquino, Fidel Ramos, Joseph Estrada, and now, Gloria Macapagal Arroyo, the Philippines has evolved into a lively democracy, with a critical press, strong political opposition, a large number of vocal NGOs, a vibrant civil society, and greater community participation. In this context, environment-oriented agencies of the state, international organizations, and NGOs have more input and influence. Environmental norms and networks of social trust have grown among community members. At an aggregate level, greater institutional input from environmental agencies and stronger social capital have contributed to important improvements in forest management. It has also allowed more scope for alternative views and approaches to increase community participation, and decrease community insecurity. One example of this more inclusive and responsive approach is the Community Forestry Program. Yet not all is well in the Philippines. Many reforms have come too late. Many have failed. Rather than reducing local insecurity, some reforms have angered residents, even at times contributing to violent protests. And in pockets of the country that still contain valuable commercial forests, local loggers, sometimes in conjunction with political and military allies, continue to degrade forests, and as in the past leave behind widespread environmental problems.

This chapter is divided into two empirical sections: the Philippines; and Sarawak and Indonesia, where the patterns of forest management have been remarkably similar. The Philippine section begins with some essential background, and then outlines the ties between state elites and loggers, state responses to forest degradation and community insecurity, and ongoing problems with forest management. The section on Sarawak and Indonesia also begins by sketching some necessary background. It then provides evidence of environmental insecurity, before outlining the ties between state officials and loggers, state responses to environmental problems, and state conceptions of and reactions to the links between forest management and community insecurity. The conclusion then considers recommendations that arise from this study, with particular attention to building social capital and reinforcing a vibrant civil society to help combat environmental insecurity within forest communities. Before proceeding to these studies, the next two sections define state, society, civil society, social capital, community insecurity, and environmental insecurity, all of which are central to the analysis.

State, Society, Civil Society, and Social Capital: Definitions

In the tradition of Weber, a state is an organization that includes an executive, legislature, bureaucracy, courts, police, military, and in some cases, schools and public corporations. A state is not monolithic, although some are more cohesive than others. A society is the arena in which state and non-state organizations compete over the official and unofficial rules of the game. States aim to control societies; non-state organizations aim to restructure states; and both states and non-state organizations aim to control the economy (market). Inevitably, to varying degrees, state agencies and non-state organizations shape the interaction and structure of each other. By definition, a state has a legitimate monopoly over the use of violence, and therefore, has coercive tools to get individuals and groups within society to obey and conform. To preserve legitimacy and stability, a state also seeks to raise revenue, minimize domestic and foreign threats, maintain internal cohesion and coordination, and mediate and deflect societal pressures and demands. State output is a result of contests and compromises across agencies and levels of the state, and with relevant non-state organizations in society.[3]

Civil society is a subset of society. It is 'that part of society that connects individual citizens with the public realm and the state. Put in other words, civil society is the political side of society'.[4] It is political in that groups within civil society are trying to promote societal change, such as helping the poor, rather than trying to maximize profits for an individual or group. The bonds that hold individuals together within civil society groupings are sometimes partly financial, such as trade unions, but often the concerns are moral, altruistic, or simply a sense that something is missing in their lives. The associations and groups that comprise civil society – such as churches, neighborhood committees, and voluntary support groups – are independent of the state, even though they may receive some state support. It is important to avoid overstressing the word 'civil'. Many of these groups may have the goal of improving community life; but some groups within civil society may aim to change societal interaction based on decidedly uncivil notions, such as racism or elitism.

Civil society is the arena that both reflects and shapes social capital. Writers, especially within the development community, frequently blur the analytical distinction between social capital and civil society. The concept of social capital is most useful as an analytical tool when it is kept analytically distinct from civil society. Most broadly it 'refers to the normative values and beliefs that citizens in their everyday dealings share'.[5] More specifically, according to Robert Putnam, it 'refers to features of social organization such as networks, norms, and social trust that facilitate coordination and cooperation for mutual benefit'.[6] Along similar lines, Francisco Magno defines it 'as the set of social resources, built on norms of trust and webs of cooperation, which facilitate the pursuit of collective action'.[7] Focusing more on societal and economic outcomes, a recent World Bank (WB) Occasional Paper defines social capital as 'an amalgam of individual and institutional relationships that determines why one society is more effective than another in transforming a given endowment into sustained well being'.[8] In more operational terms, the Canadian International Development Agency (CIDA) defines it as 'the measure of the willingness to cooperate with other individuals and institutions'.[9]

Integrating these various definitions suggests that social capital is most usefully conceived of as a type of social connectedness that facilitates the development of trust, cooperation, identifications, and norms of interaction, which in turn are crucial for decisive action – such as promoting economic growth or managing environmental resources. In this way, social capital is a positive force behind collective action, although depending on the nature of the underlying norms and values these actions could well offend or even hurt individuals 'outside' of the networks of cooperation and institutional manifestations of these norms. It is important to accept this multifaceted understanding of social capital to remove any explicit normative bias, especially when analyzing a region like SEA where claims of distinctive 'Asian values' are common.

Forms of social capital include churches, neighborhoods, trade unions, voluntary associations, and 'the most fundamental form of social capital...the family'.[10] Large corporations not embedded in the local social setting are best seen as analytically outside of social capital. On the other hand, small locally based firms can be an important form of social capital and a key arena for community participation. Important signs of a decline in social capital can include, for example, the loosening of bonds within families and neighborhoods, or falls in the number of members in trade unions and voluntary organizations. Building social capital is a necessary ingredient for empowering a civil society – that is, promoting the direct and genuine participation and input of citizens into the process of political and social change. Civic engagement, norms and networks of collaboration, and social trust are in turn, in the view of most writers on social capital and civil society, essential for economic success as well as the maintenance and consolidation of democracy.

Community and Environmental Insecurity: Definitions

Community insecurity arises when there is an absolute or relative deterioration in social relations and human security, which includes sustainable livelihoods, personal safety, shelter, human rights, health, education, and gender equity. It can also arise when a community perceives the actions of an 'outsider' – such as the central government, a corporation, or an ethnic group – as unreasonable or unjust. These relative and absolute changes and negative perceptions sometimes trigger or fuel conflicts. But they can also just create a bubbling discontentment, a particularly difficult form of community insecurity to identify. High levels of social capital (sometimes phrased as high densities of civic engagement), and the accompanying high levels of cooperation and social trust that develop within communities also, logically, tend to enhance community security and help communities tackle the effects of environmental insecurity. Environmental insecurity is defined broadly, focusing on how environmental change contributes to community insecurity rather than on how war, conflict, or threats contribute to degradation. It includes conventional disputes and conflicts between states over environmental problems, such as water flows across borders, air pollution, and waves of environmental refugees. It also incorporates how environmental degradation contributes to internal security problems, including violence (such as insurgencies and ethnic conflicts), organized resistance (such as protests and blockades), and everyday resistance. Everyday resistance is unorganized, diffuse, individualistic, and covert resistance, such as trespassing, arson, illegal farming, and theft.[11]

The Philippines

Background

The Philippines has about seven thousand islands with a total land area of 30 million hectares. Illegal and legal loggers have contributed to widespread deforestation. Less than 19 per cent of the Philippines now have significant forest cover, down from 70-80 per cent at the start of the 20th century. Only around 700,000 hectares is old-growth forest, less than three per cent of total land area. With little accessible old-growth forest left, the commercial timber industry has collapsed and Philippine tropical log imports are now larger than domestic log harvests.[12] Most of this degradation occurred during the Marcos regime.

Filipino elites and timber under President Marcos (1965-86) Philippine logging peaked during the rule of President Marcos, reaching 11.6 million cubic meters in 1968, and averaging over ten million cubic meters per year from 1965 to 1973.[13] Marcos cronies such as Alfonso Lim and Herminio Disini had substantial timber empires. Some senior state leaders, such as Defense Secretary Juan Ponce Enrile and Armed Forces Chief of Staff General Fabian Ver, were also directly involved in illegal logging.[14] With little supervision from the top, state implementors ignored violations in exchange for bribes, gifts, and personal security. In this context, loggers made windfall profits, in part by disregarding environmental and harvesting guidelines. In the 1960s and 1970s, the Philippines lost much of its remaining old-growth forests that in turn triggered widespread deforestation. Over this time, deforestation in the Philippines was well over the average global tropical rate.[15]

Filipino elites and timber under Aquino (1986-92) and Ramos (1992-98) When Aquino took over from Marcos in 1986 the Philippine timber industry was already in sharp decline. In the first half of the 1980s, as accessible stocks grew scarce, log production dropped steadily. By 1989 it was below three million cubic meters. By 1994 it had fallen to less than one million cubic meters. And by 1997 it was only about 500,000 cubic metres.[16] Annual deforestation also dropped from about 300,000 hectares in the 1960s and 1970s to around 150,000 hectares in the early 1980s. By the early 1990s, it was down to less than 100,000 hectares. To some extent, at least since the early 1990s, lower logging and deforestation rates reflect stronger laws and better management. But in many ways these changes are simply a result of fewer forests to deforest.

The fall of Marcos, along with the depletion of commercial forests severed many of the ties between loggers and top political leaders. President Aquino did not have direct links to loggers during her term. At one time Fidel Ramos had logging interests, but he broke these before becoming president in 1992. As is documented later, however, some loggers did manage to survive the transition after Marcos, especially in pockets of the country that still contain valuable timber. In these places, loggers still have considerable political influence, sometimes through a member of Congress, a provincial leader, or a local mayor.[17] Of 200 congressmen elected in 1992, 17 were connected to logging operations.[18] They are also still able to avoid and manipulate rules by bribing or coercing local implementors.

Philippine state responses to environmental degradation During the Marcos years the state did little to manage commercial forests, conserve biodiversity, or impede deforestation. There was also little sense that commercial forest practices or environmental degradation was in any way a security problem, in part because officials and state agencies (including the military) were often key actors in logging forests quickly and recklessly. Since the fall of Marcos, forest management has improved. Many factors have contributed to these changes. Since the mid-1980s global concern for environmental problems has grown considerably. Environmental concern within the Philippines has also increased.[19] International donors – such as the Asian Development Bank (ADB), the Japan Overseas Economic Cooperation Fund, and the WB – have provided substantial funds for environmental protection. The institutionalization of democratic practices has also had a significant impact. Environmental NGOs have proliferated, gaining increasing influence through a critical media and strong opposition political parties.[20]

Relatively little valuable timber, fewer high-level political and military patrons protecting loggers, stronger internal and external pressure for environmental protection, greater concern with environmental problems, a more dynamic civil society, and the strengthening of democratic practices have contributed to major reforms in commercial timber management. The government has cut the number of logging licenses, stopped issuing new licenses, and banned logging in the few remaining old-growth forests and in provinces with less than 40 per cent tree cover. The government has also collected more accurate forest statistics, increased commercial forest taxes, and implemented major reforestation programs. In 1987 there were 143 timber licenses; by July 1997, only 20 were still active, although these still covered 1.2 million hectares.[21] In addition, to reduce illegal logging the government has strengthened laws, seized illegal logs, rewarded informers, and prosecuted offenders.[22] Although it is difficult to discern absolutely, compared to the Marcos years, state officials also appear to accept a broader understanding of the effects of commercial forest management and environmental degradation, including the impact on community security. Both the Aquino and Ramos governments developed policies and programs to improve environmental quality, tighten environmental controls, and increase local participation in environmental management. Although the governments did not make most of these changes primarily for security reasons, many have the implicit objective of reducing community and environmental insecurity. Two Aquino government policies that have been especially important for reshaping the environmental management of forests are the 1991 Local Government Code and the Community Forestry Program. These also indicate fundamental changes in the attitudes of state elites towards communities and environmental management.

1991 Local Government Code and the Community Forestry Program

The 1991 Local Government Code devolved powers to provinces, cities, towns, and villages (*barangays*). It gives communities the power to protect forests, control reforestation and natural regeneration programs, operate parks and nature reserves, and enforce environmental and forest management laws. It also allows local governments to manage community-based forestry projects. This Code has had significant effects on local environmental politics. In 1995, a government-NGO study found that local officials were now more active in environmental management, diverting more funds and staff to support environmental projects, including reforestation.[23]

Besides the Code, the Aquino government also developed specific programs to increase the participation of communities and NGOs in environmental decisions, research, monitoring, and technology transfers. A particularly important initiative for the environmental management of forests is the Community Forestry Program. This program is one of many programs that comprise the Community-Based Forest Management Strategy (CBFM) and the People-Oriented Forestry Programs and Projects.[24] The motto of CBFM is 'People First and Sustainable Forestry Will Follow'. According to a Philippine Department of Environment and Natural Resources (DENR) brochure, 'Social justice is a basic principle underlying CBFM in granting forest communities tenure and comprehensive rights to use and develop forest resources'. DENR started the Community Forestry Program in 1989 to rehabilitate and conserve secondary and primary forests, shift from large to small-scale forest operations, and increase local participation and training in forest management. It is also designed to make access to forests more equal and democratic, generate work in rural communities, and enhance the institutional capacity of DENR, local government units, and NGOs. These projects provide upland communities with twenty-five year Community Forestry Management Agreements, which can be renewed once. The agreements provide communities with timber management rights conditional on approval from DENR. Communities must obey DENR guidelines and follow a plan to maintain sustainable yields (defined as the annual amount loggers can extract that will regenerate over the cutting cycle and provide equal commercial volumes in subsequent harvests).

The Program is divided into three phases. In the first phase, DENR – in conjunction with local government units and communities – provides information, identifies sites, conducts forest inventories, and selects participants. In the second phase, DENR awards Community Forestry Management Agreements, develops alternative livelihood options, and helps train and organize communities. In the third phase, with DENR assistance and supervision communities reforest, harvest, and regenerate forest areas. NGOs play a key role in this program. They assist in training, organizing, planning, managing, and marketing. With funds from the WB and the ADB, 48 projects were started in 1989; with funds from the United States Agency for International Development another 17 began in 1992.[25]

Environmental Failures, Environmental Insecurity, and Pockets of Resistance

Although the Philippines has taken important steps to make environmental management more inclusive and effective, considerable problems still exist. Decentralizing environmental management and embracing communities and NGOs have not always improved management or alleviated community insecurity. Many community reforestation sites, for example, have failed. Several studies show that after three years only 40 per cent of trees survived. Many trees have died; some are never planted. And occasionally, angry locals have ripped out or burned down plantation trees.[26] In some areas decentralization has, at least temporarily, made the situation even worse. In Agusan, for example, until his death in 1995, Governor D.O. Plaza, who funded his political empire with logs, used the new powers under the 1991 Local Government Code to increase his personal control. He took over logging checkpoints from DENR to conceal illegal logging by his allies and family.[27] Sheila Coronel argues: 'Agusan demonstrates the mixed blessings of democracy and devolution. It dramatizes how, in many parts of the country, the right to make use of increasingly scarce natural resources remains in the hands of a rich and powerful few who also have privileged access to political office'.[28]

Illegal and destructive legal loggers also remain a serious problem. State capacity to monitor and control them is still undermined by links between DENR officials and timber operators. Few staff, limited funds, and inadequate equipment, especially in remote areas that still contain valuable commercial timber, also hamper enforcement. In total, the Philippines only has around 4000 forest guards. Palawan, which contains about one-third of the remaining old-growth forests, only has about 135 guards. In this setting, illegal loggers, sometimes protected by political, military, and bureaucratic elites, continue to destroy primary forests and national parks. In Palanan, Isabela, for example, illegal logging has apparently accelerated since the 1994 ban on logging in protected areas. Other parts of the Philippines have similar problems.[29] As a result of these practices, illegal logs may well account for around half of Philippine total timber consumption. Besides illegal logging, other ongoing problems include tax evasion, inefficient processors, and bogus environmental NGOs. Government officials and corporate operators also continue to intimidate and threaten people who oppose forest management and reforestation projects, especially indigenous forest dwellers.[30] Some environmental measures, such as plantations, have even triggered violence and upheaval, rather than alleviated community insecurity. For example, Alcantara and Sons Company (Alsons) ended up fighting the Matigsalug tribe over the development of a 19,000-hectare timber plantation in Tala-ingod, Davao, Mindanao. According to Federico Magdalena, 'the consequent conflict resulted in the death of many tribesmen and 12 Alsons workers in 1994. The conflict is still raging and no solution is in sight'.[31] The Philippines, then, clearly still has problems with forest management. Yet compared with Sarawak and Indonesia substantial changes have occurred, including changes in attitudes, decision-making, policies, and to a lesser extent, practices.

Sarawak and Indonesia

Background

Like the Philippines, Sarawak and Indonesia have legal control over official forest areas. Unlike the Philippines, however, expansive tracts of commercial forests still remain, although both are heading down the Philippine path. In Sarawak, loggers harvested around 30 per cent of Sarawak's forests from 1963 to 1985.[32] By the end of the 1980s old-growth forests only covered four to five million hectares.[33] Sarawak now has about 8.7 million hectares of forests (out of a total land area of 12.3 million hectares). Around six million hectares are set aside for sustainable timber production. Since the late 1980s Sarawak's old-growth forests have been steadily logged. Commercial log production in 1997 was over 16 million cubic meters, approximately two and a half times higher than sustainable levels. Environmentalists claim that loggers have already degraded 70 per cent of the remaining forests.[34] If these rates and harvesting practices continue, Sarawak will deplete the rest of its valuable commercial timber stocks in less than a decade, leaving behind widespread environmental problems.

Indonesia, with a land area of 190 million hectares, is much larger than Sarawak. Officially, forestlands cover 143 million hectares, but it is more likely that 'natural forests' are only between 90 to 110 million hectares. About 64 million hectares are classified as production forests, accounting for around 60 per cent of legal commercial timber in SEA. According to the International Tropical Timber Organization (ITTO), in 1996 commercial log production was 31.2 million cubic meters. A WB study estimated that it was more likely over 40 million cubic meters, almost two times higher than sustainable levels.[35] At this rate, Indonesia, which has one of the largest commercial tropical log stocks left in the world, could deplete this stock in about three decades. Even more troubling, commercial logging is the most important factor driving deforestation, which is now around one million hectares per year.[36]

The Asian financial crisis that began in mid-1997 lowered demand for tropical timber in Japan and South Korea, contributing to a drop in aggregate log production over the following year across the tropical Asia Pacific. The ITTO estimates that legal log production fell almost three million cubic meters in 1997, to 28.5 million cubic meters.[37] Yet at the same time illegal logging escalated and may now even exceed the ITTO estimate of legal production.[38] Moreover, the drop in overseas demand was a temporary respite and as Asia's economies began to rebound in 1999 legal log production again started to accelerate. Coupled with moves to expand plantations and the pressure on rural land and water resources of the increasing number of poor people, forests may soon face even greater pressures than before the crisis.

Environmental Insecurity in Sarawak and Indonesia

Forest management practices and widespread forest degradation in Sarawak and Indonesia have contributed to significant levels of community and environmental insecurity, triggering everyday resistance, protests, and even violence. The most visible conflicts in Sarawak have been between loggers (backed by the state) and the Penan tribe. Indonesia has similar security problems. As Charles Victor Barber notes, Indonesia's 'forests have become the arena for increasing levels of sometimes violent social conflicts'.[39] Conflicts are sometimes triggered by state and corporate actions (such as when loggers or plantation companies displace communities) and sometimes by environmental degradation itself. These conflicts often occur between state or corporate groups and local residents. For example, Yamdena (Maluku) islanders were furious when in 1991, with no consultation or notice, the government granted the P.T. Alam Nusa Segar Company a 172,000-hectare logging concession, even though the 535,000-hectare island had been a protected area for 20 years. In late 1992, Yamdena islanders attacked the logging company, killing one person and injuring several others. Logging operations were suspended and as of 1996 the situation was still tense.

This is not an isolated case. Conflicts and disagreements between locals and loggers (often with the support of state officials) have occurred in Bentian (East Kalimantan), Sugapa (North Sumatra), and Benekat (South Sumatra).[40] Forest management practices and environmental degradation also sometimes trigger, or at least aggravate conflict between ethnic groups. For example, according to Amri Marzali of the University of Indonesia, the 1997 ethnic clash in Kalimantan between the Dayaks and the Madurese was in part a result of the social and psychological effects on the Dayaks of years of commercial forest exploitation. He explains: 'Land has special meaning for them, not just in an economic sense but is inseparable from the social and religious life within Dayak communities. A vital part of their life has been taken by other people'.[41] Inappropriate state policies, corporate actions, and environmental degradation do not just contribute to domestic insecurity. Although not as common, these can also trigger regional and even international insecurity, as demonstrated by the regional crisis created by raging fires in Kalimantan and Sumatra in the second half of 1997.

Elites and Timber in Sarawak and Indonesia

In both Sarawak and Indonesia, timber operators have maintained close ties to high-level politicians, including current Chief Minister Datuk Patinggi Tan Sri Abdul Taib Mahmud and former President Soeharto. Timber is the backbone of Sarawak's economy and timber money pervades the entire state structure. Chief Minister Taib is the Minister of Forestry, which gives him the exclusive power to grant timber concessions. He has used this power to distribute timber concessions to his allies, friends, and family.[42] The Minister of the Environment and Tourism, Datuk Amar James Wong Kim Min, is the majority shareholder in the group of companies that includes Limbang Trading, which controls around 300,000 hectares of timber concessions in Sarawak. Datuk Tiong Hiew King, the head of the Rimbunan Hijau Group, is the largest logger in Sarawak, controlling about 800,000 hectares. In the mid-1990s his net worth was about M$2 billion. Like the other six major Malaysian Chinese loggers in Sarawak, he has close ties to state leaders (including Chief Minister

Taib and Environment Minister James Wong), providing money in exchange for licenses, political protection, and bureaucratic favors.[43]

The situation is similar in Indonesia. There are hundreds of concessionaires, although most are tied to corporate groups, and according to a WB study, as a result, five or six conglomerates have dominated timber production.[44] Bob Hasan and Prajogo Pangestu have been especially powerful.[45] In the mid-1990s Hasan had logging rights to about two million hectares. Prajogo's concessions covered about 5.5 million hectares. Both Hasan and Prajogo have had close ties to the Soeharto family, including former President Soeharto. They also have extensive networks of allies within the bureaucracy, including forest enforcement officers and customs officials.[46]

Besides ties to politicians and bureaucrats, loggers have also had close ties to Indonesian military officers since the late 1960s. In 1967, Soeharto distributed timber concessions to reward generals, appease potential opponents within the military, and supplement the military budget. By 1978, the armed forces controlled at least 14 timber companies.[47] In the 1980s military involvement in timber operations declined somewhat. In the 1990s, however, substantial timber operations were still run by the military. For example, in the early 1990s the International Timber Corporation of Indonesia operated the country's largest concession (600,000 hectares in East Kalimantan). The armed forces controlled 51 per cent of this company; a conglomerate chaired by Soeharto's son, Bambang Trihatmodjo, controlled 34 per cent; and Hasan controlled 15 per cent.[48] With such powerful interests behind logging, it is hardly surprising that over the last few decades Indonesia and Sarawak have angered marginalized indigenous groups and responded to widespread environmental degradation with half-hearted measures.

State Responses to Environmental Degradation in Sarawak and Indonesia

Under pressure from international critics, Sarawak and Indonesia have developed new environmental and forest policies since the early 1990s. Sarawak has strengthened enforcement agencies, passed stronger penalties for illegal loggers and smugglers, and hired more forest guards. In Indonesia, the government has rescinded some licenses and punished a few illegal loggers. After the fall of Soeharto in mid-1998 these reforms gained momentum. A new overarching forestry law was passed in 1999, replacing the 1967 Basic Forestry Act. Specific measures have also been taken, such as canceling some timber licenses linked to corruption and nepotism, auctioning some concessions, and reviewing the allocation of funds set aside for reforestation.

Despite these changes, however, in both places many loggers still ignore environmental and harvesting guidelines and the overall impact on log production and harvesting practices has been minor. The Sarawak and Indonesian governments have mostly pursued small-time loggers or swidden farmers rather than large well-connected companies, although some larger companies with links to Soeharto have been pursued since mid-1998.[49] Not surprisingly, tight restrictions on civil society and indigenous peoples – combined with the interests of powerful elites – have left little scope for alternative or more inclusive approaches to forest management. As a result, although

Sarawak and Indonesia have social and community forestry programs, these are not nearly as comprehensive or inclusive as those in the Philippines.[50] Unlike the Philippines, there is little concern that forest practices are contributing to community insecurity. In the case of Indonesia, Barber argues that even though local conflicts over forest resources 'are pervasive, they do not particularly disturb the government. Local conflicts are largely treated as local matters'. He maintains that 'a cohesive alliance of timber firms, local governments, and the local police and military apparatus controls the communities in question through a combination of repression and cooptation offers of land compensation, jobs, or outright bribes'.[51] Also, unlike the Philippines, there is little sense that improving environmental management could enhance security.

Since 1989 the Indonesian central government has also started several development programs 'designed to directly address social and environmental problems at the local (village) level'.[52] According to Aleksius Jemadu who conducted a detailed study from 1989 to 1996, many of these efforts, however, have failed, partly because they are based on inappropriate assumptions, and partly because of the dominance of the central government. The Forest Village Development Program announced by the Ministry of Forestry in 1991, for example, is based on the assumption that traditional agricultural practices should be replaced with permanent agricultural activities and employment in commercial forest projects. Timber companies are required to finance and manage Forest Village Development Programs, which generally involve establishing tree crops (such as coffee, cloves, and rubber), social forestry schemes (such as eucalyptus plantations), irrigated rice fields, or forest conservation. These programs can involve hiring locals for logging operations, plantations, or perhaps as tourist guides. They can also involve building local infrastructure, such as roads and bridges. Jemadu shows that these programs are not well integrated into community development plans and have been largely imposed on local governments and communities. These programs also rely heavily on the commitment and performance of timber firms; in some ways they are not so much 'programs' as financial 'subsidies'. Local officials are not even required to confirm the accuracy of corporate progress and financial reports that are submitted to the central government. Corporations are supposed to keep villagers and local leaders involved and informed, but often this appears perfunctory. Although these programs have provided some local monetary and employment benefits, they have done little to resolve conflicts over access and exploitation of forestlands. Overall, they are more for corporations than communities, reflecting the central government priorities rather than the interests of local people.[53]

State Conceptions of Environment-Security Links in Sarawak and Indonesia

Both Sarawak and Indonesia strongly resist the idea that environmental degradation leads to insecurity – or that it in any way contributes to community tension, resistance, and violence. Instead, the governments in both places have linked security and environmental degradation, not to improve environmental management and enhance community security, but to use environmental language and policies to control dissident and outlying groups. For example, the Sarawak and Indonesian governments partly justify measures to confine and control indigenous groups by claiming that slash-and-burn farmers are the primary cause of deforestation and widespread fires. Of course, Indonesia and Sarawak are too sophisticated and intricate to employ environmental measures to just increase control. Some environmental reforms are genuine attempts to protect the environment. There are also diverse views within Sarawak and Indonesia, although the voices that support better environmental management, for any reason, are relatively peripheral. At the same time, it is important to note that the Philippines is also, of course, too complex and multifaceted to implement environmental policies just to improve environmental management and enhance community security; some measures are also simultaneously, or even surreptitiously, designed to increase control.

Conclusions and Recommendations

The conclusions of this study point to various practical policy recommendations for governments, groups within civil society, and bilateral and multilateral donors.

1. **As environmental problems become more acute, as global environmental concern mounts, and as international and local funds increasingly support environmental measures, the rhetoric of Southeast Asian states is shifting in support of sustainable management.** Most states now employ the language of sustainable development, environmental protection, and biodiversity conservation. It is important to recognize, however, that the effect of this new rhetoric differs significantly across political and economic systems, both *between* and *within* countries.

2. **In the Philippines since the late 1980s, a free press, an independent judiciary, democratic practices, and stronger social capital and NGOs have contributed to substantial, although inconsistent, changes to the process of environmental management.** The Aquino, Ramos, and Estrada governments have been relatively open and accountable. Public opinion has also shifted, and now strongly opposes environmentally destructive industries like logging. The central government has decentralized environmental management, and integrated local governments, communities, and NGOs. Involving a broad base of local people in the Philippines has to some extent diffused tensions, helped build social capital, and contributed to improving the basic needs of residents. More and more local politicians have come to power that support environmental protection, or at least no longer have direct ties to environmentally-destructive enterprises. The Philippine DENR has also undergone major reforms and to some extent at the national level it 'has shown that it can act as an impartial administrator and arbiter of environmental disputes'.[54] Although it is difficult, if not impossible, to isolate the main reasons for these changes, they appear partly motivated by new environmental attitudes, and partly by a need to appease vocal international and domestic NGOs and angry local communities. Whatever the underlying reasons, however, as the Community

Forestry Program demonstrates, it is clear that forest management in the Philippines is now far more transparent, inclusive, and responsive to community needs than in Sarawak and Indonesia. This process of reform in the Philippines is ongoing, however, and still requires financial, technical, and institutional support from the international community, especially as internal resources are diverted to help cope with the current financial crisis in the Asia Pacific.

3. **Over the last decade, some changes have also occurred in Sarawak and Indonesia, especially to the *content* of environmental and forest policies.** Both states have increased forest fees, tightened regulations, and launched campaigns to crack down on illegal and destructive loggers. These reform efforts gained some important ground in Indonesia after the fall of Soeharto in 1998. But until then these changes had little impact on large, well-connected companies and, even after Soeharto's downfall, there have been few changes to harvesting practices. Illegal logging also escalated during the 1997-99 financial crisis and may now exceed the volume of legal production. Moreover, as the Asian economies resurge and demand for tropical timber rises reforms in Indonesia appear to be losing momentum. This suggests that as long as valuable timber remains, as long as tight state-business alliances exist, and as long as the state overwhelms civil society and indigenous peoples, state and business leaders are likely to oppose and undermine far-reaching environmental reforms. They are also likely to continue to ignore or resist the evidence that environmental degradation is contributing to community insecurity, even when it leads to violence and protests.

4. **This chapter shows that significant variations arise in community approaches and environmental management within particular countries.** At an aggregate level, the Philippines has certainly implemented far greater reforms to community forest management than, for example, Indonesia or Sarawak. To some extent the Philippines has also moved to alleviate some of the community and environmental insecurity prevalent during the Marcos era. Yet many of these changes have come too late. Moreover, considerable problems remain. Widespread corruption, incompetence, and straightforward mismanagement continue, especially in local DENR offices.

5. **It is important to encourage governments like Sarawak and Indonesia to accept that environmental degradation creates insecurity.** Further empirical studies along this line would be an important first step. Without this evidence, it will be difficult to convince governments to channel funds allocated for security to environmental protection.

6. **Yet convincing governments like Indonesia and Sarawak that improving environmental conditions is necessary to maintain local security will not be easy, even with abundant evidence.** One of the most disturbing findings in this research is that when Indonesia and Malaysia have linked security and environmental degradation it was generally done to justify and legitimize campaigns to increase control in outlying regions, not to improve environmental management. In this way, these governments have simultaneously employed environmental ideas to increase international legitimacy and suppress internal dissent.[55]

7. **Moreover, both the governments of Indonesia and Sarawak perceive local insecurity as a primary cause of environmental degradation.** This leads these governments to use labels like 'slash-and-burn' farmers. It also justifies the use of state conservation tools to control outlying indigenous groups. This suggests that while it is important to encourage governments to examine the links between environmental degradation and security, this task must be pursued with great care to avoid inadvertently bolstering the tools of state suppression.

8. **This chapter shows that the main cause of forest degradation in Southeast Asia is destructive logging in the context of the politics of patronage and market failures.** The resulting community insecurity then feeds back into a cycle of degradation and deforestation through, for example, destitute farmers burning areas to plant crops. These communities are not, then, the main initial cause of environmental degradation, but are primarily struggling to cope with the after-effects of that degradation.

9. **This study adds further evidence that decentralization does not automatically improve management and alleviate community insecurity.** In many cases in the Philippines, decentralization has helped integrate communities and improve environmental management. But in other cases it has increased insecurity as local elites fought over control and rewards, as local environmental programs (such as plantations) triggered resistance or violence, and as local NGOs and communities struggled at cross-purposes. Decentralization works best in settings with strong social capital and civil societies, and effective state and international support.

10. **Bilateral and multilateral donors and non-governmental actors need to evaluate systematically any project labeled as 'community forestry'.** Some of these have supported genuine community participation and control, such as many in the Philippines, while others, such as many in Sarawak and New Order Indonesia, have enhanced the control and power of logging and plantation companies. Community forestry projects designed to meet the needs of corporations could well enhance community insecurity, not alleviate it.

11. **Important changes are occurring and can occur in places practicing coercive conservation.** Over time, environmental language and policies that are part of this process can reorient towards genuine attempts to improve environmental conditions and community welfare. With the fall of Soeharto, for example, there is great potential for change in Indonesia. As post-Marcos Philippines shows, a lively civil society is an important source of change. Yet it is equally important to recognize that even in countries with a vibrant civil society and strong norms of trust and cooperation, commercial interests can co-opt and divide groups within civil society. This partially explains why exploitation and degradation continue in the pockets of remaining commercial forests in the Philippines, Indonesia, and Sarawak.

12. **Ultimately, communities must participate extensively in forest management to alleviate community insecurity that accompanies environmental degradation.** Promoting the development of social capital and supporting the

associations that comprise civil society will bolster effective participation. Left alone, community members or leaders are often as tempted to seek personal gain as central elites. Developing and maintaining a consistent set of community beliefs and norms that integrate environmental concerns is a crucial ingredient for effective community involvement and ultimately effective environmental management. This is consistent with Magno's extensive study of the links between social capital and tenurial security in the forest of Northern Philippines. He concludes that: 'The legal acknowledgment of the resource rights and duties of villagers are bound to be meaningless if they are not implemented. Therefore, the presence of strong local institutions which enforce these rights and duties is crucial in the effective implementation of resource protection programs'.[56] Building social capital, through such means as education, training, and programs to enable people to interact in person, is only the first step, however. It is equally crucial to develop and maintain the associational arrangements that will allow these values and beliefs to be translated into action. This could involve, for example, financial or technical support for community, non-governmental, or voluntary associations that work to enhance community security or those that work to improve environmental conditions. This is also consistent with Magno's overall recommendation that 'In the coming years, making community forestry socially-viable, and therefore, environmentally-sustainable would require serious efforts to prioritize investments in local institution-building, as well as in human and social capital formation'.[57]

13. **Finally, the findings in this chapter suggest that effective societal input into environmental management is most likely to succeed in areas where large corporate interests are weak.** This occurs partly because of the greater scope for international organizations, aid donors, and environmental sectors within states to support communities; partly because of the relatively weak resistance of corporate forces, and partly because central politicians no longer view the area as a source of financial (either state or personal) windfalls. This means that civil societies tend to have greater potential input in areas with severe environmental degradation, especially if the groups within civil society receive external financial or technical support. More pessimistically, this chapter shows that finding ways to integrate civil society into environmental management in areas where environmental resources still retain significant commercial value – such as old-growth forests – is far more difficult as corporations and state patrons block or undermine genuine attempts to enhance community participation and form social capital, both ultimately essential for community and environmental security.

Notes

1   The core ideas in this paper were presented at Echo Seminars at the Manila Hotel, Manila, 29 July 1997; the Centre for Strategic and International Studies, Jakarta, 24 July 1997; and the Eduardo Development Center, Cebu City, the Philippines, 26 May 1998. These seminars provided invaluable input from state officials, non-governmental representatives, and academics from Indonesia and the Philippines. This paper draws on more than two

years of research, involving numerous drafts and visits to the Southeast Asian region. It builds on 'Environmental Insecurity, Forest Management and State Responses in Southeast Asia' in A. Dupont (ed.) (1998), *The Environment and Security: What Are The Linkages?*, Strategic and Defence Studies Centre, Research School of Pacific and Asian Studies, The Australian National University, Canberra, chapter 4, pp.45-64 which was published as part of this research process.

2   Peluso, N. L. (1993), 'Coercing Conservation? : The politics of state resource control', *Global Environmental Change: Human and Policy Dimensions*, vol.3, no.2, June, pp.199-217.

3   The definitions of state and society are from Dauvergne, P. (1998), 'Weak States and the Environment in Indonesia and the Solomon Islands', in P. Dauvergne (ed.), *Weak and Strong States in Asia-Pacific Societies*, Allen and Unwin, Sydney, pp.137. For similar definitions of state and society, see Migdal, J. S. (1988), *Strong Societies and Weak States: State-Society Relations and State Capabilities in the Third World*, Princeton University Press, Princeton, New Jersey; Migdal, J. S. Kohli, A. and Shue, V. (eds) (1994), *State Power and Social Forces: Domination and Transformation in the Third World*, Cambridge University Press, New York; and Grindle, M. S. (1996), *Challenging the State: Crisis and Innovation in Latin America and Africa*, Cambridge University Press, Cambridge.

4   Hyden, G. (1997), 'Civil Society, Social Capital, and Development. Dissection of a Complex Discourse', *Studies in Comparative International Development*, vol.32, no.1, Spring, pp.4.

5   *Ibid.*, pp.5.

6   Putnam, R. D. (1995), 'Bowling Alone: America's Declining Social Capital', *Journal of Democracy*, vol.6, no.1, pp.67.

7   Magno, F. A. (1998), *Environment and Security: The Philippine Mining Sector*, draft paper for the 'DSSEA Project', Manila, December.

8   This definition was quoted in Dixon, J. A. and Hamilton, K. (1996), 'Expanding the Measure of Wealth', *Finance & Development*, vol.33, no.4, December, pp.15. For a World Bank overview of the concept of social capital see 'Social Capital: The Missing Link?' in World Bank (1997), *New Measures of Wealth: Expanding the Measure of Wealth, Indicators of Environmentally Sustainable Development*, CSD Ed., Draft-for-Discussion, April.

9   This is the working definition provided by CIDA for the DSSEA project.

10   Putnam (1995), 'Bowling Alone: America's Declining Social Capital', pp.73.

11   The term everyday resistance is from Scott, James C. (1985), *Weapons of the Weak: Everyday Forms of Peasant Resistance*, Yale University Press, New Haven. For a recent study of the importance of everyday resistance in diluting state control of forests in Asia (especially Burma), see Bryant, R. L. (1997), *The Political Ecology of Forestry in Burma 1824-1994*, Hurst & Company, London.

12   Based on data and interviews at the Department of Environment and Natural Resources, Quezon City, July 1997 and May 1998. Also, see Poffenberger, M. and Stone, R. D. (1996), 'Hidden Faces in the Forest: A 21st Century Challenge for Tropical Asia', *Sais Review*, vol.16, no.1, Winter-Spring, pp.204.

13   Calculated from Food and Agriculture Organization data, various yearbooks.

14   Vitug, M. D. (1993), *Power from the Forest: The Politics of Logging*, Philippine Center For Investigative Journalism, Manila, pp.16-24, 29-32, 44.

15   For background on logging and deforestation in the Philippines, see Kummer, D. M. (1991), *Deforestation in the Postwar Philippines*, The University of Chicago Press, Chicago.

16 International Tropical Timber Organization (ITTO) (1999), *Annual Review and Assessment of the World Timber Situation: 1998*, ITTO, Yokohama, pp.98.

17 Vitug, M. D. (1993), 'Is There a Logger in the House?', in E. Gamalinda and S. Coronel (eds), *Saving the Earth: The Philippine Experience*, third edition, Philippine Center for Investigative Journalism, Manila, pp.62-8.

18 Coronel, S. S. (1996), 'Unnatural Disasters', in S. S. Coronel (ed.), *Patrimony: 6 Case Studies on Local Politics and the Environment in the Philippines*, Philippine Center for Investigative Journalism, Manila, pp.13.

19 Miller, M. A.L. (1995), *The Third World In Global Environmental Politics*, Lynne Rienner Publishers, Boulder; and Porter, G. and Brown, J. W. (1996), *Global Environmental Politics*, second edition, Westview Press, Boulder. For a discussion of the emergence of environmental concerns in the Philippines, see Magno, F. A.(1993), 'The Growth of Philippine Environmentalism', *Kasarinlan: A Philippine Quarterly of Third World Studies*, vol.9, no.1, 3rd Quarter, pp.7-18. For an analysis of the impact of the globalization of environmentalism on forest management in the Asia-Pacific, see Dauvergne, P. (1998), 'Globalisation and Deforestation in the Asia-Pacific', *Environmental Politics*, vol.7, no.4, Winter, pp.113-34.

20 Teehankee, J. C. (1993), 'The State, Illegal Logging, and Environmental NGOs in the Philippines', *Kasarinlan: A Philippine Quarterly of Third World Studies*, vol.9, no.1, 3rd Quarter, pp.19-34; and Ragragio, C. M. (1993), 'Sustainable Development, Environmental Planning and People's Initiatives', *Kasarinlan: A Philippine Quarterly of Third World Studies*, vol.9, no.1, 3rd Quarter, pp.35-53.

21 The 1997 information is from the Forest Management Bureau, Department of the Environment and Natural Resources, Quezon City, Philippines (obtained by the author in August 1997).

22 For details, see Philippine Department of Environment and Natural Resources, *1992 Philippine Forestry Statistics*, pp.xi; Vitug (1993), *Power from the Forest: The Politics of Logging*, pp.59-60; and Belcher, M. and Gennino, A. (1993) (eds), *Southeast Asia Rainforests: A Resource Guide & Directory*, Rainforest Action Network, San Francisco, pp.37.

23 Coronel (1996), 'Unnatural Disasters', pp.11.

24 See the Philippine Department of Environment and Natural Resources (1995), 'Integration of the CBFMs and POFP into the DENR Regular Structure', Administrative Order, No. 96-30. Also see Philippine Department of Environment and Natural Resources, 'Rules and Regulations For the Implementation of Executive Order 263, Otherwise Known As The Community-Based Forest Management Strategy', Administrative Order, No. 96-29, July 1995.

25 Bennagen, P. C. (1996), 'NGO and Community Participation in Environmental Programs: A Case Study of the Community Forestry Program', *Philippine Social Sciences Review*, vol.53, nos.1-4, January-December, pp.53-7; and Department of Environment and Natural Resources (DENR) (1993), *Policies, Memoranda and Other Issuances on the National Forestation Program Volume VI*, National Forestation Development Office, Department of Environment and Natural Resources, Quezon City, pp.88-107.

26 For a critique of reforestation programs in the Philippines, see Korten, F. F. (1994), 'Questioning the Call for Environmental Loans: A Critical Examination of Forestry Lending in the Philippines', *World Development*, vol.22, no.7, pp.971-81. For a study of some of the typical problems of community forestry, see Vitug, M. D. (1996), 'A Tortuous Trek To Community Forestry', in S. Coronel (ed.), *Patrimony: 6 Case Studies on Local Politics and the Environment in the Philippines*, Philippine Center for Investigative Journalism, Manila, pp.121-41.

27 Severino, H. G. (1996), 'The Rise and Fall of a Logger's Political Empire', in S. Coronel (ed), *Patrimony: 6 Case Studies on Local Politics and the Environment in the Philippines*, Philippine Center for Investigative Journalism, Manila, pp.21-44.

28 Coronel (1996), 'Unnatural Disasters', p.12.

29 Robles, A. and Severino, H. G. (1997), 'Way to a Crisis', in C. C.A. Balgos (ed.), *Saving the Earth: The Philippine Experience*, fourth edition, Philippine Center for Investigative Journalism, Pasig City, pp.21. Also see Robles, A. 'Logging and Political Power', pp.22-6, Batario, R. 'The Pillage of Isabela', pp.27-30, and Severino, H. G. 'Fraud in the Forests', pp.36-42, in ibid.

30 'The Philippines: Human Rights and Forest Management in the 1990s', *Human Rights Watch/Asia*, vol.8, no.3, April 1996.

31 Magdalena, F. V. (1996), 'Population Growth and the Changing Ecosystem in Mindanao', *Sojourn*, vol.11, no.1, pp.120.

32 Hong, E. (1987), *Natives of Sarawak: Survival in Borneo's Vanishing Forest*, Institut Masyarakat, Pulau Pinang, Malaysia pp.128-9; Brookfield, H. Potter, L. and Byron, Y. (1995), *In Place of the Forest: Environmental and Socio-economic Transformation in Borneo and the Eastern Malay Peninsula*, United Nations University Press, Tokyo, pp.101.

33 Interviews, World Wildlife Fund (WWF) Malaysia, Petaling Jaya, 10 March 1994.

34 Duff-Brown, B. (1999), 'Nomadic Rain-forest Tribe in Borneo Fears Extinction', *Associated Press*, 15 August.

35 Summarized in Della-Giacoma, J. (1996), 'Indonesia Says Improving Logging Practices', 20 May, Reuters News Service, Reuters Business Briefing.

36 For government figures and information on forest management in Indonesia, see Departemen Kehutanan (Ministry of Forestry) (1992), *The Timber Industry in Indonesia*, Ministry of Forestry, Republic of Indonesia, Jakarta; Ministry of Forestry, Directorate General of Reforestation and Land Rehabilitation (1993), *Overview: The Strategy of Reforestation and Land Rehabilitation*, Ministry of Forestry, Republic of Indonesia, Jakarta, February; Departemen Kehutanan (Ministry of Forestry) (1992), *Forestry in Indonesia and Forestry Research and Development*, Ministry of Forestry, Republic of Indonesia, Jakarta; and Ministry of Forestry (1995), *Indonesian Forestry*, Ministry of Forestry, Republic of Indonesia, Jakarta, December.

37 ITTO, *Annual Review*, pp.114.

38 Tickell, O. (1999), 'Forest Crisis in Indonesia', *Timber & Wood Products International*, August.

39 Barber, V. C. (1997), *The Case Study of Indonesia*, Project on 'Environmental Scarcities, State Capacity, and Civil Violence', A Joint Project of the University of Toronto and the American Academy of Arts and Sciences, Valerie Percival, Manuscript Editor, The Academy of Arts and Sciences, Cambridge, MA.

40 *Ibid.*, pp.62-6.

41 Quoted in Walters, P. (1997), 'Borneo's Tribal Backlash', *The Australian*, 22-23 February, pp.28.

42 See Ching, Y. L. (1987), *Sarawak: The Plot That Failed 10 March 87 - 17 April 87* [A collection of newspaper articles] Summer Times, Singapore; and Institut Analisa Sosial (1989), *Logging Against the Natives of Sarawak*, Institut Analisa Sosial (INSAN), Selangor, Malaysia, pp.73-4.

43 For background on some of the companies operating in Sarawak, see Pura, R. (1993), 'Timber Companies Blossom On Malaysian Stock Market', *Asian Wall Street Journal*, 30 November, pp.12; and Pura, R. (1994), 'Timber Baron Emerges From the Woods', *Asian Wall Street Journal*, 15 February, pp.1, 4.

44 World Bank (1993), *Indonesia Forest Sector Review*, Jakarta, April, pp.27, cited in Poffenberger, M. (1997), 'Rethinking Indonesian Forest Policy: Beyond the Timber Barons', *Asian Survey*, vol.XXXVII, no.5, May, pp.456.

45 For background on Apkindo, see Dauvergne, P. (1997), 'Japanese Trade and Deforestation in Southeast Asia', in R. De Koninck and C. Veilleux (eds), *Southeast Asia and Globalization: New Domains of Analysis/L'Asie du Sud-Est face à la mondialisation: les nouveaux champs d'anlayse*, GÉRAC, Université Laval, Québec, pp.133-56.

46 For additional background on Hasan and Prajogo, see Pura, R. (1995), 'Bob Hasan Builds an Empire in the Forest', *Asian Wall Street Journal*, 25 January, pp.4; Schwarz, A. (1994), *A Nation in Waiting: Indonesia in the 1990s*, Allen and Unwin, St Leonards, NSW, Australia; Barr, C. M. (1998), 'Bob Hasan, the Rise of Apkindo, and the Shifting Dynamics of Control in Indonesia's Timber Sector', *Indonesia*, no.65, April; and Dauvergne, P. (1997), *Shadows in the Forest: Japan and the Politics of Timber in Southeast Asia*, The MIT Press, Cambridge, MA.

47 Robison, R. (1978), 'Toward A Class Analysis of the Indonesian Military Bureaucratic State', *Indonesia*, no.25, April, pp.28.

48 See International Timber Corporation Indonesia (ITCI) (1992), *PT. International Timber Corporation Indonesia*, ITCI, Jakarta.

49 'Government Revokes Vast Forest Concessions', *Jakarta Post*, 9 July 1999.

50 For background on social and community forestry in Indonesia, see Sarido, M. A. (1996), 'Social/Community Forestry Development in Indonesia', in Department of Environment and Natural Resources and the International Tropical Timber Organization, *Community Forestry: As a Strategy for Sustainable Forest Management*, Proceedings of the International Conference, Manila, Philippines, 24-26 May 1996, pp.111-21. For background on Malaysia, see Awang, K. and Hamzah, M. B. (1996), 'Community Forestry in Malaysia: Overview, Constraints, and Prospects', in *Community Forestry*, pp.175-90. Indonesia is now working on reforming its community forestry program. It is, however, too soon to evaluate these changes.

51 Barber (1997), *The Case of Indonesia*, pp.67.

52 Jemadu, A. (1996), *Sustainable Forest Management in the Context of Multi-Level and Multi-Actor Policy Processes: Case Studies of the Incorporation of the Environmental Dimension into Sustainable Forest Management in East Kalimantan-Indonesia*, Katholieke Universiteit Leuven, Leuven, Belgium, pp.146.

53 This paragraph is based on Dauvergne, P. (1998), *Sustainable Forest Management* (book review of Jemadu), *Pacific Affairs*, vol.71, no.3, Fall, pp.445-7.

54 Coronel (1996), 'Unnatural Disasters', pp.13.

55 A similar pattern is found in Burma. See Bryant, R. (1996), 'The Greening of Burma: Political Rhetoric or Sustainable Development?', *Pacific Affairs*, vol.69, Fall, pp.341-59.

56 Magno, F. A. (1997), *Crafting Conservation: Forestry, Social Capital, and Tenurial Security in the Northern Philippines*, University of Hawai'i, Hawai'i, pp.163.

57 *Ibid.*, pp.173.

References

Awang, K. and Hamzah, M. B. (1996), 'Community Forestry in Malaysia: Overview, Constraints, and Prospects', in Department of Environment and Natural Resources and the International Tropical Timber Organization, *Community Forestry: As a Strategy for Sustainable Forest Management*, Proceedings of the International Conference, 24-26 May,

Manila, Philippines, pp. 175-90.

Barr, C. M. (1998), 'Bob Hasan, the Rise of Apkindo, and the Shifting Dynamics of Control in Indonesia's Timber Sector', *Indonesia*, no. 65, April.

Batario, R. (1997), 'The Pillage of Isabela', in C. C.A. Balgos (ed.), *Saving the Earth: The Philippine Experience*, fourth edition, Philippine Center for Investigative Journalism, Pasig City, pp. 27-30.

Belcher, M. and Gennino, A. (1993) (eds), *Southeast Asia Rainforests: A Resource Guide & Directory*, Rainforest Action Network, San Francisco, pp. 37.

Bennagen, P. C. (1996), 'NGO and Community Participation in Environmental Programs: A Case Study of the Community Forestry Program', *Philippine Social Sciences Review*, vol. 53, nos. 1-4, January-December, pp. 53-7.

Brookfield, H. Potter, L. and Byron, Y. (1995), *In Place of the Forest: Environmental and Socio-economic Transformation in Borneo and the Eastern Malay Peninsula*, United Nations University Press, Tokyo, pp. 101.

Bryant, R. L. (1997a), *The Political Ecology of Forestry in Burma 1824-1994*, Hurst & Company, London.

Bryant, R. L. (1996b), 'The Greening of Burma: Political Rhetoric or Sustainable Development?', *Pacific Affairs*, vol. 69, Fall, pp. 341-59.

Coronel, S. S. (1996), 'Unnatural Disasters', in S. S. Coronel (ed.), *Patrimony: 6 Case Studies on Local Politics and the Environment in the Philippines*, Philippine Center for Investigative Journalism, Manila, pp. 13.

Dauvergne, P. (1998a), 'Weak States and the Environment in Indonesia and the Solomon Islands', in P. Dauvergne (ed.), *Weak and Strong States in Asia-Pacific Societies*, Allen and Unwin, Sydney, pp. 137.

Dauvergne, P. (1998b), 'Globalisation and Deforestation in the Asia-Pacific', *Environmental Politics*, vol. 7, no. 4, Winter, pp. 113-34.

Dauvergne, P. (1997c), 'Japanese Trade and Deforestation in Southeast Asia', in R. De Koninck and C. Veilleux (eds), *Southeast Asia and Globalization: New Domains of Analysis/L'Asie du Sud-Est face à la mondialisation: les nouveaux champs d'anlayse*, GÉRAC, Université Laval, Québec, pp. 133-56.

Dauvergne, P. (1997d), *Shadows in the Forest: Japan and the Politics of Timber in Southeast Asia*, The MIT Press, Cambridge, MA.

Departemen Kehutanan (Ministry of Forestry) (1992a), *Forestry in Indonesia and Forestry Research and Development*, Ministry of Forestry, Republic of Indonesia, Jakarta.

Departemen Kehutanan (Ministry of Forestry) (1992b), *The Timber Industry in Indonesia*, Ministry of Forestry, Republic of Indonesia, Jakarta.

Department of Environment and Natural Resources (DENR) (1993), *Policies, Memoranda and Other Issuances on the National Forestation Program Volume VI*, National Forestation Development Office, Department of Environment and Natural Resources, Quezon City, pp. 88-107.

Dixon, J. A. and Hamilton, K. (1996), 'Expanding the Measure of Wealth', *Finance & Development*, vol. 33, no. 4, December, pp. 15.

Dupont, A. (ed.) (1998), *The Environment and Security: What Are The Linkages?*, Strategic and Defence Studies Centre, Research School of Pacific and Asian Studies, The Australian National University, Canberra, pp. 45-64.

Grindle, M. S. (1996), *Challenging the State: Crisis and Innovation in Latin America and Africa*, Cambridge University Press, Cambridge.

Hong, E. (1987), *Natives of Sarawak: Survival in Borneo's Vanishing Forest*, Institut Masyarakat, Pulau Pinang, Malaysia pp. 128-9.

Hyden, G. (1997), 'Civil Society, Social Capital, and Development: Dissection of a Complex Discourse', *Studies in Comparative International Development*, vol. 32, no1, Spring, pp. 4.

Institut Analisa Sosial (1989), *Logging Against the Natives of Sarawak*, Institut Analisa Sosial (INSAN), Selangor, Malaysia, pp. 73-4.

International Tropical Timber Organization (ITTO) (1999), *Annual Review and Assessment of the World Timber Situation: 1998*, ITTO, Yokohama, pp. 98.

Jemadu, A. (1996), *Sustainable Forest Management in the Context of Multi-Level and Multi-Actor Policy Processes: Case Studies of the Incorporation of the Environmental Dimension into Sustainable Forest Management in East Kalimantan-Indonesia*, Katholieke Universiteit Leuven, Leuven, Belgium, pp. 146.

Korten, F. F. (1994), 'Questioning the Call for Environmental Loans: A Critical Examination of Forestry Lending in the Philippines', *World Development*, vol. 22, no. 7, pp. 971-81.

Kummer, D. M.(1991), *Deforestation in the Postwar Philippines*, The University of Chicago Press, Chicago.

Magdalena, F. V. (1996), 'Population Growth and the Changing Ecosystem in Mindanao', *Sojourn*, vol. 11, no. 1, pp. 120.

Magno, F. A. (1997a), *Crafting Conservation: Forestry, Social Capital, and Tenurial Security in the northern Philippines*, University of Hawai'i, Hawai'i, pp. 163.

Magno, F. A. (1993b), 'The Growth of Philippine Environmentalism', *Kasarinlan: A Philippine Quarterly of Third World Studies*, vol. 9, no. 1, 3rd Quarter, pp. 7-18.

Migdal, J. S., (1988), *Strong Societies and Weak States: State-Society Relations and State Capabilities in the Third World*, Princeton University Press, Princeton, New Jersey.

Migdal, J. S., Kohli, A. and Shue, V. (eds) (1994), *State Power and Social Forces: Domination and Transformation in the Third World*, Cambridge University Press, New York.

Miller, M. A.L. (1995), *The Third World In Global Environmental Politics*, Lynne Rienner Publishers, Boulder.

Ministry of Forestry (1995), *Indonesian Forestry*, Ministry of Forestry, Republic of Indonesia, Jakarta, December.

Ministry of Forestry Directorate General of Reforestation and Land Rehabilitation (1993), *Overview: The Strategy of Reforestation and Land Rehabilitation*, Ministry of Forestry, Republic of Indonesia, Jakarta, February.

Peluso, N. L. (1993), 'Coercing Conservation?: The politics of state resource control', *Global Environmental Change: Human and Policy Dimensions*, vol. 3, no 2, June, pp. 199-217.

Poffenberger, M. (1997), 'Rethinking Indonesian Forest Policy: Beyond the Timber Barons', *Asian Survey*, vol. XXXVII, no. 5, May, pp. 456.

Poffenberger, M. and Stone, R. D. (1996), 'Hidden Faces in the Forest: A 21st Century Challenge for Tropical Asia', *Sais Review*, vol. 16, no. 1, Winter-Spring, pp. 204.

Porter, G. and Brown, J. W. (1996), *Global Environmental Politics*, second edition, Westview Press, Boulder.

Pura, R. (1995a), 'Bob Hasan Builds an Empire in the Forest', *Asian Wall Street Journal*, 25 January, pp. 4.

Pura, R. (1993b), 'Timber Companies Blossom On Malaysian Stock Market', *Asian Wall Street Journal*, 30 November, pp. 12.

Pura, R. (1994c), 'Timber Baron Emerges From the Woods', *Asian Wall Street Journal*, 15 February, pp. 1, 4.

Putnam, R. (1995), 'Bowling Alone: America's Declining Social Capital', *Journal of Democracy*, vol. 6, no. 1, pp. 67.

Ragragio, C. M. (1993), 'Sustainable Development, Environmental Planning and People's Initiatives', *Kasarinlan: A Philippine Quarterly of Third World Studies*, vol. 9, no. 1, 3rd

Quarter, pp. 35-53.

Robison, R. (1978), 'Toward A Class Analysis of the Indonesian Military Bureaucratic State', *Indonesia*, no. 25, April, pp. 28.

Robles, A. (1997), 'Logging and Political Power', in C. C.A. Balgos (ed.), *Saving the Earth: The Philippine Experience*, fourth edition, Philippine Center for Investigative Journalism, Pasig City, pp. 22-6.

Robles, A. and Severino, H. G. (1997), 'Way to a Crisis', in C. C.A. Balgos (ed.), *Saving the Earth: The Philippine Experience*, fourth edition, Philippine Center for Investigative Journalism, Pasig City, pp. 21.

Sarido, M. A. (1996), 'Social/Community Forestry Development in Indonesia', in Department of Environment and Natural Resources and the International Tropical Timber Organization, *Community Forestry: As a Strategy for Sustainable Forest Management*, Proceedings of the International Conference, 24-26 May, Manila, Philippines, pp. 111-21.

Schwarz, A. (1994), *A Nation in Waiting: Indonesia in the 1990s*, Allen and Unwin, St Leonards, NSW, Australia.

Scott, James C. (1985), *Weapons of the Weak: Everyday Forms of Peasant Resistance*, Yale University Press, New Haven.

Severino, H. G. (1996a), 'The Rise and Fall of a Logger's Political Empire', in S. Coronel (ed), *Patrimony: 6 Case Studies on Local Politics and the Environment in the Philippines*, Philippine Center for Investigative Journalism, Manila, pp. 21-44.

Severino, H. G. (1997b), 'Fraud in the Forests', in C. C.A. Balgos (ed.), *Saving the Earth: The Philippine Experience*, fourth edition, Philippine Center for Investigative Journalism, Pasig City, pp. 36-42.

Teehankee, J. C. (1993), 'The State, Illegal Logging, and Environmental NGOs in the Philippines', *Kasarinlan: A Philippine Quarterly of Third World Studies*, vol. 9, no. 1, 3rd Quarter, pp. 19-34.

'The Philippines: Human Rights and Forest Management in the 1990s', *Human Rights Watch/Asia* vol. 8, no. 3, April 1996.

Vitug, M. D. (1996a), 'A Tortuous Trek To Community Forestry', in S. Coronel (ed.), *Patrimony: 6 Case Studies on Local Politics and the Environment in the Philippines*, Philippine Center for Investigative Journalism, Manila, pp. 121-41.

Vitug, M. D. (1993b), *Power from the Forest: The Politics of Logging*, Philippine Center For Investigative Journalism, Manila, pp.16-24, 29-32, 44.

Vitug, M. D. (1993c), 'Is There a Logger in the House?' in E. Gamalinda and S. Coronel (eds), *Saving the Earth: The Philippine Experience*, third edition, Philippine Center for Investigative Journalism, Manila, pp. 62-8.

Walters, P. (1997), 'Borneo's Tribal Backlash', *The Australian*, 22-23 February, pp. 28.

World Bank (1997), *New Measures of Wealth: Expanding the Measure of Wealth, Indicators of Environmentally Sustainable Development*, CSD Ed., Draft-for-Discussion, April.

Chapter 5

Development and (In)security: The Perspective of a Philippine Community

Pia C. Bennagen[1]

Introduction

In an attempt to make the Philippines a Newly Industrialized Economy (NIE) by the turn of the century, the government has embarked on a number of projects involving the construction of power plants across the country. These plants are intended to supply much-needed energy to boost the country's efforts at industrialization. However, this type of development has come at a cost to both the environment and to members of affected communities. Due to disastrous experiences, such as in Calaca, Batangas,[2] any proposal to construct a new plant is usually met by protest. Most of the time the government is able to convince residents to accept a proposed project, but resistance from local communities has sometimes led to a search for an alternate project site.

The Problem

One of the most significant energy projects during the 1990s is the Sual Coal-Fired Thermal Power Plant (SCFTPP) in Pangasinan. Launched in 1994, the plant was scheduled to be operational by mid-1999. It is intended to provide some 1,000-1,200 megawatts of energy for the island of Luzon. Initially, the residents of Sual resisted the idea of having a power plant in their backyard. However, after some persuasion on the part of government, the people eventually agreed. A year before operations were scheduled to commence, residents were reconsidering and asking themselves whether they made the right decision in allowing the government to build what was touted as the biggest power plant in the Philippines.

This chapter examines the development and security implications of such an energy project, primarily from the perspective of members of affected communities. It delves into the question of how the construction of the SCFTPP has and will continue to affect the development and security of households and communities as perceived by the residents themselves. Policy recommendations are also drawn from data generated through field visits, interviews, and literature surveys. This research is intended to contribute to an understanding of the linkages between development and security at the community level and within the context of energy projects and the environment.

Development, Security, and the Environment: Analytical Framework

How are development and security linked in the context of the particular concerns of this research? The pursuit of development (that is, defined largely in the economic sense) has, in many instances, led to the degradation of the environment and the dislocation of communities. Infrastructure projects, industrialization, and urbanization have been seen to cause or worsen water, soil, and air pollution, land degradation, deforestation, global warming, and so on. Consequently, while development projects may contribute to the economic wealth of a country, they may also create insecurity in society as they threaten people's livelihood, health, general living conditions, housing, and the environment. More concretely, the development goals of the Philippine government, which in this case are manifested in the construction and operation of a power plant, have a significant impact on the level of development and sense of security of the nation, especially of the members of the community hosting the project. The benefits the people derive from the project do somewhat improve their conditions, but residents also suffer a sense of insecurity as a result of the probable environmental consequences of the plant's operation.

In several similar cases, communities have rallied against environmentally critical projects and consequently, the government was forced to alter its plans. So far, no such change has happened to the SCFTPP project. However, if the people perceive this project as creating more problems than benefits, they have voiced their willingness to protest against the continued operation of the plant. This case study reveals the links between development and security at the levels of the state and province, on the one hand, and the community, on the other. Likewise, it illustrates the relationship between a community's level of development and sense of security as seen by its members.

For the most part, this chapter relies on data generated from field visits to Sual, Pangasinan. Between 1994 and 1998, five visits were made to the affected community and two visits to the plant site. Interviews were conducted with community residents, past and present local government officials, and plant engineers. Data were also obtained from published literature and from government documents, particularly the Department of Environment and Natural Resources (DENR), the DENR-Environmental Management Bureau (EMB), the National Economic and Development Authority (NEDA), the Department of Energy (DoE), the National Power Corporation (NAPOCOR) and the Build-Operate-Transfer (BOT) Projects Center.

Sual, Pangasinan and the SCFTPP

The Province and the Community

Located on the western coast of Luzon, Pangasinan occupies the northern part of the island's central plains. It has a total land area of 5,368.20 square kilometers and an estimated population of 2,178,412.[3] Lingayen is the capital of the province which has a total of three cities, 45 municipalities, and 1,364 *barangays*. Farming and fishing are the province's major industries. Among its primary products are rice, tobacco, sugarcane, corn, and salt. Almost half of the province's land area is devoted to agricultural activities. Pangasinan also hosts a number of cottage industries such as blanket weaving, basketry, bamboo craft, furniture making, and shell craft.

Pangasinan, along with the provinces of Ilocos Norte, Ilocos Sur, La Union, and Baguio, form the Northwestern Luzon Growth Quadrangle (NWLGQ), also known as the Quad. This area is being developed as a financial center and tourist attraction in the short term, and as part of a larger growth quadrangle including China, Hong Kong, and Japan in the long term. Once set into motion, it is hoped that this emerging area will contribute to the country's economic growth through agro-based industrialization. Furthermore, the Quad is also envisioned as a tool to promote socio-economic development in the region.[4] To pursue these objectives, four growth nodes with either a high level of industrial or commercial activity, or a proposed industrial site have been identified: (1) Laoag-Currimao zone; (2) San Fernando-Bacnotan-Bauang zone; (3) Baguio-La Trinidad zone; and (4) Sual-San Fabian zone.

Sual, a municipality of some 19,594 residents with a land area of 201.8 square kilometers, has been identified as a site for an industrial estate,[5] of which the SCFTPP is a part. More specifically, the power plant is located in Sitios Bangayao, Buyog, and Pao of *Barangay* Pangascasan, Sual. Pangascasan, with an estimated 1,397 residents, has a total land area of 680 hectares and is one of the coastal areas in Sual.[6] It is precisely because of its strategic location and topographical characteristics that it was chosen as the site of a power plant. The key industries in Sual are agriculture, fishing, cottage industries, and tourism. In the area of education, it is estimated that Sual has a literacy rate of 94.6 per cent with the majority having at least finished primary schooling. There are 15 elementary schools in the area and one is located in *Barangay* Pangascasan.[7] As for health services, only five *barangay* health centers can be found in Sual, not one of which is located in Pangascasan. The residents of the area have to share the services offered by the health center in *Barangay* Cabalitian (which is an island that can be reached only by boat) with three other *barangays*.[8] With regard to sources of water and power, the majority of the residents get their water from deep wells and some 60 per cent of Sual's *barangays* are supplied electricity by the Pangasinan Electric Cooperative. However, only 29.8 per cent of households use electricity for lighting purposes. In 1992, residents paid 3.45 pesos per kilowatt-hour. As for the area's road network, an estimated 82.6 per cent of Sual's roads are considered as *barangay* roads. This means that the maintenance of these roads, the surface pavement of which is gravel and earth fill, is the responsibility of the *barangays* concerned.[9]

In compliance with government requirements, alternative houses were built. Among those who have free occupancy of land are the residents who live along the shores of Baquioen Bay and those who formerly worked as farm hands in agricultural lands that now form part of the project site. The roofs of these houses are usually made of cogon, nipa, and anahaw, while walls are of bamboo, sawali, cogon, and nipa (all of which are native materials). Energy sources include wood for cooking and kerosene for lighting. At the time the environmental impact assessment (EIA) was conducted, the affected *barangays* did not have electricity. This is one of the major problems cited by residents of Pangascasan. Other key concerns are the reduction in fish catch, the poor quality of roads, unemployment and lack of livelihood opportunities, lack of health services, unavailability of transportation, lack of teachers in schools, and displeasure with the presence of the NAPOCOR in the area.[10] When the government campaigned for the approval of the project among the affected communities, these concerns were precisely the ones that the government promised to address. Along with the immediate gain of having electricity in their homes, the residents were also offered an attractive package of benefits if they agreed to the construction and operation of a coal-fired power plant in Pangascasan.

Philippine Development and Energy Projects

The development agenda of the Ramos government was articulated in the *Medium-Term Philippine Development Plan: 1993-98* and the *Updated Medium-Term Philippine Development Plan: 1996-98*. Both documents seek the goals of increasing the country's economic growth rate and GNP per capita, and decreasing the incidence of poverty. One of the strategies to be implemented to attain these objectives is the creation of regional development centers and growth zones. Partly as a response to criticisms of urban bias and Metro Manila imperialism, the establishment of regional development centers is also an attempt to ensure that the benefits of development are shared equitably across the nation.

The NWLGQ or the Quad, of which Pangasinan is a component province, has been identified as one of the growth zones. According to the Master Plan for the North Quad, this area is going to serve as the country's springboard to the industrialized economies of Asia. The advantages of the area are its strategic export trade location and high tourism potential. Among the projects that have been identified for both the short-and long-terms are economic and free port zone development, sea port zone development, agro-industrial growth centers, road construction, water and irrigation system development, and eco-tourism and national park development.[11] These projects will put pressure on the energy-generating capacity of existing power plants in the region, raising the need to augment the present capacity through the construction and operation of new power plants.

The growing Philippine economy of the mid-1990s meant increasing energy demands. Consequently, the DoE prioritized the construction of new power plants and the promotion of the use of indigenous energy sources. According to former President

Fidel V. Ramos: 'Energy will always be at the forefront of our national activities as we march towards full industrialization'. To that, former Secretary of Energy Francisco L. Viray added: 'As the country moves closer to its vision of industrialization by the turn of the century, energy has become a vital engine in sustaining overall economic growth'.[12] To put the country on the road to Philippines 2000 and industrialization, the government approved the construction of power plants that, upon completion and operation, would mean a total energy capacity of 102,424 megawatts for the Philippines.[13]

Currently, oil-based power plants dominate the scene, providing more than half of the country's energy needs. In 1999, there were nine coal-fired plants in operation with a capacity of 1,460 megawatts or 13.8 per cent of the total national capacity. Of this figure, 610 megawatts were generated from plants using local coal, while 850 megawatts were generated from plants consuming imported coal. Up to 2005, most of the additional plants will be coal-based ones. Some 600 megawatts will be generated through plants using local coal. These projects are in Cebu, Negros, Panay, and Mindanao. Meanwhile, a total of 2,150 megawatts will come from plants running on imported coal. These include two 300-megawatts plants in Masinloc, Zambales, a 350-megawatt independent power producer-owned plant, a 200-megawatt plant in Mindanao, and the 1,000-megawatt (with an additional capacity of 200 megawatts) plant in Sual, Pangasinan.[14]

The Power Plant Project

President Ramos launched the SCFTPP, the biggest power plant in the country in terms of energy generating capacity, in 1994. This project entailed the construction of two 500-megawatt power plants with the potential to provide an additional 200 megawatts should the need arise. Undertaken through the BOT scheme, the SCFTPP was developed and would be operated by the Pangasinan Electric Corporation (PEC) for 25 years, after which it would be turned over to the government at no cost. The SCFTPP was projected to cost US$1.36 billion. The project sponsors and owners of the PEC are Consolidated Electric Power Asia (CEPA) Pangasinan Electric Ltd., a subsidiary of CEPA, and the International Finance Corporation.[15] A total area of 280 hectares in *Barangay* Pangascasan had been allotted for the power plant and other plant facilities and storage areas (for example, coal yard, turbine and boiler area, chimney, switchyard, and the proposed ash disposal area). The coal to be used for the plant's operation would be imported from Australia, Indonesia, or China. The plant was scheduled to become operational by mid-1999.[16]

The construction and operation of the SCFTPP were governed by two important documents: (1) the BOT agreement between the PEC and NAPOCOR, and (2) the Memorandum of Agreement (MOA) with representatives of the PEC and NAPOCOR and provincial, municipal, and *barangay* officials as signatories. Both documents enumerate the responsibilities of all parties concerned with the construction and operation of the SCFTPP. Among other responsibilities, the PEC shoulders the development, design, construction, commissioning, and testing of the plant. PEC will also finance the project, operate and maintain it until such time that it is turned over to the government. For its part, NAPOCOR is responsible for providing the project site, the transmission lines linking the plant to the grid, and the fuel for operation purposes. Moreover, NAPOCOR will handle the resettlement and provision of livelihood projects to affected households.

Meanwhile, the representatives of the province, municipality, and *barangay* are mandated to conduct dialogues among their constituencies regarding the acceptability of the SCFTPP. These entities are also required to suggest community development projects to the NAPOCOR, who will fund these projects under the financial assistance program. Aside from these actors, the DENR was also given a role. The department was assigned to review the EIA prepared for the project, to issue the Environmental Clearance Certificate (ECC) once compliance with environmental standards has been ascertained, and to monitor the construction and operation of the power plant. However, the monitoring of the project is not the task of DENR alone. A representative management group of all parties to the MOA is responsible for monitoring activities throughout the project cycle.[17] With the signing of the BOT agreement and the MOA and the ground breaking ceremonies graced by President Ramos in 1994, the SCFTPP was on its way to becoming a reality.

Development and Security and the SCFTPP: A Community Perspective

From the time they first heard about the possibility of a power plant being constructed and operated in their hometown, the residents of Pangascasan have been concerned about the possible effects that such a project would have on their lives. Those who favored the project saw the economic benefits that would accrue to them and the province of Pangasinan once the power plant became operational. On the other hand, resistance came from residents who have heard of the problems in Calaca, Batangas and have become wary of the probable environmental consequences of operating a power plant in their backyard. The opposition even conducted a rally against the project in front of the town hall.

Laws mandate that aside from being technically sound, a proposed project must also be socially acceptable. In view of this requirement, the government, specifically the NAPOCOR, embarked on a campaign to sell the SCFTPP project to the residents of Pangascasan. While NAPOCOR may have convinced some critics of the advantages of the project, it appears that it was President Ramos' efforts at promoting the plant that finally won the people over. According to a former *barangay* official, the people finally accepted the project when President Ramos gave them his personal assurance that the project will not harm the people and the environment.[18] Even Sual Mayor Luis Agbayani acknowledged that the President played a crucial role in convincing his fellow residents of the province to accept the project.[19] As resistance eventually died down, NAPOCOR and the PEC finally got the seal of approval that they needed. This did not mean, however, that the concerns raised by the residents regarding the probable effects of the project on their lives and the environment were finally put to rest. While there may have been a general sense of resignation at that time, to this day, some people continue to have reservations regarding the construction and operation of the SCFTPP.

Community Concerns During the Pre-SCFTPP Period

The proposal to build a power plant in their *barangay* was met with mixed reactions by the residents of *Barangay* Pangascasan. Data from the EIA survey reveals that while the majority (56.9 per cent) favored the project due to the benefits that it may bring, there was a significant number (21 per cent) who opposed the project. Reasons for the negative answer included the project's possible effects on the environment and on the people's livelihoods. However, there were an equally considerable percentage of respondents (21.7 per cent) who, at the time they were interviewed, did not have a definite opinion on the project. These were the residents who were not certain about the project's effects, who expected they will not directly benefit from the project, and who wanted to seek the opinion of others (for example, heads of households, neighbors, *barangay* and municipal officials) before deciding for themselves.[20]

The key concerns that were articulated by the residents as regards the proposed project included the following: (1) relocation or resettlement of affected households; (2) electrification of the *barangay*; (3) employment and livelihood opportunities; (4) environmental consequences; (5) health effects; and (6) migration of outsiders to Sual. Relocation of households residing in the project site is the most immediate consequence of the SCFTPP. Resettlement will not only mean losing their original homes, but also losing their land, which for some families is their only source of livelihood. According to the provisions of the MOA, NAPOCOR is required to provide each of the affected households with at least a 30-square meter housing unit on a 200-square meter lot in the resettlement area located in Sitio Tubag, *Barangay* Pangascasan.[21] Should a household opt to resettle somewhere else, it will be paid the cash equivalent of its original house and a 200-square meter lot. In addition, the household will also receive Relocation Incentive Assistance (RIA) that is equivalent to two months average gross income. Since resettlement will also affect the residents' livelihood, the MOA also required the provision of financial assistance amounting to 9,464,500 pesos for livelihood projects and training programs. These programs were aimed at equipping eligible community members with skills that will qualify them for employment during the construction phase of the SCFTPP.[22]

It is to be expected that those who favored the project also expressed willingness to relocate, while those who opposed it preferred to stay in their original residence. Those who were willing to relocate said they would do so because they would receive compensation, and there was an available resettlement site. However, 18 respondents said they would relocate because they had no choice. They expressed the view that whether they wanted to or not, the government would send them to the relocation site anyway; so it was better to accept the offer of the compensation package. On the other hand, those who were unwilling to move cited reasons such as loss of livelihood, lack of alternative places to go, and the problems caused by having to adjust to a new lifestyle. And those who where uncertain said that their final decision will eventually depend on the amount of the compensation package, on the location of the resettlement site, and on the decision of their landlords and/or the community. The respondents pointed out that in order to make the relocation proposal more acceptable, the NAPOCOR should offer a comprehensive relocation program and adequate compensation based on the fair market value of the real property and improvements.[23]

The lack of electricity in Pangascasan was considered to be one of the problems that will be addressed by the project. For the most part, residents used fuel wood, kerosene, and batteries for their energy needs. The SCFTPP would not only add to the energy capacity of the Luzon Grid, but would also finally lead to the provision of electricity in the affected *barangays*, a development which residents associated with progress. Moreover, it was projected that the operation of the SCFTPP would lower the cost of power by about 1-1.50 pesos per kilowatt-hour, because the power generated by the plant would be sold at reduced prices.[24]

Employment and livelihood concerns also ranked high on the agendas of the affected households. Since relocation would mean losing agricultural lands, the residents wanted assurance from the government that the compensation package offered would include provisions for livelihood programs. Residents also wanted top priority in the hiring of workers during the construction phase of the SCFTPP. As mentioned earlier, the MOA mandates the NAPOCOR to set aside funds for livelihood projects for relocated households. Moreover, NAPOCOR is required to allocate 300 million pesos as financial assistance for the host local government units. Of this amount, 60 per cent (180 million pesos) would go to the provincial government, 35 per cent (105 million pesos) to the municipal government, and five per cent (15 million pesos) to the *barangay*. These amounts were to be disbursed within a four-year period (that is, from 1995 to 1998). As regards employment opportunities, one of the responsibilities of the PEC as project proponent is to give priority to the local residents in the hiring of semi-skilled, skilled, and professional workers during the construction and operation of the SCFTPP, provided that they meet the basic qualifications for the job. Skills training programs funded by the NAPOCOR would help in equipping the residents with the necessary competence.[25]

As for the environment, the Calaca experience is not lost on the residents of Pangascasan. Those who expressed worry about the environmental consequences of the SCFTPP often cited the experience of the residents of San Rafael, Calaca when explaining their reasons for opposing the power plant. Many were worried about the polluting effects that the construction and subsequent operation of the plant might cause. Air and water pollution, destruction of marine life, soil erosion, loss of agricultural lands and the consequent effects on livelihood, community life, health, tourism, and national patrimony were the top concerns of residents. During the construction phase, the most obvious changes in the landscape would take place in the project site: a coastal area with hilly anteriors having slopes ranging from 5-40 per cent. According to the project plan, a portion of the seacoast would be reclaimed to permit the leveling off of the site. A land use survey of the area directly affected by the project (or the direct impact zone) characterized it generally as open grasslands, brush lands, and patches of coconut, mango, and other fruit bearing trees. On the other hand, the areas within a five-kilometer radius of the project site (identified as the probable impact zone) were found to consist mostly of open grass, non-irrigated rice fields, shrubs, and patches of trees. Due to construction activities, fruit bearing trees such as mangoes, bananas, and coconuts will be cut down, burnt, and disposed of. Some fishponds and rice lands will also be affected. Clearing the project site will be done through blasting procedures using dynamite.[26] Prior to the full operation of the SCFTPP, the residents could not determine whether the Calaca experience would be replicated in their *barangay*.

Due to the changes in the environment and in their lifestyles, the people of Pangascasan were also quite wary of the probable consequences such changes will have on their health, particularly the health of children. The decrease in fish catch may mean less food on the table unless the heads of households are able to find other sources of livelihood. Air and water pollution due to emissions from the project site may lead to respiratory problems and the spread of communicable diseases. An aggravating factor is the absence of a permanent health service unit in the *barangay*. With the high cost of health services, if and when available, the residents were worried that the construction and operation of the SCFTPP would cause them more harm than good.

During the construction phase, the PEC and NAPOCOR needed a large pool of skilled and unskilled workers. Projections indicated that during the first year, 800 workers would be required while during the second and third years, 3,000 and 1,000 workers would be needed, respectively. Of these figures, 20 per cent were engineers, 15 per cent were office personnel, 25 per cent were skilled workers, and 40 per cent were semi-skilled workers. Given the level of skills of Sual residents, it cannot be expected that they would be able to fill up positions that required a high level of technical competence and knowledge. Also, since farming and fishing were the top income sources in the area, the skills that residents possessed were not compatible with the requirements of the project.[27] This implies that the firms sub-contracted for construction activities will bring in people from outside to meet the project's manpower needs. The influx of outsiders caused concern among the residents due to changes in community life. Relations among community members are largely built on the kinship system. For instance, particularly in the countryside, several families related either by consanguinity or affinity may occupy an entire street. Such social networks make it easier to relate to one another. Residents fear the entry of migrants may alter the already established relations in their town.

The Sual power plant project is 'envisioned to alleviate the power shortage in the Luzon Grid and to sustain the country's economic development whose power demand is expected to reach an average growth rate of eight per cent per annum from 1990 onwards'.[28] Moreover, the project is geared to promote growth in Pangasinan and the host community. Pangascasan residents who supported the project were aware of the benefits that the project may bring such as employment opportunities, livelihood programs, electrification, and roads. To supporters of the project, these are signs that progress had finally come to their *barangay*. However, while they looked forward to development, they continued to worry about the adverse consequences that the project's construction and subsequent operation would bring. Environmental pollution, loss of agricultural livelihood, changes in community life, and increased influx of outsiders were problems that bring about a sense of insecurity among the residents. To them, the challenge is to reconcile their desire for progress and development with the costs that would inevitably follow.

Community Concerns During the Construction Phase

More than four years after the groundbreaking rites for the SCFTPP, some residents of Pangascasan remained ambivalent about the project. Although, NAPOCOR and the PEC have delivered on some of their contractual obligations, problems continued to hound the residents as they adapted to their new lives in a changed environment. Interviews with residents in the resettlement area and in the coastal zone conducted in January-February 1996 and April and December 1998 revealed the concerns that they had as a result of the construction activities in relation to the project[29] – see Table 5.1 for summary findings.

Table 5.1 Development and Insecurity Among the Residents of *Barangay* Pangascasan, Sual, Pangasinan in Relation to the SCFTPP Project

	Indicators of Development	Indicators of Community Insecurity
Employment in the Plant	• more regular work • more regular income source	• cases of delayed wages • non-remittance of SSS contributions • contractual basis of employment in the plant • lack of employment opportunities for unskilled residents and women • reduced need for unskilled and semi-skilled workers once plant is operational
Infrastructures / Electrification	• provision of electricity, transmission lines, and connectors	• not all households have electric supply as yet • additional expense due to payment for electric use
Housing	• provision of houses made of more durable materials and lots	• ownership titles have not been issued to residents • coastal zone residents may be relocated due to the international seaport project

Roads	• clearing of certain portions of hilly areas to serve as dirt roads • cementing of parts of the road leading to the town proper • improvements in transportation to and from town proper	• roads in *Barangay* Pangascasan remain dirt roads • relatively expensive transport fare
	Indicators of Development	**Indicators of Community Insecurity**
Water	• provision of water pumps	• lack of potable water due to excessive demand • impact of chemicals and other hazardous materials from the plant on water sources
Basic Facilities Health Services	• doctors visit the *barangay* every so often	• absence of a permanent health service unit • nearest *barangay* health center can only be reached by boat • health problems arising from over-crowding, lack of potable water, garbage collection problems, air pollution, etc.
Education/ Training Services	• training programs to equip residents with skills for employ-ment in the plant	• lack of opportunities for women given the nature of jobs in the plant
Marketing Services	• construction of a market structure to serve food needs of the residents and workers	• partially operational market • food prices still high
Livelihood Programs	• provision of financial assistance for the setting up of livelihood programs	• not financially rewarding due to administrative problems • program operation has stalled

Sources of Income	• continued farming and fishing • additional sources of income such as houses and rooms for rent, sari-sari stores, and transportation	• decreased fish catch and lower farm productivity • increased income from new 'business ventures' is temporary • increased income does not make much difference due to the increasing prices of goods and to residents' new lifestyles
	Indicators of Development	**Indicators of Community Insecurity**
Environment Construction Phase		• loss of lands planted to rice and fruit-bearing trees • disturbance of terrestrial and marine flora and fauna • air, water, and noise pollution • increased siltation/sedimentation of river systems
Operation Phase		• emissions of toxic and hazardous materials into the air, land, and water • death of marine resources land degradation • health problems

Among residents now living in the resettlement area, the most significant benefit they have derived from the project is the house and lot awarded to them as part of the resettlement package. Whereas they used to live in houses that were made of materials such as cogon, bamboo, sawali, and nipa, the houses they currently live in are of concrete hollow blocks, cement, and G.I. sheets.[30] Since their houses are now made of more durable materials, this has given them more protection against harsh natural elements such as typhoons. However, the residents have so far not yet been awarded titles of ownership to their house and lot. What they have in their possession is a certificate of award from the NAPOCOR. The titles are to be awarded to them after they have lived in the resettlement site for five years.

Electricity has finally come to *Barangay* Pangascasan, particularly in Sitio Tubag where the resettlement area is located. In addition to the houses and lots, the electrification of the area is deemed to be an invaluable outcome of the project. While the SCFTPP is not yet operational, the NAPOCOR has already provided transmission lines and connectors that give the residents access to the existing power generators in the province. No longer do they have to depend on kerosene, fuel wood, and batteries for their energy needs. However, there are some residents in the coastal zone who complained that even now they do not have electricity in their homes because they do not have the equipment that will enable them to get connected to the power lines. NAPOCOR was supposed to provide them with this equipment, but supplies were not sufficient to cover all the affected households.[31]

Employment opportunities, particularly for semi-skilled and skilled individuals, and livelihood programs are other benefits that came as a result of the SCFTPP. In 1996, an engineer of Sampaguita Builders Inc., a firm sub-contracted for the project, estimated that 80 per cent of their employees were local residents.[32] While the income from construction work may not be substantially more than the income from farming and fishing, what the residents appreciate more is the fact that cash flow in their households became more regular, whether at the end of every week or every 15th and 30th of the month. For some residents, while the income derived from employment in the plant has become their main source of livelihood, they continue to earn from farming and fishing activities. What has changed is that less time is now devoted to agricultural work. Also, women now do more work on the farms since the men have been hired for construction work.[33] Residents who operate *sari-sari* (convenience) stores also say that they benefit indirectly from the employment given to the townspeople. Customers are now able to pay their debts on time and have increased in number due to the influx of workers from outside. Other business ventures that provide additional sources of income have also risen around the project site, such as restaurants, eateries, and drinking pubs.[34] Aside from employment in the plant, continued farming and fishing, and *sari-sari* store business, another source of income is the enterprise of renting out rooms and/or houses to migrant workers and their families. For instance, one interviewee said that he built five temporary housing units (made of concrete flooring, plywood walls, and G.I. sheets roofing) purposely to be rented out to outsiders. On average, he earned about 500 pesos per month for every unit. Some charge as much as 900 pesos, depending on the size of the unit and the available facilities.[35] Due to the increased demand for housing, some units are occupied beyond capacity. Also, the shore of Baquioen Bay, which in September 1994 was dotted only by a number of houses some meters apart, is now overcrowded. Due to the demand for temporary housing, residents are renting out even some units in the resettlement area.

Regarding livelihood programs, income-generating projects funded by NAPOCOR have been established. Residents have also organized the Pabuyao Association to handle the livelihood programs to be undertaken in the resettlement area. The initial project of the organization was the construction of a fishpond where milkfish would be raised for community consumption and for sale. When asked about the present status of this project, a resident replied that the project has been suspended due to administrative problems. They are currently looking at other alternative projects that will generate income for the relocated households.[36] Another project is being implemented by an association of married women in *Barangay* Pangascasan. This project is funded by the United Nations Development Programme (UNDP) and has been in operation since 1991. At present, the group is conducting livelihood and training programs for women with the assistance of the Department of Education, Culture, and Sports (DECS).[37]

Training programs have also been conducted by NAPOCOR. These are conducted either in Lingayen or Dagupan, Pangasinan. The end goal of such programs is to equip the residents with the skills that will make them employable in the construction and even operation phases of the SCFTPP. Some of those who have successfully completed such training programs have been given employment in the plant. The majority of those who benefited from the skills training are male residents. This is to be expected given the nature of jobs available during the construction phase. Some female residents bemoaned the fact that the training programs usually targeted the men. While there were few opportunities open for single women, it was even tougher for married women with children. Even though the training programs were open to men and women, the married women were not able to take advantage of such programs because they were responsible for the care of their children and homes.[38]

The residents of Pangascasan also expressed appreciation for the other infrastructure developments that have taken place in the area due to the funds from NAPOCOR. Part of the road network leading to the project site has already been asphalted. However, the roads in Pangascasan itself remain dirt roads. This makes travelling quite difficult, especially during the rainy season. During the summer months, dust becomes a significant problem due to trucks carrying construction materials to and from the project site. Residents are still awaiting improvements on the *barangay* roads. A market has been constructed near the resettlement village to make it easier for the residents to procure food at a cheaper price. Before the market was constructed, residents had to travel to the town proper for their marketing, incurring significant travel costs. The problem with the market structure at the project site is that the rent is not affordable. Up until December 1998, the market was only partly operational. Some residents continue to travel all the way to the town center because the price of foodstuffs there is much cheaper than in their own market.[39] A new and bigger *barangay* hall has also been constructed. In addition, the construction of a covered basketball court-*cum*-multipurpose hall was also undertaken by the *barangay*.

Alongside the so-called signs of progress that have resulted from the SCFTPP, residents continued to feel insecure about their future. In both the resettlement area and the coastal zone, overcrowding is a major concern. Not only have migrant workers brought their families with them, but also household members who used to work in other parts of the country have decided to return home due to the availability of work at the project site. The growth in population size has resulted in an inadequacy of potable water and an excessive generation of waste. The drainage system that was installed in the area has also proved to be inadequate, in addition to the fact that the original design drained waste materials directly into one of the main rivers in the *barangay*. The potential for diseases and illnesses resulting from the lack of basic facilities required to maintain a clean environment has led the relocated households to complain to local authorities. Although design alterations have been made to the drainage system, water and garbage problems continued to be unresolved. No move has been made as yet to establish a permanent health service unit in the area. This inaction causes added apprehension among residents, especially since overcrowding in the resettlement site may cause communicable diseases to spread faster.

In terms of the lay out of the resettlement site, some residents appreciate the fact that adjacent lots place them closer to their neighbors. Others, however, allege that due to the migration of workers and the arrival of new families, the resettlement site (and even the coastal zone) now resembles a squatters' colony. This has also affected the peace and order situation in the *barangay*. When the outsiders first arrived, there were some significant skirmishes with the native residents. Unfamiliar with the others' lifestyles, the entry of outsiders was seen by some as a threat to their community. After the initial tension, *barangay* officials have been able to establish order, and community relations normalized to a certain extent.[40]

For the people living in the coastal zone, life has not been without worries. They have heard of plans to develop the area into an international seaport as part of the Sual Industrial Estate. Should this materialize, they will also be relocated in the same way as those already residing in Sitio Tubag. Residents would prefer to remain where they are now, since they continue to have easy access to the coastal waters. However, they said that if the government asks them to move, they have no choice but to comply, as they do not own the land they live on. What matters to them is that the community members develop a common position on the matter. Residents will also request a compensation package to enable them to rebuild their lives wherever they may be relocated. What adds to their anxiety is the lack of information coming from NAPOCOR, the PEC, and government officials regarding this matter. Hence, they feel unprepared for the future.[41]

Another major consequence of relocation is the change in lifestyle. Unlike the relatively simple subsistence life on farms, residents now face a life that is far more complicated than they had expected. In their new circumstances, everything from transportation to water has to be paid for. Whereas households used to share or exchange their agricultural produce with one another, now most everything has to be bought from the town market. Used to earning a living through farming and fishing, they now have to find other sources of income. Those who are not equipped for employment in the plant continue to farm or fish. However, agricultural production has been decreasing of late due to irrigation problems. Residents also claim fish catches have declined through the years. This is attributed to the disturbance caused by the ongoing construction of the power plant combined with years of environmentally-hazardous practices such as dynamite fishing, trawl fishing, and the use of different kinds of fishing gear.[42] Moreover, the Logolog River which gives the fishermen access to the Pao Bay, has become too shallow for the *bancas* (small boats). Residents counted on the NAPOCOR to deliver on its promise to dredge the river, but according to project engineers, there is no existing plan for such an activity.[43] Consequently, due to lack of income sources in the project and resettlement sites, other residents (particularly those who do not have any formal schooling or vocational training) have had to find jobs elsewhere in Pangasinan or other parts of the country.[44] With the disturbance compensation given to relocated households long gone, there is increasing pressure to find any available source of livelihood.

Employment at the plant site, mostly for male residents, had eased the people's financial troubles to an extent. Nevertheless, some employees reported delays in the release of their wages and even non-remittance of contributions to the Social Security System (SSS) by the construction firms. Such contributions are deducted from the monthly salaries of workers and as yet were not remitted to the SSS.[45] Also, due to the low skill levels of the residents and those demanded by construction work, employment was only on a contractual basis. Hence, a concern among those who had become dependent on earnings from employment in the SCFTPP is the reality that once the plant became operational, they would be unemployed again. The plant's operation would require less unskilled and semi-skilled workers and more technical and office personnel. In fact, towards the latter part of 1998, some companies already began to terminate some employees whose services were no longer required. In the view of one resident, it was some consolation that at least the first ones to have been laid off were the migrant workers.[46] Despite employment instability, people were looking forward to job opportunities in the new establishments expected to open once the Sual Industrial Estate is finally built.

As for the women community members, they have taken over the cooperative, which was left inactive as a result of their husbands' employment in the plant. Two officers of the cooperative reported that while most members were quite enthusiastic about the projects run by their organization, as of December 1998, funding problems prevented them from doing anything concrete. They have had difficulty in accessing money to fund their projects due to the vast amount of paperwork required. Also, while the project proponent offered them work once the plant started to operate, the kind of work offered was not acceptable to some members. As a result, some members are already losing interest in the activities of the cooperative.[47]

Problems were also raised regarding compensation for properties used for the plant. One resident said that his land was taken over by the NAPOCOR for purposes of building transmission lines. While he and his family have given up their land and already moved to the resettlement site, they have not yet been paid despite representations with the appropriate authorities.[48] While cases such as these may be the exception, it nevertheless points to the fact that the release of compensation funds has not been accomplished with reasonable efficiency.

In terms of the environmental hazards posed directly by the construction of the plant, residents pointed out that thus far their main concern has been air and water pollution. Blasting procedures undertaken to level the plant site and the heavy use of dirt roads by trucks and other big vehicles have increased the amount of dust particles in the air. Some mothers noted that this might have contributed to their children's susceptibility to respiratory problems. The use of dynamite for blasting has also caused noise pollution. As for water resources, residents noted the increasing amount of waste materials that are thrown into the sea. Fishermen have also observed increased sedimentation and siltation of the river system. They blame this in part on construction activities, on inefficient garbage collection, and on the increasing population, particularly in the coastal zone.

In the resettlement site, residents expressed fear that a landslide might occur during the typhoon season, because trees have been cut down in the higher parts of Sitio

Tubag. This section is being cleared to serve as one of the ash disposal sites. Aside from these concerns, the residents feel that thus far, the construction of the plant has not led to any serious environmental problems, at least not like those that happened in Calaca, Batangas. But while they have not yet experienced such problems, they remain cautious about the environmental effects that the SCFTPP may bring once it became operational in 1999. One female resident said that at first, they rejected the power plant project because of fears that an environmental disaster might occur in their town. But due to former President Ramos' assurance, they finally agreed to the project. However, once they observe that the SCFTPP is causing harm to their lives and the environment, they will not waste time in mobilizing and organizing community members to protest against the continued operation of the plant.[49]

To allay the residents' fears, several mitigating measures to prevent adverse effects on the environment during the construction and operation stages were suggested in the EIA and endorsed by the DENR-EMB. During the construction phase, the following measures were recommended: (1) heavy construction activities to be carried out during day time; (2) construction of a seawall prior to excavation activities to prevent increased sedimentation of the river system and to protect coastal and marine resources; (3) provision of drainage systems to augment natural drainage ways; and (4) use of low energy explosives for blasting procedures. As for the operation phase, the EIA required the following measures: (1) construction of a stack of 220 meters or higher to disperse emissions and keep ambient concentration levels within allowable limits; (2) utilization of high-grade coal to reduce polluting emissions; (3) implementation of an appropriate coal yard operation and maintenance program; (4) implementation of proper wastewater treatment facility; (5) construction of drainage system for proper disposal of waste materials; and (6) undertaking continuous monitoring and maintenance of environmental quality and living conditions in surrounding areas especially in the resettlement site.[50] It is hoped that the adoption of these measures will minimize the adverse effects that the construction and operation of the plant will have on the people's lives and on the environment.

Development and Security: The Short-Term Versus the Long-Term

In the Filipino language, the words that perhaps best approximate 'development' are *pag-unlad* or *maunlad*. When residents were asked whether they feel that their plight has been improved since the launching of the SCFTPP in 1994, most of the respondents replied in the affirmative. Their sentiment is that '*mas maunlad na ang lugar nila sa ngayon*' (their place is more developed now). They have observed certain improvements in their *barangay* and in their lives. While they do not as yet consider their area to be fully developed (relative to the town centers in Pangasinan), they feel that the electrification of their *barangay*, the improvements in the road network, the awarding of houses and lots, employment opportunities in the plant, and livelihood assistance have all made them better off than before. To the residents of Pangascasan, development is attained once they have improved access to the basic necessities of life and/or once there are observable improvements in their way of life.

Hence, in the short term, the people of Pangascasan feel that the SCFTPP project has resulted in the gradual development of their *barangay* as indicated by improvements in employment and other income sources, such as housing and infrastructure.

However, these improvements have come at a price. Interview responses of the residents reveal a sense of insecurity regarding their present status and the future, particularly once the SCFTPP became operational. Technically, they still do not own their homes, because the titles to their houses and lots have not been issued to them, as earlier noted. Residents in the coastal zone are not sure how long they will be able to live there due to the possibility of relocation once the international seaport project begins.

Overcrowding in both the resettlement site and the coastal zone has resulted in lack of potable water, garbage collection problems, and tense community relations. Employment in the plant, while it has given workers a more regular source of income, is only on a contractual basis. Once the plant begins operations, there will be less need for unskilled and semi-skilled workers. Business ventures such as houses and rooms for rent and *sari-sari* stores will take in less money once the construction activities end and the migrant workers move out. NAPOCOR has provided access to electricity although not all households have electricity at present. Also, to this day, there is no permanent health service unit in the *barangay*. Market structures have been established near the resettlement site, but due to the high rent, the market is not being used as planned.

Skills training programs have been conducted, but the women complain about the lack of opportunities given to them under such programs. Livelihood programs have been implemented (for example, fish ponds), but due to administrative failures, such attempts have not been financially rewarding. And there is a sense of community insecurity that stems from environmental problems caused by the construction of the SCFTPP, and from the probable adverse environmental consequences that the plant's operation will bring. These are the problems that have prompted one resident to say: '*Mas mabuti pa ang buhay noon sa bukid. Kahit na mas mahirap ang trabaho, mas sigurado kang may kakainin ka at mas kaunti ang problema*'. ('Life was much better on the farm. Although work was more difficult, at least we were sure that we always had something to eat and we had less problems').

The government's pursuit of development, defined for the most part in economic terms, may have resulted in improvements in *Barangay* Pangascasan. Nevertheless, residents feel that life can be better. For instance, people explain that while they acknowledge the government's (particularly NAPOCOR's) assistance in making life easier for them, their region will only be fully developed once they have access to the following: (1) security of residential tenure; (2) permanent sources of livelihood which may not necessarily be inside the plant; (3) adequate supply of clean water, regular garbage collection, and working drainage systems; (4) a permanent *barangay* health service unit especially for the children; (5) asphalted roads and cheaper transportation costs; (6) market and grocery stores selling affordable food and other supplies; (7) a regular supply of electricity at reduced costs; and (8) financial assistance for farmers and fishermen. Of course, the residents are awaiting the operation of the plant to see whether the promises of former President Ramos and the

PEC and NAPOCOR will be fulfilled. Should environmental safety suffer and problems begin to manifest themselves as a result of the plant's operation, the respondents said they would not hesitate to protest against the operation of the plant. They said that they will monitor the plant's operations diligently to prevent the Calaca experience from happening in their own backyard.

But due to their failed attempts at rejecting the project in the first instance, there is no assurance that the residents will be able to mobilize the entire community and to forge a united stance against a plant that may possibly be environmentally-disastrous. At present, there are two organizations, the Pabuyao Association and the Mothers' Association that exist in the area. Both these groups were established to implement livelihood programs designed to give financial assistance to the residents of Pangascasan. Outside of these, there is no existing institutional mechanism through which the residents can channel their complaints regarding SCFTPP-related issues. A *barangay* official said that when they have any grievance regarding the conditions in the resettlement site, for example, they could lodge these complaints through the *barangay*, which then would relay them to the municipal or provincial officials. It is also the *barangay* officials who communicate with the project officials and personnel.

However, due to some problems between the current *barangay* captain and the project officials arising from allegations that the former was involved in anomalous activities inside the plant, the relations between the *barangay* and project officials have been quite strained of late. Consequently, security in and around the project site has been tightened. It is the people who are caught between the 'warring' parties, and it is they who are affected by the lack of communication between the community leaders and the project handlers. Some residents say that because of the lack of communication, they are left in the dark regarding new developments concerning the SCFTPP.[51] In fact, given that the *barangay* government is one of the primary sources of information for community members, and that current relations between the local government and the project proponents are strained, residents say that very little information trickles down to them about future project plans, livelihood programs, financial assistance, health services, among others. Thus, this makes the residents uneasy about the future. Also, without access to information, they are afraid of being suddenly evicted from their homes to give way to new infrastructure developments.

Inadequate flow of information has long been an issue in *Barangay* Pangascasan. In September 1994, an NGO worker reported that one of the reasons NAPOCOR had a relatively easy time getting the people's 'approval' for the project was that people did not have a chance to weigh the pros and cons of the SCFTPP. They only heard one side of the story: NAPOCOR's. In his words: '*Naunahan ng pamahalaan ang mga NGOs na gusto sanang pumasok sa Pangascasan*'. ('The government was a step ahead of the NGOs who wanted to mobilize the people of Pangascasan.')[52] With NAPOCOR winning the information drive and former President Ramos' successful attempt at weakening whatever resistance existed, the SCFTPP project pushed through as planned. That the project was finally implemented is not a sign of acceptance on the part of the people: it was more a sign of resignation. '*Wala na kaming magagawa.*

Nandiyan na iyan'. ('We cannot do anything about it. The project's already final'.) That sums up the sentiment among Pangascasan residents.

One of the key factors that make the experience in other communities facing the same predicament quite different from that in Pangascasan is the people's access to information and their level of organization or mobilization. One success story is that of Bolinao, Pangasinan where a cement plant was to be built. From June 1994 to August 1996, the municipality of Bolinao was embroiled in a controversy surrounding the proposal to build a cement plant funded by a Taiwanese company. The cement plant complex would have consisted of a quarry site, power plant, cement factory, and wharf for water transport of unbagged cement to Taiwan. This project was to be implemented as part of the NWLGQ project of the Ramos government.

The proponents argued that the cement plant would boost the industrialization of Bolinao while the critics pointed to the probable harm the project would bring to the people and the environment. A group of concerned citizens organized themselves and fought against powerful political and business interests who were pushing for the project's approval. The opposing camps traded allegations of bribery and misinformation drives. A crucial factor that changed the tide in favor of the opposition was the vigorous environmental awareness program that they implemented. This resulted in a mass advocacy movement that called for the rejection of the cement plant project. On 6 August 1996, after almost 27 months of campaigning, the opposition claimed victory as former DENR Secretary Victor Ramos issued a final denial to the project proponents' request for an ECC.[53] The law prohibits the implementation of any environmentally-critical project without an ECC.

Among the lessons that can be drawn from the Bolinao experience, perhaps the most relevant to the case of *Barangay* Pangascasan is the importance of a well-informed and organized citizenry. When people have access to information, they have the capacity to make decisions for themselves, and not have decisions imposed on them by authorities. In this way, the people become empowered, because they can determine for themselves the kind of development that they want for their families and their community. Moreover, being well informed means that project proponents (usually the government) would not be able to mislead the people, because they are now made aware of the costs and benefits of suggested projects. As for the power plant in Sual, now that the project is already underway, there is no longer any chance of revoking the ECC that has been issued unless there is sufficient evidence to prove that the project does not comply with established environmental standards. To be able to monitor any activity related to the construction and operation of the SCFTPP, Pangascasan residents and other concerned citizens need to be organized and to exercise vigilance. The first step that can be undertaken is to establish a core group (apart from the existing ones) that will purposely devote its efforts towards institutionalizing communication links between all concerned parties (for example, NAPOCOR, PEC, construction firms, local governments units, and residents) and handle SCFTPP-related matters that concern the affected residents. Once established, this group will serve as the mechanism by which grievances can be relayed and information can be exchanged and shared.

As of now, communication channels between the residents and the project and local government officials are quite informal. Hence, any change in leadership in the local government units or in the project offices means changes in the working relations between them. Again, it is the residents that are caught in between. While during the initial phase of the SCFTPP the residents may have appeared as passive recipients of the government's development project, the problems they have experienced and continue to face have made them realize that they cannot remain passive throughout. The fact that they are aware of the possibility that the plant's operations may be harmful to them and the environment, and that they are willing to oppose the plant once they find it to be environmentally disastrous, indicate the level of concern that the residents have regarding the future of their community and the environment. The challenge now is to transform that concern into action, equipping the people with information about possible scenarios and strategies, organizing them, and ensuring that such action will be sustained.

Organizing themselves is a vital step in making the residents' voices heard. Without being organized, the people will just be overpowered by 'the entrenched political and economic structures' in society. Being organized gives the people the capacity to influence the policy direction taken by government and to make policy choices more favorable to them.[54] However, in the case of Pangascasan, because they lack experience in organizing and mobilizing their own members, community residents need to undergo local capacity-building. This task may be accomplished through the assistance of more established local and/or international NGOs or local government units. This is the case with the two existing groups in the area, the Mothers' Association having been established through the auspices of the UNDP, and the Pabuyao Association formed with the help of the NAPOCOR.

Based on the concerns articulated by the residents of *Barangay* Pangascasan, it appears that although they acknowledge the benefits they have enjoyed so far as a consequence of the SCFTPP, they continue to face certain problems arising from the project. In the short run, they have witnessed changes in their lives and in their community, changes that for them indicate that development has arrived in Pangascasan. Nevertheless, they recognize the costs that they have had to pay and may pay in the future. In the long run, the people will be preoccupied with the costs that may arise due to the operation of the plant. At the present time, there is an air of uncertainty about the future in the resettlement site and in the coastal zone of *Barangay* Pangascasan. The problems they continue to face make the people wonder whether the promises made by the government in 1994 will become a reality when the power plant becomes operational in 1999. The residents remain hopeful the promises will hold. Only then will development coexist with a sense of community security.

Policy Implications

'*Ang problema sa pamahalaan, iba ang konsepto nila ng* development *kaysa sa amin. Maaaring pag-unlad nga siya para sa kanila, pero problema ang dala nito para sa mga tao*'. ('The problem with government is that it sees development in a different manner compared to the people. A project may mean development for government, but for us it only causes problems').[55] Sentiments like this point to the need to reconcile national and community development goals. Many development projects in the Philippines have been criticized for failing to take into consideration the sentiments of the people that will be affected. To some, people protesting against development projects may seem ironic given that they are the target beneficiaries of these projects. It should be noted, however, that the people are not against development projects *per se*. In fact, the EIA survey for the SCFTPP showed that 56.9 per cent of the respondents were in favor of the project.[56] Among other reasons, they approve of the project because they realize the need for energy and/or electricity, and they are aware of the benefits arising from such a project. What they reject is the government's practice of top-down decision-making, government planning, and imposition of such projects on them. It is because of this practice that people get the sense that they have no role in development planning. Moreover, while the law requires that consultations and dialogues be held between the government and the people, the parties involved often have varying views about what a consultative process should be. The latter expect that their input will find their way into the final policy, while the former insists that no matter what transpires during dialogues, the final decision is theirs to make. The problem boils down to the issue of participatory development.

The 1987 Philippine Constitution and the 1991 Local Government Code recognize the critical role in nation building and development played by actors outside of the national government. These actors include local government units, the private sector, NGOs and people's organizations (POs), community organizations, indigenous peoples, women's groups, youth, and the labor sector. The rights of these entities to participate in decision-making are given primacy under a decentralized system of governance. More specifically, the law provides that these actors shall be directly involved in the making of plans and projects concerning the delivery of basic services and facilities, joint ventures and cooperative programs, financial and other forms of assistance, and financing, construction, maintenance, operation, and management of infrastructure projects. These groups also have the right to representation in local planning bodies. In addition, preferential treatment shall be extended to organizations and cooperatives, including fisherfolk's cooperatives.[57]

One means by which these proclamations have been enacted is the government's policy of inducing growth in the rural areas, primarily through: (1) enhancing the participation of the residents (especially the marginalized sectors such as fisherfolks and farmers), not only in project implementation but also in policy-making; (2) granting equitable access to the rural residents to natural resource-use and benefits; (3) providing infrastructure and support services to increase rural productivity and expand markets; (4) establishing growth centers to serve as bases for industrial and commercial activities that will provide alternative livelihood and increased economic opportunities; and (5) improvements in the delivery of social services such as education, health, and nutrition.[58] People's participation is also encouraged in the EIA system which is a requirement in the project cycle. Defined as 'the evaluation of the various impacts and the resultant natural and induced changes as simply and as precisely as possible for optimizing the total benefit to the development and the environment'. An EIA is designed to examine the positive and negative consequences of a project's construction, operation, and decommissioning on the biophysical, geophysical, and socio-economic environment. Basically, it looks at the benefits and adverse impacts of a project on development and the environment.[59]

Aside from a physical survey of the proposed project site, a key component of any EIA statement is a survey of the people's perceptions about the project. The EIA is also a means of determining the social acceptability of a project. In practice, however, the conduct of EIA has not been without difficulties. While the issue of social acceptability has always been associated with energy projects because of the unfortunate experiences in both local and foreign power plants, the problem of accurately determining and assessing people's attitudes towards such projects remains. Part of the EIA process is the conduct of public hearings and consultations to serve as a venue for the people to articulate their reactions towards a proposed project. Ideally, such consultations should be broad-based and conducted in a democratic manner. A major problem is that 'resource constraints have made the actual conduct of public hearings non-regular and unsustained'.[60] Difficulties such as these hamper the participation of community residents in the decision-making process. And before suggestions are made that new laws need to be legislated to make development more open to participation, it is better to examine and strengthen the existing legal documents.

A participatory development process also entails responsive policy makers. Even during the implementation of development projects, policy makers need to be continuously aware of the situation in project sites. In this way, the proper authorities can more easily address the grievances of residents (especially those who are relocated as a consequence of a project). Moreover, there is a need for a regular dialogue mechanism between the residents and the project implementors. Consultations should not be held only during the EIA process. In Pangascasan, for instance, some residents complained that it takes a long time before NAPOCOR or the municipal officials attend to their problems. At times, they get no response at all. While project proponents were very keen on providing the demands of the community members during the negotiation stage, once the project was approved, it became harder and harder for the community members to gain access to these officials.

On the whole, genuine (as opposed to token) participatory development requires that the people be given the opportunity to play a substantial part in determining the government's policy choices. Therefore, decisions are based not solely on the interests of the national government, but on the interests of all parties concerned. Resistance to the government's development efforts may be reduced if the people are part of the decision-making process and they are no longer viewed as passive actors. As stakeholders in the development process, they have the right to determine for themselves the kind of development that they want. But corollary to that right is the people's responsibility of equipping themselves with the proper skills, information, and know-how so that they may responsibly participate in the political process. Participatory development will not become a reality even if the law provides for it as long as the people remain apathetic to government. In the final analysis, participatory development is the task of both government and the people.

Concluding Remarks

The pursuit of development in the Philippines has led past and present administrations to embark on various programs that seek to address the needs of the country and its people. The construction of a power plant in Sual, Pangasinan is one such endeavor. The SCFTPP is a BOT project that the government hopes will: (1) address the energy needs of the island of Luzon; (2) fuel the country's industrialization efforts; and (3) contribute to the development of the host province and community. There is no denying that the 1,000-megawatt energy capacity of the coal-fired power plant will add immensely to the existing capacity of the Luzon Grid. The power that will be generated from the plant will be utilized by the various agro-industrial projects that are being planned under the NWLGQ program. As for Pangasinan and *Barangay* Pangascasan, the financial assistance that was given to them under the MOA was to serve as a start-up fund to compensate for whatever 'inconveniences' the project may bring. Launched in 1994, the first unit of the SCFTPP is nearing completion and is already operational. All parties concerned are hoping that the benefits to be derived from the project will be maximized and costs minimized.

While the project is still in the construction phase, the residents of Pangascasan already experienced both the positive and negative consequences arising from the SCFTPP. Some community members perceive that their *barangay* is now being developed as a result of the assistance extended to them by the NAPOCOR and the PEC. New and better houses, electricity, regular employment, paved roads, water pumps, a new *barangay* hall and multipurpose hall, and a market are indicators of community development. But alongside these positive impacts of the SCFTPP are the costs: environmental degradation, physical and social disruption, and the uncertainty of the sustainability of economic benefits from the project.

The adverse effects of development programs on the people's lives and on the environment may be considered as a non-military threat to the security of communities in particular and societies in general. In the Philippines, the construction of a coal-fired thermal power plant in Pangasinan, a component of the provincial and national governments' development programs, may have resulted in development in the short run, but alongside this has evolved a sense of community insecurity as regards the future. This is because the experiences of other communities hosting power plants have proven that the time when the plant begins operation is usually more potentially disruptive than the construction phase. It is during operation when adverse environmental consequences, livelihood and health problems, and socio-economic difficulties become more evident. Therefore, the residents of Pangascasan are on the alert. They are ready to take action once things turn for the worse.

Before they can take action, however, the most immediate challenge they face is to organize themselves. In the absence of any community organization outside of the two livelihood groups in existence, it is imperative for the residents to identify a core group composed of community leaders and members who will assist them in articulating their demands and identifying strategies of actions to ensure that their interests are protected. This is one means by which they can secure their welfare. Assistance can be obtained from the more established NGOs and POs whose expertise lie in community organizing and mobilization. The residents have articulated their resolve to protest against the continued operation of the plant if they find it to be more harmful than beneficial to them and the environment. This may be taken as a sign of the vigilant tendencies of the residents. The next step is to cultivate and sustain this orientation. By acting as watchdogs, it is the residents themselves who will make the future secure for this and future generations. For now, it is too soon to tell whether the operation of the SCFTPP will have disastrous effects on the environment and the people of Pangascasan. Only time will tell whether their fears of a Calaca-like experience are unfounded or not. In the meantime, they wait and hope that the project will be all that the government promised it to be: economically beneficial and environmentally friendly.

Government usually envisions development as a means to ensure the security of its people. Through development projects, the goals of economic growth, infrastructure development, better living conditions, and improved environmental quality are to be attained. However, if the very projects which are designed to contribute to development result instead in human, community, and environmental insecurity, then something must be done to change the development process and make it more responsive to the people's well being.

Notes

1 The researcher would like to acknowledge the assistance of CIDA and ISDS, Dr. Carolina G. Hernandez, Ms. Mylene Rivera (DENR-EMB), Mr. Jhoel P. Raquedan, and Mr. Lailo Sotero and the residents of *Barangay* Pangascasan, Sual, Pangasinan.

2 Calaca, Batangas is the site of two 300-megawatt coal-fired power plants. The continued operation of these power plants was opposed by affected residents and some local government officials due to the adverse effects on livelihood, community life, health, and the environment. The operation of Calaca I has been found to have resulted in the relocation of residents, environmental pollution, a decrease in fish catch, depletion of marine resources, contamination of potable drinking water, health problems, and a decrease in agricultural productivity. Doyo, M.C. P. (1992), 'Postmortem: Calaca', *Sunday Inquirer Magazine*, 12 January, and Baes, A. V. (1991), 'Project CALABARZON and Environmental Degradation', *Midweek*, 25 December.

3 Data as of 1995 from the National Statistics Office, Republic of the Philippines.

4 Louis Berger International Inc. (1995), 'Preparation of a Master Plan for the Northwestern Luzon Growth Quadrangle', *PAPSP Studies*, February. The master plan was undertaken through the Philippine Assistance Program Support Project.

5 Data as of 1990 from the National Statistics Office, Republic of the Philippines.

6 Data as of 1995 from the National Statistics Office, Republic of the Philippines.

7 BHP Engineering Philippines Inc. (1994), *Environmental Impact Statement for the*

Proposed Sual Coal-Thermal Power Plant, BHP Engineering Philippines, Inc., Quezon City, pp.214.

8 *Ibid.*, pp.200.

9 *Ibid.*, pp.214.

10 *Ibid.*, pp.222-7.

11 'The Northwestern Luzon Growth Quadrangle', *CPPAP Reports*, Northwestern Luzon Growth Quadrangle Commission Program, 1997.

12 Statements taken from messages of the President and the Energy Secretary on the occasion of the launching of the Department of Energy's Philippine Energy Plan: 1996-2025.

13 As of 1996, total energy capacity was placed at 10, 286 megawatts. Between 1996 and 2025, the period covered by the energy plan, the government hopes to add 92,138 megawatts. Department of Energy (1996), *Philippine Energy Plan: 1996-2025*, Manila, Republic of the Philippines, pp.30.

14 *Ibid.*, pp. 30-31 and National Power Corporation (NAPOCOR) (1998), *Power Development Program* National Power Corporation, Manila, pp.1.

15 BHP Engineering Philippines Inc. (1994), *Environmental Impact Statement for the Proposed Sual Coal-Thermal Power Plant*, pp.25.

16 *Ibid.*, pp.34 and 36.

17 *Ibid.*, pp.25 and 'Memorandum of Agreement: The Sual-Coal Fired Thermal Power Plant Project', Pangasinan, 3 December 1994, pp.1, 4-6.

18 In an interview conducted by the author in September 1994, this former *barangay* official said that the residents of the area finally supported the project when President Ramos promised them that he will make sure that the SCFTPP will not have adverse consequences on the people's lives and on the environment. The people believed that because President Ramos hails from Pangasinan himself, he will not approve a project that will be disadvantageous to his province.

19 Jatayna, E. A. (1995), 'The Sual Coal-Fired Power Plant: Lessons From the Past', *Politik*, vol.2, no.1, August, pp.29.

20 BHP Engineering Philippines Inc. (1994), *Environmental Impact Statement for the Proposed Sual Coal-Thermal Power Plant*, pp.228-9.

21 When the EIA was being prepared, it was estimated that 64 families from the project site and 12 families from the ash disposal areas will have to be relocated to Sitio Tubag. In 1998, a resident in the resettlement site estimates that there are some 85-100 households living in the area. This figure does not include the workers (and their families) brought in from outside by construction firms subcontracted for the SCFTPP.

22 'Memorandum of Agreement : The Sual-Coal Fired Thermal Power Plant Project', 1994, pp.2.

23 BHP Engineering Philippines Inc. (1994), *Environmental Impact Statement for the Proposed Sual Coal-Thermal Power Plan*, pp.229-30 and 232. While there are no exact figures, a sizable number of households who used to reside in the project site do not own the land where they live. Hence, as farm workers, the decision to move out is not theirs to make. A consequence of this is that compensation for the agricultural lands and crops that will be destroyed due to the construction of the plant will not accrue to them but to the actual land owners.

24 This plan may have already been overtaken by events. In September 1998, NAPOCOR announced that as of October, its selling price will increase by an average of 2.7 centavos per kilowatt-hour. Part of the reason for the price hike is the increased utilization of NAPOCOR's coal-fired power plants in the Luzon Grid. Velasco, M. M., 'NPC Hikes Power Rates in Luzon Grid', Manila.

25 'Memorandum of Agreement: The Sual-Coal Fired Thermal Power Plant Project', 1994, pp.2-3.

26 BHP Engineering Philippines Inc. (1994), *Environmental Impact Statement for the Proposed Sual Coal-Thermal Power Plan*, pp.232, 234, 236, and 238 and National Power Corporation (NAPOCOR) (1994), *Resettlement Program: Sual Coal-Fired Thermal Power Plant*, Social Engineering Department, May.

27 BHP Engineering Philippines Inc. (1994), *Environmental Impact Statement for the Proposed Sual Coal-Thermal Power Plan*, pp.34 and 229. Among residents who said they possessed certain technical skills, the top responses were carpentry (8.1 per cent), driving (1.2 per cent), and mechanic (1.1 per cent).

28 NAPOCOR (1994), *Resettlement Program: Sual Coal-Fired Thermal Power Plant*, pp.1.

29 Data from 1996 interviews were generated by Karen Soriano for her thesis at the University of the Philippines. Data from all other interviews were generated by the author.

30 NAPOCOR (1994), *Resettlement Program: Sual Coal-Fired Thermal Power Plant*, pp.3 and 6.

31 Interview with a *barangay* councilor, *Barangay* Pangascasan, April 1998.

32 Interview with engineer Ronald Garing, SCFTPP project site, February 1996.

33 Interview with a female resident, coastal zone, *Barangay* Pangascasan, April 1998. According to this resident, she has had to do more farm work since her husband began working in the plant. She is not complaining, however, since her husband's employment has given them additional income. However, she laments the fact that between her and her husband, they still have difficulty making ends meet. In addition, farming and fishing activities are done in different places now due to the dislocation caused by the plant's construction.

34 Interview with a male resident, coastal zone, *Barangay* Pangascasan, April 1998.

35 Interview with a male resident who is also a former *barangay* councilor, coastal zone, *Barangay* Pangascasan, April 1998.

36 Interview with a male resident, resettlement site, *Barangay* Pangascasan, April 1998.

37 Interview with the president of the Mothers' Association, *Barangay* Pangascasan, April 1998. The current project of the group has members making pickled papaya and banana catsup. These are primarily for home consumption. The president of the organization also explained that aside from this project, they also conduct environmental activities such as clean-up drives and beautification programs. At one point, they also had a piggery project.

38 Interview with two female residents, coastal zone, *Barangay* Pangascasan, April 1998. One of the interviewees stated that she had a female relative who was enrolled in a training program for welding, a male-dominated activity. Hence, whether male or female, interested residents were given training in jobs that are traditionally done by males. This is due to the skills required during the construction phase. However, another resident said that once the Sual Industrial Estate becomes a reality and other businesses such as factories, eating establishments, and shopping malls are brought in, she hopes that there will be more employment opportunities for women, especially married ones like herself. Another resident said that she was interested in joining one of the training programs but was unable to because the programs were usually held in the town centers. If she joins, nobody would look after the needs of her two children.

39 Interview with two female residents, coastal zone, *Barangay* Pangascasan, December 1998.

40 Interview with a married couple, resettlement area, *Barangay* Pangascasan, April 1998. Asked as to what they preferred, life in the farm or in the resettlement area, this couple said that they prefer to go back to their land and to farming. Although the project proponents of the SCFTPP have given them homes and electricity, among other advantages, life has been more difficult now due to the conditions in the resettlement area. And though this couple had a *sari-sari* store (small convenience shop) and a jeep which they use for

transport, they said that it is easier for them to earn money these days, but that money is also spent faster due to needs arising from changes in their lifestyles. At least on the farm, once they have harvested the rice and other crops, they are assured that they will have something to eat until the next harvest season. As regards community relations, they reported that there were some serious conflicts in the past year – one even involved the death of a community resident. Incidences of theft have also been reported by some residents. Fortunately, they noted, there have been improvements in recent months.

41 Interview with a female resident, coastal zone, *Barangay* Pangascasan, April 1998.

42 BHP Engineering Philippines Inc. (1994), *Environmental Impact Statement for the Proposed Sual Coal-Thermal Power Plant*, pp.232 and Interview with a female resident, resettlement site, *Barangay* Pangascasan, January 1996.

43 Interview with a NAPOCOR-Sual engineer, project site, *Barangay* Pangascasan, February 1996.

44 According to a female resident in the resettlement area, some women members of the community used their compensation to set up *sari-sari* stores. However, a visit to the site will show that almost every household has its own store. Due to the excessive number of stores catering to the needs of community members, some have had to close down their shops.

45 Interview with a female resident, resettlement area, *Barangay* Pangascasan, February 1996. The husband of the interviewee is a worker of one of the construction firms involved in the SCFTPP construction. In another interview conducted in December 1998, some female residents still reported the problem of non-remittance of SSS contributions by the employers.

46 Interview with a male resident, coastal zone, *Barangay* Pangascasan, December 1998.

47 Interview with two female residents, coastal zone, *Barangay* Pangascasan, December 1998. During the interview, the respondents expressed their interest in training programs that are offered by NGOs. They said that if they have the necessary skills and knowledge, they may have an easier time obtaining funds from government. Such responses reveal that some residents are not indifferent to their plight. Rather, what makes it difficult for them to participate more actively in their community is their lack of information, skills, and training.

48 Interview with a male resident, resettlement area, *Barangay* Pangascasan, April 1998.

49 Interview with a female resident, coastal zone, *Barangay* Pangascasan, April 1998. Among residents interviewed in April 1998, this appears to be a common sentiment. While most of them are grateful that the construction of the power plant has not been that harmful to the environment, they said that they are willing to campaign against the continued operation of the plant should they find it adversely affecting environmental quality in their area. According to the interviewee: '*Kapag may* pollution *na, magkakaisa din kami sa pagpapaalis sa kanila.*' ('Once the plant pollutes our town, we will unite in getting them out of here.')

50 BHP Engineering Philippines Inc. (1994), *Environmental Impact Statement for the Proposed Sual Coal-Thermal Power Plant*, pp.15-24.

51 Interview with a *barangay* councilor, coastal zone, *Barangay* Pangascasan, April 1998.

52 Interview with an NGO worker, resettlement site, *Barangay* Pangascasan, September 1994.

53 Interview with an official of the group of concerned citizens that campaigned for the rejection of the cement plant project, Bolinao, September 1995, and Talaue-McManus, L., Yambao, A. C., Salmo, S. III, and Altilde, P. (1998), *Participatory Coastal Development Planning in Bolinao, Northern Philippines: A Potent Tool for Conflict Resolution*, Conflict Management Case Study, IDRC. According to the authors, the Community-Based Coastal Resources Management Project in Bolinao that was sponsored by the International Development Research Center of Canada and implemented in part by the University of the

Philippines-Marine Science Institute (UP-MSI) proved to be a crucial means by which information regarding the project and its probable environmental effects were disseminated to the people. Equipped with the necessary information, the residents of Bolinao were able to organize themselves and make an independent decision regarding the project. Thus, they were not just resigned to accept the plans formulated by the national government.

54 Co, E. A. (1996), 'Reinterpreting Civil Society: The Context of the Philippine NGO Movement', in A. G. Alegre (ed.), *Trends and Traditions, Challenges and Choices: A Strategic Study of Philippine NGOs*, Ateneo Center for Social Policy and Public Affairs and Philippines-Canada Human Resource Development Program, Quezon City, pp.195-6.

55 Interview with a male resident, resettlement site, *Barangay* Pangascasan, April 1998.

56 BHP Engineering Philippines Inc. (1994), *Environmental Impact Statement for the Proposed Sual Coal-Thermal Power Plant*, pp.229.

57 *1987 Constitution of the Republic of the Philippines*, Article II, Sections 13-4, 18, 20, and 22-3 and *1991 Local Government Code of the Philippines*, Article 62.

58 Department of Environment and Natural Resources (1990), *Philippine Strategy for Sustainable Development: A Conceptual Framework*, Quezon City, Republic of the Philippines, pp.11.

59 United Nations Environmental Program (UNEP) (1980), *Environmental Assessment Statement: A Test Model Presentation*, UNEP Regional Office and United Nations Asian and Pacific Development Institute, Bangkok, March, pp.217, and DENR-Environmental Management Bureau (1994), *Philippine Environmental Impact Statement System Guide: Policies and Procedures*, Quezon City, Republic of the Philippines.

60 DENR-Environmental Management Bureau, (1992), *A Report on Philippine Environment and Development: Issues and Strategies*, Quezon City, Republic of the Philippines, pp.2-51. For example, when asked whether they participated in any consultations or hearings prior to the approval of the SCFTPP, some residents were not even aware that there were dialogues between the project proponents and the community. What aggravates the situation is that residents are not aware that they have the right to request the holding of consultations because this is mandated under the EIA system. This is not to deny that there are residents who are indifferent to the point that although they know of such consultations, they do not participate.

References

Baes, A. V. (1991), 'Project CALABARZON and Environmental Degradation', *Midweek*, 25 December.

BHP Engineering Philippines Inc. (1994), *Environmental Impact Statement for the Proposed Sual Coal-Thermal Power Plant*, BHP Engineering Philippines, Inc., Quezon City, pp. 214.

Co, E. A. (1996), 'Reinterpreting Civil Society: The Context of the Philippine NGO Movement', in A. G. Alegre (ed.), *Trends and Traditions, Challenges and Choices: A Strategic Study of Philippine NGOs*, Ateneo Center for Social Policy and Public Affairs and Philippines-Canada Human Resource Development Program, Quezon City, pp. 195-6.

Department of Energy (DoE) (1996), *Philippine Energy Plan: 1996-2025*, Manila, Republic of the Philippines pp. 30.

Department of Environment and Natural Resources (DENR) (1990), *Philippine Strategy for Sustainable Development: A Conceptual Framework*, Quezon City, Republic of the Philippines pp. 11.

DENR-Environmental Management Bureau (DENR-EMB) (1994a), *Philippine Environmental Impact Statement System Guide: Policies and Procedures*, Quezon City, Republic of the Philippines.

DENR-Environmental Management Bureau (DENR-EMB) (1992b), *A Report on Philippine Environment and Development: Issues and Strategies*, Quezon City, Republic of the Philippines, pp. 2-51.

Doyo, M.C. P. (1992), 'Postmortem: Calaca', *Sunday Inquirer Magazine*, 12 January.

Jatayna, E. A. (1995), 'The Sual Coal-Fired Power Plant: Lessons From the Past', *Politik*, vol. 2, no. 1, August, pp. 29.

Louis Berger International Inc. (1995), 'Preparation of a Master Plan for the Northwestern Luzon Growth Quadrangle', *PAPSP Studies*, February.

National Power Corporation (1998), *Power Development Program*, National Power Corporation, Manila, pp. 1.

National Power Corporation (NAPOCOR) (1994), *Resettlement Program: Sual Coal-Fired Thermal Power Plant*, Social Engineering Department, National Power Corporation, Manila, May.

Northwestern Luzon Growth Quadrangle Commission Program (1997), *The Northwestern Luzon Growth Quadrangle*, CPPAP Reports.

Talaue-McManus, L., Yambao, A. C., Salmo, S. III, and Altilde, P. (1998), *Participatory Coastal Development Planning in Bolinao, Northern Philippines: A Potent Tool for Conflict Resolution*, Conflict Management Case Study, IDRC.

United Nations Environmental Program (UNEP) (1980), *Environmental Assessment Statement: A Test Model Presentation*, UNEP Regional Office and United Nations Asian and Pacific Development Institute, Bangkok, March, pp. 217.

Chapter 6

Human and Ecological Security: The Anatomy of Mining Disputes in the Philippines

Francisco Magno

Introduction

A new mining law was passed in the Philippines in 1995. It aims to liberalize investment criteria in mineral development ventures. Through state incentives, it was expected that the mining industry, whose contribution to national income has been steadily declining since the 1980s, would be awakened from its deep slumber. However, rather than the expected mining boom, expansion efforts have instead precipitated a storm of conflicts.[1] The anatomy of these disputes could be dissected in at least three ways. First, mining income and employment are generated while simultaneously threatening the health and ecological security of host communities. Social discontent especially simmers when mining firms pass on the burden of paying the social costs of pollution to local residents. Second, perceptions of inequities in the allocation of mining rights have damaging effects on social cohesion. Tensions are ignited when large mining corporations are awarded development permits in the same area claimed by tribal groups as part of their ancestral domain. Third, mining conflicts are produced when other rural land uses such as those associated with agricultural, forestry, and fishery systems are dislocated.

Through the lens of development, mining could be seen as an economic enterprise with both positive and negative effects. Ranked among the richest nations in the world in terms of its mineral endowments, the Philippines is second only to South Africa in gold density and third to Chile and Poland in copper density. Tapping the vast mineral reserves of the country could yield favorable economic returns especially in creating jobs and raising public revenue through the collection of real property taxes from mining companies. The other side of the balance sheet, however, points to the likely displacement of local communities and their livelihood systems from mining ventures. Likewise, the downstream impact of mining waste on croplands, rivers, and coastal resources are potentially enormous.

Looking at mining as a security issue entails an understanding of the multiple threats to human safety and environmental sustainability engendered by reckless mining practices. Human security refers to the sense of well being enjoyed by people and communities when they have adequate access to food, freedom, health, and sustainable livelihood. Left unchecked, the environmental degradation and resource competition fostered by mineral-development activities could create conflicts that endanger security. In the absence of strong regulatory institutions and conflict-resolution mechanisms, competing claims over access rights in mining zones may lead to confrontations, pitting big mining firms against other resource users, including small-scale miners and indigenous communities. Already, instances of aggressive rivalry have erupted among stakeholder groups in pursuit of competing claims to resource privileges in mining sites. Development disputes in the mining sector are transformed into security concerns when the contending parties threaten to abandon peaceful means in settling their differences.

To resolve mining conflicts peacefully, there is a need for the state to adopt a strategic stance that is sensitive to the integration of development, environment, and security concerns. To this end, this chapter suggests policy and institutional measures to manage the risks to human and environmental security arising from mineral development activities. It also assesses how social capital could be employed as a strategic asset in implementing accountability, transparency, and participatory processes in the administration of mining projects. Social capital is defined as a set of social resources, constituted by networks of trust and webs of cooperation, which facilitates collective action. In the past, state failure to internalize the social costs of environmental degradation, and the incapacity to apply equitable criteria in the distribution of user rights over mineral resources, contributed to the outbreak of security crises. Averting violent resolution of mining disputes would require the adoption of a broad view of security, which considers the well being and participation of host communities and civil society associations in establishing rules and norms governing mining operations.

New Security Risks

The demise of the cold war has enlivened efforts to expand the security agenda beyond the narrow preoccupation with the strategic containment of external military aggression. Given the reduced risk of military confrontation following the decline in bipolar politics, proponents of the broad view of security suggest the need to pay closer attention to non-military threats as potential sources of conflict. The trend towards a more inclusive understanding of security is evident in the assertion that resource degradation threatens the security of people. Growing human demands on a shrinking resource base provide the groundwork for igniting conflicts inside and outside the borders of nation states.[2]

With the emphasis on geopolitical and military concerns, traditional security perspectives often fail to account for the environmental threats that endanger human well being.[3] The literature on the environment-security interface seek to address this gap by emphasizing the need to safeguard ecological systems as a preventive measure against conflict eruption.[4] In the conventional notion of security, the state is summoned to defend the nation's territorial integrity against foreign assault. Ironically, even without armed invaders, the nation state is often compelled to surrender the resources within its boundaries to the silent forces of environmental decay. According to Norman Myers, the commitment not to cede a single meter of national territory as a matter of security policy sounds hollow, especially when hundreds of square miles of topsoil are lost each year through state failure to regulate forest and watershed destruction.[5]

Grappling with the security consequences of contemporary development and environmental processes involves the questions of 'security for whom'? and 'security for which' values?[6] The concept of security has to specify a referent object and determine a set of values that requires protection.[7] Increasingly, security is being defined with reference to the security of citizens seen as human beings and not simply as members of a particular state.[8] This coincides with the move to disentangle security from the state's monopolistic embrace.[9] Security as defined by the state may not necessarily conform to the security of people. In certain cases, inappropriate state policies and actions generate greater threats to those who live within their borders than the armed forces of neighbors.[10] Rather than seen as the automatic guarantor of security, the state should be viewed as the institutional terrain where dynamic policy struggles to define the security agenda are waged.

Situated within the context of state-society relations, the implications of environmental degradation on human security are considered in this chapter. As stated earlier, human security is understood as the sense of well being enjoyed by people when they have sufficient income, food, health, freedom, and livelihood. Here, emphasis is placed on the broad security of citizens. Security policy is established not only to preserve the state's political autonomy and territorial integrity, but also to protect a wide range of other values that include citizen-safety, economic welfare, democratic participation, and ecological sustainability. In order to avert the instability and breakdown afflicting many countries in the world, the design of human security policy should take into account the complex web of social, economic, and environmental factors that define the issue. Compared to traditional military security, human security is much less about procuring arms and deploying troops than it is about strengthening the social and environmental fabric of societies and improving their governance.[11]

The defense of human security involves serious efforts to protect people against the social and environmental hazards resulting from unsustainable development activities. In the mining industry, poor compliance with environmental standards has been generally attributed to weak administrative institutions. Holding mining polluters accountable for their actions would, therefore, rely heavily on the presence of an independent and competent state, capable of monitoring and regulating mineral-development activities. Nevertheless, the intensity of competing claims and resource conflicts in mining sites indicates that the reform of formal administrative structures may not be enough. In responding to the security challenges in areas torn by mining disputes, there may be a need to investigate the role of social capital as an asset in mobilizing conflict resolution processes to improve development outcomes.

Social Capital

Social capital is created within the context of institutional rules and norms in society. People come together to participate in collective action based on the calculation of strategic gains as well as the identification with community norms.[12] Where there exists a sense of community and social responsibility, cooperation prevails based on a notion of altruism that promotes group interests.[13] However, where levels of sociability are low, institutions induce coordinated actions through the application of both formal rules (for example, constitutions, laws, and property rights) and informal constraints (for example, sanctions, taboos, customs, traditions, and codes of conduct).[14]

Institutions are important in forging common goals and facilitating their achievement. They are created not only to formulate rules, but also to enforce them not only to structure relationships, but also to make them work. As instruments for realizing objectives, and not just for reaching consensus, institutions operate under given political and historical circumstances. While influencing the conduct of socio-political interactions, institutions themselves are historically constituted by changes in the political, economic, and cultural landscape. Within the context of environmental governance, institutions provide the framework of rules and conventions that construct people's relationship to resources, converting interests into claims, and claims into rights.[15]

Institutions are significant forces in implementing participatory processes in mining-development activities. In order to make the development process sustainable, the strengthening of local participation is imperative.[16] Towards this end, it is clearly necessary to acquire a better understanding of the micro-institutional foundations of development. Recognizing the importance of institutions, as well as social capital in making people collectively productive, should provide a clearer understanding.[17]

The smallness of scale has been acknowledged as a significant factor in facilitating collective action. It has been argued that small groups, compared to large ones, are in a better position to monitor the behavior of fellow members in such a way that mutual assistance and cooperation is cultivated.[18] Mancur Olson has conceded that the free-rider problem could be solved in a small group where a collective good could often be provided through the voluntary, self-interested action of its members.[19] However, in small communities characterized by heterogeneity, collective action may also prove to be difficult.[20] While the possibilities of generating collective action may indeed be greater in small-scale societies, this is not guaranteed in the absence of strong institutional rules and conventions that nourish mutual trust and cooperative behavior.

The term social capital was initially used by Glenn Loury to refer to a set of social resources within a household or community that serve as important assets in the development of human capital.[21] Incorporating the concept of social capital within a general theory of social action, James Coleman has depicted it as a productive collection of structural resources, embedded in social relations, which facilitate the achievement of certain ends that would not have been attainable in its absence. Forms of social capital include norms, obligations, information potential, and voluntary associations that promote trust and cooperation.[22]

Robert Putnam, elaborating on the theme that voluntary cooperation is better in a community with large reserves of social capital founded on norms of reciprocity and networks of civic engagement, has asserted that 'for political stability, for government effectiveness, and even for economic progress social capital may be even more important than physical or human capital'.[23] In a comparative study of regional governments in Italy, he linked measures of social capital with variations in democratic and development gains. Following Putnam's lead, a host of scholarly efforts has been undertaken to explain critically the impact of social capital on political and economic processes and to account for the mixed levels of social capital existing in particular contexts.[24] For instance, Francis Fukuyama has argued that a high-trust society is most likely to register a better economic performance than a low-trust society. In this regard, social capital is generated by trust, which is the expectation produced by regular, honest, and cooperative behavior anchored on shared norms prevailing among members of a community.[25]

The main factors contributing to the creation and sustainability of social capital include the closure of social networks, stability of social relations, continuity of mutual aid arrangements, maintenance of regular communications, and existence of government incentives. Stable social relations prevent disruptions that could potentially lead to the devaluation of social capital. On the other hand, the continuity of mutual-aid arrangements increases the amount of social capital in circulation through the reinforcement of norms of cooperation. Just like human capital and physical capital, social capital depreciates over time and demands constant renewal.[26]

Within voluntary organizations, the maintenance of communications through regular meetings serves as an important channel for information exchange. The mechanism for distributing information is a form of social capital that facilitates collective action. The state also participates in the making and recreation of social capital through the generation of policy incentives.[27] In this sense, the state could play a vital function in providing the opportunity for cross-cutting ties to flourish in communities and across society in general.

Mining Policy and Governance

The authority of the state in allocating mining rights in the Philippines was established under Spanish colonial rule. By virtue of an 1846 decree, the supreme control of mineral lands was placed under the domain of the Royal Crown. The right to utilize the mines could be granted through the special concession of the colonial government. Through this imposition, the legitimacy of traditional small-scale mining activities in the Philippines was nullified.[28] This also coincides with the Regalian Doctrine which asserts that all lands of the public domain, including mineral lands belong to the state. For the purpose of distributing rights to mineral concessions, the *Inspeccion General de Minas* was formed by the Spanish regime.[29]

Under American colonial rule, an exception to the Regalian Doctrine was introduced through the freehold system, which granted title and ownership over mineral lands to private individuals who discovered and located mining claims. To conform with the 1935 Constitution, however, the Mining Act of 1936 reiterated that 'all mineral lands of the public domain and minerals belong to the State, and their disposition, exploitation, development or utilization, shall be limited to citizens of the Philippines, or to corporations, associations, at least sixty per centum of the capital of which is owned by such citizens, subject to the Government established under the Constitution'. The law also limited concessions to a 25-year renewable lease.[30]

The Mining Act of 1936 remained in effect even during the post-colonial period. Under the presidency of Ferdinand Marcos, a number of presidential decrees were issued to streamline the mining industry. Presidential Decree No. 463, for instance, pushed for the intensified discovery, exploitation, development, and wise utilization of the country's mineral resources. However, it also declared that all rights to land, whether ownership of or right to use for agricultural, logging, industrial, commercial, residential, and petroleum-exploration purposes, excludes the right of ownership or right to develop, exploit, or utilize the mineral deposits found therein or under the surface of such lands. This decree is intended to stress that all mineral deposits in public and private lands belong to the state.

With respect to small-scale miners, the thrust was to control their further expansion. For this purpose, Presidential Decree No. 1150 sought to regulate gold panning and sluicing to ensure that there would be no loss to the government of foreign exchange or taxes generated by gold production. However, small-scale mining was only officially acknowledged by the government as a new dimension in mineral development in 1984. Through Presidential Decree No. 1899, the capacity of small-scale mining to create employment was recognized in the context of the economic crisis engulfing the country at that time. Small-scale miners referred to any single unit mining operation having an annual production of not more than 50,000 metric tons of ore.[31]

Under the administration of President Corazon Aquino, Executive Order No. 279 was signed in 1987. It was designed to authorize the Secretary of the Department of Environment and Natural Resources (DENR) to negotiate and conclude joint venture and production-sharing agreements for the exploitation, development, and utilization of minerals. Provisions on environmental preservation, community development, and personnel training were outlined in the executive issuance. Through the Mineral Production Sharing Agreement (MPSA), a contractor is given the exclusive right to conduct mining operations within a specified area. DENR Administrative Order No. 57 (series of 1989) and DENR Circular No. 6 (series of 1989) provide the implementing guidelines for the MPSA. It is striking to note that nowhere in the implementing rules and guidelines could any provision be found relating to community participation in the conduct of the mining operations. The recognition and respect for the rights, customs, and traditions of indigenous communities over their ancestral lands are, however, contained in DENR Administrative Order No. 57.[32]

In 1991, Congress enacted Republic Act No. 7076. Otherwise known as the People's Small-Scale Mining Act, this legislation made it a declared policy of the state to promote, develop, protect, and rationalize viable small-scale mining activities. Small-scale miners are defined as Filipino citizens who voluntarily formed a cooperative, duly licensed by the DENR to engage in the extraction or removal of minerals from the ground. The Provincial or City Mining Regulatory Board is tasked to declare and set aside people's small-scale mining areas, subject to review by the DENR Secretary. The Board is composed of representatives coming from the DENR Secretary, the provincial or city mayor, the small-scale mining sector, the large-scale mining sector, and the non-governmental organization (NGO) sector. It should be emphasized that ancestral lands are not to be declared as people's small-scale mining areas without the prior consent of indigenous communities.

The current policy framework for mining is anchored on the Environment Impact Statement (EIS) System established by Presidential Decree No. 1586 and Republic Act No. 7942 or the Philippine Mining Act of 1995. The EIS determines potential environmental impacts of development activities like mining, and provides for mitigating mechanisms to minimize or eliminate such impacts. It is designed to ensure that environmental concerns are addressed in all stages of project implementation. Initially proposed during the Aquino administration, the Mining Act was signed into law by President Fidel Ramos in 1995. This legislation allowed the state to enter into three key modes of mining rights: Exploration Permit (EP), Mineral Production Sharing Agreement (MPSA), and Financial or Technical Assistance Agreement (FTAA).[33]

An EP grants the right to conduct exploration for all minerals in specified areas. The Mines and Geo-sciences Bureau (MGB) of the DENR shall have the authority to grant an EP to a qualified party. The permit is good for a period of two years, subject to annual review and relinquishment or renewal upon the recommendation of the MGB Director. The EP holder shall undertake exploration work on the area as specified by its permit based on an approved work program. On the other hand, the MPSA is an instrument providing the contractor with the exclusive right to conduct mining operations within a contract area and to shares in the gross output. The contractor is responsible for supplying the financing, technology, management, and personnel necessary for the implementation of this agreement. The FTAA shall be negotiated by the DENR and executed and approved by the President. It shall have a term not exceeding 25 years, and renewable for another 25 year term. Under the FTAA, the minimum capitalization requirement is $4 million. Table 6.1 identifies the distinguishing features of these mineral resource agreements.

Under the 1995 Mining Act, the areas that are open to mining applications are public or private lands not covered by valid and existing mining rights and mining applications, lands covered by expired mining and quarrying rights, mineral reservations, and timber lands as defined in existing laws. However, the law also recognizes that there are limits to resource access by mining firms. The following areas are closed to mining applications: (1) areas covered by valid and existing mining rights and applications; (2) old growth forests, proclaimed watershed forest reserves, wilderness areas, mangrove forests, mossy forests, national parks, provincial municipal forests, tree parks, green belts, game refuges, bird sanctuaries and areas proclaimed as marine parks, and identified initial components of the National Integrated Protected Areas System (NIPAS); and (3) areas which the DENR Secretary may exclude based on proper assessment of their environmental impact and implications for sustainable land uses such as critical watershed areas.

Under the revised Implementing Rules and Regulations (IRR) of the Mining Act, mining companies are constrained from operating without getting the prior informed consent of indigenous peoples, especially in areas covered by ancestral domain claims. In the event that the indigenous people give their consent, the community will receive royalties arising from mining operations equivalent to at least 1 per cent of the annual gross revenues. Issued following the Marcopper mining disaster, the revised guidelines also placed heavy emphasis on improving environmental guarantees and monitoring mechanisms. For instance, the Environmental Work Program for Exploration aims to respond to any potential disturbance during the exploration stage. On the other hand, the Environmental Compliance Certificate and the prescribed environmental procedures seek to ensure that environment-related infrastructures are in place even before the inauguration of mining activities.

Table 6.1 Key Types of Mining Rights

Mining Rights	Maximum Area (hectares)	Term	Qualifications Of Contractor	Benefit Sharing
Exploration Permit	32,000 onshore 81,000 offshore	2 years; renewable to a maximum of 6 years	Individuals / Filipino corporations /Foreign corporations	research data collection
Mineral Production Sharing Agreement	16,200 onshore 40,500 offshore	25 years; renewable for another 25 years	Individuals / Filipino Corporations	40% company 60% government
Financial and Technical Assistance Agreement	81,000 onshore 324,000 offshore	25 years; renewable for another 25 years	Filipino Corporations / Foreign corporations	40% company 60% government (to start after recovery of initial operating expenses)

Sources: Philippine Mining Act of 1995 (Republic Act No. 7942); Ramos, *The Mining Regulatory Framework*, 1998

The stress on mining rehabilitation measures is exhibited in the establishment of the Contingent Liability and Rehabilitation Fund, which addresses the need to build the financial capacity to confront the progressive rehabilitation of areas affected by mining through the Mine Rehabilitation Fund, and compensation for damages to lands through the Mine Wastes and Tailings Fund. A Multi-Partite Monitoring Team, which includes local government and NGO representation, is envisioned to strengthen transparency in monitoring the operations of mining firms. The corporations are also asked to submit a comprehensive Decommissioning Plan in order to guarantee that all affected areas will be restored as near as possible to the original state or to a pre-agreed productive end-use, following consultations with the local government and the host community. The Plan shall also include financial guarantees to cover long-term maintenance and minimize the economic impact of the mine's eventual closure to the host and adjoining community.[34] These rules, of course, are only as good as the capacity of regulatory institutions to implement them.

In this chapter, the security implications of the environmental disputes in the following mining towns will be analyzed: (1) Boac, Marinduque, (2) Sipalay, Negros Occidental, (3) Siocon, Zamboanga del Norte, and (4) Tampakan, South Cotobato. These cases were selected because they provide varied snapshots of the intense conflicts occurring in Philippine mining communities. The examination of the conflicts in these areas would focus on the threats posed by mineral-development activities on human and environmental security. It will also look into how social capital, or the lack of it, affects the proliferation or mitigation of conflicts in the mining sites.

Boac, Marinduque

In 1996, ecological disaster hit the Southern Luzon island-province of Marinduque. Leaks from an open pit-mining site managed by Marcopper Mining Corporation resulted in huge volumes of mine tailings being dumped into the Makulapnit and Boac rivers in this Southern Luzon island-province. Precipitated by a damaged drainage tunnel in the Mount Tapian copper mine pit, the massive discharge of mining waste led to the eradication of the plant and animal life in the two rivers, and the inundation of several hectares of crop land. The complete loss of aquatic life and biological productivity from within the Makulapnit and Boac River systems downstream from the outfall was caused by the physical process of sedimentation.[35] Given its bad mining practices and lack of concern for human security in the past, the Marcopper spill was simply a disaster waiting to happen.

Marcopper began its mining operations in Marinduque in 1969. Its initial base of operation was the Mount Tapian deposit that was mined until its resources were depleted in 1990. Thereafter, extraction activities shifted to the San Antonio copper ore body that is located some three kilometers north of the previous mine site. Mt. Tapian eventually became the storage system for the tailings generated by the San Antonio reserve. Such a disposal scheme was seen as a temporary arrangement pending further research on the submarine disposal option as indicated in the company's EIS.

In Marinduque, mining interests are veritably ranged against the health and livelihood concerns of fishing communities. Marcopper's lack of respect for community security was exhibited when the firm used Calancan Bay as a dumping ground for its mine tailings. Since 1975, the mining firm had released around 84 million metric tons of its wastes into the bay. With their sheer volume, the tailings now form a 4.7 kilometres long causeway in the middle of this water artery.

The Canadian firm Placer Dome, Inc. owns 40 per cent of Marcopper. During the period of authoritarian rule in the Philippines, a majority of the company's shares were owned by President Marcos through legal front Jose Yao Campos.[36] This explains the high-handed attitude exhibited by the corporation, especially in refusing to heed the complaints of fishing groups whose livelihood resources were degraded due to the failure of Marcopper to contain the pollution generated by its mining activities. Even then, the mining firm failed to provide compensation to the fishermen for the loss of their livelihood.[37]

The health security of local people had also been adversely affected by the mining operations. In 1997, tests were conducted by a composite team from the Department of Health and the National Poison Control and Information Service of the University of the Philippines to evaluate the health of Boac and Calancan Bay villagers. The findings indicate that children and adults exposed to mine tailings register high toxicity levels in their blood stream. They complained of numbness, weakness, paleness, and frequent headaches. Health officials further suspect that more Marinduque residents could be suffering from poisoning as a result of the prolonged years of mining activities in the province.

In the past, the social capital that was built in challenging the mining practices of Marcopper featured the alliance between the fishermen and the local church.[38] With the support of a national NGO like the *Lingkod Tao Kalikasan*, the civil society coalition was successful on two occasions in getting the environmental regulatory agency to issue a directive urging the mining firm to refrain from dumping its tailings in the Calancan Bay. In 1981, Commissioner Guillermo Pecache of the National Pollution Control Commission (NPCC) ordered Marcopper to 'cease and desist' from discharging its waste into Calancan pending further investigation. However, Marcos reversed the order upon the representation made by Marcopper president Garth Jones who asked the NPCC to lift all restrictions on the company. Seven years later, in 1988, the Pollution Adjudication Board, headed by DENR Secretary Fulgencio Factoran Jr., issued another cease and desist order that sought to restrain Marcopper from discharging mine tailings into the bay. President Aquino similarly overturned Factoran's directive on the strength of an appeal made by Marcopper board chairman Nemesio Prudente. Nevertheless, the company was required to deposit P30,000.00 for every day that the disposal system operated into a fund for the rehabilitation of Calancan Bay.[39]

The failure of previous coalitions to defend human security in Marinduque could be attributed to the limited nature of the networks of civil society organizations to challenge the negative impact of mining activities on local livelihood, health, and environmental well being. Civil society in this case was unable to cultivate the social capital needed to engage in collective action to compel Marcopper to clean up its act and be more transparent in its operations. At the level of civil society itself, it is only lately that the local union of miners is being challenged to be more sensitive to environmental concerns. It is significant to note that the Marcopper Employees Union (MELU) is affiliated with the National Mines and Allied Workers Union (NAMAWU). This union signed a memorandum of agreement with the Labor Advisory Consultative Council and the Trade Union Congress of the Philippines in 1997 committing to pursue the goals of sustainable development. This stance is based on the premise that mine workers who are at the first line of environmental risk should be seen as strategic stakeholders in the mining sector. In this regard, mine workers can be an asset for environmental protection since they work at the interface between the mining company and the local community.[40]

Another policy stakeholder thrown into the center of engagement in the aftermath of the mine spill was the local government. In the past, the opponents of mining pollution had a difficult time in getting local officials to sympathize with the value of environmental protection. However, the municipal government of Boac has become more assertive in voicing its position on mining activities. Its town mayor, Roberto Madla, insists that the Marcopper mines should not be reopened even after the clean-up and rehabilitation of the Boac River. Instead, he calls for the conversion of the Marcopper concession area into a 'non-mining' economic zone.

The erosion of trust in Marcopper's capacity to act responsibly if allowed to resume its mining operations could be attributed to the company's lack of transparency and failure to inform local stakeholders of the environmental risks posed by its development activities. The approach adopted by Marcopper in building social capital between the mining company and the local community revolved around the provision of social infrastructures such as schools and roads. However, a missing element in such an effort was the institution of a transparent information system involving community participation. The absence of monitoring mechanisms to oversee the firm's mining procedures eventually resulted in serious human security and environmental problems for the local residents, especially as a consequence of the mining spill.

Sipalay, Negros Occidental

Sipalay is a mining town that is located some 187 kilometers to the south of Bacolod, the capital of Negros Occidental province. Marinduque Mining Corporation have been undertaking mineral-development activities in the *barangay* (village) of San Jose since 1953. Mining rights were transferred to the Maricalum Mining Corporation in 1986. The history of mining in this site reveals how the lack of corporate responsibility has brought great risks to the security of people and the environment in Sipalay. Just like any other open pit mine operation, the two sources of wastes and effluents are the mine site and the mill site. Mine effluents that come from the various peripheral sumps at the Cansibit pit are pumped out and recycled as industrial water for the mill's water requirements. During the dry season, this water is discharged into the Tao-angan River. Siltation of rivers due to silt and sand that come from the various waste dumps and unprotected excavation slopes is the negative impact observed in the mine's operation. The main river systems affected are the Tao-angan River and the Cartagena River.

The instability of the mining area's tailings pond poses imminent danger to the surrounding communities. That Maricalum has not been mitigating the threats presented by its tailings ponds is evidenced by its recurrent history of being issued 'cease and desist' orders by government monitoring teams due to the pollution caused by its operations. The mining firm has argued, on the other hand, that the mining sites, having existed since the 1950s are exempted from the new environmental laws. The municipal government and civil society groups contest this view and stress the responsibility of Maricalum for the social impacts and environmental hazards arising from their mining operations.

Environmental and human security has been severely affected by Maricalum's mining activities in Sipalay. Local residents report that the agriculture and fishing industry have been affected by pollution from the mines. Small farmers in the area were paid minimal fees to compensate for damages incurred as a result of the overflow of mine tailings into cropland areas. Maricalum's unwillingness to assume full responsibility for the social costs of its pollution-generating activities reinforced the long-standing rift between the company and its surrounding communities. Its bad mining practices and lack of transparency in its operations have resulted in the rise of opposition against continued mining in the area.

Anti-mining sentiments within the province have gained significant support, especially after the passage of the 1995 Mining Act and the Marinduque disaster. The local church mobilized its parishioners and members in a Negros-island wide caravan in 1997. In a joint statement on mining and ecology by the Social Action Centers in the Diocese of Bacolod and San Carlos, an alarm was sounded about the disregard for the indigenous people's ancestral domains and the farmers' right to own land guaranteed under the agrarian reform program. The anti-mining activists also stressed that the said legislation will be tantamount to selling the country's mineral resources to foreign firms while the impact of the mining projects could aggravate landlessness, food shortage, and chemical contamination of the environment.

During the martial law years, the province of Negros Occidental was a bastion of the underground left movement. Military operations in the 1980s were associated with the provision of protection and security to the mining companies. In this regard, coercive methods became the preferred option in safeguarding the continuity of mining activities rather than securing community consent by building social capital between the company and the local residents. Even as the strength of the armed left groups has diminished in importance, military presence continues in the province. Civil society groups believe that this step was taken to facilitate the expansion of mineral-extraction activities in the province.

Siocon, Zamboanga del Norte

The municipality of Siocon lies in the southwestern part of Zamboanga del Norte province. Its original inhabitants are the Subanen people. At present, the town is made up of the Christian settlers (60 per cent) who live in farmlands, the Muslims (25 per cent) who reside in the coastal areas, and the indigenous Subanens (15 per cent) who have moved into the mountainous interiors. Migrants to Siocon multiplied with the entry of timber companies in the 1960s. However, as logging declined, the settlers branched into agricultural and mining pursuits.[41]

In the upland *sitio* of Canatuan, the Subanens have long engaged in gold panning.[42] In the late 1980s, small-scale mining intensified as people from a neighboring mining town and retrenched workers from cancelled timber concessions began panning and tunneling activities. Seeking to defend their claim to mineral resources, the Subanens applied for a small-scale mining permit from the DENR. In 1990, the indigenous miners gave in to suggestions by a tunnel financier named Ramon Bosque to form a corporation, in the belief that it will facilitate the processing of their mining claims. They signed the incorporation papers establishing the Bosque Mining Corporation (BOMICO) with Bosque as Chairman of the Board. As it turned out, Bosque simply used their names to acquire mining rights for himself on more than 500 hectares of land. The Declaration of Location pertaining to the proposed mining site contained only his name.

The small-scale miners contested the mining privileges awarded to Bosque and insisted on the validity of their own claims having been in the area for a much longer period of time. However, the DENR replied that the Provincial Mining Regulatory Board (PMRB) should first declare the Canatuan site as a people's small-scale mining area before their mining permit could be processed. The problem was that the PRMB of Zamboanga del Norte was organized only in 1995. Yet, even after its formation, the Board has refused to address the small-scale miners' petition. With their lack of organizational clout and the absence of allies in government, the miners were unsuccessful in pressing their demands.

After Bosque's mining claim was affirmed by the state, he proceeded to transfer his rights to Benguet Mining Corporation (BMC). Financial difficulties later on forced BMC to cede mining rights to Toronto Ventures Pacific, Inc. (TVI), a Canadian company whose 13 subsidiaries are involved in the development of more than 20 mining projects in the country.[43] TVI undertook exploration activities to search for gold in land that is also claimed by the Subanen people. While the area coverage of the TVI gold project in Siocon appeared to be limited, the foreign firm counted on the prospective high financial returns from what was seen as a relatively low capital venture. The potential net profit of the company was pegged at $12 million annually.

The Subanens attempted but failed in successive moves to secure a small-scale mining permit as well as a Certificate of Ancestral Domain Claim (CADC) in the area. A CADC would have given them the right to occupy, cultivate, and utilize land and natural resources covered by the ancestral domain which is determined through a set of delineation and mapping procedures specified under DENR Administrative Order No. 2 (Series of 1993). Communities with CADCs are empowered to negotiate the terms and conditions for the exploitation of natural resources in their respective areas within the context of national laws and customary rules.

Poorly organized and lacking advocacy skills, the local people through the Siocon Federation of Subanen Tribal Councils tried to register their opposition to the mining project during the public hearings organized by the Environmental Management Bureau (EMB). Despite the conflicting resource claims, the DENR decided in favor of the application of TVI for a MPSA. Under the MPSA granted to TVI, the firm was given the exclusive right to conduct mining operations within the contract area of 508 hectares. In return, the government receives a share from the revenues generated through the imposition of an excise tax on mineral products as provided in the Revised National Internal Revenue Code.

Rather than actively seeking community cooperation and building social capital in support of its activities, TVI resorted to coercive methods in establishing its monopoly-control over resource-use in the area. This has resulted in intensified resource-disputes and heightened security risks. In response to the barricade set up by small-scale miners protesting TVI's mining exploration, the firm countered with a food and economic blockade in early 1997. Former members of the military and police force were recruited as company guards who were eventually organized into a Special Civilian Armed Auxiliary (SCAA) unit. Seen as the replacement of the Civilian Armed Forces Geographical Unit (CAFGU), the SCAA is similarly trained by the Armed Forces of the Philippines (AFP). Companies based in remote areas could request the services of these civilian militia groups. Tasked to defend the mining interests of TVI, the SCAA placed checkpoints along the Zamboanga del Norte provincial road in R.T. Lim leading to the town of Siocon. Local miners passing through the checkpoints were prevented from bringing in food items, mining tools, and housing materials into the area. The residents had to smuggle their food into the forest through alternative passages. Some of the restrictions on the entry of food were eventually lifted. However, a weekly rice quota per family is still in place.

Aside from instituting controls on local food supplies, TVI likewise imposed prohibitions on the transport of mine tailings from the mining site. These are the mineral extracts where gold could still be recovered. TVI had earlier offered to buy the tailings from the small-scale miners at a price lower than the rates offered elsewhere. Eventually, the small-scale miners decided to sell their mine wastes to the outside market. In this context, the company's checkpoints forced the local miners to sell their accumulated sacks of tailings at a cheap rate to TVI. The coercive techniques, ranging from the food blockade to the direct intimidation of local residents practiced by the SCAA, have succeeded in forcing families to flee the area.

Fact-finding missions conducted by civil society organizations in 1997 noted that people were displaced from their land because of the harassment conducted by the SCAA. Interviews conducted by the human rights team revealed that spikes were planted along the foot trails used by community people in evading the checkpoints. Through forcible means, TVI did not have to worry about compensating people who had to relocate because they happened to be in the way of mining operations. The aggressive use of force by TVI against the local community has shattered the foundations for building social capital as an input in the pursuit of mineral-development efforts. Such a high-handed approach only fuelled the opposition of the indigenous people and small-scale miners against the mining activities of TVI and raised the potential for violent confrontation. This has also generated negative effects on community security as people's homes and livelihood systems were displaced. In the absence of trust and a shared understanding that health and environmental concerns matter for their common protection, norms for the responsible use of resources had no chance of prospering in the area. In the absence of a firm system of accountability, both the TVI and the small-scale miners were unrestrained in the reckless release of mercury and mining discharges into the river systems.

Tampakan, South Cotabato

Together with Arimco Corporation, the Western Mining Corporation (WMC) was one of the first two companies to receive a FTAA under the new mining law passed by the Philippine government in 1995. A top mining firm in Australia, WMC initially came to the country in 1988. In 1990, WMC established ties with Tampakan Mining Corporation, Sagittarius Mining Corporation, and South Cotabato Mining Corporation. With an option agreement forged with the local partners, the Australian firm successfully negotiated the grant of an MPSA to undertake exploration activities in 15,000 hectares of land in Tampakan, South Cotabato.

The B'laans, upland farmers whose produce includes cacao, corn, sweet potato, and other root crops originally inhabited Tampakan. Through time, the authority of the indigenous people over their ancestral domain was eroded by the arrival of lowland settlers from the Visayas and other parts of Mindanao. In the 1960s, logging companies such as the Habaluyas Enterprises, Inc. and the Malalag Lumber Company, Inc. were awarded Timber License Agreements (TLAs) to operate in the area. They built logging roads that destroyed the forest and penetrated deeply into B'laan territory. These same roads proved useful in providing easy access to WMC in tapping mineral reserves. With the departure of the timber concessionaires, mining has replaced logging as the main resource-extraction activity posing potential threats to the security of the people and environment of Tampakan.

The WMC first put up a base camp in Tampakan to undertake survey work in 1990. The B'laans residing in the nearby *barangay* of Pulabato were hired by the firm to perform various jobs, ranging from the reconstruction of logging roads to the hauling of drilling equipment. However, the employment of local residents only lasted for a short period of time, because they were not qualified for the other positions available within the mining firm. The local people whose services were terminated went back to farming to sustain their livelihood.

The MPSA, which was the original legal instrument secured by WMC to undertake mineral-development activities, was converted into an FTAA in 1995. The new agreement covered a much bigger area of about 99,387 hectares. Under the 1995 Mining Act and the 1997 Indigenous People's Rights Act (IPRA), especially in cases where indigenous people inhabit the area, community consent to mining activities in their area is required. The mining company is also encouraged to contribute to community-based development, provide compensation for mining-related damages, and devise revenue-sharing schemes for the local residents. In this context, WMC was compelled to undertake active efforts to get the B'laan tribal leaders to sign a memorandum of agreement pertaining to the conduct of mining in the area and the corresponding distribution of costs and benefits to be derived from the development effort.

In the town of Tampakan, the contract area assigned to WMC covers the villages of Pulabato and Danlag. While the villagers of Danlag approved the contents of the document prepared by the mining firm, the Pulabato Tribal Council, led by *Datu* (Leader) Willy Gulaya, failed to reach a consensus with the WMC proposal. The B'laans of Pulabato believe that the proposed agreement would lead to the destruction of their village and that they would not get a fair share in the exploration activities.[44] To gain better social acceptability for its mining venture, WMC had initiated moves to render development assistance to the local community. For example, the company rented a truck to transport the B'laan residents to lowland markets every week. It spearheaded the detachment of a regular medical mission to the upland areas. The mining firm likewise extended its support to the Demolan Foundation, an NGO that conducted education and agricultural training programs for the B'laan people.[45]

The community development activities pursued by WMC are acceptable ways of winning the trust and confidence of the villagers. However, the motives behind these forms of development intervention were questioned when viewed in the context of simultaneous company efforts to undermine social capital in Pulabato by creating rifts between the villagers and their leaders. In this regard, WMC attempted to remove Willy Gulaya as head of the Pulabato Tribal Council when he remained steadfast in refusing to sign the agreement with the mining company. Instead of addressing the concerns of the B'laan community in Pulabato, WMC sought to avoid a lengthy negotiation process by supporting the bid of its ally, Raymundo Calanao, to unseat Gulaya as tribal chief.

The municipal government joined hands with WMC in ousting Gulaya from his position. In 1996, Tampakan Mayor Emilio Escobillo recognized Calanao as the new village leader. To dispel the controversy about who the real council head was, an election was announced by the government's Office of Southern Cultural Communities (OSCC). Gulaya won the election, but he was still dropped by WMC and the OSCC Regional Director in favor of Calanao. In 1997, Gulaya asked the help of the Justice and Peace Desk of the Catholic Church based in Koronadal, South Cotabato and the Legal Rights and Natural Resources Center in petitioning the OSCC to declare him as the legitimate village chief. Eventually, the OSCC Executive Director issued a Certificate of Accreditation declaring Gulaya as the legitimate *datu* of Pulabato.[46]

Aside from the B'laan people, the Christian settlers also asserted their position as a stakeholder in the mining area. To emphasize their resolve to be part of the negotiations, they set up roadblocks that temporarily stopped the operations of WMC in late 1996. The settlers demanded that the company should not exclude them in the effort to gain social acceptability for its mining project in Tampakan. In this regard, WMC failed to adopt a comprehensive approach toward stakeholder participation in development planning. While the mining firm made moves to secure the consent of the host community, it was done in a manner that lacked trust, participation, and transparency.

Conclusion

While mining corporations in the Philippines may have environmental standards, these are generally not followed. Risk assessment and sound environmental management systems are neglected. While mining companies may have developed environmental and social codes of conduct, these are rendered meaningless when they do not provide detailed technical or scientific standards that must be met, nor do they describe the means by which independent monitoring of compliance would be conducted.[47]

A large part of the reason why mining firms are not compelled to undertake good environmental practices lies in the poor regulatory environment in the country. Environmental risk-assessment procedures are not seriously implemented, as in the case of the Marcopper operations in Marinduque. This could be attributed to the lack of prudent and effective regulation on the part of state institutions. Where nobody is penalized, mining rules are easily trampled upon. It is imperative that resource-users are held accountable, billed, and charged for the pollution caused by their mining operations.

The government should enhance its regulatory and monitoring capacities in order to ensure that companies comply with environmental procedures and, thereby, safeguard the security of host communities in the mining sites. In the interest of democratic participation in mining development projects, the consent of local communities should be secured before mining exploration and extraction is allowed in an area. Fortifying structures of trust and transparency could even minimize transaction costs for mining enterprises. As the more organized communities are now able to tap into networks that enable them to access the services of public interest lawyers in defending their environment and livelihood, mining firms may end up spending more to pay for litigation costs. Given the flurry of capability-building efforts by local communities and civil society organizations, mining companies may find out that it would be more cost-effective in the long run to adopt sound environmental practices in their mining ventures.

Strengthening reserves of social capital as a major resource in governing corporate-community relations could be facilitated if there is transparency in corporate governance. Such an approach also requires that local communities share and participate in the development gains from mining activities. Safeguarding participatory processes and mobilizing social capital could be the best defense against the environmental risks that may endanger human security. The cultivation of social capital between civil society organizations and the local government could increase the bargaining power of local stakeholders in dealing with large corporations on issues arising from mineral-development activities. This bodes well for efforts to democratize development planning and management.

Increasing the capabilities of local institutions in development and environmental monitoring would put more teeth into the current regulatory model adopted by the EMB in controlling pollution in local areas. The multipartite monitoring system involves the joint participation of the government, civil society, and the company itself in auditing and regulating mining ventures. This would allow for greater transparency in company operations. The availability of adequate information regarding the environmental management systems of firms would enable the various stakeholders in the local community to participate in the process of responding to the risks posed by mining for ecological and human security.

Notes

1   The contribution of mining and quarrying to gross national product (GNP) even went down from 1.2 per cent in 1995, the year the mining law was signed, to 1.1 per cent in 1997.

2   See Mathews, J. T. (1989), 'Redefining Security', *Foreign Affairs*, vol.68, no.2, pp.162-77; Myers, N. (1989), 'Environment and Security', *Foreign Policy*, no.74, Spring, pp.23-41; Romm, J. (1993), *Defining National Security: The Non-Military Aspects*, Council on Foreign Relations Press, New York; Sands, P. (1993), 'Enforcing Environmental Security: The Challenges of Compliance with International Obligations', *Journal of International Affairs*, vol.46, no.2, Winter; Homer-Dixon, T. (1994), 'Environmental Scarcities and Violent Conflict', *International Security*, vol.19, no.1, pp.5-40; and Maddock, R.T. (1995), 'Environmental Security in East Asia', *Contemporary Southeast Asia*, vol.17, no.1, June.

3   Soroos, M. (1994), 'Global Change, Environmental Security, and the Prisoner's Dilemma', *Journal of Peace Research*, vol.31, no.3, pp.317-32.

4   Lodgaard, S. and af Ornas, A. (eds) (1992), *The Environment and International Security*, PRIO Report No. 3, International Peace Research Institute, Oslo.

5   Myers, N. (1996), *Ultimate Security: The Environmental Basis of Political Stability*, Island Press, Washington, DC, pp.21.

6   Baldwin, D. (1997), 'The Concept of Security', *Review of International Studies*, vol.23, pp.5-26.

7   Buzan, B. (1991), *People, States and Fear: An Agenda for International Studies in the Post-Cold War Era*, second edition, Lynne Rienner, Boulder, pp.26.

8   Graeger, N. (1996), 'Environmental Security?', *Journal of Peace Research*, vol.33, no.1, pp.109-16.

9   Dalby, S. (1992), 'Security, Modernity, Ecology: The Dilemmas of Post-Cold War Security Discourse', *Alternatives*, vol.17, no.1, pp.95-134.

10 Booth, K. (1996), '75 Years On: Rewriting the Subject's Past – Reinventing the Future', in S. Smith, K. Booth and M. Zalewski (eds), *International Theory: Positivism and Beyond*, Cambridge University Press, Cambridge, pp.328-39.

11 Renner, M. (1997), 'Transforming Security', in *State of the World 1997*, W.W. Norton and Company, New York, pp.115-31.

12 Anderson, L. (1994), *The Political Ecology of the Modern Peasant: Calculation and Community*, Johns Hopkins University Press, Baltimore, pp.28.

13 Margolis, H. (1982), *Selfishness, Altruism, and Rationality: A Theory of Social Choice*, Cambridge University Press, Cambridge, pp.11.

14 North, D. (1991), 'Institutions', *Journal of Economic Perspectives*, vol.5, pp.97-112.

15 Gibbs, C. and Bromley, D. (1989), 'Institutional Arrangements for Management of Rural

Resources: Common Property Regimes', in F. Berkes (ed.), *Common Property Resources: Ecology and Community-Based Sustainable Development*, Belhaven Press, London, pp.22-24.

16 See Redclift, M. and Sage, C. (eds) (1994), *Strategies for Sustainable Development: Local Agendas for the Southern Hemisphere*, John Wiley and Sons, Chichester.

17 Evans, P. (1996), 'Introduction: Development Strategies Across the Public-Private Divide', *World Development*, vol.24, pp.1033.

18 Taylor, M. (1982), *Community, Anarchy, and Liberty*, Cambridge University Press, Cambridge, pp.34.

19 Olson, M. (1965), *The Logic of Collective Action: Public Goods and the Theory of Goods*, Harvard University Press, Cambridge, MA, pp.34.

20 Massey, R. I. (1994), 'Impediments to Collective Action in a Small Community', *Politics and Society*, vol.22, pp.421-34.

21 Loury, G. (1977), A Dynamic Theory of Racial Income Differences', in P. Wallace and A. LaMond (eds), *Women, Minorities, and Employment Discrimination*, Lexington Books, Lexington, pp.153-86.

22 See chapter 12 of Coleman, J. (1990), *Foundations of Social Theory*, Harvard University Press, Cambridge.

23 Putnam, R. (1993), *Making Democracy Work: Civic Traditions in Modern Italy*, Princeton University Press, Princeton, New Jersey, pp.183.

24 See Tarrow, S. (1996), 'Making Social Science Work Across Space and Time: A Critical Reflection on Robert Putnam's Making Democracy Work', *American Political Science Review*, vol.90, pp.389-397; Goldberg, E. (1996), 'Thinking About How Democracy Works', *Politics and Society*, vol.24, pp.7-18; Heller, P. (1996), 'Social Capital as a Product of Class Mobilization and State Intervention: Industrial Workers in Kerala, India', *World Development*, vol.24, pp.1055-71; Fox, J. (1996), 'How Does Civil Society Thicken?: The Political Construction of Social Capital in Rural Mexico', *World Development*, vol.24, pp.1089-103; and Brown, L. D. and Ashman, D. (1996), 'Participation, Social Capital, and Intersectoral Problem Solving: African and Asian Cases', *World Development*, vol.24, pp.1467-79.

25 Fukuyama, F. (1995), *Trust: The Social Virtues and the Creation of Prosperity*, The Free Press, New York, pp.26. Fukuyama's application of social capital to corporate culture, however, has been criticized on the basis of the observation that executives and directors do not constitute an appropriately dense network of social interactions to foster the trust necessary in developing social capital. See Fellmeth, A. X. (1996), 'Social Capital in the United States and Taiwan: Trust or Rule of Law?', *Development Policy Review*, vol.14, pp.151-71.

26 Coleman (1990), *Foundations of Social Theory*, pp.321.

27 Schneider, M., Teske, P., Marschall, M., Mintrom, M. and Roch, C. (1997), 'Institutional Arrangements and the Creation of Social Capital: The Effects of Public School Choice', *American Political Science Review*, vol.91, pp.82-93.

28 Caballero, E. (1996), *Gold from the Gods: Traditional Small-Scale Miners in the Philippines*, Giraffe Books, Quezon City.

29 Royo, A. and Gatmaytan, D. (1991), 'The Philippine Mining Policy: A Case of Obscured Environmental and Social Impacts', *Philippine Natural Resources Law Journal*, vol.4, no.2, pp.24-38.

30 *Ibid.*, pp.26.

31 *Ibid.*, pp.28-9.

32 *Ibid.*, pp.30-1.

134 *Development and Security in Southeast Asia*

33 Ramos, H. (1998), *The Mining Regulatory Framework,* Chamber of Mines of the Philippines, Pasig City, 25 June.
34 *Ibid.*, pp.8.
35 UNEP-Water Branch (1996), *Final Report of the United Nations Expert Assessment Mission to Marinduque Island, Philippines*, United Nations Environment Programme, Nairobi, September.
36 Alibutud, R. (1993), 'Rough Winds Over Calancan Bay', in E. Gamalinda and S. Coronel (eds), *Saving the Earth: The Philippine Experience*, third edition, Philippine Center for Investigative Journalism, Makati, pp.69-79.
37 Coumans, C. (1998), 'Mining Industry Responses to the Debate on Mining in the Philippines', *Intersect*, July, pp.13-25.
38 Coumans, C. (1995), 'Ideology, Social Movement and Organization, Patronage and Resistance in the Struggle of Marinduquenos Against Marcopper', *Pilipinas*, no.24, Spring, pp.37-74.
39 Alibutud (1993), 'Rough Winds Over Calancan Bay', pp.73.
40 National Mines and Allied Workers Union (1997), *Case Study on the Mine-Related Environmental Disaster in Marinduque*.
41 For an account of the mining-related problems faced by indigenous people in Zamboanga del Norte, South Cotabato, and Sultan Kudarat, see Montiflor, M. and Alano, M. L. (1998), 'Mining in Mindanao: Issues and Prospects', *Mindanao Focus*, no.1.
42 In Philippine local administration, the *barangay* (village) is constituted by various *sitios*.
43 The subsidiaries of TVI in the Philippines include the Alberta Resource Development Corporation, CAL Mining Ventures, Inc., ESCAF Minerals Corporation, Exploration Drilling Corporation, FILCAN Mining Corporation, Goldcrest Asia Mining Ventures, Inc., Lake Bonavista Mining Corporation, Miracle Mining Corporation, Paramount Copper-Gold Corporation, Pico Minerals Corporation, Southeast Gold Resource Corporation, TVI Mineral Processing, Inc., and TVI Resource Development, Inc.
44 Montiflor and Alano (1998), 'Mining in Mindanao: Issues and Prospects', pp.20.
45 See Floretino-Hofileña, C. (1996), 'Searching for Gold in B'laan Country', in S. Coronel (ed.), *Patrimony: 6 Case Studies on Local Politics and the Environment in the Philippines*, Philippine Center for Investigative Journalism, Pasig City, pp.97-119.
46 Montiflor and Alano (1998), 'Mining in Mindanao: Issues and Prospects', pp.22.
47 Coumans (1998), 'Mining Industry Responses to the Debate on Mining in the Philippines', pp.14.

References

Alibutud, R. (1993), 'Rough Winds Over Calancan Bay', in E. Gamalinda and S. Coronel (eds), *Saving the Earth: The Philippine Experience*, third edition, Philippine Center for Investigative Journalism, Makati, pp. 69-79.
Anderson, L. (1994), *The Political Ecology of the Modern Peasant: Calculation and Community*, Johns Hopkins University Press, Baltimore, pp. 28.
Baldwin, D. (1997), 'The Concept of Security', *Review of International Studies*, vol. 23, pp. 5-26.
Booth, K. (1996), '75 Years On: Rewriting the Subject's Past – Reinventing the Future', in S. Smith, K. Booth and M. Zalewski (eds), *International Theory: Positivism and Beyond*, Cambridge University Press, Cambridge, pp. 328-39.
Brown, L. D. and Ashman, D. (1996), 'Participation, Social Capital, and Intersectoral Problem

Solving: African and Asian Cases', *World Development*, vol. 24, pp. 1467-79.

Buzan, B. (1991), *People, States and Fear: An Agenda for International Studies in the Post-Cold War Era*, second edition, Lynne Rienner, Boulder, pp. 26.

Caballero, E. (1996), *Gold from the Gods: Traditional Small-Scale Miners in the Philippines*, Giraffe Books, Quezon City.

Coleman, J. (1990), *Foundations of Social Theory*, Harvard University Press, Cambridge, MA.

Coumans, C. (1998a), 'Mining Industry Responses to the Debate on Mining in the Philippines', *Intersect*, July, pp. 13-25.

Coumans, C. (1995b), 'Ideology, Social Movement and Organization, Patronage and Resistance in the Struggle of Marinduquenos Against Marcopper', *Pilipinas*, no. 24, Spring, pp. 37-74.

Dalby, S. (1992), 'Security, Modernity, Ecology: The Dilemmas of Post-Cold War Security Discourse', *Alternatives*, vol. 17, no. 1, pp. 95-134.

Evans, P. (1996), 'Introduction: Development Strategies Across the Public-Private Divide', *World Development*, vol. 24, pp. 1033.

Fellmeth, A. X. (1996), 'Social Capital in the United States and Taiwan: Trust or Rule of Law?', *Development Policy Review*, vol. 14, pp. 151-71.

Floretino-Hofileña, C. (1996), 'Searching for Gold in B'laan Country', in S. Coronel (ed.), *Patrimony: 6 Case Studies on Local Politics and the Environment in the Philippines*, Philippine Center for Investigative Journalism, Pasig City, pp. 97-119.

Fox, J. (1996), 'How Does Civil Society Thicken?: The Political Construction of Social Capital in Rural Mexico', *World Development*, vol. 24, pp. 1089-103.

Fukuyama, F. (1995), *Trust: The Social Virtues and the Creation of Prosperity*, The Free Press, New York, pp. 26.

Gibbs, C. and Bromley, D. (1989), 'Institutional Arrangements for Management of Rural Resources: Common Property Regimes', in F. Berkes (ed.), *Common Property Resources: Ecology and Community-Based Sustainable Development*, Belhaven Press, London, pp. 22-4.

Goldberg, E. (1996), 'Thinking About How Democracy Works', *Politics and Society*, vol. 24, pp. 7-18.

Graeger, N. (1996), 'Environmental Security?', *Journal of Peace Research*, vol. 33, no. 1, pp. 109-16.

Heller, P. (1996), 'Social Capital as a Product of Class Mobilization and State Intervention: Industrial Workers in Kerala, India', *World Development*, vol. 24, pp. 1055-71.

Homer-Dixon, T. (1994), 'Environmental Scarcities and Violent Conflict', *International Security*, vol. 19, no. 1, pp. 5-40.

Lodgaard, S. and af Ornas, A. (eds) (1992), *The Environment and International Security*, PRIO Report No. 3, International Peace Research Institute, Oslo.

Loury, G. (1977), A Dynamic Theory of Racial Income Differences', in P. Wallace and A. LaMond (eds), *Women, Minorities, and Employment Discrimination*, Lexington Books, Lexington, MA, pp. 153-86.

Maddock, R.T. (1995), 'Environmental Security in East Asia', *Contemporary Southeast Asia*, vol. 17, no. 1, June.

Margolis, H. (1982), *Selfishness, Altruism, and Rationality: A Theory of Social Choice*, Cambridge University Press, Cambridge, pp. 11.

Massey, R. I. (1994), 'Impediments to Collective Action in a Small Community', *Politics and Society*, vol. 22, pp. 421-34.

Mathews, J. T. (1989), 'Redefining Security', *Foreign Affairs*, vol. 68, no. 2, pp. 162-77.

Montiflor, M. and Alano, M. L. (1998), 'Mining in Mindanao: Issues and Prospects', *Mindanao Focus*, no.1.

Myers, N. (1996a), *Ultimate Security: The Environmental Basis of Political Stability*, Island Press, Washington, DC, pp. 21.

Myers, N. (1989b), 'Environment and Security', *Foreign Policy*, no.74, Spring, pp. 23-41.

National Mines and Allied Workers Union (1997), *Case Study on the Mine-Related Environmental Disaster in Marinduque*, National Mines and Allied Workers Union.

North, D. (1991), 'Institutions', *Journal of Economic Perspectives*, vol. 5, pp. 97-112.

Olson, M. (1965), *The Logic of Collective Action: Public Goods and the Theory of Goods*, Harvard University Press, Cambridge, MA, pp. 34.

Putnam, R. (1993), *Making Democracy Work: Civic Traditions in Modern Italy*, Princeton University Press, Princeton, New Jersey, pp. 183.

Ramos, H. (1998), *The Mining Regulatory Framework*, Chamber of Mines of the Philippines, Pasig City, 25 June.

Redclift, M. and Sage, C. (eds) (1994), *Strategies for Sustainable Development: Local Agendas for the Southern Hemisphere*, John Wiley and Sons, Chichester.

Renner, M. (1997), 'Transforming Security', *State of the World 1997*, W.W. Norton and Company, New York, pp. 115-31.

Romm, J. (1993), *Defining National Security: The Non-Military Aspects*, Council on Foreign Relations Press, New York.

Royo, A. and Gatmaytan, D. (1991), 'The Philippine Mining Policy: A Case of Obscured Environmental and Social Impacts', *Philippine Natural Resources Law Journal*, vol. 4, no. 2, pp. 24-38.

Sands, P. (1993), 'Enforcing Environmental Security: The Challenges of Compliance with International Obligations', *Journal of International Affairs*, vol. 46, no. 2, Winter.

Schneider, M., Teske, P., Marschall, M., Mintrom, M. and Roch, C. (1997), 'Institutional Arrangements and the Creation of Social Capital: The Effects of Public School Choice', *American Political Science Review*, vol. 91, pp. 82-93.

Soroos, M. (1994), 'Global Change, Environmental Security, and the Prisoner's Dilemma', *Journal of Peace Research*, vol. 31, no. 3, pp. 317-32.

Tarrow, S. (1996), 'Making Social Science Work Across Space and Time: A Critical Reflection on Robert Putnam's Making Democracy Work', *American Political Science Review*, vol. 90, pp. 389-397.

Taylor, M. (1982), *Community, Anarchy, and Liberty*, Cambridge University Press, Cambridge, pp. 34.

UNEP-Water Branch (1996), *Final Report of the United Nations Expert Assessment Mission to Marinduque Island, Philippines*, United Nations Environment Programme (UNEP), Nairobi, September.

Chapter 7

Food Production and Environmental Security in Indonesia

Mary Young

A growing awareness of environmental problems in Southeast Asian countries has given impetus to a rethinking of development and security issues. The environmental implications of current agricultural practices in Indonesia suggest that we are facing new challenges with respect to pursuing development and security in the long term. Hence, environmental perspectives offer more than new academic insights to the ongoing debate of how development and security can be achieved across a number of different geographical spaces; they also question existing assumptions underlying the very meanings of development and security.

The broadening of security to encompass new problems that do not necessarily constitute a direct threat to the national security of the state has substantially increased the number of issues that constitute security concerns. Security analysts have tied environmental degradation to the possibility of increased violent conflict among peoples and states, thereby producing a new linkage between the environment and national security. However, criticisms of the state-centric bias in security studies has led to the inclusion of new research that attempts to understand more extensively the range of security concerns facing people today. The concept of development has been subject to an even more dynamic debate, much of its discourse being laden with normative assumptions that certain social, economic, and political relationships and institutions should emerge within less industrialized countries. Criticisms of conventional perspectives about security that have been introduced in the past decade have encouraged fresh perspectives on the numerous ways in which people's security can be enhanced and, related to this, the different dimensions of development projects and research.

The challenge is jointly directed at our intellectual understanding of problems facing Southeast Asia (SEA) and the corresponding task of formulating appropriate policies. The difficulty arising from the consideration of the environmental problems associated with the development and security of Southeast Asian countries is that environmental change, economic development, and national security-building are all processes that produce social differentiation when they are located in a specific historical context. Questions of 'security for whom' or 'which groups benefit the most from a certain national development program' demonstrate that behind these broad analytical concepts are material processes that can create or simply intensify existing social differences within national communities. As such, these differences make concepts of environmental sustainability, development, and security contestable and subject to ongoing political debate. This presents some difficulty for constructing effective and equitable policies in Southeast Asian countries.

The prioritization of environmental quality within this and other chapters in this volume stems from the perspective that environmental problems jeopardize human security, and ideally these problems should be addressed before they become crises. Because environmental problems frequently have local manifestations that are more immediately apparent than their repercussions for national security or development, one needs to consider how deterioration in environmental quality endangers human security at the individual and community levels. Human security includes the provision of basic human needs such as access to sustainable livelihoods, health, food, shelter, education, human rights, and gender equity. Therefore, our assessment of environmental problems and their possible solutions requires analysis at different levels; this is likely to reveal the disjuncture between local and national level economies and environments.

The issue of food production in Indonesia reflects the dilemmas of preventing further environmental deterioration, ensuring equitable development, and crafting comprehensive mechanisms for ensuring security for the nation-state and the diverse population contained within its borders. Therefore, the debates surrounding food production in Indonesia have a wide applicability. They reflect the new challenges to the regulatory capabilities of nation-states presented by the increasingly integrated global economy of food production and the transnational nature of environmental problems.

This chapter argues that the difficulty of dealing with environmental problems associated with food production lies in the multitude of roles food production plays in national development and security. The chapter first examines the way that food has historically become politicized as a result of occupying a critical juncture between facilitating industrial development and ensuring economic and political stability in rural areas. Next, the pressures on national agriculture arising from efforts to restructure the Indonesian economy as it becomes more integrated into the global market economy will be examined. The restructuring process brings to the fore the ecological and economic contradictions of the postwar food system in Indonesia. The following section discusses these contradictions and demonstrates how they have infused a great deal of uncertainty and ambiguity into current discourses on food and security. Finally, the possibilities that seem present in the existing social order by drawing on the emerging concept of social capital are explored. However, all possibilities must be considered in conjunction with an evaluation of the probable obstacles to implementing environmental protection, especially those stemming from the Asian financial crisis. Therefore, policy options will be discussed with reference to both the capabilities of the Indonesian state and international institutions in providing developmental assistance.

The Indonesian case is a particularly timely study, given the pressures on former President Soeharto's New Order regime from global market forces. The 1997-98 financial crisis focuses our attention on the urgent situation of food shortages and demonstrates the importance of having reliable food policies that can quickly respond to changing domestic and international circumstances in place. In fact, one may be reluctant to treat the subject historically and instead wish to focus on the immediacy of the situation. But this chapter argues that the food problems facing Indonesia today, like the financial crisis, emerge from the interplay of historically based forces and events. Indonesia may be in a period of significant transition, but agriculture and environmental policies are shaped from past experiences with national food production.

Food Insecurity in the Indonesian Context

The concept of food security in Indonesia has long been centered on providing rice to the general population. Direct state intervention in the rice trade can be traced back to the colonial period when the Dutch established the *Stichting Het Voedingsmiddelenfonds* (VMF) in the 1930s to restrict imports of rice, signifying a move towards a system of self-sufficiency in rice.[1] The primacy of rice in Indonesian food security was further entrenched in 1952 with a new policy which gave partial salary payments in rice.[2] This policy was to have a significant bearing on all postwar food production in Indonesia. According to Walter Falcon and C. Peter Timmer:

> The move to making partial salary payments in rice, while perfectly understandable and indeed laudable on welfare grounds, clearly served over time to politicize further a commodity that was already nearly beyond the control of normal market forces.[3]

State control over the distribution and production of a key crop can hardly be seen as extraordinary. Philip McMichael observes that modern nation-states have an important stake in agriculture that is set apart from all other economic sectors. Whether this is due to the critical contribution of agriculture in providing resources for the industrial sector through a secure food supply or for reasons of territorial integrity, the reluctance of national governments to relinquish regulatory powers over food production has been demonstrated time and time again. Most recently, this tendency was evident in the struggles over the inclusion of agricultural products in the Uruguay Round negotiations.[4]

In Indonesia, food issues became explicitly linked to national security with the agricultural and rural development strategies of the New Order. Frans Hüsken and Benjamin White claim that the survival of the post-1966 regime was based on the overriding imperatives to achieve and maintain political control in rural areas, and ensure food availability at relatively stable prices in the cities.[5] The creation of the Indonesian Food Logistics Agency (BULOG) in 1967 to stabilize the supply of rice, which can fluctuate with seasonal production cycles, established a key institution to serve these goals.

The history of BULOG reveals some of the important successes and the weaknesses of national agricultural and rural development policy. Food security[6] in Indonesia has traditionally been defined by the availability of rice for consumption. Hence, in BULOG's early years the stabilization of rice prices through policies to support farm prices in rural markets and to defend ceiling prices in urban retail markets took priority.[7] This was a daunting task given the financial and logistical resources required. It should be noted that BULOG's share in the domestic rice market is less than 10 per cent, but the importance of its role should not be underestimated. Besides introducing stabilizing floor and ceiling prices for rice, BULOG has also been the dominant importing body for sugar, wheat flour, and soybeans.

In the 1970s, international food crises precipitated by the 1973 Soviet-American grain deals alerted many to the dangers of food import dependency for national security. Indonesia, facing poor harvests in 1972-73, was forced to buy 1.6 million tons of imports at high prices, double the previous year's figure of 0.73 million tons. The government's response was to launch an intense program of technical and financial support for domestic rice production through the National Rice Intensification Program (BIMAS). Guidance, credit, and production inputs – including seeds of high-yielding varieties (HYVs), fertilizers and pesticides – were provided to farmers on concessional terms as part of Indonesia's embrace of the 'green revolution'.[8] This public investment in rice production was aimed at supporting the current trends in rice consumption. Complementary policies included continuing rice pricing polices that ensured minimum payments to farmers as well as market intervention through the use of buffer stock and trade as stabilizing measures to protect consumers.

The normalization of world rice markets in the late 1970s combined with the accumulation of Indonesia's foreign exchange reserves through oil exports allowed BULOG to purchase imports to meet the rising demand for rice in urban centers.[9] At the same time, these conditions were favorable for agricultural policies aimed at increasing production. Between 1971 and 1981, real gross domestic product (GDP) grew over seven per cent per year and the oil revenues were directed towards supporting investment in the agricultural sector. A study by the International Food Policy Research Institute estimates that the cost of irrigation was subsidized at more than 75 per cent; the average implicit subsidy of the domestic price of fertilizer was 55 per cent in 1980-82 (though it declined in the mid-1980s to approximately 35 per cent); and the pesticide subsidy before the government began its promotion of integrated pest management in the late 1980s was over 60 per cent.[10]

The results of the green revolution as demonstrated in figures provided by the Indonesian Central Bureau of Statistics (BPS) were impressive, showing that rice production from 1970 to 1988 grew at a rate of 4.8 per cent per year. Since the actual increase in area cultivated was only 1.3 per cent during these 18 years, this growth was mainly attributed to the intensification of agricultural production that was made possible with new fertilizer-responsive 'modern varieties' or HYVs. The achievement of 'self-sufficiency' in 1983-84 led to the recognition of Indonesia's accomplishments by the UN Food and Agricultural Organization (FAO).[11]

Indonesia did not need to import rice for the next five years; however, rice overproduction presented a new set of problems. For BULOG, the maintenance of a large buffer stock was very expensive due to the high cost of storage in humid, tropical climates. BULOG's warehouses were so full in 1985 with the 1984 surplus harvest that domestic market prices were forced to drop so much that in some areas they were 20-30 per cent below the official floor price. As a result, part of the 1985 stock had to be exported despite low world market prices. The widespread adoption of green revolution technology contributed to the attainment of self-sufficiency in rice, but it could not solve the fundamental problem of balancing productive activities with consumer needs. As Timmer points out, in none of the years from 1970 to 1988 was domestic production ever exactly equal to consumption. Moreover, excess production in one year could not guarantee self-sufficiency in the following year. For example, by 1986, national consumption was already higher than production so BULOG stocks were once again being depleted. By 1989, external supplies had to be secured once again.[12]

A concept of food security premised on a notion of self-sufficiency, defined in terms of zero imports in rice, holds inherent difficulties for policymakers trying to balance agricultural production in a country of diverse ecological and geographical characteristics with the pressures of declining prices of rice in global markets. Generally, the achievement of food security is premised on the ability to secure a supply of food that meets consumption needs. Food security in the historical context of Indonesia was defined through one key commodity – rice – and this concept was also biased towards consumption. This is not to say that production did not receive an adequate share of attention; rather, the contradictory relationship between consumption needs and productive ability was manifested in the state's dual commitment to providing cheap rice to urban consumers and promoting farmers' welfare. The trick was to utilize state resources to finance food policy at both ends, but this required the state to protect the domestic market from global economic pressures. Essentially, BULOG had to continually balance the ongoing gaps in consumption with domestic production through its buffer stocks or resort to trade. Furthermore, this strategy required not only the continued pumping of state revenues into the agricultural sector, but also increasing productivity of the agricultural sector to match the demand that accompanied population growth. By the late 1980s, changing economic and ecological conditions threw both requirements into doubt and launched a new debate over what constituted food security in Indonesia.

The Push for Restructuring

At the center of the mainstream debate over the future of Indonesia's self-sufficiency in rice was the issue of the program's costs. While advocates of trade liberalization and the World Bank had continually called for the reduction of state intervention, oil revenues had granted Indonesian policymakers the financial resources to carry out development programs with a high degree of autonomy. However, by the early 1980s budgetary pressures arising from the drop in petroleum prices led officials in the Finance Ministry to join the chorus of World Bank analysts to cut expenditures beginning with the fertilizer subsidy package.[13]

The move towards deregulation in the agricultural sector gathered momentum with the increasing integration of Indonesia into the global economy and the inclusion of agricultural products in the Uruguay Round negotiations. The General Agreement on Tariff and Trade (GATT) negotiations were concluded in December 1993 and ratified by most signatories by the end of 1994. In the same year, Indonesia formally joined the World Trade Organization (WTO). Indonesia is also a member of the ASEAN Free Trade Area (AFTA) that has been planning to implement its own free trade agreement over a 15 year period beginning in January 1992. The practice of defining food security as self-sufficiency has repeatedly been at the center of trade disagreements. The question of whether food security could be *better* achieved through imports, given that much of the problem with food access was not a problem of global underproduction *per se* but disproportionate distribution, remains a contested point between the protectionist and neo-liberal camps. The latter contend that global production of food according to the principle of comparative advantage would lead to greater efficiency in a country's allocation of resources.

The logic behind arguments for moving towards the use of food imports to counter domestic shortages looks solid from an economic point of view. Moreover, such arguments hold greater weight if one considers the new constraints and possibilities for the Indonesian economy under WTO and Asia-Pacific Economic Cooperation (APEC) trade reforms. Accelerated reforms within Indonesia that will allow the competition of certain Indonesian exports under a liberalized trade regime are seen as a way of providing the foreign exchange earnings needed to purchase food imports.[14] Since very few Indonesian agricultural products are competitive in the world market, continued public investment in the production of food crops that have limited export potential is seen as wasteful and inefficient. Furthermore, the demands of the domestic market have made the import of commodities such as sugar, soybeans, and milk products necessary on a regular basis.[15]

The globalization of agricultural markets has affected the degree to which any nation-state can protect and regulate its agricultural sector; thus, globalization challenges the underlying premise of *national* food security. Moreover, as national food production and distribution systems are increasingly subject to the impact of global agricultural production, the dominant position enjoyed by domestic crops stands to diminish. A globalized food system undermines the steadfast commitment of the Indonesian government to rice as the representative commodity of food security. Therefore, a change in the spatial dimensions of agricultural production is a historical process that transforms normative understandings and subsequent attitudes towards the qualitative aspects of food security. These qualitative aspects include not only the psychological attachment to one particular commodity – rice – but also some subjectivity in a spatial and temporal sense. Falcon and Timmer write that 'the time period and region for which self-sufficiency is measured are issues', citing that

'Indonesia has nearly always been more than self-sufficient in rice from March to October'. Equally important for them is the fact that 'some households and regions are always in surplus, while others, especially in urban areas, are constantly in deficit'.[16] The economic rationalization for achieving food security through imports and not necessarily limiting those imports to rice comes up against the historical weight of nation-state's political prerogatives and the social/cultural association with rice as the primary signifier of food availability.

In Indonesia, the attainment of self-sufficiency entails a process that has historically been characterized as national in scope, consumer-biased in orientation, and rice-centered in its focus. The strength of protectionist forces stemmed from the shared historical understanding of food security and self-sufficiency in this sense. This consensus soon received another blow from a different direction. The environmental effects of the green revolution technology also influenced understandings of food security and related development policies. Environmental critiques ran along two related lines of discussion: first, the negative effects of pursuing increased agricultural productivity within the existing scientific paradigm and second, the implications of liberalized agricultural trade for sustainable development of countries in general, and local communities in particular.

Addressing Environmental Contradictions: Problems of Spatiality and Temporality

The changing ecological conditions within Indonesia and a growing global awareness of the negative impact of biotechnology in agriculture have prompted fresh debates over the meaning of food security. Alternative conceptions of food security have expanded beyond the notion of consumer access to food supply. The expansion of definitions is characterized by spatial and temporal changes. This is exemplified in a World Wildlife Fund (WWF) discussion paper which calls for a long-term view towards food security and argues that it has to be assessed at the local rather than the national level.[17] If we shift the focus of security and development to a more localized level and deploy a longer temporal frame of reference, then food security in rural areas cannot be limited to only food accessibility since it is also linked to problems of sustainability. Human security with respect to food cannot only come from meeting consumptive needs, but must also consider the long-term implications of our productive activities, including the capacity for sustaining the livelihoods of farming communities.

Agricultural practices in Indonesia in the mid-1980s came under criticism for being unsustainable, primarily because heavy amounts of inputs were needed to increase food-crop yields. Rice production naturally drew the most attention as the only other food crop to demonstrate an impressive growth rate was corn. However, since corn is consumed mostly by people in the bottom fifth of the Indonesian income distribution in rural areas and is used more as a feed in the chicken industry, it seemed less significant in food security terms.[18] In addition, public resources were most heavily

144   *Development and Security in Southeast Asia*

invested in rice inputs and irrigation facilities, effectively encouraging farmers to maximize the potential of fertile lowland fields for highest possible yields of rice.

These practices generated a great deal of concern because they frequently involved an indiscriminate use of synthetic pesticides, fertilizers, and other chemicals considered harmful to the environment. Pesticide abuse became obvious when natural predators of the targeted pests were eliminated and both pests and diseases demonstrated an unforeseen capability to mutate and become resistant. The widespread planting of IR 20 and IR 24 'miracle rice' led to severe brown plant hopper outbreaks throughout Java, and the hoppers' transmission of grassy stunt virus destroyed many rice fields. The Indonesian government's response was to ban 57 broad-spectrum pesticides in 1986. Farmers were then encouraged to plant resistant varieties (IR 36 and IR 48) and spray pesticide Applaud (buprofezin) on all affected crops.[19]

Critics have charged that the use of new biotechnology to treat existing problems firmly places farmers on a chemical treadmill. When farmers get hooked on the new super seeds and inputs to get maximum yields, other problems arise. Chemical fertilizers seem to have sped up the loss of soil fertility and there has yet to be any research revealing exactly why the loss occurs or how it can be halted. Meanwhile, organizations such as the International Rice Research Institute (IRRI) have introduced a new strain of rice – the 15 ton 'super rice' – that is supposed to increase yields by 15-25 per cent. IRRI claims that this new rice will not have to be used with pesticides as the plant will make some of its own.[20] However, the long-term dependability of new engineered plants remains questionable. There is still the hazardous possibility that herbicide-tolerant genes may be transferred to surrounding weeds and these herbicide-tolerant weeds could present new difficulties, including higher expenses.[21]

In addition, the question of what local environments are able to support is crucial. Much of the controversy over this new super rice has to do with the amount of nitrogen fertilizer that will be needed. Past experience shows that the application of increasing amounts of fertilizer does not always help stagnating yields. This phenomenon of diminishing returns on rice crops makes it doubtful that new biotechnology will be able to fix all environmental problems. Yields of rice HYVs began to slow down around 1988 despite the continuation of high investment in production. From 1988 to 1993 rice productivity did manage to increase at a rate of three per cent per year, although by 1994, BULOG once again had to resort to imports when drought hit the rice harvest. The peak performance of these modern varieties and fertilizers resulted in the same rice shortages that had been experienced so many years ago. In doing so, the environmental contradictions of rice production demonstrated to policymakers and the general public the need to think about linkages between environment, security, and development.

However, at the local level these links can also be seen in ways other than the leveling off of rice yields. Problems of chemical contamination and pollution in places of limited water supply have affected public health and destroyed other animal species such as fish in paddy fields. Despite government attempts to implement an Integrated Pest Management program in 1989, reports of pesticide poisoning continue, particularly among illiterate farmers and women. This is in part due to the weakness of environmental legislation in Indonesia. While the pesticide subsidy has been eliminated, numerous pesticides including banned substances are supposedly still available in local markets.[22]

A number of studies conducted by a well-known local non-governmental organization, Pesticide Action Network-Indonesia (PAN), have traced the relationship between pesticides and women, as women frequently lack knowledge about pesticides due to their lower level of formal education and lower rate of participation in agricultural extension seminars. The damage to human health stems from overuse, a lack of precautionary measures (for example, wearing protective clothing, washing hands after spraying), and a lack of awareness of chemical residue on food crops. Given the degree to which women's work revolves around food, either in terms of direct production or household preparation, their exposure to chemicals raises questions about individual security.

These studies also point to the underlying problem that new technologies often originate outside of the rural communities in which they are applied. The lack of knowledge about inputs and technology translates into less control over one's productive and consumptive activities. Access to a secure supply of food assumes that the food itself does not pose a risk to public health. Similarly, if food policies are designed to increase farmers' welfare (even if they tend to have an urban consumer bias) then one presumes that the production of these food crops should be safe for those involved as well.

Recognizing the importance of reasserting some local control over food production and consumption has led environmental and rural development groups within Indonesia to articulate the view that food security is 'best assured when food is locally produced, processed, stored, and distributed, and is available on a continuous basis regardless of climatic and other variations'.[23] By engaging in environmentally-sustainable farming practices, communities actively participate in creating a local supply of food that is secure insofar as this supply will not be as affected by national and global market forces. A localized source of supply may also be more secure with respect to food safety, as well as protecting lands and human health.

The vulnerability of local communities, both as producers and consumers, to shifting prices of commodities and inputs in national and global markets is at the heart of environmental fears over the differential impact of free trade in agricultural products. The general concern is that the shift to a market-oriented global agricultural regime will further expose domestic markets to international price pressures. There are also fears that increased market liberalization will lead to greater competition from transnational agribusinesses which could negatively affect the livelihood security of small farmers and the food security of poor urban and rural consumers.[24] Of particular concern for producers are international standards of product quality as demonstrated in the growing presence of imported fruits and vegetables in supermarkets and smaller stores throughout major cities in Indonesia. But to grow uniform produce in order to compete with imports, Indonesian producers would have to turn to hybrid varieties and utilize greater amounts of chemical inputs. With respect to consumers, whether through price increases or long-term structural changes in agro-food production, there are issues regarding the consequences of increased exposure of domestic markets to global market forces on those segments of society who have limited access to savings and income-generating activities.

The degree to which farming communities in Indonesia will be affected needs to be explored through further studies. It has been pointed out by some analysts that state trading enterprises (STEs) such as BULOG will not be affected by the GATT/WTO rules established at the Uruguay Round because of the 'green box' provisions which allow STEs dealing in strategic food commodities to keep their domestic subsidies and intervention practices. Therefore, Indonesia has not been required to implement structural adjustment measures with respect to agriculture under this agreement.[25] This situation suggests that some continuity in food policy can be expected. In AFTA talks, the Indonesian government displayed a strong protectionist position in its reluctance to allow rice and other significant food crops such as sugar and soybeans to be included within a liberalized trade scheme.

Neither globalization nor national agricultural programs have uniform effects. Both are processes of social differentiation insofar as certain segments of society benefit disproportionately from the resultant economic and social changes. BIMAS in the context of national economic development may have helped bring about an overall increase in rural standards of living but it also actively created socioeconomic differences within and across villages and regions. These differences can also be seen in the unevenness of the current economic crisis across different regions. Producers across Java are hard-hit by the rising costs of imported inputs, especially animal feed, fertilizers, and seeds. For consumers, problems of food security are especially acute in cities and in those rural areas where large numbers of people do not have access to the means of production for self-subsistence. In contrast, some women interviewed by the author in two villages (one in East and one in Central Java) claim that there was relatively little hunger in their communities because most villagers had access to a bit of land, sometimes only in the form of a garden, on which they could rely to buffer the effects of rising food prices.[26] Such variations present numerous challenges for policymakers at present.

Individuals working in agricultural and environmental sectors have continually grappled with the contradictory impact of the national rice program on rural development. The environmental problems of intensive rice production are well recognized and few would deny that a long-term and broad view of food security is problematic when biased towards urban needs, failing to take into account the issue of sustainable development that most directly affects peasants. Yet at the same time, the national rice program is recognized for its attempts to provide some degree of support towards the agricultural community, even if it tends to be the relatively well-off farmers that have benefited the most from BIMAS assistance.[27] This tension also underlies attitudes towards the regulatory capabilities of the state. On the one hand, environmental critics sympathize with the argument made by free trade advocates that the inefficiencies in the national rice program and other food crops subject to state intervention waste limited resources and may do little to benefit some farmers. On the other hand, within a historical context of state support for the agricultural sector, there is a tendency to look towards the state to protect the interests of domestic producers despite the flaws of past policies. This tendency is prevalent when dealing with environmental issues, as the state remains the key authority capable of instituting new regimes of governance with regard to sustainable development.

There is some concern that the opening of domestic markets will further erode the ability of the state to protect agricultural producers as well as remove any incentive for pursuing more environmentally-sustainable practices given the increased competitiveness associated with the increased exposure of national and local markets. The issue is not simply one of how Indonesia's farmers and food security programs will fare under GATT/WTO rules. Rather, more important is the extent to which the changing global economic climate interacts with domestic economic factors to bring about the restructuring of national policies towards agriculture and the environment. Indeed, it was the internal contradictions of national development (such as uncontrollable ecological responses to existing agricultural technology in the form of soil depletion, disease, and droughts) together with externally influenced circumstances (such as the drop in oil revenues) that created the need for a structural transformation of the domestic economy. But it is uncertain how restructuring will take place. The central issue is over the direction of national development policy that, by definition, includes the role of agriculture within the economy and the degree of commitment to dealing with environmental problems.

At this point, debates over food security reveal the difficulty of conceptualizing a single, coherent definition since the spatial and temporal boundaries for judging food security are contested. Global, regional, national, and local spaces of economic and environmental interaction all become important considerations in examining the different lengths of time needed to buffer against shortages, plan investments, advance new agricultural research, and protect environments. State efforts to restructure national agriculture in ways to address the widening implications of food security policy further reveal some of the contradictions and limitations within Indonesia's structures for food production.

Policies Moving in Two Directions

At present, the official strategy for tackling the problems of rice self-sufficiency has been through diversification. The diversification concept has actually spanned two decades of official policy, although it received much greater attention in the late 1980s when the rice self-sufficiency program appeared to be under stress. Formulated in the context of rice shortages in the mid-1970s, diversification first appeared in Repelita III (Five Year Development Plan, 1979/80-1983/84) in which food and nutrition policy was aimed at diversifying food consumption to reduce the national reliance on rice. This policy was followed and strengthened in Repelita IV (1984/85-1988/89) and Repelita V (1989/90-1993/94) in which the diversification in consumption was accompanied by new possibilities in the area of production.

According to one analyst at the National Development Planning Agency (BAPPENAS), diversification involves the following four steps:

1. Creating a climate conducive to the increase of non-rice food production, processing, distribution, and consumption through price, marketing, and investment policies;
2. Continuing and strengthening efforts to defend local food consumption patterns which do not depend on rice as a staple food;
3. Developing and spreading the use of simple and suitable food processing technology; and
4. Continuing and intensifying extension on food diversification in order to improve nutrition status.[28]

From these four points it appears that the food diversification policy could have a significant impact on the restructuring of agricultural production in ways that could serve the interests of environmental and human security. Diversification appears consistent with environmental interests in preserving biodiversity. The loss of biodiversity, as a result of mono-crop agriculture, was seen as a factor in bringing about the loss of access to sustainable livelihoods. As both diversification and biodiversity indicate a need to move away from HYV rice production, one is tempted to think that if farmers could engage in the ecologically-sustainable practice of mixed farming, ideally, this could reduce consumers' and farmers' dependence on the seasonal productivity of a single food staple and enhance environmental security.

Actual implementation of such a broad approach is far from easy. It is tremendously difficult to get a clear grasp of what diversification really entails. Is diversification primarily a risk-aversion mechanism for farmers, an attempt to raise rural incomes, or a return to traditional methods of more sustainable farming with an emphasis on productive decision making at the farm household level? Or is the main purpose to reduce national consumption of rice, thereby taking resources away from the rice self-sufficiency program and allowing greater imports in other cereals, such as wheat, to become dominant in Indonesian diets? An alternative scenario is that diversification could center on restructuring national agriculture towards export-oriented production, a pattern established earlier by some of the more industrialized countries in Asia.

Diversification of agriculture is extremely difficult to delineate precisely because of the extensive nature of agricultural production at present. Again, the spatial and temporal dimensions across which food production takes place are as significant as the transformation of raw materials into the forms in which we find food commodities. According to Harold F. Breimyer, modern agriculture must be understood as a composite of three separate and distinct economies that sequentially create products. For him, the first economy constitutes the classic view of agriculture, namely, crop production. The second economy of agriculture involves the production of livestock, a subsequent enterprise to that of crop production as it is the process of converting bulky materials into less bulky goods. The third economy involves the complex process of marketing through which crops and livestock, as raw materials, are 'assembled, transformed, stored, conveyed, and distributed'.[29] Even if we limit our understanding of diversification to the greater production of non-rice crops, this does not help establish which stage in the interconnected levels of food and agricultural production should be targeted for regulation.

If we use the broadest definition of diversification such as the one proposed by Faisal Kasryno, then diversification includes technological, resource, regional, crop-livestock, energy, institutional, product, and employment dimensions.[30] Even considering that diversification of agriculture as a strategy has numerous components, this is perhaps the most problematic interpretation of diversification because it is too broad. Kasryno's assertion that transmigration can be seen as one example of the diversification policy is interesting in that it highlights the ways food and agriculture policy overlap with other development issues, indicating another obstacle for effective policy formation and implementation.

Kasryno's claim that Indonesia needs a strong regional diversification policy in agricultural development because of the over concentration of production on an increasingly limited space in Java appears to have been taken seriously by state authorities. In 1995, the Indonesian government began implementing the expansion of one million hectares of peat land in Central Kalimantan for agricultural use. The purpose of this development is primarily to sustain rice self-sufficiency, although it is also supposed to be directed at the promotion of social equity as farmers from Java will be transmigrated to Kalimantan. The project is clearly a huge undertaking given the scale of operations involved and it will require the coordination of nine ministries. Environmental concerns include the impact of rice fields on ground water levels, soil fertility, pollution from pesticides, unexpected growth or alterations in the pest population, and the general decrease in the ecological value of the wet swampland ecosystem.[31]

The project has been questioned on the grounds that it may undermine the sustainable practices of indigenous peoples in the area who combine rattan and palm leaf cultivation with the production of pond fish, tree resin, medicinal plants, and traditional rice.[32] Competition between locals and transmigrants over land that could be used for rice fields planted with HYVs or traditional crops illustrate some of the problems inherent in such a broad approach to diversification. In this case, the specific measures taken to implement regional diversification come into conflict with the preservation of diverse crop production within local spaces.

This points to some of the inherent contradictions of diversification that are produced by spatial and temporal levels of analysis. Should diversification be a response to trends in market demand and, if so, how broad a time frame should be taken? This is an important issue as the time frame being used will influence state credit and investment policy. Another consideration is whether regional, national, or provincial market trends should be the basis for planning. This requires decision-making over the focus of diversification, whether it is self-sufficiency through the domestic production of non-rice food crops or a shift towards export promotion of select, high-value agricultural commodities. The latter has been more common among nations such as Japan, Taiwan, and Thailand because items such as poultry, fish, fruits, and vegetables have greater potential for growth in consumer demand. Whether the state encourages the growth of these commodities through foreign investment in plantation-style agribusiness enterprises or through small-holder farm sub-contracting schemes, it is necessary for the state to decide how it will balance the welfare of its numerous small farmers while moving towards the production of commodities that depend on economies of scale for competitive advantage. Furthermore, what role will the state carve out for itself within this new strategy regarding investment and research?

Much of this uncertainty can only be resolved by determining the limits and possibilities that lie within the structures of Indonesian agriculture. The case of the land conversion in Kalimantan presents an example in progress. The degree to which one ecosystem can be infrastructurally adapted for growing rice on an intensive basis is one side of the major questions surrounding crop diversification. In Java, a related problem is raised. What is the potential for farmland that was previously dominated by rice to be converted for the production of other crops? However, these individual issues frame a broader set of policy choices. As one writer points out, diversification must not be seen as just an agronomic issue of what can grow where, nor is it purely an economic issue of how to make this diversification profitable. Rather, the 'issue is wrapped up with a broader agricultural development strategy, especially the interplay between short-run policy designed to meet government obligations for the sector and the longer-run relationship of agriculture to the rest of the economy during structural change'.[33] Crafting an appropriate balance between private and public sectors will be difficult for the state in the current crisis situation which has environmental as well as economic dimensions.

Food security in Indonesia has become somewhat of an ambiguous concept at present, carrying the historical legacy of self-sufficiency in rice production through to the mega-projects such as that in Kalimantan. At the same time, the problems arising from the dominant practice of defining food security in terms of rice self-sufficiency is driving numerous discussions about the possibilities of diversification in much of the food policy literature. Economic analyses of the potential for corn, soybean, cassava, and other cereals to satisfy domestic demand and the obstacles of developing domestic production into an export capability are becoming increasingly prevalent. Other studies on developing upland agriculture, specifically looking at the economic potential of tree crop production and livestock,[34] point to the need to diversify not only in terms of crop-livestock mix but also in a geo-ecological sense as well.

From an environmental perspective, diversification is most desirable if it can encourage biodiversity preservation at the local and national level, thus contributing to sustainable farming practices. This presents quite a task as state resources are now strained more than at any other time in the past two decades. However, as diversification essentially shifts some of the responsibility of satisfying food demand and farmers' welfare away from the rice self-sufficiency program, it removes the bulk of the pressure from existing state programs and implementing agencies. Many experts tout as desirable the notion of a more flexible agriculture because it connotes an agricultural sector capable of responding quickly to market forces. But this does not mean that the process is completely market-driven. The state is still saddled with decisions regarding the extent to which farmers will be subjected to the pressures of market forces. The decision to cut food subsidies is a politically volatile one that threatens immediate and destabilizing consequences as the 1998 riots have demonstrated. Long-term policy decisions must specifically address the question of whether farmers are to be weaned off the subsidies and price supports of the rice program and the extent to which there will be new public investments in research, extension, and infrastructure for other crops. Since it will be some time before future investments begin to pay off (i.e., in the form of export earnings), there will have to be some transitional measures in place so farmers do not have to absorb the full impact of adjustment.

It appears that if national policy is facing budgetary constraints and environmental criticisms against intensive mono-crop agriculture, then to some extent the decentralization of decision-making regarding production choices will be necessary. This is the logical consequence of a diversification strategy on a national scale. Unless the state is prepared to develop a comprehensive investment, credit, and purchasing program, the choice of what gets planted will be made on an individual basis in a country of predominantly small farmers. Of course, general policies towards foreign investment in agribusiness and credit mechanisms will affect these individual decisions. A similar logic applies to the preservation of biodiversity, since the limitations of national regulations towards the environment stem in part from the localized nature of the problems. Biodiversity seems to have the most opportunity to flourish in a context of agricultural diversification if local communities making decisions about what to grow are also encouraged to engage in sustainable practices that frequently depend on maintaining a high degree of biodiversity within a given locale.

The principles of diversification and biodiversity come into conflict when they are subject to the temporal and spatial contradictions inherent in food and agricultural policies. Diversification in this historical context represents an adjustment of the Indonesian agricultural sector to the presence of global forces, yet at the same time it also purports to enhance the position of consumers and farmers. Biodiversity appears to have greater potential under an official strategy of diversification than it would under the rice program. However, to what extent will local economies and environments be able to adjust and demonstrate flexibility as they are increasingly integrated into a globalized terrain of trade and production?

The ability and willingness of the state to mediate conflicts between local communities and global forces is also a constant source of debate. At the global level, since the mid-1990s, there have been ongoing discussions within the FAO regarding the establishment of Farmers' Rights to access and control over genetic resources. The concept of Farmers' Rights was developed in recognition of the farmers' role as creators and stewards of agricultural diversity.[35] The dramatic decrease in the number of local species as a result of greater reliance on genetically engineered seeds in modern agriculture has generated new concerns with the widespread realization that many local species of food crops such as tubers and even rice could be lost to farmers with the introduction of mono-cultures.[36] HYVs in rice and other crops are blamed because they have a very narrow genetic base and replace indigenous cultivars that contain environmentally-adapted local genes. But new recognition of the possible commercial value of many traditional species has created a potentially new area of conflict between local communities (including farmers and indigenous peoples) and transnational and national agro-industrial interests.[37]

Official recognition of farmers' roles could be seen as a sign of genuine commitment to biodiversity and environmentally sustainable forms of diversification. But as of now there is still a great deal of uncertainty surrounding Indonesian agriculture that must, in the context of a more globalized economic setting, delegate greater responsibility to local communities for structural adjustment in food production, while at the same time continue to follow the pursuit of self-sufficiency in rice with shrinking economic and ecological resources. This is the contradictory nature of the current Indonesian food and agricultural policy, indicating that the outcome of the restructuring process is far from being predetermined. Playing an equally important role in influencing the direction of change will be the societal responses discussed in the following section.

Societal Responses: Building Social Capital?

Throughout Indonesia a general decline in the proportion of income from agricultural production has created pressures on those still dependent on farming for a living. Additional sources of income may come from family members (most likely youth) migrating to urban centers or seeking employment in non-farm rural sectors. This points to agriculture's declining importance in terms of GDP contribution and overall employment, and also reflects the channeling of resources from the agricultural to the industrial sector over the past three decades.

As previously mentioned, within farming communities there are significant variations in socioeconomic status. While some rice farmers have prospered with the help of BIMAS extension programs and support, landless farm laborers and female-headed rural households have often suffered from the decrease in the availability of farm-wage labor. The diminishing amount of agricultural land has frequently led to a decline in their share of income. In their study of nine Javanese villages, Benjamin White and Gunawan Wiradi have explained that a drop in share tenancy and recent rationalizations in the labor process is perpetuating this process of differentiation and is making more common the phenomenon of part-time farming.[38] While the subject of agrarian differentiation is widely dealt with in numerous studies and an in-depth discussion is beyond the scope of this chapter, we still need to recognize the general situation of rural transformation in order to understand the specific factors involved in community responses to food security and environmental problems.

Community initiatives at the local level towards developing sustainable agricultural practices have either had an explicitly environmental focus or they have been more generally directed at increasing farmers' welfare since confronting the poverty issue has been seen as a critical component of altering environmentally destructive practices. With respect to the development of sustainable agricultural practices, some communities focus on the sharing of traditional technology and knowledge for pest control, trying to reduce reliance on industrial inputs. Throughout Indonesia, especially on Java, local community seed banks containing traditional varieties of rice have become increasingly popular in the past ten years due to growing frustration with stagnating yields and high costs (from the farmer's perspective) of inputs needed to grow modern varieties.[39] Finally, the gradual incorporation of environmental education into programs of rural development has been encouraged through funding from donor countries.

These grassroots initiatives may be considered crucial to the formation of social capital within Indonesian society. Social capital is a concept that, in the narrow sense used by Putnam, refers to the features of social organizations which include tangible elements such as networks and less concrete ones such as norms and trust.[40] Social capital is seen as desirable insofar as it facilitates coordinated actions, including spontaneous cooperation. There are two kinds of networks of social organization: vertical and horizontal. A vertical network is made up of organizations that are hierarchically ordered in society. For instance in the case of Indonesia, official state-sponsored women's organizations are vertically ordered in a manner corresponding to the administrative levels of the state. In contrast, a horizontal network is characterized by organizations that are related to each other in a non-hierarchical manner and frequently exist at the same community levels. One example would be local sports clubs or art societies. For Putnam, a vertical network 'no matter how dense and no matter how important to its participants, cannot sustain social trust and cooperation',[41] whereas under a broader definition, Coleman allows for greater flexibility within any given system, stating that 'an organization brought into existence for one set of purposes can also aid others, thus constituting social capital that is available for use'.[42]

It would seem feasible that social capital within a local community would be an important resource for the development of grassroots initiatives aiming to enhance environmental security in general and food security in particular. Networks, norms, and shared values take on an even greater importance in a context of economic crisis when state resources are unable to meet all societal needs. But what are the best ways to develop social capital? It appears to prosper best with small-scale, decentralized, grassroots initiatives, preferably existing in horizontal relations across all spectrums of society.

Coleman's notion of social capital offers some further optimism for the Indonesian case. It points to the possibility that existing structures within village communities could spawn new social relations for countering rural poverty, as well as environmental and food production problems. However, Putnam's conceptualization seems more realistic since he recognizes that any community has deep historical roots. This is not to suggest that Indonesian society lacks social capital. Rather, the question at hand is whether we can find within Indonesian communities the civic organizations that Putnam deems instrumental in building social capital which are based on trust, cooperation, and reciprocity.

There does appear to be both horizontal and vertical organizations that build bonds of social kinship and community reliance if we look at religious organizations, schools, state-sponsored rural activities, and women's development programs in Indonesia.

Regarding vertical organizations, Coleman's suggestion that they can operate as the springboard for other activities seems more likely if these organizations do not serve as instruments of social control over rural populations. Moreover, another question is whether vertical or horizontal organizations are as broad-based and as demographically inclusive as these two authors imply. Civic organizations such as 'neighborhood associations, choral societies, cooperatives, sports club, mass-based parties'[43] assume some degree of voluntary participation which is only possible if individuals can afford the time and energy to attend. Women working in the fields or non-farm industries are still responsible for housework and childcare. Their contribution to family income includes activities in the informal sector and 'invisible' work that is carried out in the 'private' sphere of the home. Therefore, women's active participation in the kinds of civic organizations suggested by Putnam seems unlikely.

The ways in which women may participate differently in food production and consumption remains an area requiring further study. For example, there is a gendered division of labor in agricultural production in which women participate primarily in certain tasks such as planting, weeding, and harvesting. Changes in production practices, whether in response to environmental or economic conditions, will have a significant impact on women's access to sustainable livelihoods. Therefore, the restructuring of agriculture as a process of social differentiation has important implications for gender relations.

It appears that the development of social capital could be useful in organizing community activities around sustainable farming, biodiversity issues, and food security both on a productive and a consumptive level. In times of limited budgetary options, it seems that governments should be encouraging decentralized approaches that can tailor small-scale development projects to specific local economic and environmental needs. Advocating decentralized communities does not absolve the state from responsibility for making policies to enhance farmers' welfare or protect the environment on a broad scale. Rather, policies tailored at both the national and local level are needed as action taken at one level affects the effectiveness of policy at the other.

Current Crisis: Policy Options and Possible Obstacles

It is unfortunate that after more than a decade of having achieved self-sufficiency in rice production, Indonesia is now struggling with a record food deficit due to environmental factors and a serious financial crisis. According to an FAO report released in April 1998, Indonesia faced an import requirement of 3.5 million tons for the fiscal year 1998-99 but the report warned that this number could easily top 4 million tons.[44] The financial crisis has exacerbated difficulties for farmers as the price of inputs such as quality seeds and fertilizer have risen due to the 70 per cent devaluation of the rupiah. This has caused the prices of food and other commodities to rise, as an increase in the price of rice is one of the biggest contributors to inflation. Shortages also developed along with price hikes because some farmers refused to sell their unhulled paddy rice for fear that they will not be able to purchase rice again for consumption because of ongoing inflationary pressures. There were also rumors of the smuggling or re-exporting of imported rice by profit-seeking individuals.[45]

According to the head of the Indonesian Central Statistics Agency (BPS), Suwito Sugito, the agricultural sector is in fact the least dependent on imports and actually provides a shield against the dropping value of the rupiah.[46] Climatic aberrations in 1997, such as the lack of rain, led to a drop in the amount of paddy area planted because the farmers shifted production to *palawija* (secondary food crops) such as maize, soybeans, tubers, and roots. The FAO had originally expected that this increase in secondary crops would cushion food security needs, but by July 1998 it was becoming clear that original estimates for secondary crops were too high. BULOG continued to negotiate deals to import rice from other countries such as Vietnam.[47] By the end of the 1998 calendar year, 4.3 million tons of rice had been imported to Indonesia. However, the end of the prolonged drought in 1998 had led to more optimistic forecasts for 1999. It was expected that BULOG would import between 2 to 2.5 million tons in 1999.[48] By mid-1998, BPS claimed that 79.4 million people or about 40 per cent of Indonesia's population were living below the poverty line.[49] Since Indonesia's economy is not expected to recover quickly from the crisis and the subsidization of essential goods, which includes food, is depicted as responsible for the year's budget deficit, a reworking of food security may result despite the political risks associated with subsidy cuts.

Yet we are likely to witness some significant lines of continuity. The prominent role played by BULOG in ensuring supplies and stabilizing prices in recent months has been praised for preventing further social upheaval.[50] The sudden widespread appreciation for the state agency at this time illustrates two important aspects of food policy: (1) the persistent centrality of rice as representative of food accessibility and consumer demand, and (2) the likelihood of continued state direction over this key commodity. Even the strength of IMF pressure on Indonesia does not appear, at least for the time being, to be able to alter BULOG's dominance in this area. Moreover, subsidy cuts on other BULOG commodities (sugar, wheat and fishmeal) were supposedly on hold until 1999. However, BULOG's future activities and the question of access to rice as representative of food security in Indonesia will remain a source of ongoing debate over state intervention in a changing economic and environmental context.

The current economic crisis represents a combination of structural change within the Indonesian economy and shifts at the global level. While analyses of the crisis focus on the weaknesses of the financial sector and its detachment from the real economy, the lessons for understanding food production and environmental security lie in how the contradictions between spatial and temporal configurations of economic and environmental structures emerge and render a system vulnerable to collapse. Lessons from this crisis could inform future policies aimed at enhancing human security. Even though the present situation hinders the ability of the Indonesian state to fully protect the economy and environment with its national jurisdiction from global pressures, the state will still have to make some critical policy decisions regarding food policy and agricultural development in the long term. Donor countries and organizations should also consider what kind of assistance could effectively assist community efforts to enhance human and environmental security on a sustainable basis.

Policy objectives should focus on enhancing household and community-level food security and encouraging sustainable agricultural practices. An integrated approach is best, as adoption of any one of the following measures suggested without additional support may be ineffective. Furthermore, this list of policies is by no means a comprehensive one; it simply aims to highlight some possible areas of activity for strengthening human security with regard to food production and the environment.

1. **Investigate the feasibility of establishing community food security councils.**
   The logistics of trying to ensure food security on a national level in a country the size of Indonesia are overwhelming even if food security is defined only in terms of rice self-sufficiency. With a diversification policy in which a broad range of food crops are included, food security is an issue that needs to be decentralized to some extent. Moreover, an ongoing dialogue about food security based on a broad range of food commodities at the local level could address issues of affordability and sustainability as well as those of self-sufficiency.
   Admittedly, there is some risk since such efforts could lead to the consolidation of local-level authority in the hands of the state bureaucracy rather than in the hands of the community at-large.

2. **Use the framework of diversification to further encourage small-scale business activities in the rural areas.**
   Support for small businesses in rural areas could help ease the economic disparity between urban and rural spaces and contribute to environmentally sustainable development away from cities provided that strict regulations regarding land conversion and resource use are put in place, accompanied by measures to limit the scope of large enterprises in the interests of protecting small businesses against competition that would jeopardize their existence. Admittedly, this is an immensely difficult task for policymakers in any country. However, it needs to be considered if rural development is to proceed on an environmentally sustainable and socially equitable basis.[51]

3. **Encourage the development of credit and savings programs for farmers and rural entrepreneurs.**
   This may facilitate new productive activities such as the processing of agricultural products in home industries, or may allow farmers to develop animal breeding efforts alongside their crop production. Such programs are especially important as smallholder farmers or landless farm laborers do not have the land and/or collateral to meet the formal requirements for bank loans.

4. **Recognize the role of women in food security.**
   This role encompasses women's productive, distributive, and consumptive activities and may reach across Breimyer's 'three economies of agriculture'. It is not uncommon to find women who live in rural areas engaging in farm work when there is seasonal demand for wage labor or assisting in household farm production, and they are also active in food processing industries and food trade. Despite their

productivity, women still tend to be concentrated at the bottom end of all sub-sectors in rural industries, receive relatively less formal education than their male counterparts and have low rates of participation in official women's groups and farmers' organizations. Moreover, as female-headed households are generally among the most impoverished, the problem of rural household food security is felt most severely among this group.

Specific policies for women could include:

(a) *Educational programs developed and offered at the community level.* These programs should be tailored to the specific needs of the community and special attention should be given to the needs of the most disadvantaged groups of women, such as older women or heads of households. Their access to sustainable livelihoods and food security should be evaluated and practical skills training and environmental education should be provided.

(b) *Extension of credit to female farmers and entrepreneurs.* As mentioned above, lack of access to credit is especially a problem of those who do not possess property or education.

(c) *Facilitation of women's involvement in decision-making processes,* especially those regarding community-level food security.

5. **Promote biodiversity enhancement through donor support for seed banks, community-based research, development and dissemination of local knowledge especially in the areas of environmentally appropriate technologies which may require lower external input and therefore, more likely to be sustainable.**

   Examples would include exploring alternatives to chemical fertilizers through the use of household livestock programs. There should also be financial support for farmer innovation in the conservation and production of seeds. This may include a formal recognition of the FAO Farmers' Rights.

6. **Sponsor community-based research on the possibilities of improving marketing systems within and between local communities, especially for seeds and crops such as traditional rice varieties.**

   Much of this research should come from farmers' organizations or non-governmental institutions as their participation is more likely to increase social capital within a community as they develop initiatives in a 'bottom up' manner.

7. **At the national level, research efforts should be interdisciplinary and address the following problems**:

   (a) Under a diversification policy, to what degree can public resources be invested in non-rice crops and in the development of upland agro-systems (most emphasis to date has been on lowlands)? Given that uplands are considered to be even more complex and fragile, environmentally sustainable practices will have to be developed for them.

   (b) There must be consistent coordination among state bureaucracy in dealing with the problem of land conversion (most severe on Java), agricultural policies aimed at maintaining self-sufficiency in rice, and environmental protection laws.

(c) National research and extension systems in environmental and agricultural education at numerous universities should be encouraged to work with local communities on an ongoing basis, thereby allowing investment in higher education to have a spillover effect into rural communities as well.

Like many of its other Southeast Asian neighbors, Indonesia is being pushed to face the national consequences of global and local level structural change. The process of adjustment will deeply affect human security in the immediate sense as people's access to basic needs is threatened. But we also need to think seriously about security and development in the long term. It is by using this time frame that action towards environmental sustainability can be taken. The extent to which the Indonesian society and economy are undergoing a period of real transition makes the policy choices of the present all the more urgent as they will shape the future socio-environmental relationships through the production of food.

Notes

1 Timmer, P. (1991), 'Institutional Development: Indonesia's Experience in Stabilizing Rice Market', *Indonesian Food Journal*, vol.11, no.1, pp.56.

2 Wahab, R. D. (1989), 'Overview on Food and Nutrition Policy in Indonesia', *Indonesian Food Journal*, vol.1, no.1, pp.7.

3 Falcon, W. P. and Timmer, C. P. (1991), 'Food Security in Indonesia: Defining the Issues', *Indonesian Food Journal*, vol.11, no.1, pp.10.

4 McMichael, P. (1994), 'Global Restructuring: Some Lines of Inquiry', *The Global Restructuring of Agrofood Systems*, Cornell University Press, Ithaca, N.Y., pp.285.

5 Hüsken, F. and White, B. (1989), 'Java: Social Differentiation, Food Production and Agrarian Control', in G. Hart, A. Turton and B. White (eds), *Agrarian Transformations: Local Processes and the State in Southeast Asia*, University of California Press, Berkeley, pp.249.

6 The concept of 'food security' remains highly contested because state efforts to enhance the security in terms of the interests of food consumers may come into conflict with the economic security interests of food producers. However, food security is still conventionally discussed in terms of security of consumers' access to an adequate supply of food. In the particular historical context of Indonesia, food security has become closely associated with the concept of national self-sufficiency in rice production. The difference has critical policy implications. Whereas it could be argued that the ability to import a regular supply of food for the general population would adequately fulfill food security needs, the Indonesian government has been wary of relying on imports because this is seen as being too vulnerable to fluctuations in supply, market prices, and exchange rates.

7 Timmer, C. P. (1989), 'Indonesia's Experience with Rice Market Interventions', *Indonesian Food Journal*, vol.1, no.1, pp.14.

8 Amat, S. (1982), 'Promoting National Food Security: The Indonesian Experience', in A. H. Chisholm and R. Tyers (eds), *Food Security: Theory, Policy and Perspectives from Asia and the Pacific Rim*, DC Heath and Company, Lexington, Mass., pp.147.

9 Timmer (1991), 'Institutional Development: Indonesia's Experience in Stabilizing the Rice Market', pp.66.

10 Gonzales, L. A., Kasryno, F., Perez, F. and Rosegrant, M. W. (1993), *Economic Incentives and Comparative Advantage in Indonesian Food Crop Production*, International Food Policy Research Institute, Washington, DC, pp.13-4.

11 Handoko, S. B. (1995), '*Beras, Antara Harapan dan Kenyataan*', *Business News*, 12 August, pp.1C.

12 Timmer (1989), 'Indonesia's Experience with Rice Market Interventions', pp.19.

13 *Ibid.*, pp.20.

14 See Pangestu, M. and Feridhanusetyawan, T. (1996), *Liberalization of the Agricultural Sector in Indonesia: External Pressures and Domestic Needs*, paper presented at the 'Conference on Food and Agricultural Policy: Challenges for the Asia-Pacific', Manila, 1-3 October 1996; and Ferry, I. T. (1988), 'Performance of Indonesia's Agriculture: Food Self-Sufficiency and Beyond', *The Indonesian Quarterly*, vol.XVI, no.4.

15 Booth, A. and Baharsyah, S. (1986), 'Indonesia', *Food Trade and Food Security in ASEAN and Australia*, ASEAN-Australia Joint Research Project, Canberra, pp.21-2.

16 Falcon and Timmer (1991), 'Food Security in Indonesia: Defining the Issues', pp.11.

17 World Wide Fund for Nature International Discussion Paper (1986), *Agriculture in the Uruguay Round: Implications for Sustainable Development in Developing Countries*, WWF, Gland, Switzerland.

18 Gonzales *et al.* (1993), *Economic Incentives and Comparative Advantage in Indonesian Food Crop Production*, pp.73.

19 van de Fliert, E. and Wiyanto (1996), 'A Road to Sustainability', *ILEIA: Newsletter for Ecologically Sound Agriculture*, vol.12, no.2, July, pp.7.

20 GRAIN (1996), 'IRRI's 15-Ton Super Rice', *Seedling*, vol.13, no.3, pp.12.

21 Correspondence between Hope Shand, RAFI USA and PAN Indonesia, reprinted in 'RAFI and GRAIN: Herbicide-Tolerant Rice Successfully Introduced, But Have Not Yet Been Commercialized', *Terompet*, no.3, November-December 1993, pp.7-10.

22 Information gathered by the author from interviews with the owner of a chemical inputs store and various farmers in East Java in April 1999.

23 Taken from *NGOs Declaration Food For All*, NGOs Draft Declaration to the World Food Summit in Quebec Canada on 10 October 1995, reprinted in *Terompet*, Pesticide Action Network (PAN) Indonesia, vol.3, no.3, pp.11.

24 GRAIN (1996), 'Free Trade Versus Food Security', *Seedling*, vol.13, no.3, October, pp.8.

25 For example, see Pangestu and Feridhausetyawan (1996), *Liberalization of the Agricultural Sector in Indonesia: External Pressures and Domestic Needs*, pp.12.

26 Interviews conducted in a focus group discussion in January 1999 in Central Java and in March 1999 by the author.

27 Edmundson, W. C. and Anderson, S. (1986), 'Geographic Variation and Changing Economic Status in Two Javanese Villages', *Singapore Journal of Tropical Geography*, vol.7, no.1, pp.33-4.

28 Wahab (1989), 'Overview on Food and Nutrition Policy in Indonesia', pp.10.

29 Breimyer, H. F. (1962), 'The Three Economies of Agriculture', *Journal of Farm Economics*, vol.XLIV, no.3, August, pp.680.

30 Kasryno, F. (1990), *Diversification as Future Policy Instrument: In Agricultural Development for Indonesia*, paper presented to the World Bank and at the 'Regional Workshop on Diversification' in Bogor, Indonesia, 20-22 March 1990. Reprinted in *Indonesian Food Journal*, vol.1, no.2, 1990, pp.31.

31 Dahuri, R. (1996), 'Environmental Impact of One Million Hectare of Swampland and Its Management Strategy', *Farmer Irrigation Newsletter*, no.11, pp.6-7.

32 See Kusnadi and Riza V.T. (1997), 'Rice Mega-Project Pressing to Local People', *Terompet*, vol.IV, no.10.

33 Timmer, C. P. (1990), 'Crop Diversification in Rice-Based Agricultural Economies' *Indonesian Food Journal*, vol.1, no.2, pp.16.

34 See Kelompok Penelitian Agro-Ekosistem (KEPAS) (1985), *The Critical Uplands of East Java: An Agroecosystems Analysis*, KEPAS/ Brawijaya University Research Center, Malang.

35 GRAIN (1997), 'The Year of Agricultural Biodiversity Revisited', *Seedling*, vol.14, no.1, March, pp.6-7.

36 Sugiartoto, A.D. (1996), 'The Loss of Agricultural Biodiversity: Do Farmers Have the Right to Conserve It?', *Ecosounder*, no.16, October, pp.8.

37 Abraham, M. (1988), *The Pesticide Portfolio: Lessons for the Gene Revolution from the Green Revolution*, Proceedings of the 'Asian Regional Workshop on Plant Genetic Resources' Conservation and Development and the Impact of Related Technologies' in Malang, East Java, 6-11 December 1987, Southeast Asia Regional Institute for Community Education (SEARICE), Manila, pp.42-3.

38 White, B. and Wiradi, G. (1989), 'Bases of Inequality in Javanese Villages', *Agrarian Transformations: Local Processes and the State in Southeast Asia*, in G. Hart, A. Turton and B. White (eds), University of California Press, Berkeley, pp.298-9.

39 For one example of a seedbank projects in Central Java see Rice, D. (1992), 'Living seed banks: a resource for the entire community', *Inside Indonesia*, December, pp.31-2.

40 Putnam, R. D. (1994), *Making Democracy Work: Civic Traditions in Modern Italy*, Princeton University Press, Princeton, N.J., pp.167.

41 *Ibid.*, pp.174.

42 Coleman, J. S. (1990), *Foundations of Social Theory*, Belknap Press, Cambridge, Mass., pp.312.

43 Putnam, *Making Democracy Work: Civic Traditions in Modern Italy*, 1994, pp.172.

44 FAO (1998), 'Drought and financial crisis leave Indonesia facing record food deficit', 24 April, World Wide Web document, *URL: http://www.fao.org/News/GLOBAL/ GW9810-e.htm*.

45 Kompas (1998), 'The Rice Price the Biggest Trigger of Inflation Increase', Kompas Online, 1 September, world wide web document, *URL: http://www.kompas.com/kompas-cetak/9809/01/ENGLISH/her.htm*.

46 'Economy shrinks for the first time in 30 years', *Jakarta Post*, 8 July 1998, pp.1.

47 Associated Press (1998), 'Indonesia to buy rice from Vietnam', *China News*, 6 October, pp.9.

48 'Rice imports halve last year's figure', *Jakarta Post*, 23 February 1999.

49 In urban areas BPS judges people do not have a minimum daily calorie intake of 2,100 calories per person and a minimum monthly income of 52,470 Rupiah to be living below the poverty line. In rural areas, the lower monthly income of 41,600 is given. See 'Number of poor people hits 79.4 million', *Jakarta Post*, 3 July 1998, pp.1.

50 McBeth, J. (1998), 'Monopoly of Virtue', *Far Eastern Economic Review*, 30 July, pp.49-50.

51 According to some analysts, this problem has been exacerbated with the series of deregulation packages that have appeared since 1983. See Utrecht, A. and Sayogyo, P. (1992), 'Policies and Interventions', in M. Grijns *et al.* (eds), *Gender, Marginalisation and Rural Industries: Female entrepreneurs, wage workers and family workers in West Java*, Akatiga, Bandung, pp.49-50.

References

Abraham, M. (1988), *The Pesticide Portfolio: Lessons for the Gene Revolution from the Green Revolution*, Proceedings of the 'Asian Regional Workshop on Plant Genetic Resources' Conservation and Development and the Impact of Related Technologies' in Malang, East Java, Southeast Asia Regional Institute for Community Education (SEARICE), Manila, 6-11 December, pp. 42-3.

Amat, S. (1982), 'Promoting National Food Security: The Indonesian Experience', in A. H. Chisholm and R. Tyers (eds), *Food Security: Theory, Policy and Perspectives from Asia and the Pacific Rim*, DC Heath and Company, Lexington, Mass., pp. 147.

Associated Press (1998), 'Indonesia to buy rice from Vietnam', *China News*, 6 October, pp. 9.

Booth, A. and Baharsyah, S. (1986), 'Indonesia', *Food Trade and Food Security in ASEAN and Australia*, ASEAN-Australia Joint Research Project, Canberra, pp. 21-2.

Breimyer, H. F. (1962), 'The Three Economies of Agriculture', *Journal of Farm Economics*, vol. XLIV, no. 3, August, pp. 680.

Coleman, J. S. (1990), *Foundations of Social Theory*, Belknap Press, Cambridge, Mass., pp. 312.

Dahuri, R. (1996), 'Environmental Impact of One Million Hectare of Swampland and Its Management Strategy', *Farmer Irrigation Newsletter*, no. 11, pp. 6-7.

Edmundson, W. C. and Anderson, S. (1986), 'Geographic Variation and Changing Economic Status in Two Javanese Villages', *Singapore Journal of Tropical Geography*, vol. 7, no. 1, pp. 33-4.

Falcon, W. P. and Timmer, C. P. (1991), 'Food Security in Indonesia: Defining the Issues', *Indonesian Food Journal*, vol. 11, no. 1, pp. 10.

Ferry, I. T. (1988), 'Performance of Indonesia's Agriculture: Food Self-Sufficiency and Beyond', *The Indonesian Quarterly*, vol. XVI, no. 4.

Gonzales, L. A., Kasryno, F., Perez, F. and Rosegrant, M. W. (1993), *Economic Incentives and Comparative Advantage in Indonesian Food Crop Production*, International Food Policy Research Institute, Washington, DC, pp. 13-4.

GRAIN (1997a), 'The Year of Agricultural Biodiversity Revisited', *Seedling*, vol. 14, no. 1, March, pp. 6-7.

GRAIN (1996b), 'IRRI's 15-Ton Super Rice', *Seedling*, vol. 13, no. 3, pp. 12.

GRAIN (1996c), 'Free Trade Versus Food Security', *Seedling*, vol. 13, no. 3, October, pp. 8.

Handoko, S. B. (1995), 'Beras, Antara Harapan dan Kenyataan', *Business News*, 12 August, pp. 1C.

Hüsken, F. and White, B. (1989), 'Java: Social Differentiation, Food Production and Agrarian Control', in G. Hart, A. Turton and B. White (eds), *Agrarian Transformations: Local Processes and the State in Southeast Asia*, University of California Press, Berkeley, pp. 249.

Kasryno, F. (1990), *Diversification as Future Policy Instrument: In Agricultural Development for Indonesia*, paper presented to the World Bank and at 'Regional Workshop on Diversification' in Bogor, Indonesia, 20-22 March 1990. Reprinted in *Indonesian Food Journal*, vol. 1, no. 2, 1990, pp. 31.

Kelompok Penelitian Agro-Ekosistem (KEPAS) (1985), *The Critical Uplands of East Java: An Agroecosystems Analysis*, KEPAS/ Brawijaya University Research Center, Malang.

Kusnadi and Riza V.T. (1997), 'Rice Mega-Project Pressing to Local People', *Terompet*, vol. IV, no.10.

McBeth, J. (1998), 'Monopoly of Virtue', *Far Eastern Economic Review*, 30 July, pp. 49-50.

McMichael, P. (1994), 'Global Restructuring: Some Lines of Inquiry', *The Global Restructuring of Agrofood Systems*, Cornell University Press, Ithaca, N.Y., pp. 285.

Pangestu, M. and Feridhanusetyawan, T. (1996), *Liberalization of the Agricultural Sector in Indonesia: External Pressures and Domestic Needs*, paper presented at the 'Conference on Food and Agricultural Policy: Challenges for the Asia-Pacific', Manila, 1-3 October.

Putnam, R. D.(1994), *Making Democracy Work: Civic Traditions in Modern Italy*, Princeton University Press, Princeton, N.J., pp. 167.

Rice, D. (1992), 'Living seed banks: a resource for the entire community', *Inside Indonesia*, December, pp. 31-2.

Sugiartoto, A.D. (1996), 'The Loss of Agricultural Biodiversity: Do Farmers Have the Right to Conserve It?', *Ecosounder*, no. 16, October, pp. 8.

Timmer, C. P. (1991a), 'Institutional Development: Indonesia's Experience in Stabilizing Rice Market', *Indonesian Food Journal*, vol. 11, no. 1, pp. 56.

Timmer, C. P. (1990b), 'Crop Diversification in Rice-Based Agricultural Economies', *Indonesian Food Journal*, vol. 1, no. 2, pp. 16.

Timmer, C. P. (1989c), 'Indonesia's Experience with Rice Market Interventions', *Indonesian Food Journal*, vol. 1, no. 1, pp. 14.

Utrecht, A. and Sayogyo, P. (1992), 'Policies and Interventions', in M. Grijns *et al.* (eds), *Gender, Marginalisation and Rural Industries: Female entrepreneurs, wage workers and family workers in West Java*, Akatiga, Bandung, pp. 49-50.

van de Fliert, E. and Wiyanto (1996), 'A Road to Sustainability', *ILEIA: Newsletter for Ecologically Sound Agriculture*, vol. 12, no. 2, July, pp. 7.

Wahab, R. D. (1989), 'Overview on Food and Nutrition Policy in Indonesia', *Indonesian Food Journal*, vol. 1, no. 1, pp. 7.

White, B. and Wiradi, G. (1989), 'Bases of Inequality in Javanese Villages', *Agrarian Transformations: Local Processes and the State in Southeast Asia*, in G. Hart, A. Turton and B. White (eds), University of California Press, Berkeley, pp. 298-9.

World Wide Fund for Nature International Discussion Paper (1986), *Agriculture in the Uruguay Round: Implications for Sustainable Development in Developing Countries*, WWF, Gland, Switzerland.

Chapter 8

The New Age of Insecurity: State Capacity and Industrial Pollution in the Philippines[1]

Eliseo M. Cubol

Recent scholarly works in the field of regional and international security studies suggest that there is more to societal, national, regional, and global security than military security.[2] Some scholars saw the need to redefine the concept of security in explaining the behavior of the nation-state, while others have attempted to explain security-related issues that bring potential threat against people and nature.[3] While modern technological advances and industrial development have significantly improved the quality of life on the planet, many of the problems that gave rise to environmental decline and social conflict in the post-cold war era signal the beginning of the *'new age of insecurity'*.[4] The increased levels of insecurity, however, are more salient in developing countries including in Southeast Asia (SEA).

This chapter explores the inescapable link between environmental and social decline and rising insecurity and conflict brought about by the problem of industrial pollution in the Philippines. It argues that the level of state capacity and the nature of policy responses aimed at preventing industrial pollution determine the degree of efficiency and effectiveness of environmental governance in the Philippines. This argument draws inspiration from the struggles of the various stakeholders in Philippine environmental protection who believe that environmental management in the country is long on legislation, but short on implementation, monitoring, and innovative approaches, resulting from a weak Philippine state.[5] At present, the policy of pollution control is implemented mainly through the imposition of regulatory measures.[6]

The problem of state capacity in ensuring the security of its people and environment from threats of industrial pollution requires specific policy interventions and innovative approaches. This chapter focuses only on the industrial pollution of the manufacturing and food processing industries in Metro Manila, Metro Cebu, and Davao City. It does not cover the subject of pollution from the mining sector and from power plants. Industries in the Philippines are traditionally agro-based, such as sugar mills and coconut mills, or resource-extractive in nature, such as mining, forest extraction, and wood processing. Light manufacturing and electronic industries are growing, particularly in the new economic zones and industrial estates in the country. The unbridled dumping of chemical wastes and toxic substances in major industrial centers is increasingly becoming a serious problem in some parts of the country. Environmental management experts believe that the early stages of industrial development in the Philippines present better opportunities for policy intervention than more advanced stages of industrial development which may have already wreaked havoc and irreparable damage to the environment.[7] In the face of this worsening environmental situation, much is left to be desired in the prevention of industrial pollution in the Philippines.

State, Social Capital, Security, and Development: Some Conceptual Definitions

Most definitions of the state draw heavily from Max Weber.[8] The concept of state is defined in this chapter as 'a set of organizations invested with the authority to make binding decisions for peoples and organizations juridically located in a particular territory and to implement these decisions using, if necessary, force'.[9] The state, in its wider sense, refers to 'a set of institutions that possess the means to legitimate coercion, exercised over a defined territory and its population, referred to as society. The state monopolizes rule-making within its territory through the medium of an organized government'.[10] The continuing relevance of the state in contemporary social science is seen in both conceptual and empirical terms. At the conceptual level, the theoretical refinements of state-in-society model developed by Migdal[11] offers a striking image of power relations in society. This perspective allows social scientists to engage in systematic theorizing by linking specific institutions within the bureaucracy or the state in general with other variables that may have direct or indirect relations with the state-in-society. From an empirical standpoint, the conceptual categories used to describe and analyze the state help uncover its real nature through observable patterns of behavior or actions. These patterns demonstrate the state's potential strengths or inherent weaknesses, particularly in the areas of promoting human security and sustainable development.

The institutional centrality of the state in local, national, and international affairs or its 'stateness in an era of globalization'[12] becomes increasingly more pronounced in the manner it authoritatively manages depleting natural resources. These resources have been depleted over time as a result of increased integration of the economies of nation-states into the global market. This is particularly true in response to the challenges and pressures of the globalization of production, distribution, and exchange.

Of particular interest to the various stakeholders of sustainable development in the Philippines is a critical appraisal of state capacity. This chapter adopts Dauvergne's definition of state capacity as 'the ability of the state to maintain social control, make policies, impose rules, provide basic services, and manage the national economy (including natural resources)'.[13] He argues that a weak state 'has particular problems providing essential services, such as education, health care, protection from random violence, and internal and communication' while a strong state 'requires coordinated actions among state agencies, technical competence, and a high-level of state autonomy from societal pressures'. The state should be able to provide effective and efficient regulation of the entry and exit of various non-military sources of security threats against people and the environment in an increasingly globalized economy. How effective and efficient is the Philippine state in the area of environmental governance? What policy interventions are necessary to enhance state capacity in preventing industrial pollution in the country? The importance of state capacity in the current discourse on environmental politics in the Philippines can be seen in its role of protecting and advancing the constitutional 'right of the people to a balanced and healthful ecology'.[14]

State responses to environmental problems in the form of meaningful and relevant policy interventions could effectively enhance environmental governance in the country and decisively transform the elite-dominated politics of environmentalism in the Philippines. The concept of state capacity is useful in the analysis of environmental issues where the 'state and other social forces may be mutually empowering'.[15] It also serves as a conceptual bridge in linking security, development, and the environment. In fact, various modes of popular 'interactions between state segments and social segments can create more power for both', and these could potentially help build diverse forms of social capital. The concept of social capital is defined in this chapter as the 'norms of trust and reciprocity and the networks of repeated interaction [that] operate interpersonally and within communities'.[16] Contemporary theorists of social capital such as Robert Putnam[17] argue that these norms and networks are potentially valuable economic assets. In a country like the Philippines where the structure of synergistic relations between the state and local organizations and institutions (LOI) is yet to be strengthened, 'norms of cooperation and networks of civic engagement among ordinary citizens can be promoted by public agencies and used for developmental ends'.[18]

One can argue, therefore, that the increased vitality of civil society and the increased capacity of the state are positively, rather than conversely, correlated. Migdal, however, argues that 'as civil society grows more robust, the capacity of the state to govern is increased. Conversely, as the state disengages from society, the possibilities for civic action decline'.[19] It is relevant, therefore, to test here Migdal's contention if there is a positive correlation between the increased vitality of civil society and the increased capacity of the state in addressing the problem of industrial pollution in the Philippines.

Over the years, scholars from various disciplines have seriously engaged in a lively debate on various conceptualizations of security. Such conceptualizations are now to be found in 'discourses of security'.[20] One of the most recent contributions to this continuing discourse, for example, argues that the perceived dependence of war economies on extra-legal transborder trade, globalization, and market liberalization has created a 'new development-security complex'.[21] The concept of security used in this chapter pertains specifically to human security. Viewed largely as an integral part of environmental quality, human security is threatened by environmental problems when the latter pose fundamental challenges to basic human needs such as access to sustainable livelihoods, health, food, shelter, human rights, and gender equity in both absolute and relative terms.

Michael Klare offers fresh insights on the meaning of security. He believes that the battle lines of the future can be secured by eliminating the threats from within, arguing that:

> The major international schisms of the 21st century will not always be definable in geographic terms. Many of the most severe and persistent threats to global peace and stability are arising not from conflicts between major political entities but from increased discord within states, societies, and civilizations along ethnic, racial, religious, linguistic, caste, or class lines. The intensification and spread of internal discord is a product of powerful stresses on human communities everywhere. These stresses – economic, demographic, sociological, and environmental – that are exacerbating the existing divisions within societies are creating entirely new ones. As a result, we are seeing the emergence of new or deepened fissures across international society, producing multiple outbreaks of intergroup hostility and violence.[22]

On the subject of state capacity, Klare believes that 'states also vary in their capacity to cope with environmental crisis and the depletion of natural resources' and that 'poor countries are much less capable' in the enterprise of environmental security.[23] According to Gareth Porter,[24] proponents of environmental security argue that 'the increasing stresses on the earth's life-support systems and renewable resources have profound implications for human health and welfare that are at least as serious as traditional military threats'.[25] The views of Klare and Porter are shared by Thomas Homer-Dixon who believes that 'environmental scarcity sharply raises financial and political demands on government by requiring huge spending on new infrastructure'.[26] Since many developing countries 'are much less capable' in meeting such expenditures, 'the potential for a widening gap between demands on the state and its financial ability to meet these demands' could lead to internal conflict between competing groups in society. The problem of having a 'less capable state', therefore, could easily generate other problems that would increase the levels of human and environmental insecurity in the developing world.[27]

Development, Security, and Industrial Pollution in the Philippines

Philippine industrialization strategies that were implemented in the country during the last four decades establish a strong link between development and security. This trend can be characterized as industrialization without development. Many local environmentalists believe that the pattern of industrial development in the Philippines has resulted in unmitigated environmental destruction. Philippine industrialization strategies demonstrate how industrial development has aggravated environmental decline, resulting in social conflicts in the form of binary oppositions. These conflicts often occur between local communities and 'dirty' industries, state authorities and polluting industries, non-governmental organizations/people's organizations (NGOs/POs) and industries that pollute the environment, or against local government units (LGUs) and state functionaries.

A case in point is the Import-Substitution Industrialization (ISI) strategy, adopted in the 1950s. The ISI was intended to encourage domestic production of capital goods like machines, machine parts, and tools, as well as the exportation of primary agricultural products like logs, minerals, sugar, banana, pineapples, mangroves, abaca, coconut, and coconut-related products. However, the capital-intensive nature of the ISI imposed heavy burdens on the environment and natural resources. Huge quantities of agricultural products were needed by the local import-substituting industries, as well as a significant expansion of mining operations for mineral exports such as gold, copper, magnesium, iron ore, and zinc. The massive and indiscriminate extraction of these resources greatly contributed to the destruction of forests and mountains. The ISI also required extensive expansion of agricultural lands for export crops that eventually resulted in land degradation, soil erosion, water pollution of pristine frontier lands, and environmental contamination due to waste dumping and toxic industrial emissions. The Export-Oriented Industrialization (EOI) strategy replaced the ISI strategy in 1972. It marked the shift from the heavy exportation of traditional products to exportation of new products like garments, shoes, furniture, handicrafts, and electronics. This shift helped to generate foreign exchange as well as to promote small and medium-scale enterprises (SMEs) that are also geared towards export production. The Marcos regime (1965-86), however, did not stop exporting primary agricultural products since the implementation of the EOI. The administrations of President Corazon Aquino (1986-92), President Fidel Ramos (1992-98), and President Joseph Estrada (1998-2001 January) adopted the same industrialization strategy.

Like the ISI, the EOI also exacted a heavy toll on the environment and natural resources. Massive conversion of large tracts of land for the establishment of industrial estates, export processing zones, and special economic zones forming the new industrial habitat for EOI significantly damaged the environment. This strategy aggravated the already worsening environmental situation in the country during the ISI period. During the last 25 years, EOI brought industrial pollution to the Philippines significant enough in degree to threaten the security of human lives and destroy the precious sanctuaries of the environment. Since most of the exporting industries are polluting and/or hazardous as well, it follows that the expansion of trade and investment, as a result of the policy of export promotion, raises the potential for worsening industrial pollution. It can be argued, therefore, that increased pollution is a negative result of development that threatens human security. Thus, an industrial pollution prevention policy must complement industrialization to bring about a more sustainable type of industrial development. The following section examines the state of the Philippine environment with reference to the major types of industrial pollution in various parts of the country.

The State of the Philippine Environment

Since the onset of Philippine industrial development in the late 1950s, polluting industries have inflicted major burdens on the environment. The harmful effects of industrial development can be seen in the amount of pollutants in the environment. These pollutants refer to 'all non-product outputs, irrespective of any recycling or treatment that may prevent or mitigate releases to the environment'.[28] The three major types of pollution generated by industries in the Philippines are air pollution, water pollution, and solid wastes. Each of these types of pollution is examined below to determine the impacts and implications of industrial pollution for human security in selected industrial centers in the country.

Air Pollution

There are two main sources of air pollution – the mobile sources (motor vehicles) and the stationary sources (industry). While the former emit the largest amount of carbon monoxide (CO), total organic gases (TOG), and nitrogen oxides (NOx), the latter contributes the most sulfur oxides (SOx). Since this chapter focuses primarily on the impacts on and implications of industrial pollution for human security, more attention will be paid to stationary or industrial sources of pollution.

According to the Emissions Inventory of the Environmental Management Bureau (EMB), stationary sources are still the major emitters of SOx in Metro Manila, contributing 88 per cent of the total airborne SOx from all sources. The other sources of pollutants are paper and allied industries, food manufacturing, textile, clay and glass manufacturing, primary metal industries, lumber and wood products, and chemical manufacturing plants.

Stationary sources also contribute 68 per cent of the NOx, while the high SOx emissions (limited by current fuel standard to 4.0 per cent by weight) are attributed to the high sulfur content of the fuel used. As for other types of pollutants, stationary sources contribute 11 per cent of particulate matter, less than ten microns (PM10), 17 per cent of the NOx, and less than two per cent of the TOG and CO emissions.

In Metro Manila, air quality is among the worst in the world. Sixty per cent is attributable to mobile sources (transport sector), and the rest to industrial sources (manufacturing and power sectors). Ambient air-quality data suggests that the most significant environmental problems are particulate and lead pollution. Available data show that the transport sector generates 100 per cent of the lead and 87 per cent of NOx emissions, while the industrial sector accounts for 84 per cent of the total annual SOx production in 1990.[29]

Abracosa argues that while gaseous pollutants like SOx, NOx, and CO are not observed at serious levels at present, the projected doubling of emission rates of these pollutants during the next 15 years will certainly threaten the people unless the government respond vigilantly to mitigate the impacts of these pollutants. It has been documented that lead concentration has now been brought within permissible levels, which until recently was twice as high as the limit set by the World Health Organization (WHO). This change is due to the wider availability and use of unleaded gasoline by both the transport and industrial sectors (at 20 per cent of the market), low-lead gasoline (80 per cent of the market), and the total elimination of high-leaded gasoline from the market.[30]

Even the government admits that urban areas like Metro Manila are facing serious air-pollution problems.[31] Through the years, particulate matter concentration in ambient air, primarily dust, metallic particles, and smoke has been increasing. The Philippine Environmental Quality Report (PEQR) claims that the 1980s closed with the highest level of particulate matter recorded at 250 *ug*/NCM, or three times the allowable standard of 90 micrograms per cubic meter. In 1994, this level rose to 322 *ug*/NCM, which is also above the set standard of 90 *ug*/NCM. The PEQR also concludes that the trend in the Total Suspended Particulate (TSP) levels in Metro Manila has been generally increasing and, in contrast to Abracosa's findings, this trend could be partly attributed to the growing number of diesel-powered industries and vehicles.[32]

Metro Cebu has a better environment quality compared to Metro Manila's. But 'it's actually getting worse because the government doesn't acknowledge that there is a problem. It's moving from bad to worse'.[33] Abracosa[34] offers a more succinct description: Metro Cebu's geographic and climatic conditions are generally favorable with regard to natural dispersion of air pollution. Breezy winds from the sea regularly remove accumulated air pollutants. Still, high concentrations of dust have been measured, particularly along the principal thoroughfares. Total suspended solid concentrations have been found to exceed the standard of 180 *ug*/SCM over a 24-hour period in some parts of Metro Cebu. This is attributed to the heavy vehicular traffic, industrial emissions, and poor road conditions.[35]

The Regional Office of the Department of Environment and Natural Resources (DENR) in Cebu City has been monitoring air quality in the region since 1990 but 'it is limited only to some particulates because we don't have the necessary equipment to monitor the other types of air pollutants'.[36] The problem of monitoring is only one of the most important issues facing the DENR in the region, as is also true in other parts of the country. Fortunately for Metro Cebu, there is a Philippine-German Project, *Industrial Pollution Control Cebu* (IPCC), which, according to Abracosa's study, has estimated that based on the annual fuel consumption in Metro Cebu, some 24,000 kgs of lead are being emitted into the atmosphere every year. According to the IPCC, this amount may be reflected in the high lead concentrations found in the rivers as a result of the lead being washed down by rainfall. It has also been estimated that nearly one-fifth of Metro Cebu's population is exposed to lead emissions above the allowable limit.[37] The causes of excessive smoke and dust emissions are also traceable to inadequate and unreliable exhaust gas-monitoring systems and lack of pollution control devices. It has been estimated that 92 per cent of the SOx load and 20 per cent of PM10 comes from industry and that 30 per cent of Metro Cebu's population is exposed to PM10 concentrations above the allowable limit.[38]

Davao City has relatively good air quality compared to Metro Manila and Metro Cebu. In fact, an official of the DENR Regional Office in Davao City claims that 'it is not really a problem because the industries in Davao are somewhat dispersed'.[39]

Water Pollution

The Philippines has 421 rivers. All four major river systems in Metro Manila are biologically dead. With the exception of some upstream portions, these rivers are now unable to sustain aquatic life due to low levels of dissolved oxygen.[40] The Pasig River, a 25-kilometer river connecting Manila Bay to Laguna de Bay, runs through Metro Manila and has an average Biological Oxygen Demand (BOD) load of 23 to 80 mg/l. According to the Report of the ASEAN Environmental Improvement Project, this is many times in excess of the standard of 7 to 10 mg/l for its class of waters.[41] Laguna de Bay, also known as Laguna Lake, is Southeast Asia's second largest inland body of water, covering 90,000 hectares and receiving water from 21 river systems. Laguna Lake is reported as suffering from severe water quality alteration by siltation and chemical contamination from domestic sewage, agricultural run-off, and industrial waste.[42]

The watershed that supplies water to Laguna Lake covers about 482,000 hectares and, based on estimates by the Laguna Lake Development Authority (LLDA), is home to an industrial hub of 1,600 industries. According to Lumbao, most of these companies are involved in the production of food products, pulp and paper, livestock, beverages, dyes and textiles, chemicals, and metals. Her case study on the LLDA shows that these industries contribute about 30 per cent of the pollution of Laguna Lake, whereas agricultural activities, including livestock procedures and feed lots, contribute 40 per cent and domestic sources make up the remaining 30 per cent.[43]

The LLDA area, which includes parts of Metro Manila and three adjacent provinces surrounding Laguna Lake, currently adds about 30 per cent to the country's total manufacturing output, contributing to the country's gross national product (GNP) by about seven per cent.

Abracosa claims that industry is a major source of water pollution because it contributes roughly 40 per cent of the BOD load in Metro Manila's waterways. This load is equal to about 300 tons per day, which is discharged after wastewater treatment. The raw or untreated BOD generated by industries is about 560 tons per day. BOD reduction is, therefore, about 46 per cent, well below what could be expected if the wastewater treatment facilities were properly established or maintained.[44]

Official reports from the DENR in 1996 show that water quality in Metro Manila has been deteriorating at a considerable rate, and that industry contributes a slightly higher BOD load (48 per cent) than has been shown by other studies.[45] One study claims that a survey of the 100 most polluting firms in Metro Manila showed that wastewater treatment facilities, though in place in many firms, were often neglected or unused. On average, treatment efficiency was found to be a low 50 per cent. Philippine environmental regulation requires industries to install wastewater facilities before they can operate. The problem, however, is that these facilities are often not properly maintained or regularly used. Aside from industries, domestic sewage and solid waste contribute the other 60 per cent of the BOD load in Metro Manila's waterways – roughly 40 per cent from domestic wastewater and 20 per cent from solid wastes. This situation implies that efforts to manage industrial wastewater would be negated if the effort to control domestic wastewater and solid wastes is inadequate.[46]

The sewage system in Metro Manila is well known for being antiquated and inadequate. Sewage collection and treatment serve only approximately one million people, or about 15 per cent of the population. The rest rely on communal or individual septic tanks. Properly maintained, septic tanks can remove about 30 per cent to 40 per cent of BOD. However, most household septic tanks are not maintained and may be operating at or below 10 per cent BOD removal efficiencies. Effluent from septic tanks ends up in waterways, or else pollutes the groundwater. In part because of wastewater pollution, water-related diseases are still the largest cause of morbidity among urban populations. According to the World Bank, the estimated productivity loss from water pollution related illnesses in Metro Manila is in the order of US$100M annually.[47]

According to the ASEAN-EIP 1994 Report, groundwater has been critically affected by over extraction. This has resulted in the lowering of the underground water table. Without the pressure of freshwater in the water table, seawater is beginning to seep in; the process is called saltwater intrusion or salinization. Deterioration of fresh water quality is attributable to domestic liquid waste and sewage (40 per cent), solid waste (22 per cent), and industrial waste (38 per cent).[48]

In the Central Visayas region, about 85 per cent of the potential water polluting firms are located in Metro Cebu.[49] They consist of pig raising, fish processing, prawn hatching, and food canning industries. Some 4,000 tons of BOD and about 3,000 tons of suspended solids are produced annually by these industries. By comparison, the domestic waste load from Metro Cebu's one million residents is estimated to be 13,500 tons of BOD and 9,000 tons of suspended solids. Metro Cebu's four major rivers are in a serious state of deterioration due both to untreated wastewater discharges and dumping of garbage. These rivers are now declared to be biologically dead, i.e., unable to support aquatic life due to oxygen depletion. A 1993 study by the IPCC Project also found alarming levels of heavy metals and other toxic elements in Metro Cebu's rivers, suspected to come from electroplating industries.[50]

A conventional sewage system equipped with sewer collectors and a centralized wastewater treatment facility is largely non-existent in Metro Cebu. In the urbanized areas, wastewater from houses and commercial establishments is collected in individual septic tanks. Due to lack of space, very few of these septic tanks have seepage or leaching devices, such that effluent from the tanks flows out directly into natural watercourses. All wastewater conveyed by the drainage systems eventually find its way into the Mactan Channel and the Cebu-Bohol Strait. As a consequence, the natural waterways and artificial drainage systems serve as combined sewer and storm water collectors. Areas in which the drainage systems have been developed for such combined use are limited to the core of the cities and municipal centers. However, the inadequate capacity of these systems frequently results in overflows into surrounding streets, inundating these areas with highly polluted water during heavy rains. Cholera, dysentery, and diarrhea are among the leading causes of morbidity in Cebu City.[51]

There is no existing sewage system for Davao City. Some large residential subdivisions are equipped with a sewer system, but without centralized waste treatment facilities. Domestic wastewater is commonly stored in septic tanks. Overflow from these tanks goes directly into the storm drainage system, which discharges into the rivers and eventually into Davao Gulf.[52]

Although water pollution has not yet reached a point where rivers can be considered biologically dead, the sewage coming from households has adversely affected the beaches in terms of bacteriological quality. In 1992, DENR data from 11 beach monitoring stations around Davao City showed that fecal coliform reached as high as 2,400 in some stations, rendering some beaches unsuitable for contact recreation. Unlike Cebu, with its large electroplating industry, the electroplating industry in Davao City is relatively small. The impact of toxic and hazardous wastes from this industry is probably low in comparison with water pollution problems that have been observed in Cebu.[53]

Solid Wastes

Data from the ASEAN-EIP Report suggest that solid waste management presents the most serious pollution concern.[54] This was corroborated by Abracosa's study which shows that some 5,000 to 6,000 tons of garbage is generated daily in Metro Manila. This volume is estimated by DENR nearly to double by the year 2014. The uncollected garbage of more than 1,000 tons per day, and its resulting leachate, as well as the industrial wastes released into the environment present serious hazards to human health. Much of this waste is thrown into vacant lots, storm drains, riverbanks, and canals. The volume of uncollected garbage obstructs drainage and exacerbates flooding during the rainy season. They also add significantly to the organic pollution load. It is estimated that 20 per cent of the total BOD load in Metro Manila waterways is due to solid wastes. It was also estimated that at an average density of 330 kgs. per cubic meter, Metro Manila's current solid waste production requires about 18,000 cubic meters of disposal space daily.[55]

Households generate nearly 50 per cent of solid waste in Metro Manila. This situation suggests a need for a state policy that would require LGUs to plan for the proper management of solid, including hazardous wastes produced by residential areas and the industrial sector. Solid waste studies done in 1992 show a steady increase (11 per cent of the total) of food waste from 32 per cent to 44 per cent in the early 1980s. It was also noted that plastics account for the second largest contributor to solid waste in the metropolitan area. Aside from households, market areas are also considered major sources of food wastes and screenings while commercial, industrial, and institutional entities produce mainly plastic and paper wastes.[56]

As noted above, the availability of dumpsites is increasingly becoming a perennial problem. The Metro Manila Development Authority (MMDA) has estimated that nearly 50 hectares of disposal area is needed every year to cope with Metro Manila's solid wastes. In fact, the practice of overusing existing dumpsites has been observed in the past owing to the availability of limited dumpsites in the national capital region (NCR).

Experts in Philippine environmental management argue that solid waste management in the country has traditionally been viewed as mainly a disposal problem, and thus the emphasis has been on landfill solutions. As a result, very little effort has so far been devoted to looking at waste source reduction and waste reuse approaches as cost effective alternatives to solid waste management.[57] The concluding portion of this chapter offers specific policy tools and interventions that seek to strengthen state capacity in the area of solid waste management that is the most serious problem caused by industrial pollution in the Philippines at present.

Abracosa's study also shows that only 60 per cent of the solid waste generated in Metro Cebu is disposed of in dumps while the remaining 40 per cent is uncollected. This is usually burned, buried, or composted by households while the rest is dumped along streets and alleys, or thrown into canals and waterways. When the rainy season comes, the garbage dumped in waterways, along with septic tank leachate is washed out into the sea endangering aquatic life and other marine resources. In the dry season, fires in the open dumps also contribute to air pollution and thus, threaten the health and sources of livelihood of nearby communities.[58]

In 1979 an open dumpsite was closed in Cebu and a new dumpsite was established near the coastal area approximately eight kilometers away from the central business district. Common sense suggests that the location of the new dumpsite is likely to pollute the marine water. Abracosa's accounts show that disposal was originally envisioned as a sanitary landfill, but the city decided to revert to open dumping due to lack of funds needed to cover the high cost of materials and proper equipment. Except for the component cities of Lapu Lapu and Mandaue, other component municipalities of Metro Cebu do not have their own garbage disposal facilities. In these areas, garbage disposal is done through dumping in backyards or vacant lots, burying, burning, and composting.[59]

Like other metropolitan jurisdictions in the country, Metro Cebu lacks a proper disposal facility for industrial and hazardous wastes, although the IPCC is helping to set up such facility. The problem, however, is that hazardous wastes are presently being dumped along with ordinary household and industrial solid wastes. A number of private waste management contractors serving industries haul industrial wastes from the factory sites. These contractors purchase these materials for a price, based on the contractors' estimate of the value of the reusable material in the factory waste. Since hazardous and toxic materials, such as PCBs, lead solder slags, and asbestos wastes often have little or no market resale value, they most often end up in the dump site where they threaten the health of scavengers, or find their way into water bodies, resulting in contamination.[60]

In Davao City, the dominant method of solid waste disposal among households is still the traditional 'throw and burn' approach and the garbage collected by the city's dump trucks is brought to an open landfill for disposal. According to Abracosa, the present landfill was leased from a private owner and the city is examining alternatives for another garbage disposal site. Davao City's fleet of 84 dump trucks collects an average of 1,200 to 1,400 cubic meters of garbage daily. One important development in Davao City is that solid waste management is high on the environmental sanitation agenda of the city government. In fact, the City Planning Officer disclosed that assistance is needed in locating and assessing alternative sites for a sanitary landfill, including the possible construction of an incinerator operating in tandem with the landfill for the disposal of hospital and other toxic and hazardous wastes.[61]

Development, Security, and Environmental Governance in the Philippines

Based on the report prepared by the Department of Health in 1996, environmental pollution is considered to be a major hazard to the health of the Filipino people. The continued exposure of children to lead, for example, has been affecting their physical and intellectual development. Air pollution from mobile and stationary sources has caused severe pulmonary diseases and respiratory problems to urban and rural populations. Water pollution and land contamination due to uncollected garbage have caused major outbreaks of diarrhea and other types of diseases. In short, industrial development and urbanization in the Philippines have greatly contributed to the problem of industrial pollution.

The Philippine state, however, has taken a number of steps to respond to environmental health risks. These measures include the establishment of the Inter-agency Committee on Environmental Health chaired by the Secretary of Health. This initiative aims to bring together the statutory powers, skills, and resources of a wide range of government agencies with relevant responsibilities to improve environmental health. In addition, the DOH has strengthened its capacity to address environmental health risks and has responded to episodic outbreaks of cholera. The government has also formulated and begun to implement a number of measures related to the quality of air and water, and the abatement of pollution from transport and industrial sources. The report indicates, however, that government needs a clearer idea of the nature and dimensions of the health problems caused by pollution, their sources, and the affected populations. This clearer understanding will help develop cohesive policy tools and interventions towards effective and efficient environmental governance in the country.

The same study offers a stunning revelation about the share of the burden of morbidity and premature mortality in 1990 that are attributable to pollution. A conservative estimate of the identified populations exposed to industrial pollution include: (1) 294 million days of healthy life lost caused by bronchitis due to dust; (2) 47 million days of healthy life lost caused by heart disease due to dust; (3) 54 million days of healthy life lost caused by diarrhea due to poor water supply and sanitation; (4) average five points of I.Q. loss among all children caused by lead exposure; and (5) 184, 000 years of life lost caused by premature mortality due to bronchitis, diarrhea, and heart disease. It has also been estimated that the present value of the loss of discounted future earnings due to premature death in 1990 of people participating in the work force amounted to 2 to 4 per cent of the gross domestic product (GDP).

Since environmental health involves 'public goods', such as the air that people breathe, there is a legitimate role for the government and the private sector in the promotion of a clean and healthy environment, a safety net for a sustainable society.

In response to this challenge, the Inter-agency Committee on Environmental Health (IACEH) identified five priority areas for the prevention or reduction of the impact of pollution on health. These areas include: (1) dust (particulate matter) from industrial, transport, and household sources affecting respiratory diseases; (2) lead exposure from transport and other sources affecting child development; (3) contamination of drinking water and poor sanitation leading to diarrhea and skin diseases; (4) pesticide exposure affecting the health of farm and plantation workers due to inappropriate use; and (5) food contamination leading to diarrhea.[62]

These figures and findings suggest that the hazardous and toxic pollutants generated by industries threaten a large section of the urban and rural population in the Philippines. While industrial development is essential to meet the demands of a growing economy and population, development must not be pursued at the expense of the health and security of people and the environment. While this is easier said than done, government must seriously engage in building 'networks of cooperation' that will allow for an effective implementation of policy tools and interventions with local organizations and institutions (LOIs).

In recent years the Philippine government has developed major environmental laws and regulations in response to popular demands for environmental protection. These include: (1) Republic Act (RA) 6969 or the Toxic Substances and Hazardous Wastes Control Act of 1990, which prohibits the importation, storage, or transport of toxic nuclear wastes into or through the Philippines; (2) RA 7587 or the National Integrated Protected Areas System Law, which aims for biodiversity conservation and sustainable development against a backdrop of the rapid loss of forest cover and other critical areas; (3) House Bill (HB) 8622 or the Act to Revise the Philippine Environment Code, which endorsed emission and water pollution charge systems by promoting cooperation and self-regulation among industries through the application of disincentives and market-based instruments; (4) HB 5668 or the Imposition of Environmental Hazard Fee, which penalizes all chemical, thermal, and industrial plants and factories found to be violating environmental protection laws by five per cent of their gross income; (5) DENR administrative order 28 or the Interim Guidelines for the Importation of Recyclable Materials Containing Hazardous Substances; and (6) House Resolution 766 or the Investigation on pollution of water bodies by industrial establishments operating without waste treatment facilities.

The Philippine state has also forged ties with other countries to prevent environmental degradation. The alliances and agreements to which the Philippines is a signatory include the Basel Convention on the Control of Transboundary Movement of Hazardous Wastes and their Disposal, the Montreal Protocol, the United Nations Environmental Program Convention on Climate Change, and the Earth Summit in Rio de Janeiro, Brazil. These laws and resolutions only lay the framework for environmental protection and most of these measures await decisive implementation. Most officials of the DENR in the NCR, as well as in various regional offices, admit that the biggest challenge to implement the many environmental laws in the country is the problem of financial affordability. In short, the government agencies involved in the implementation of environmental regulations such as the DENR, Department of

Health (DOH), Department of National Defense (DND), Department of Tourism (DOT), Department of Education, Culture and Sports (DECS), and the Department of Interior and Local Government (DILG), among others, are not only competing for resources for their respective offices and programs, but can only deliver the goods to a limited extent even if they are expected to deliver more with less resources. In this context, environmental governance simply becomes an exotic icon in the menu of public sector administration in the Philippines.

The problem of state capacity in ensuring the security of its people and the environment from the threats generated by industrial pollution is also deeply rooted in both the institutional and procedural requirements of environmental governance in the Philippines. Some of the problems that retard state capacity in its task of preventing industrial pollution in the Philippines include insufficient budget for the implementation of environmental programs, lack of technologies, equipment, and trained personnel to monitor the activities of polluting firms, persistence of obsolete approaches to environmental management, lack of cooperation between government, industry, and NGOs and POs in solving the problem of industrial pollution, and corrupt practices in the bureaucracy.

The solutions to these problems are to be found for the most part, in what the state and the private sector (including the NGOs/POs) would commit to accomplish in the future. Estimates made by the Securities and Exchange Commission show that there are about 58,000 non-stock, non-profit organizations in the country.[63] These organizations are a potentially huge social capital that can be tapped for environmental governance. Only a few NGOs, however, are actively involved in the campaign against industrial pollution. Most NGOs are involved in multi-sectoral issues like women, education, livelihood projects, children's issues, and other development oriented initiatives.

While there is a thin line that divides environmental NGOs between green and brown issues, most of them are interested in mining and deforestation. Some NGO leaders believe that 'maybe this is because industrial pollution does not affect your life in the short- run compared to the range of other problems like unemployment and lack of livelihood. People are more concerned about their jobs. A little bit of pollution is not a problem as long as they have their jobs. People don't think ahead what this might do to their health or the environment'.[64] On many occasions, the LGUs and other government agencies saw the need to promote GO-NGO interactions, because they also recognize the need to involve civil society groups in the task of cleaning up and protecting the environment, such as the cleaning of Butuanon River in Mandaue City, and the Pasig River under the Pasig River Rehabilitation Program (PRRP). Both rivers are now biologically dead but various stakeholders such as the DENR, the LGUs, NGOs, and the private sector are getting involved in saving these rivers.

In the face of the changing political climate after the EDSA revolution of 1986, the traditional political elites in the Philippines have learned to accept the important role played by NGOs in environmental governance. The populist political culture that characterizes post-EDSA governance somehow convinced the elites that it is in their best interest to sound and look green to win electoral support. Groups attracted to environmental causes range from church organizations to indigenous peoples. Some local politicians have a positive view of NGO involvement in their programs and they believe that 'the NGOs are helping the [local] government through tapping their members and organizing people. They are pushing for the cleaning and greening of the barangay'.[65] Even officials of the DENR in the regional offices (particularly in Regions VII and XI) see the need for greater involvement and participation of the NGOs in environmental governance. However, the DENR is more concerned about their capacity to respond to the numerous challenges facing the Department in terms of budgets and implementation of environmental laws and regulations. This is where the state that has a preponderance of political power can strike a balance between the public and private divide and bring all the concerned sectors and stakeholders towards a higher level of interaction. The promise of empowerment through decentralization is not enough if LGUs lack understanding in the area of environmental legislation. LGUs and local communities must be empowered alike in various aspects of local administration and no amount of devolution will bail them out of their powerlessness if the resources they need are nowhere to be found.

In this day and age where environmental destruction threatens not only the security of nature and human lives, but also the power of local and national authorities, state capacity must move beyond the terrain of environmental legislation. Opportunities for vertical and horizontal partnerships between the state and/or local government units and community-based environmental NGOs/POs must be explored to broaden the scope of peoples' participation in environmental governance. The Philippine state may start charting the road to human security and development by designing an integrated approach to environmental governance that will encourage greater involvement by civil society groups within the context of decentralization and popular participation. This strategy could serve as a catalyst towards building a strong chain of 'norms of cooperation and networks of civic engagement' across the public-private divide. Thus, a 'state-society synergy'[66] would facilitate the formation of viable social capital that will ultimately safeguard the requirements of a sustainable society.

Selected Policy Recommendations

While it is true that Philippine industrialization has significantly improved the productive capacity of the national economy, the strategies that were adopted to propel industrial development in the country have left deep scars and painful wounds on the environment. Such policy mishaps require decisive and immediate action from the state and its functionaries, together with civil society groups and the private sector. In this context, the state and local authorities will have to define their position and priorities much more carefully in the face of rapid destruction of the country's natural resources. The state, with all the problems and challenges posed by a gaping budget deficit, declining investment, and foreign reserve need not only protect the interests of industrial capital but also the lives and sources of livelihood of the people whose common future is rendered increasingly insecure by industrial pollution and depletion of the natural resources. It is for this reason that environmental quality becomes crucial to human security. The capacity of the state to respond to the challenges brought about by increasing levels of mobile and stationary source pollutants raises important policy options that will help deliver the society from the crisis caused by industrial development. Environmental quality ultimately affects the people's quality of life. The nature of policy responses by the state amidst rapid environmental decline could also raise equally serious questions about the effectiveness of environmental governance in the country.

The alarming levels of industrial pollution in the Philippines require policy interventions that would help prevent, if not totally eliminate, the worsening environmental threats against human security. Various stakeholders of sustainable development, including the state and its functionaries and civil society groups, have important roles to play in the campaign to clean and save the environment from further decline. There is a need for a new set of environmental policy tools and interventions that would strengthen the capacity of the state to redress environmental problems in the country. Across the public-private divide, there is a vibrant spectrum of stakeholders who strongly believe that these initiatives would generate greater norms of cooperation and networks of civic engagement among ordinary citizens that can be promoted by public agencies for development and security.

All of the major types of pollution discussed above have reached critical levels. However, as shown by the ASEAN-EIP Report[67] solid waste presents the most serious pollution concern. Expected to reach 11,705 tons per day by the year 2014, it is certainly one of the biggest challenges that will test the capacity of the Philippine state – in partnership with other stakeholders of environmental protection – in eliminating this threat against human security. This phenomenon clearly demonstrates the inescapable link between development and security in contemporary Philippine society. It is, therefore, to the best interest and future of Philippine development and security concerns if the state will consider prioritizing solid waste, if it cannot address all the major types of pollution simultaneously with equal attention and resources in its action list. The seriousness of environmental decline caused by solid waste may be attributed to the following: (1) the increased quantity of solid waste generated daily in the major metropolitan areas; (2) the large amount of uncollected garbage that ends up in vacant lots and bodies of water; (3) the future demand for dumpsites/sanitary landfill as a result of the increasing levels of waste generation in large cities; (4) the lack of cost-effective alternatives to solid waste management; and (5) its long-term implications for development and human security. More city dwellers have been complaining of the foul smell coming from uncollected garbage than the smoke emitted by vehicles and industrial plants. More and more households and environmental watchdogs in metropolitan areas are complaining about the inefficiency of garbage collection, the delays in collection schedule, and lack of foresight of both the national and local government officials in setting up an integrated solid waste management in the country. This situation creates an '*ecology of fear*' among Filipinos.

A comprehensive fine-tuning of industrial pollution prevention measures is necessary to ensure that environmental policy goals are met. As a matter of policy expediency, the state – through Congress and the DENR – must adopt and implement an Integrated Waste Management Act that will provide for, among other things, the legal and procedural requirements of source reduction and recycling element (SRRE) and residential and industrial hazardous waste element (RIHWE). This proposed policy retooling aims to revise and integrate into a new law the archaic and separate provisions on certain aspects of solid waste management in the Philippines contained in various legislative and policy frameworks, namely: the Philippine Environmental Code (Presidential Decree or PD 1152); Garbage Disposal Law (PD 825); Code of Sanitation (PD 856); Pollution Control Law (PD 984); Definition of the Scope and Coverage of the Environmental Impact Statement System (PD 2146); MMDA Law (RA 7942); Memorandum Circular 30, November 1987; Local Government Code (RA 7160 of 1991); and Administrative Order 90, 1993. It also seeks to strengthen state capacity by adopting national waste management standards and procedures and involving various sectors to provide a safe, environmentally-friendly, and cost-efficient way of disposing wastes collected from various sources.

State capacity could be greatly enhanced through National and Regional Waste Boards that will serve as the state's implementing and monitoring agencies towards an effective and efficient solid waste management system. The state may appoint members of the LGUs, NGOs/POs, and industry to Regional Task Forces (RTFs) that will aid the National and Regional Waste Boards in policy implementation, monitoring, and regulatory reform. These RTFs will also serve as state conduits in the utilization and integration of various social capital assets in environmental governance.

A number of environmental policy tools and interventions may be prioritized by a National Integrated Waste Management Board (NIWMB) such as the following: (1) require LGUs to implement waste diversion goals (from dumpsites/landfills) by 25 per cent in the short-term and 50 per cent in the long-term. LGUs will be required by this waste diversion policy to develop and implement recycling, reuse, and composting programs. Under the auspices of the Department of Trade and Industry (DTI), the private sector may spearhead the development of secondary market of recycled materials; (2) require LGUs and industry to adopt waste-to-energy programs. The state may consider entering into an agreement with the private sector or foreign firms to build waste-to-energy plants that would provide electricity while meeting air quality standards; and (3) explore the use of alternative technology which takes mixed solid wastes, grinds the solids, blends the liquids, and uses polymers to bind these elements together to produce building products (for example, bricks, slabs, blocks, retention walls, or energy materials). Unless the Philippines state retreats from the standpoint of an 'ecology of denial', – by adopting the necessary policy responses that will enhance its capacity to promote human security and solve the problems of environmental decline – the nation's hope for a sustainable future will remain an elusive dream. In view of the foregoing discussions, the study proposes the following policy recommendations:

1. **Strengthen the monitoring functions of the DENR.**
   The state may involve other government agencies such as the DTI, DILG including the Philippine National Police (PNP), DOH, DOT, Department of Transportation

and Communications (DOTC), DND, and DECS. The Bureau of Investments has been periodically monitoring environmental compliance among firms.

2. **Design an integrated approach to environmental governance.**
This approach will avoid confusion among government agencies in the implementation of environmental regulations and also avoid the duplication of their functions.

3. **Strengthen the capability of the DENR in responding to industrial pollution accidents.**
The government can save considerable sums of money as well as human lives and property if this need can be addressed immediately.

4. **Strictly implement existing industrial pollution laws, including RA 6969.**
RA 6969 is officially known as 'An Act to Control Toxic Substances and Hazardous and Nuclear Wastes Providing Penalties for Violations Thereof, and for Other Purposes'. Section 1 of this Act provides for its common and shorter title known as 'Toxic Substances and Hazardous and Nuclear Wastes Control Act of 1990' as it was approved by the Philippine Congress on 26 October 1990. This is a landmark legislation in the field of environmental health and human security in the Philippines because it tasked the DENR with specific powers, functions, and responsibilities (Section 6) that serve as the cornerstone of Philippine environmental policy in terms of regulation, 'use and disposal of chemical substances and mixtures that present unreasonable risk and/or injury to health or the environment' (Sec. 2). The full text of RA 6969 is available online at <http://www.chanrobles.com/ra6969.htm>.

5. **Actively involve the LGUs and NGO/POs in the implementation of industrial pollution laws and regulations.**
Cognizant of the sheer size and important role played the NGOs in the country, there is a need to raise the level of participation of civil society groups in the implementation of environmental regulations. This policy recommendation addresses the need to enhance the role of social capital and technology diffusion in sustainable development. The Local Government Code of 1991 mandates the participation and representation of NGOs/POs in special local bodies (SLBs) and local governments would be better off if they could maximize their efficiency by utilizing to the fullest the available resources and expertise in the NGO/PO community.

6. **Conduct regular training for LGUs in environmental legislation, monitoring, and implementation.**
The State through the DENR, in cooperation with other public/private agencies/institutions (for example, University of the Philippines Institute of Public Health and the National College of Public Administration and Governance, Asian Institute of Management, Institute for Strategic and Development Studies, etc.), may provide training modules for LGU officials in environmental policy and management. Some local officials in the Philippines, if not all, enter politics without sufficient background and experience in environmental law in particular, and the legislative process in general, among other matters. The Environment Training Programs (ETPs) such as the ABC of toxic and hazardous wastes and

their effects on human health would enhance local environmental governance in the country.

7. **Require firms to establish industrial pollution-prevention training programs.** These programs would increase employee awareness and involvement in environmental governance.

8. **Launch public awareness campaigns targeted at exposed populations.** The DECS, DENR, DILG, DOTC and DENR may jointly spearhead this program.

9. **Adopt market-based instruments for more cost-effective/efficient industrial pollution prevention measures.** The Philippine regulatory regime can be characterized as having a 'top down' approach to environmental management. The State implements policies that leave industry without any choice or room for alternative compliance even if there are available or alternative environmental technologies and market-based instruments. Advanced countries have developed market-based instruments and incentives in recent years that offer greater flexibility to the private sector in complying with environmental regulations and evidence have shown equally significant results.

10. **Adopt and strictly implement an Integrated Waste Management Act.** Up to now, the Philippines lacks an Integrated Waste Management Policy. Waste management guidelines in the country are vaguely written in archaic laws such as the Philippine Environmental Policy of 1977 (P.D. 1151) and the Philippine Environmental Code of 1988 (P.D. 1152) that produced the horrible 'Payatas trash slide' incident. Environmental tragedies of historic proportions such as this demand that government agencies (for example, DENR, DECS, DOH, DND, others) their regional offices, including the LGUs get their act together under an integrated policy that provides for a nationwide waste management plan (from trash disposal by households and industries to recycling programs and compliance monitoring as well as R&D of waste disposal problems and application of appropriate technologies).

Notes

1   This chapter is part of the Development and Security in Southeast Asia (DSSEA) program which is funded by the Canadian International Development Agency (CIDA) and coordinated by the York Centre for International and Security Studies (YCIS, Canada), the Institute for Strategic and Development Studies (ISDS, Philippines), and the Centre for Strategic and International Studies (CSIS, Indonesia). I wish to thank CIDA for funding and all our collaborators in this project. I acknowledge the excellent research assistance of Ma. Cecilia T. Ubarra. The ideas and conclusions articulated in this paper do not necessarily represent the views of CIDA, ISDS and DSSEA Research Staff and the errors, therefore are entirely mine.

2   Acharya, A., Dewitt, D., and Hernandez, C. (1995), *Sustainable Development and Security in Southeast Asia: A Concept Paper, CANCAPS Papier Number 6*, Canadian Consortium on Asia Pacific Security Centre for International and Strategic Studies (CSIS), York University, North York, Ontario, Canada; Hernandez, C. G. (1995), 'Linking Development

and Security in Southeast Asia', *Konrad-Adenauer Stiftung Occasional Papers: Southeast Asia: Security and Stability*, vol.3, no.1, pp.33-47.

3   Maddock, R.T. (1995), 'Environmental Security in East Asia', *Contemporary Southeast Asia*, vol.17, no.1, June, pp.20-37; Porter, G. (1995), 'Environmental Security as a National Security Issue', *Current History*, May, pp.218-222; Klare, M. (1996), 'Redefining Security: The New Global Schisms', *Current History*, vol.95, no.604, pp.353-358; Magno, F. A (1997), 'Environmental Security in South China Sea', *Security Dialogue*, vol.28, no.1, pp.97-112.

4   Renner, M. (1996), *Fighting for Survival: Environmental Decline, Social Conflict, and the New Age of Insecurity*, W. W. Norton, New York.

5   Coronel, S. S. (ed.) (1996), *Patrimony: 6 Case Studies on Local Politics and the Environment in the Philippines*, The Philippine Center for Investigative Journalism, Pasig City, Philippines; Magno, F. A. (1998), 'Forest Protection in the Caraballo Sur, Northern Philippines', *Mountain Research and Development*, vol.18, no.1, pp.63-70.

6   Israel, D. (1997), *Industrial Policy and the Environment: The Case of the Manufacturing Sector in Metro Cebu*, Philippine Institute for Development Studies, Manila.

7   For a detailed and comprehensive discussion of environmental policy and regulations of the Philippines and other ASEAN countries, see United States International Development Agency (USAID) (1994), *Environmental Policy, Regulations, and Institutions of the ASEAN Member Countries*, Report of the ASEAN Environmental Improvement Project submitted to the United States Agency for International Development (USAID), Washington, DC.

8   Weber, M. (1968), *Economy and Society*, Bedminster Press, New York; Skocpol, T., Evans, P. and Rueschmeyer, D. (eds) (1985), *Bringing the State Back In*, Cambridge University Press, New York; Migdal, J. S. (1988), *Strong Societies and Weak States: State-Society Relations and State Capabilities in the Third World*, Princeton University Press, Princeton; Migdal, J. S., Kohli, A. and Shue, V. (eds) (1994), *State Power and Social Forces: Domination and Transformation in the Third World*, Cambridge University Press, New York.

9   This definition of the State is from Evans and Reuschmeyer (1985).

10 World Bank (1997), *World Bank Development Report 1997*, Washington, DC, USA.

11 Migdal, *et. al.* (1994), *Power and Social Forces: Domination and Transformation in the Third World*.

12 Evans, P. B. (1997), 'The Eclipse of the State?: Reflections on Stateness in an Era of Globalization', *World Politics*, vol.50, no.1, pp.62-87.

13 Dauvergne, P. (1997), *Weak States and the Environment in Indonesia and the Solomon Islands*, Working Paper 1997/10 presented at a 'Workshop on Weak and Strong States in Southeast Asia and Melanesia', The Australian National University, August 1997.

14 *Philippine Constitution*, 1987.

15 Migdal, *et. al.*, (1994), *State Power and Social Forces: Domination and Transformation in the Third World*, pp.4.

16 Evans, P. B. (ed.) (1997), *State-Society Synergy: Government and Social Capital in Development*, International and Area Studies, Berkeley, CA., pp.2.

17 Putnam, R. (1993), *Making Democracy Work: Civic Traditions in Modern Italy*, Princeton University Press, Princeton, NJ.; and his article, 'The Prosperous Community', *American Prospect*, no.13, Spring 1993, pp.35-42.

18 Evans (1997), *State-Society Synergy: Government and Social Capital in Development*, pp.178.

19 Lipschutz, R. D. (ed.) (1995), *On Security*, Columbia University Press, New York, pp.8.

20 Duffield, M. (1999), 'Globalization and War Economies: Promoting Order of the Return of History', *The Fletcher Forum of World Affairs*, vol.23, no.2, pp.29.

21 Klare (1996), 'Redefining Security: The New Global Schisms', pp.354.

22 Some scholars like Ronald Bailey (1995) are more optimistic about the future. He argues that 'many of the looming threats predicted in the early days of the environmental movement turned out to be exaggerated.' He also believes that 'the problem with the past twenty years of environmentalism has been a simple one: a failure of theory' and blames the followers of Malthusianism like Rachel Carson and Paul Erlich for contributing to this failure.

23 Klare (1996), 'Redefining Security: The New Global Schisms', pp.358.

24 Porter (1995), 'Environmental Security as a National Security Issue', pp.218.

25 Homer-Dixon, T. (1993), 'Environmental Security and Intergroup Conflict', in M. Klare and D. C. Thomas (eds), *World Security: Challenges For a New Century*, St. Martin's Press, New York, pp.298-299.

26 Asian Development Bank (ADB) (1994), *Climate Change in Asia: Indonesia*, ADB, Manila.

27 Environmental Management Bureau-Department of Environment and Natural Resources (EMD-DENR) (1996), *Philippine Environmental Quality Report 1990-1995*, Quezon City, Republic of the Philippines.

28 For a discussion of urban and industrial environment in the Philippines, see Abracosa, R. (1998), *Philippine Urban and Industrial Environment*, Asian Institute of Management, Makati.

29 Abracosa (1998), *Philippine Urban and Industrial Environment*, pp.4.

30 EMB-DENR (1996), *Philippine Environmental Quality Report (PEQR) 1990-95*.

31 Abracosa (1998), *Philippine Urban and Industrial Environment*, pp.4.

32 Interview with Ms. Marit Remonde, Cebu Environmental Initiatives for Development Center, Inc. (CEIDEC), Cebu City, Philippines, 3 August 1998.

33 Abracosa (1998), *Philippine Urban and Industrial Environment*, pp.7.

34 See also DENR (1996), *Environment and Natural Resources Accounting Project (ENRAP)*, Quezon City, Philippines.

35 Interview with Mr. Alan Arranguez, DENR Region VII, Cebu City, Philippines, 3 August 1998.

36 Abracosa (1998), *Philippine Urban and Industrial Environment*, and DENR (1996).

37 *Ibid.*, pp.7.

38 Interview with Engr. Bienvenido Lipayon, Chief of Environmental Quality Division, DENR Region XII, Davao City, Philippines, 5 August 1998.

39 Abracosa (1998), *Philippine Urban and Industrial Environment*, pp.2.

40 USAID (1994), *Environmental Policy, Regulations, and Institutions of the ASEAN Member Countries*.

41 *Ibid.*, pp.5-1.

42 See Kircher-Lumbao, L. (1997), 'Laguna Lake Development Authority: Tackling Water Pollution', *Competitive Advantage*, vol.11, no.1, pp.18.

43 Abracosa (1998), *Philippine Urban and Industrial Environment*, pp.2.

44 EMB-DENR (1996), *Philippine Environmental Quality Report 1990-95*.

45 Abracosa (1998), *Philippine Urban and Industrial Environment*, pp.3.

46 *Ibid.*

47 USAID (1994), *Environmental Policy, Regulations, and Institutions of the ASEAN Member Countries*.

48 Water pollution data for Metro Cebu and Davao City are from Abracosa (1998), *Philippine Urban and Industrial Environment*, pp.6-9.
49 *Ibid.*, pp.6.
50 *Ibid.*
51 *Ibid.*, pp.8.
52 *Ibid.*
53 Aside from sources drawn from USAID (1994), most of the data on solid waste management discussed in this section are from Abracosa (1998).
54 Abracosa (1998), *Philippine Urban and Industrial Environment*, pp.3.
55 *Ibid.*
56 *Ibid.*, pp.4.
57 *Ibid.*, pp.6.
58 *Ibid.*, pp.7.
59 *Ibid.*
60 *Ibid.*, pp.9.
61 Department of Health (DOH) (1996), *Philippines: Health and the Environment*, Republic of the Philippines.
62 *Ibid.*
63 David, K. C. (1997), 'A History of NGOs in the Philippines', in S. Silliman and L. Noble (eds), *Non-Governmental Organizations in the Philippines: Civil-Society and the State*, University of Hawaii Press.
64 Interview with Ms. Marit Remonde, CEIDEC, Cebu City, Philippines, 3 August 1998.
65 Interview with Councilor Felixberto Rosito, Chairman of the Committee on Public Services and Environmental Protection, Cebu City, Philippines, 4 August 1998.
66 Evans (1997), 'The Eclipse of the State?: Reflections on Stateness in an Era of Globalization', pp.62-87.
67 USAID (1994), *Environmental Policy, Regulations, and Institutions of the ASEAN Member Countries*, pp.5-1.

References

Abracosa, R. (1998), *Philippine Urban and Industrial Environment*, Asian Institute of Management, Makati City, Philippines.
Acharya, A., Dewitt, D., and Hernandez, C. (1995), *Sustainable Development and Security in Southeast Asia: A Concept Paper*, *CANCAPS Papier Number 6*, Canadian Consortium on Asia Pacific Security Centre for International and Strategic Studies (CSIS), York University, North York, Ontario, Canada.
Asian Development Bank (ADB) (1994), *Climate Change in Asia: Indonesia*, ADB, Manila.
Bailey, R. (1995), *The True State of the Planet*, The Free Press, New York and London.
Coronel, S. S. (ed.) (1996), *Patrimony: 6 Case Studies on Local Politics and the Environment in the Philippines*, The Philippine Center for Investigative Journalism, Pasig City, Philippines.
Dauvergne, P. (1997), *Weak States and the Environment in Indonesia and the Solomon Islands*, Working Paper 1997/10 presented at a 'Workshop on Weak and Strong States in Southeast Asia and Melanesia', The Australian National University, August 1997.

David, K. C. (1997), 'A History of NGOs in the Philippines', in S. Silliman and L. Noble (eds), *Non-Governmental Organizations in the Philippines: Civil-Society and the State*, University of Hawaii Press.

Department of Health (DOH) (1996), *Philippines: Health and the Environment*, Republic of the Philippines.

Duffield, M. (1999), 'Globalization and War Economies: Promoting Order of the Return of History', *The Fletcher Forum of World Affairs*, vol. 23, no. 2, pp. 21-38.

Environmental Management Bureau-Department of Environment and Natural Resources (EMB-DENR) (1996), *Philippine Environmental Quality Report 1990-1995*, Quezon City, Republic of the Philippines.

Evans, P. B. (ed.) (1997a), *State-Society Synergy: Government and Social Capital in Development*, International and Area Studies, Berkeley, CA.

Evans, P. B. (1997b), 'The Eclipse of the State?: Reflections on Stateness in an Era of Globalization', *World Politics*, vol. 50, no. 1, pp. 62-87.

Evans, P. B. and Rueschemeyer, D. (1985), 'The State and Economic Transformation: Toward an Analysis of the Conditions Underlying Effective Intervention' in P. Evans, D. Rueschemeyer, and T. Skocpol (eds), *Bringing the State Back In*, Cambridge University Press, New York, pp. 44-77.

Hernandez, C. G. (1995), 'Linking Development and Security in Southeast Asia', *Konrad Adenauer Stiftung Occasional Papers: Southeast Asia: Security and Stability*, vol. 3, no. 1, pp. 33-47.

Homer-Dixon, T. (1993), 'Environmental Security and Intergroup Conflict', in M. Klare and D. C. Thomas (eds), *World Security: Challenges For a New Century*, St. Martin's Press, New York, pp. 298-299.

Israel, D. (1997), *Industrial Policy and the Environment: The Case of the Manufacturing Sector in Metro Cebu*, Philippine Institute for Development Studies, Manila.

Klare, M. (1996), 'Redefining Security: The New Global Schisms', *Current History*, vol. 95, no. 604, pp. 353-358.

Kircher-Lumbao, L. (1997), 'Laguna Lake Development Authority: Tackling Water Pollution', *Competitive Advantage*, vol. 11, no. 1, pp. 18-21.

Lipschutz, R. D. (ed.) (1995), *On Security*, Columbia University Press, New York.

Maddock, R.T. (1995), 'Environmental Security in East Asia', *Contemporary Southeast Asia*, vol. 17, no. 1, June, pp. 20-37.

Magno, F. A (1997), 'Environmental Security in South China Sea', *Security Dialogue*, vol. 28, no. 1, pp. 97-112.

Magno, F. A. (1998), 'Forest Protection in the Caraballo Sur, Northern Philippines', *Mountain Research and Development*, vol. 18, no. 1, pp. 63-70.

Migdal, J. S. (1988), *Strong Societies and Weak States: State-Society Relations and State Capabilities in the Third World*, Princeton University Press, Princeton.

Migdal, J. S. Kohli, A. and Shue, V. (eds) (1994), *State Power and Social Forces: Domination and Transformation in the Third World*, Cambridge University Press, New York.

Porter, G. (1995), 'Environmental Security as a National Security Issue', *Current History*, May, pp. 218-222.

Porter, G. and Brown, J. W. (1995), *Global Environmental Politics*, Westview Press, Boulder, Colorado.

Putnam, R. (1993a), *Making Democracy Work: Civic Traditions in Modern Italy*, Princeton University Press, Princeton.

Putnam, R. (1993b), 'The Prosperous Community', *American Prospect*, no. 13, Spring, pp. 35-42.

Chapter 9

The Textile Industry in Indonesia

Wiku Adisasmito

Introduction

After the cold war ended, several Asian countries, including Indonesia, realized that a state cannot protect its security merely by having a strong military capability and a high degree of military preparedness.[1] Security is widely used to mean safety or freedom from danger and anxiety. The traditional meaning of security is often used to refer to ideological, territorial, or political security; however, such an understanding does not reflect contemporary understandings of security threats. This chapter uses a broader concept of security that includes economic, industrial, technological, environmental, social, and cultural dimensions.

In light of this broader understanding of security, the research reported in this chapter looks at the Indonesian textile trade from an environmental security perspective. The textile industry in Indonesia has been a strong contributor to the national income. With the political and economic crisis that has affected Indonesia since late 1997, the industry is under threat of economic insecurity from future competitive trade liberalization. The global textile industry, including Indonesia's, will have to increase its product quality not only to ensure that the environmental standards are met, but also to be able to compete in the era of free trade.

Textiles have been produced in Indonesia since the 1930s and the industry receives special attention from the government since it is an important base for industrial development. This is because of its simple technology and the fact that it has a large domestic market. Automatization of the industry occurred in the mid-1960s, completely replacing the handloom that resulted in increased production. With the advent of import saturation of the local market and the decrease in oil prices, non-oil exports became increasingly important for the Indonesian economy.

Until the early 1980s, Indonesia's manufacturing sector was very inward-oriented with the exports of textile products playing an insignificant role; however, this changed by the mid-1980s. Textiles and textile-products have played an increasingly important role in the overall export performance of Indonesia. But in terms of export markets, Indonesia had to agree on a quota system for its textile exports under the Multifiber Agreement. The quota is fixed, limiting the export of textiles classified under certain categories. The destination (or quota) countries are the United States (US), the European Union (EU), Canada, and Norway. Quotas apply to them. As a result of the Uruguay Round of the General Agreement on Tariffs and Trade (GATT), the quota systems are being phased out over the next ten years to improve free trade conditions. Exports from Indonesia to quota countries constitute 56 per cent of overall exports of textile and textile-products. Europe constitutes the largest market among the quota countries, with the EU countries alone accounting for 25.3 per cent of all Indonesian textile exports.

The Indonesian Textile Industry

Over the last two decades, Indonesia has seen a boom in the growth of its textile industry. Besides supplying a basic commodity, the textile industry provides many employment opportunities. For this reason, the textile industry has always been one of the spearheads of developing countries' export thrust. The rapid growth of this sector cannot be separated from the fact that the manufacturing activities use cheap and unskilled labor for which developing countries, including Indonesia, are well known. Combined with the capability to export their products, this inexpensive source of labor has enabled the textile companies to be highly profitable.

The industry assumes special significance in Indonesia. Since the textile industry is by far the largest of the country's manufacturing sectors, it is no exaggeration to state that the industry will be the litmus test in Indonesia's efforts to diversify the economy away from its heavy reliance on oil and gas. If textile exports flounder, it is unlikely that Indonesia will be able to engineer a strategy of rapidly growing and broad-based non-oil exports, including other manufactured goods, services such as tourism, or cash crops.[2]

Location

About 85 per cent of the textile manufacturing companies are situated in Java. Geographically, this is an advantage for both the companies and the labor force, as Java is the most populated island in Indonesia. Java also has the most developed infrastructure of all of the islands, providing easy access to production activities. However, production on Java also has disadvantages since industries produce waste and pollution that have harmful effects on such a densely-populated island. Another environmental challenge to be considered is the fact that land in Java is very fertile, making it more appropriate for agricultural use than for industrial purposes.

Employment and Positional Structure

Both the textile and garment industries are for the most part labor-intensive and low-skilled activities. Value added per employee in the factory sector, the most common measurement of labor intensity, is slightly over half of the national manufacturing average for textiles, and about one-third for garments.

Textile Production

Raw Materials

Almost all of the raw materials used in the textile industry are imported. Cotton fibers, for example, are largely imported since local production does not meet the needs of the industry. Approximately 440,000 tons of cotton fibers are required, with the US, the biggest supplier, accounting for 35.1 per cent of all imported fibers. Other fibers such as synthetic fibers are produced locally.

Production

Several factors have contributed to growth in the Indonesian textile and garment industry since 1966. Improvements in productivity and efficiency include a technological revolution in weaving, a more skilled labor force, new and more efficient management practices, and the introduction of new products.

The modern spinning and weaving industries have expanded rapidly since the early 1970s. This was supported by the rapid increase in domestic and foreign investment due to the rising demand in the domestic market and favorable investment incentives such as trade protection against imports.

With regard to the synthetic fiber industry, expansion started in the late 1970s as the government promoted downstream utilization of energy resources, particularly petroleum. By 1985, locally made synthetic fibers accounted for 83 per cent of the total volume of synthetic fibers available to the spinning industry, indicating that import substitution policies were successful.[3]

The production process of the textile industry consists of five main stages: fiber production, spinning, weaving and knitting, dyeing-printing, and finishing. The first three are commonly referred to as the wet process, while the latter two make up the dry process. Most textile factories are engaged in the last four stages which are frequently vertically integrated under one management. Dying and printing activities account for the bulk of pollution.

In 1996, the export growth in the textile industry was 6.64 per cent, and total exports were valued at US$ 5226.6 million – see Figures 9.1 and 9.2. Net export figures for the period January-October 1997 increased up to 12.85 per cent from the previous year. This growth is due to the increase in exports of synthetic filament yarns by 19.78 per cent.[4] The destination of yarn exports is mostly European countries such as France, Germany, and Holland as well as others, including the U. S. and China. It is expected that this sector will continue to expand. Due to this growth, textiles have become Indonesia's top export commodity. It is not surprising that the Ministry of Industry and Trade wants to keep the stability of these industries in order to maintain Indonesia's exporting capability. The establishment of the Indonesian Textiles Association (API) in the 1970s demonstrates the government's effort to secure the sustainability of the textile industry trade.

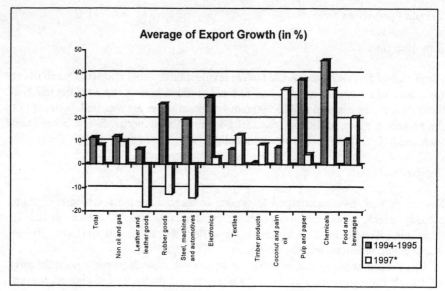

Note: * January – October 1996 January – October 1997

Source: Ministry of Trade and Industry, 1998

Figure 9.1 Export Growth in the Textile Industry

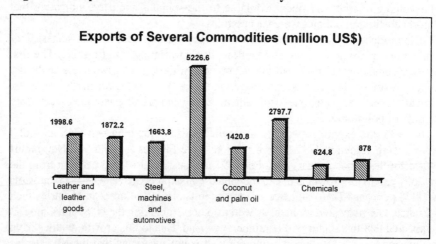

Source: Ministry of Trade and Industry, 1998

Figure 9.2 Export Growth in Industries

Since July 1997, Indonesia has been hit by an economic crisis that appears to have affected its textile exporting potential. As of November 1997, as many as 39 out of the 112 textile and garment companies in the Bandung-Majalaya area (West Java) have stopped production and are in the process of closing down. Other existing industries are limiting the number of work hours. This is due to the difficulties of finding capital at a time of rising costs of raw materials.[5] As the economic crisis continues, massive labor cuts for efficiency gains become the choice of most textile manufacturers.

However, medium-sized companies are the only ones experiencing this financial setback. Bigger companies are still able to operate and export goods abroad. The firm foundation of large textile firms has helped Indonesia weather the economic crisis. Indeed, the industry has been shaken by the difficulties of importing raw materials and chemicals, as the prices of these products have been subject to currency fluctuations since mid-1997. For small-and medium-sized companies, this has led to an even higher production cost. Tables 9.1 to 9.3 show that although Indonesia went through economic turmoil, no significant textile export change occurred in terms of its contribution to total exports in 1997. The first half of 1998 was marked by massive and sporadic student demonstrations that led to the fall of Socharto as well as a two-day riot that burned strategic locations in Jakarta. The statistics in Table 9.3 show that textile exports were not affected by the political and economic situation in Indonesia.

Table 9.1 Export Figures of January – November 1996

	Net (ton) 1995	Net (ton) 1996	Changes (1995-96) (%)	Value FOB (thousands US$) 1995	Value FOB (thousands US$) 1996	Changes (1995-96) (%)	Contri-bution to Total Export (%)
Textiles	774,018	881,847	18.52	5,586,805	5,907,240	5.74	13.09
Garments	199,463	212,621	6.60	3,049,805	3,223,893	5.72	7.14
Woven Textiles	189,954	213,981	12.65	1,436,841	1,418,419	-1.28	3.14
Other Textiles	354,601	455,245	28.38	1,100,642	1,264,928	14.93	2.00

Source: Bureau Central of Statistics

Export Quotas

To highlight the importance of exports, the State Ministry of Trade and Industry has established an Indonesian Trade Promotion Center (ITPC) and hired four high-quality trade attaches who have a good understanding of export goods, trade potentials, and databases. These steps notwithstanding, however, quotas remain a problem for the textile industry. The setting of quotas was initially aimed at establishing greater control over trade barriers by allowing the importing country to select goods meeting certain quality standards. For exporting countries, quotas can prevent severe actions such as trade embargoes. But the establishment of quotas has also had a negative impact on Indonesia's domestic trade.

Table 9.2 Export Figures of January – November 1997

	Net (ton) 1996	Net (ton) 1997	Changes (1996-97) (%)	Value FOB (thousands US$) 1996	Value FOB (thousands US$) 1997	Changes (1996-97) (%)	Contribu-tion to Total Export (%)
Textiles	881,847	802,204	-9.03	5,907,240	4,940,435	-16.37	10.14
Garments	212,621	211,888	-0.34	3,223,893	2,692,737	-16.48	5.52
Woven Textiles	213,981	177,832	-16.89	1,418,419	1,162,965	-18.01	2.39
Other Textiles	455,245	412,484	-9.39	1,264,928	1,084,733	-14.25	2.23

Source: Bureau Central of Statistics

Table 9.3 Export Figures of January – June 1998

	Net (ton) 1997	Net (ton) 1998	Changes (1997-98) (%)	Value FOB (thousands US$) 1997	Value FOB (thousands US$) 1998	Changes (1997-98) (%)	Contribu-tion to Total Export (%)
Textiles	531,810	800,410	50.51	3,378,212	3,789,564	12.18	15.42
Garments	124,590	85,112	-31.69	1,742,043	1,249,588	-28.27	5.09
Woven Textiles	131,584	129,239	-1.78	865,310	681,254	-21.27	2.77
Other Textiles	275,636	586,059	112.62	770,859	1,858,722	141.12	7.57

Source: Bureau Central of Statistics

As normally experienced in activities controlled by government authorities, the procedures for quotas are often complex and time-consuming with the obligation to accept established rules and regulations. This is considered to be a disadvantage for exporters because they have to pay additional costs to cargo companies for extensive delays.

In Indonesia, each industry has specific quantity limits for their exports to various countries. Larger firms have greater access to export destinations than small companies. This handicap for small companies is an advantage for the larger firms that buy the smaller companies' products at a cheaper price and then sell these products to their export markets. Smaller companies are forced into selling their products if they want to produce for export, since they do not have access to foreign buyers.

Security

Security Linkages

A nation's security concerns and perceptions of its security problems are shaped by both internal and external factors. Paramount among them are the internal factors including the nation's geography and its historical experience. These internal factors determine a nation's perceptions of the external factors that help determine its foreign and security policies. Foreign policy, to some extent, is a reaction to the policies of other nation-states.[6]

Insecurity is an inherent part of the global political economy. International competition, which shapes the market, offers opportunities to accumulate great wealth, but it is also replete with risks and dangers. States and businesses only prosper to the extent that they can manage or eliminate threats. Events such as restrictions on exports, inflation, currency and interest rate fluctuations, trade deficits, defaults on debts, loss of market share, technological innovations, and pressures on interest rates can challenge a country's economic health. These are not necessarily threats to national security, but rather problems to be managed.[7]

Looking at Indonesia, economic activities are under the threat of losing their export markets. The high cost of production during the last few months of Soeharto's New Order era through the Habibie and Wahid governments had resulted in currency fluctuations. This is a great disadvantage for Indonesia especially since it has committed to the ASEAN Free Trade Area (AFTA) that will be realized beginning in 2003.

Security Measures

Imported raw materials for textile production pose a problem for the environment and security. Despite the richness in natural resources, Indonesia still relies on imported goods such as cotton and dye. Domestic raw materials like cotton are available, but they are below the required standards.

One of the challenges for export industries concerns the environment. To achieve environmental goals, trade measures are often used. Indonesia participates in a number of major international agreements relating to environmental management, and has implemented numerous aspects of these agreements. In accordance with the Montreal Protocol that seeks to protect the ozone layer by controlling the production and consumption of ozone depleting substances, Indonesia has taken an initial step by prohibiting chloroflorocarbons (CFCs) in the aerosol and cosmetic industries. Another environmental agreement is the Basel Convention on the Control of Transboundary Movements of Hazardous Wastes and their Disposal. Since Indonesia is a party to the Basel Convention, the Government of Indonesia issued Government Regulation No. 19 of 1994 concerning the management of hazardous wastes.

Environmental Security Measures for B Textile Products

Since security issues in this chapter relate to the textile industry and environmental measures, the discussion is on environmental standards affecting Indonesian textile products in its main export markets.

As already noted, a significant portion of Indonesian textiles are exported to European markets; one obstacle here is the eco-labelling schemes in selected European countries. The criteria set by different eco-labelling schemes for textile products affect the production of fiber and the textile manufacturing process. There is an emerging consensus in Europe on the need to encourage organic cultivation methods for the production of natural fibers. The Swedish scheme (BM), for instance, awards the A-label to products made only of fiber which has been produced following the principles of organic agriculture. The content of pesticides in fibers also is limited under the Nordic and the EU schemes. With regard to synthetic fibers, the EU establishes requirements for certain emissions and heavy metal residues, while the Nordic scheme only requires the manufacturer to provide information about emissions.

One of the most problematic parts of the textile industry with respect to production is the use of certain harmful dyes and pigments. The Swedish and EU schemes explicitly ban the use of certain dyes and pigments and demand a declaration from the manufacturer to verify this, while the Dutch and the Nordic schemes rely on indirect measurements of the dye and pigments in the composition of the final product. Proponents of less strict standards concerning heavy metal residues base their arguments on the difficulties in the testing methods for measuring heavy metal residues in final products. The most comprehensive and detailed water emission limits are applied under the Swedish scheme that considers, among others, the dye discharges into water B a parameter not included in other schemes.

Regarding energy consumption criteria, the EU and the Nordic schemes require detailed information on the consumption of energy and water during the different production phases, with the aim of incorporating the resource consumption requirements in future criteria. A further review of the different schemes reveals that the Dutch scheme allows the highest levels of formaldehyde concentration. The Nordic scheme sets more detailed criteria concerning the consumer health effects, while the EU scheme includes several criteria for occupational exposure. However, the Dutch scheme intends to include more criteria in the future, on the condition that agreements over the minimum requirements are reached in the bodies working on that particular issue. In terms of how to control and verify the compliance of the applicants with the eco-labelling criteria, the EU relies on the manufacturer's own declarations for certain aspects, whereas the Nordic and the Dutch schemes prefer to use clearly measurable criteria.

Within the EU, an important market for Indonesian textile products is Germany. Germany's International Society of Research and Testing in Textile Technology's Oeko-Tex standard 101 defines special conditions for granting the authorization to use the label Oeko-Tex for textile fabrics for clothing, with the exception of baby clothing. Apart from internationally recognized Oeko-Tex standard, there are two other schemes in Germany of which foreign textile producers have to be aware, namely the Toxproof certification and the Eco-tex scheme. The former is generally established for garments, whereas the latter requires participation in the Eco-tex Consortium. Membership in the Eco-tex Consortium is attainable only by large export companies that can afford the membership fee. One of the advantages of this scheme is that the frequently revised information about environmentally optimized production processes is distributed to all members.

It is also important to be aware of German legislation applying to textiles. The most dangerous substances B pentachlorophenol (PCP) and formaldehyde B fall under strict regulations. Use of PCP is banned. Compulsory labelling is required for the use of formaldehyde in excess of 1500 mg/kg since 1986. As well, arsenic, a carcinogenic substance that was used in protective clothing is banned. The EU has also launched a similar PCP regulation.

Outside Europe, Japan constitutes a major market for Indonesian textile exports. In Japan, criteria to obtain an Eco-Mark exist for unbleached towels, cloth diapers, cloth shopping bags, and textiles made from waste fibers. The established criteria are also based on an impact assessment of the entire product life cycle.

Environmental Considerations

Environmental Regulations

The Government of Indonesia (GI) has adopted several rules and regulations regarding environmental management. The latest is Act No. 23 of 1997 concerning the management of the living environment. The Act basically explains the aim and objectives of the government's environmental management: the rights, obligations, and role of public agents, the responsibilities of other key actors, and the mechanisms to control environmental impacts including sanctions for non-compliance.

The State Minister of Environment is responsible for coordinating the planning and implementation of the national policy on environmental management, as well as the enforcement of environmental laws and legislation. *Badan Pengendalian Dampak Lingkungan* B Environmental Impact Management Agency (BAPEDAL) was established in order to help the President manage environmental impacts of projects. BAPEDAL reports directly to the President. One of BAPEDAL's main duties is the implementation of environmental impact assessments, called *Analisis Mengenai Dampak Lingkungan* (AMDAL). BAPEDAL also sets up technical policies to protect the environment and to restore the quality of the existing environment.

According to the law, the public plays a very important role in environmental management. Everybody has an equal right to live in a healthy environment. The public has the right to know relevant information regarding the management of the environment. On the other hand, everybody is obliged to maintain the sustainability of the environment. The public, or its representative, has the right to bring any environmental disputes to court or to report them to a law enforcer.

In order to ensure conservation of the environment, the law establishes some control mechanisms. Any activity that exceeds environmental standards, or other criteria for environmental damage is not allowed. To anticipate any environmental problems that may occur, conducting an AMDAL is obligatory for activities expected to have significant environmental impact. The company or person who is in charge of an activity is responsible for the management of the waste released from it. There is also a specific provision for the management of hazardous and toxic substances that covers their production, transportation, distribution, and storage. The provisions under this law are detailed in Government Regulations and other legislation by lower bodies. Government Regulation No. 20 of 1990 concerns the control of water pollution, No. 51 of 1993 concerns the application of AMDAL, and No. 19 of 1994 concerns hazardous and toxic waste management that was amended under Government Regulation No. 12 of 1995.

According to these regulations, waste is categorized as hazardous and toxic if it is explosive, flammable, reactive, toxic, corrosive, infectious, and proven to be so through toxicological tests. The management of hazardous and toxic waste is monitored by BAPEDAL and is the responsibility of the firm that released the waste; if it fails to comply with the regulation, BAPEDAL will restore the damaged area, but the clean-up cost is borne by the responsible firm.

To improve the environmental performance of ongoing activities, the government through Act No.23 encourages the responsible firm or person to undergo an environmental audit. Although an environmental audit is not compulsory, the government has the authority to order the firm or person responsible to carry it out if they are suspected to have violated the existing environmental law. The cost for conducting the audit is borne by the particular firm or person. The Act also regulates sanctions for non-compliance, in the form of fines or a termination of the permit to run the business. Legal disputes over the environment can be settled in or out of court. Whoever intentionally causes environmental pollution or damage can be charged with a crime and can be jailed up to ten years and face a penalty as high as 500 million rupiahs.

Furthermore, it is noteworthy that the textile industry is not specifically mentioned in the list of industrial activities for which AMDAL is mandatory.[8] Setting up a textile factory might require an AMDAL if it is planned to be located near a protected site. However, environmental regulations have set standards for effluents released from the textile industry.[9] Environmental problems that can arise in a textile factory mostly concern the wastewater. The utilization of dyes in the production process can result in a chemically complex effluent since synthetic dyes take a long time to degrade. Therefore, the organic content of textile wastewater, measured by its chemical oxygen demand (COD) is usually very high.

Besides regulations released by the State Ministry of Environment, another important regulation is a decree issued by the Ministry of Industry, No.134/M/SK/1988. The legislation lists all industrial activities requiring Preliminary Impact Studies (PIA) or an Environmental Impact Analysis (EIA). The EIA must contain a detailed explanation of the process of production, the chemicals used, and a prediction of the impact of the particular factory on the environment, as well as the measures the firm has taken to counteract these likely impacts.

Although environmental regulations in Indonesia are quite strict and comprehensive, their enforcement leaves much to be desired. A lack of monitoring by the responsible government agencies is the main reason. Also, BAPEDAL does not have adequate resources to control the environmental impacts of projects. Cases of environmental disputes are often resolved in an unsatisfactory manner. One of the hindrances is insufficient environmental knowledge and understanding by the common civil law enforcers. For example, residents who live near the Muhamad Toha Industrial Area in Bandung have often suffered from wastewater flooding and none of the factories compensate for their discomfort.[10] The government itself occasionally neglects environmental considerations for the sake of development. Sometimes government's actions contradict environmental regulations, such as a President's decree that approved a reclamation project on the north coast of Jakarta covering an area of 2,700 hectares and a coastal tourist resort covering an area of 4,000 hectares. Such large-scale development projects are believed by many scientists to have significant negative impacts on the environment, especially of the vulnerable coastal zone.

Clean Production Technology

During the 1960s, the textile and garment industry in industrial countries was relatively *padat karya*, meaning that its economic weight was of utmost importance. Technology did not undergo many changes and generally, production consisted of standard products. The competition in such industries was generally based on price competition. However, during the 1970s and 1980s, many of these industries faced obstacles and had to adapt to challenges brought about by the slow growth in demand, different demand patterns, and rising competition from the newly industrialized countries of East Asia. These decades also brought vast changes in processing and production technology.

The changes in technology that have occurred in industrial countries have altered the competition in the international market. This is because such competition is no longer based on prices, but also technological innovations.[11] Technological capability consists of effective application, management, marketing, problem-solving, and new design capabilities. The purpose of such changes in technology varies from product differentiation, upgrading product quality, improvement in product design, labor saving technology, automatization, and speed of production.

Efforts to upgrade production technology of the textile industry include the development of synthetic fiber with a more up-to-date application of weaving techniques. Moreover, Japanese industries have developed a soft silk-like fabric made from polyester filament. Ways of developing product technologies have been undertaken by European and Japanese textile industries, where the domestic market for textiles has a relatively high demand for differentiation and quality. On the other hand, changes in production technology have the objective of reducing per-unit production costs by improving the speed of ring-frame machines, of open-end spinning machines, and of automatic transfer between various operations in the spinning industry. They also include improvements of conventional shuttle looms, the use of faster water jet looms, the use of shuttle-less looms in the weaving industry, and also faster knitting operations. The introduction of new technology is possible due to the availability of standard quality synthetic fiber at a cheap price. New technology in the textile industry is also common in the US. This is understandable because the US has a relatively large domestic market for quality textile material.

To what extent are textile producers in developing countries able to face new dimensions in the international competition? The answer depends on the extent to which they are capable of obtaining, mastering, and blending new technology inputs with their production process and the goods they produce.

For many industries, technology may be a key factor in competitiveness, but this is not the case for the Indonesian textile industry. In terms of machinery, many of the machines used in the Indonesian textile industry are imported. To renew technology would cost a considerable amount of money, especially since the economic crisis has drastically increased the prices of imported goods. Only the Texmaco group has maintained its Research and Development branch to manufacture textile machinery. However, thus far, they have not claimed that their products are technologically competitive and efficient.

Only 25 per cent of the machinery used was produced in the 1980s that, at a glance, indicates insufficient technological change. Old machinery usually requires higher maintenance costs and consumes more energy and water.[12] The use of old machinery contradicts the energy efficiency program established by the State Ministry of Mining and Energy (MME). From an environmental point of view, the use of old machines has caused faulty or lack of coordination among governmental sectors as the Ministry of Industry and Trade overruled the energy efficiency program proposed by the MME.

Textile factories in Indonesia are happy to maintain their relatively old machines for economic reasons. The production activity in the industry is performed without needing new technology. Management feels that the urgency of new and better technology is not a primary concern, for they can still produce textiles with their present machinery. However, neither old nor new machines are considered to be energy-efficient. Most of the machines are powered by and consume large amounts of electricity.

Environmental Implications for the Public

Sources of pollution are classified into three main categories: wastewater, airborne, and solid waste. Indicators such as the biological oxygen demand (BOD), toxicity, acidity/alkalinity, and the presence of metals characterize wastewater from the textile industry. The wet process is the main source of wastewater where every step of the process has its own wastewater characteristics. Wet processing requires a great deal of water and chemical inputs and consists of six main activities including desizing (starch, soda, and ash), scouring, merserizing (caustic soda, hydrochloric acid, suspended solids), bleaching (chlorine, sodium hypochlorite), and finishing (silicon, dissolved solids, detergent).

Air emissions from the textile industry are not considered to be significant. One source of air contamination is the combustion of fuels used in steam generation. Air pollution occurs during spinning, and the weaving and knitting of natural fibers since these processes produce dust. These processes require a factory to be equipped with dust collectors and filters to prevent this dust from being spread to the environment. In addition, sludge comes from wet processing and the wastewater treatment plant. The sludge contains chemicals, which may be toxic, thus, requiring waste treatment. Solid waste is produced during the dry processing stages.

Industrialization has always affected society. A case study of society's response to factories in four industrial firms in the Solo district shows the relationship between industry and society. The study surveyed one hundred inhabitants who lived near a textile factory and was conducted in September to October 1998.

In response to the issue of air pollution, 43 per cent of the survey group felt that industrial residue from the factory gives off an unpleasant odor. This is a majority since only 17 per cent responded that they were not disturbed by the smell. Most of the inhabitants near the factory obtain their water necessities from the state-owned Drinking Water Company (PAM), even if they believe their well water is contaminated by industrial waste. They still use the water provided by PAM for drinking and cooking. Many of the families have built wells outside their houses. However, many of these wells are only used for cleaning. This situation compromises their health since contaminated water can lead to skin diseases and irritation. Such disorders have indeed occurred, as 71 per cent of the respondents stated that they have been affected by skin or respiration problems. Most of these respondents contracted these diseases after the establishment of the factory in their community. At the same time, the factory management built lavatories for the community in order to provide a clean lavatory using PAM water, instead of water sourced from underground. Such disorders experienced by the respondents no doubt also apply to their families that usually live under the same roof. The public awareness of health concerns is still low; therefore, few people seek medical help for their disorders. They did, however, file complaints with the industry about various problems including the dust from the spinning process, the smoke, and the unpleasant smell of liquid waste from the dyeing process. From a social perspective though, the establishment of this factory has also brought prosperity to many people in the district as it has provided job opportunities.

Trade Barriers

Tariff Barriers

Tariffs are taxes applied to certain commodities entering or leaving a country. They include Ad Valorem tariffs, specific tariffs, and a combination of both. The former is a fixed percentage of a commodity's value while the latter is a tax that is applied to a commodity based on its physical number. Ad Valorem is more appropriate for manufacturing products. The function of tariff barriers is not merely to provide revenue to governments, but to protect domestic and foreign producers. The main agreement in AFTA was to eliminate tariff barriers in ASEAN countries by the year 2003.

On the one hand, the elimination of tariff barriers will enhance competitiveness of Indonesia's textile products in the world market. On the other hand, the elimination of tariff barriers will support other textile exporting countries to compete with Indonesian products. This challenge cannot be satisfied only by cheap labor, as is Indonesia's advantage, but must also be satisfied by research and development to improve the product quality.

Non-Tariff Barriers

Other barriers to trade are described as non-tariff. They include standard-testing procedures, custom classification and valuation of procedures and purchasers, local content rules, and health and safety standards. Usually non-tariff barriers are disadvantageous for developing countries wishing to export their products to European and other advanced countries because such criteria have not been properly implemented in developing countries. According to the UN Conference on Trade and Development (UNCTAD) classifications, non-tariff barriers are Type II barriers. Such classification was made in accordance with local commercial policy and often used as a tool to limit import access and stimulate exports.

For the last two decades, the definition of trade barriers is no longer restricted to treaties or other ratification. Issues relating to ideology, human rights, environment, as well as economic, political, and social problems, that do not necessarily occur within the production line, can now be classified as trade barriers. As a simple example, a pair of shoes made by prisoners cannot be exported to certain countries. This is based on human right concerns that center around the fact that only a small part of the profit goes to the maker and while most of it goes to the penal institution.

Environmental Labelling

Indonesia has increased its economic reliance on the export of manufactured commodities. However, international trade competition and trade blocs have affected the progress of Indonesian exports. Considering the growing environmental concerns of the importing countries and the use of eco-labelling by some countries, Indonesia has to respond to the demand for environmentally friendly produced and labelled products.

As discussed above, eco-labelling informs consumers by labelling products that are environmentally friendly, or less damaging than other unlabelled products. It aims at raising consumers' awareness of the environmental effects of the products and encouraging producers to shift to more environmentally friendly production processes.

Usually, the criteria for issuing environmental labels require an assessment of the ecological impacts over the entire life cycle of the product – from production, distribution and use, to consumption and disposal, popularly known as the cradle-to-grave approach. Accordingly, producers are likely to alter their manufacturing design and integrate environmental concerns into the entire production process. The use of eco-labelling is voluntary, but in the environmentally conscious markets, it may have the same effects as those of mandatory regulation. The effect of eco-labelling on developing countries depends on the product categories selected for eco-labelled products, as well as the compliance and the administrative costs of using labels.[13] So far the impacts of eco-labelling on developing countries' exports are considered insignificant because most eco-labelled products are not exported by developing countries. However, the possibilities of applying eco-labels to their primary export products, such as textiles, tropical timber, tropical timber products, paper, and footwear are already under consideration by the EU and other Organization for Economic Cooperation and Development (OECD) countries. This prospect raises concerns among producers in developing countries.

A number of developing countries and countries in transition have established their own eco-labelling programs (for example, India, Republic of Korea, Singapore, China, and Taiwan) or are in the process of doing so. As a commitment to the International Tropical Timber Organization's Agreement (ITTA) on achieving sustainable forest targets by the year 2000 and responding to the pressure from the European markets, Indonesia has started to set up a national eco-labelling program. Two bodies are responsible for developing the criteria for an Indonesian eco-label. The Indonesian Eco-labelling Institute (*Lembaga Ekolabel Indonesia*-LEI) which is responsible for developing eco-labelling criteria for timber products, and the BAPEDAL which is responsible for developing eco-labelling criteria for all other products.

In the current free trade era, trade measures have been increasingly used to ensure the effectiveness of international environmental agreements. Principle 12 of the Rio Declaration states that trade policy measures for environmental purposes should not constitute a means of arbitrary or a disguised restriction on international trade. It is stated that the regulation of environmental issues concerning transboundary or global environmental issues should be based on international consensus. Such consensus has emerged surrounding the trade of hazardous wastes in the form of the Basel Convention.

Indonesia has participated in a number of International Environmental Agreements (IEA) and recent initiatives related to environmental protection, such as the Montreal Protocol, the Basel Convention, the ISO 14000, and the ITTA. As a participant, Indonesia's policies, including those related to trade, have been directed towards addressing environmental issues. Various domestic programs, such as the eco-labelling and the business performance-rating program, have been developed to conform to the ISO 14000. Eco-labelling has been introduced as an effective method of directing production techniques toward more environmentally friendly techniques without relying on strict instruments such as trade bans. Indonesia has been ahead of other countries in the preparation for applying eco-labelling for timber products. This is because of the increasing pressures from the consuming countries, which require an assurance that all traded timber originates from sustainably managed forests.

Free Trade and Textile Security Issues

The crucial question is whether the pace of liberalization negatively affects the state of the environment. Although Indonesia confirmed its willingness to open its economy by issuing several deregulation packages in past years, it remains to be seen whether a substantial number of controls governing foreign trade will be dismantled in the future. Existing protected industries include assembled motorcars and motorcycles, certain textiles, and agricultural food items. With regard to the environmental implications of the future foreign direct investment flows to Indonesia, a 1995 NRMP study concluded that liberalization will help spread foreign direct investment more broadly across non-natural resource-based sectors and sectors based on renewable natural resources, thus offering the opportunity to reduce the rate of natural resource use. Furthermore, installing a less distorting trade regime will also increase the degree of value added processing of natural resources. This may result in a reduction of the natural resources content of each unit of income generated in Indonesia's resource-intensive sectors. However, future liberalization strategies should be viewed within the context of an ASEAN-wide harmonization of foreign direct investment and environment policies. Current academic work has so far neglected this issue and future research could provide fruitful findings for environmental policymakers.

The industry's behavior toward the environment currently is changing. Some factories have participated in environmental management codes, and in 1991, industries established the Declaration of the Business Council for Sustainable Development, which directs business activities to a secure and sustainable environment. This environmental awareness is implemented by counting the environment as a production factor. Thus, all environmental damage is internalized as a function of production costs. Such internalization is aimed to create an optimized allocation of natural resources. Therefore, on the one hand, consumers have demanded that the product and its operating industries to be soft on the environment, and on the other hand, the government has also set industry-related environmental regulations.

With free trade, the worst possibility will be degradation of the quality of the environment. Such phenomenon leads to trade restrictions in the form of environmental standards. Of course, with domestic regulations attached, the standard will vary from one country to another. Normally, the consumer standard in industrial countries is higher than in developing countries. Moreover, governments of industrialized countries have higher environmental regulations. That is why these governments often relocate their 'dirty' factories to developing countries. This is understandable since in their own country, industries are forced to obey their regulations with a threat of heavy sanctions if the regulation is ignored. By relocating factories to a country with more moderate regulations, such as developing countries, textile companies tend to have more freedom, since the developing countries offer cheap production costs and softer regulations.

Prospects of Free Trade

The main questions for us to ponder are: are we ready for free trade and is the textile industry in Indonesia prepared to face the reality of 2003? It is almost impossible for Indonesia to compete with other countries in the current export market, but to answer these questions it is best if we look at the problem as a whole.

The main problem for the Indonesian textile industry is its environment-related performance. Although Indonesia has fared well in the world market, especially in Europe, there is no guarantee that it can maintain this level of performance. The establishment of eco-labelling and the wide perception of trade barriers indicate that the public demand in years to come will be centered on health, environmental, and social matters. The public will stress whether a product can cause damage to their health and whether the process of production is environmentally friendly. Such criteria are a result of increased environmental awareness.

As for Indonesia, attaining the required standard means a speeded-up process. This is because Indonesia still lacks basic or essential systems such as law enforcement that supports the requirements of the free trade era. Indeed, the regulations concerning environmental conservation made by the Indonesian government have been applied to industries such as textiles, but even regulations are sometimes ignored due to poor awareness in the society and also in the government. The poor enforcement is visible in the form of complaints from the public concerning polluted areas, normally pertaining to the place where they live.

Infrastructure to accommodate the basic requirements of free trade in industries is still lacking. This has been demonstrated by the continuing use of old technology in the textile industry. Indeed, the current technology can accommodate the export target, but the current machinery is far from sustainable. During the next decade, energy will become scarcer than previously due to the depletion of conventional energy sources. If this continues up to the year 2003, it is possible that Indonesia's exporting ability could no longer maintain its previous accomplishments. Thus, in terms of quality, eco-labelling standards, or even non-tariff barrier classifications, the Indonesian textile producers would not be able to meet the public demand.

Another crucial question remains. Is the public ready for free trade? As the progress for better quality production would lead to higher production costs, this would impact on consumers as they would face higher prices. The people may be aware of environmental issues relating to production, but their consumption needs might overshadow such precious knowledge. Should Indonesia be static and not do anything, since there is still a possibility of a domestic market for the companies who cannot export their goods? In terms of export, the public most affected will be the workers.

Economic constraints cannot be used as a scapegoat all the time. Indonesia will have to improve its product standards in the near future should the country want to continue to compete with other countries in the international market. Physical infrastructure such as machinery may not be able to be invented in Indonesia in the near future, but industries should be able to subsidize the purchase of new and efficient technology from other countries. What should be dealt with seriously is not the physical infrastructure, for it is obtainable, but the mental infrastructure or mind set. To establish such infrastructure is time consuming, as it is closely related to individual behavior and culture. If the current mentality continues in Indonesia, then there will not be much change by the year 2003, and hence it will fail to help its producers to keep up with trade liberalization. On the other hand, Indonesia's position in world trade has been strong. Such a firm foundation is an incentive to further improve quality, standards of production, and maintain the sustainability of the environment.

Notes

1   Habib, A. H. (1996), 'Regional Security: Trends and Prospects', in Center for Strategic and International Studies (CSIS), *Regional Security Arrangements: Indonesian and Canadian Views*, CSIS, Jakarta.

2   Hill, H. (1992), *Indonesia's Textile and Garment Industries Development in an Asian Perspective*, ASEAN Economic Research Unit, Institute of South East Asian Studies, Singapore.

3   Center for Strategic and International Studies (CSIS) (1996), *Trade and Environment Linkages: A Case Study from Indonesia*, a report prepared for the ASEAN Secretariat by the Center for Strategic and International Studies.

4   *Kompas*, 10 January 1998.

5   *Kompas*, 3 October 1997.

6   Djiwandono, J. S. (1996), 'New Concepts of Security After the Cold War', in Center for Strategic and International Studies (CSIS), *The Role of Security and Economic Cooperation Structures in the Asia Pacific Region: Indonesian and Australian Views*, CSIS, Jakarta.

7   Trood, R. (1996), 'The Asia Pacific Region, Economics and New Concepts of Security', in *Ibid*.

8   State Minister of Environments Decree No: Kep-11/MENLH/3/1994.

9   State Minister of Environments Decree No: Kep-03/MENLH/1991.

10 *Republika*, 20 October 1998.

11 Wie, T. K. (1997), *Pengembangan Kemampuan Teknologi Industri di Indonesia*, University of Indonesia Press, Jakarta.

12 Zarili, S., *et. al.*, (eds) (1997), *Eco-Labelling and International Trade*, Macmillan Press, London.

13 *Ibid*.

References

Center for Strategic and International Studies (CSIS) (1996), *Trade and Environment Linkages: A Case Study from Indonesia*, CSIS, Jakarta.

Djiwandono, J. S. (1996), 'New Concepts of Security After the Cold War', in Center for Strategic and International Studies (CSIS), *The Role of Security and Economic Cooperation Structures in the Asia Pacific Region: Indonesian and Australian Views*, CSIS, Jakarta.

Habib, A. H. (1996), 'Regional Security: Trends and Prospects', in Center for Strategic and International Studies (CSIS), *Regional Security Arrangements: Indonesian and Canadian Views*, CSIS, Jakarta.

Hill, H. (1992), *Indonesia's Textile and Garment Industries Development in an Asian Perspective*, ASEAN Economic Research Unit, Institute of South East Asian Studies, Singapore.

Trood, R. (1996), 'The Asia Pacific Region, Economics and New Concepts of Security', in Center for Strategic and International Studies (CSIS), *The Role of Security and Economic Cooperation Structures in the Asia Pacific Region: Indonesian and Australian Views*, CSIS, Jakarta.

Wie, T. K. (1997), *Pengembangan Kemampuan Teknologi Industri di Indonesia*, University of Indonesia Press, Jakarta.

Zarili, S., *et. al.*, (eds) (1997), *Eco-Labelling and International Trade*, Macmillan Press, London.

Chapter 10

Environment and Security: Mitigating Climate Change while Strengthening Security

Agus P. Sari

Introduction

International pressures on developing countries to contribute to protecting the global environment, like mitigating climate change, are intensifying. Climate change is a phenomenon of the warming of the Earth due to the accumulation of heat-trapping ('greenhouse') gases in the atmosphere. For the majority of developing countries, committing to protecting the global environment is perceived to be a threat to their sovereignty, to their right to development, and, in turn, to their security. There are two arguments that are the basis for developing countries' refusal to limit their greenhouse gas emissions. First, today's accumulation of these gases is the result of chronic emissions by the industrialized countries since the nineteenth century. Second, while most developing countries' contribution to this accumulation has been negligible, their development needs may force them to emit more of these gases in the future. From these arguments sprung the 'common but differentiated' principle in the Climate Change Convention and its Kyoto Protocol.[1] But it is not clear that in practice limiting greenhouse gas emissions poses an absolute threat to developing countries' economic or sovereignty goals.

This chapter evaluates the underlying arguments behind the refusal of developing countries to limit their greenhouse gas emissions. Specifically, it assesses whether international environmental pressure is a real threat to the sovereignty of developing countries, and thus, to their security. It is argued that the relationship between climate change and security is complex. Climate change itself, as well as the absence of efforts to address it can be as much a threat to state and community security as the perceived sovereignty and security threats from efforts to limit greenhouse gas emissions. The analysis presented is based on Indonesia's involvement in the ten years of climate change negotiation. First, the broad notions of security, the global environment, climate change, and the linkages between them are explored. Then, by examining some sectoral case studies, the chapter presents an evaluation of emission reduction in Indonesia and shows that this situation threatens Indonesia's economic development and security.

What is Security?

Security can be defined at two levels: security of the state on the one hand, and of the community on the other. The state-centered approach defines security as being strongly associated with national sovereignty, whereas the community-centric approach is closely related to the security and well being of individuals. Often, the state and community definitions of security seem to be in conflict with each other.

As part of the legacy of World War II when most developing countries were still under colonial rule, security has been strictly defined in territorial and militaristic terms, centering on the state as the main actor needing to be protected. This definition was perpetuated by the cold war between the United States (US) and the former Soviet Union. Since the end of the cold war, global geopolitics has shifted towards the north-south divide between the developed and under-developed countries. This divide, as perceived by many in the south, is closely associated with dependency theory, with the north being closely associated with the center and the south with the periphery.[2] Due to the legacy of past colonialism, it is understandable that for many developing countries security has been defined as a state of independence from foreign interests.

What are Environmental Problems?

Economic development requires inputs from the environment and also produces waste to be absorbed or stored into the environment. Environmental problems occur when this process takes more inputs than the environment can regenerate, and when it produces more waste than the environment can absorb or store. In both cases, the capacity of the environment to sustain development will diminish. Eventually, the diminished quality of the environment will hinder the capacity of future generations to experience economic development. From this concern, the Brundtland Commission defined sustainable development as 'development that meets the needs of the present without compromising the ability of future generations to meet their own needs'.[3] Following this definition, sustainability is further defined as the inheritance by future generations of at least the same amount of capital in order to ensure they have the same opportunity to develop as the current generation. This capital for development includes physical, natural, human, and social dimensions.[4]

As the world has become globalized, so have environmental problems. In general, there are two main types of global environmental problems. The first are problems resulting from multinational activities, although the problems themselves may be most noticeable at the local level. Examples of this type of global environmental problems include the environmental impacts of trade liberalization or the environmental effects of the activities of multinational corporations. The second type of consists of problems which may occur simultaneously in many locations, but have global impacts. Examples of this type include climate change, ozone depletion, desertification, and loss of biodiversity. While recognizing the importance of both types of global environmental problems, the research on which this chapter was based focuses on the second type. While most of the findings are based specifically on the climate change case – and particularly from the case of Indonesia – more general theoretical lessons can be drawn.

What is Climate Change?

Climate change is a phenomenon caused by the warming of the Earth. This is due to the so-called greenhouse effect, which is a necessary and natural phenomenon caused by the presence and accumulation of greenhouse gases in the atmosphere. These gases act like a blanket that keeps heat contained in the Earth's atmosphere. The most prominent of these gases are carbon dioxide (CO_2) and methane (CH_4). If not for the greenhouse effect, the Earth would be 32 degrees Celsius (°C) colder than it is now. Much of the greenhouse effect leads to excessive global warming and, in turn, climate change.

The accumulation of greenhouse gases in the atmosphere is caused mainly by the combustion of fossil fuels (coal, oil, and natural gas) and biomass since the beginning of the industrial revolution in the 1800s. The secondary cause of the accumulation of greenhouse gases is land-use change that leads to a reduction of forest cover, or deforestation.[5] CO_2 is released mainly by the burning of forests and wood-waste during the land-clearing process. Deforestation also leads to a release of CO_2 and other greenhouse gases from the soil into the atmosphere since wood decay in the soil releases CH_4. Finally, since forests absorb CO_2, depletion of forest cover will reduce the amount of carbon removal that offsets carbon emissions.

There is more agreement than not that there is a correlation between the increase of the concentration of these gases in the atmosphere and the increase of the Earth's average temperature. The concentration levels currently increase at a pace never experienced prior to the industrial revolution. For example, the atmospheric CO_2 concentration was about 360 ppm (parts per million, by volume) in 1990, already one-fourth higher than in the pre-industrial era. The concentration of CH_4, 1.72 ppm, was more than twice of that in the pre-industrial era.[6]

The Intergovernmental Panel on Climate Change (IPCC) expects that an increase in global mean temperature of between 1° to 3.5°C may occur when the concentration of CO_2 doubles the levels measured prior to the industrial revolution. To avoid this from happening, the IPCC suggests a deep and immediate cut of 60 to 80 per cent of current levels of greenhouse gas emissions in order to stabilize the current atmospheric concentration. Although the IPCC acknowledges the uncertainty that is inherent in its modeling, it repeatedly states that 'uncertainty does not reduce risks'.[7]

Environment and Security Nexus: Are the Pressures Real?

Climate change and attempts to address it – as with other global environmental problems – threaten security in a number of ways. First, climate change is largely due to the historical combustion of fossil fuel in the industrialized countries. The impact of this, however, will affect Indonesia and other developing as well as industrialized countries. Climate change will result in reduced agricultural productivity, which will threaten food supply. It will also result in other problems including the rise of sea levels which will increase the risks of flooding productive lands, the spread of vector- and water-borne diseases, and the increased occurrence of other natural disasters due to an increase in the average temperature and extremes of precipitation. Many countries have already experienced these impacts.

Second, abating climate change may accrue costs for Indonesia as well as other countries. These include the political and economic costs of limiting the problem itself as well as the costs of containing development options that possibly occur along the way. This argument is still the subject of a prolonged debate. Indonesia shares other developing countries' concerns that pressures for global environmental protection may hurt the nation's sovereignty, as it is perceived as derailing national development priorities, and therefore, threatening its security. There is already a deep-seated concern over whether the nation-state, as a sovereign actor with absolute authority over its physical territory, can address transboundary ecological problems.[8] Climate change may be the ultimate transboundary ecological problem since its scope is truly global.

From Science to Politics

Climate change was first discussed in an international political forum at the 1988 Conference on the Changing Atmosphere in Toronto, Canada. This conference called for 'immediate action by governments, the United Nations (UN), and their specialized agencies ...to counter the ongoing degradation of the atmosphere', and to urge 'the development of a comprehensive global convention as a framework for protocols on the protection of the atmosphere'.[9] In the same year, the United Nations General Assembly convened the First World Climate Conference, and mandated the development of the Framework Convention on Climate Change. Co-sponsored by the United Nations Environment Programme (UNEP) and the World Meteorological Organization (WMO), IPCC was established in November 1988.

In July 1989, a G-7 Summit in Paris stated that it was 'strongly advocating common efforts to limit emissions of CO_2 and other greenhouse gases which threaten to induce climate change'. At the Second World Climate Conference in 1990, Mostafa Tolba, then Executive Director of UNEP, proposed a framework climate treaty entitled 'Law of the Atmosphere'. This conference was the landmark for the formation of the Intergovernmental Negotiating Committee for a Framework Convention on Climate Change (INC-FCCC, or INC). The FCCC was finally adopted and signed by most countries at the Earth Summit in 1992, and entered into force in 1994. Six months after the Convention entered into force, the first Conference of Parties (COP) was held in Berlin, Germany.

The Third COP, held in Kyoto, Japan, was another milestone in the international politics of climate change. At this COP, a Protocol to the FCCC, the Kyoto Protocol, was adopted. However, far from the IPCC's recommendation of a 60 to 80 per cent emissions-reduction to stabilize atmospheric concentrations of greenhouse gases, the

Protocol only commits the 39 industrialized countries to reduce their collective emissions by 5.2 per cent from their average 1990 levels by the period between 2008 and 2012. The specific commitments range from a decrease of eight per cent by the European Union (EU) member countries collectively, seven per cent by the US, six per cent by Japan, to an increase of eight per cent by Australia and ten per cent by Iceland.

The pressures on developing countries The last session of the INC, just prior to the Earth Summit, mandated the First Conference of the Parties (COP) of the Convention to review the adequacy of commitments in the climate convention. In its First COP meeting in Berlin in 1995, all countries agreed that current commitments by the parties to the Convention were not adequate to meet the Convention's objectives. Some industrialized countries argued that no matter how deeply their emissions are reduced, they would not be adequate unless developing countries are committed to limiting their future emissions. The Berlin Mandate, the main result of the First COP, recognizes the inadequacy of the commitments, but calls on only the industrialized countries to reduce emissions and allows developing countries to increase their emissions.

Disregarding the Berlin Mandate, the call made mainly by the US for meaningful participation of key developing countries was prominent at the negotiation of the Kyoto Protocol. Domestic politics in the US instigated the Senate's refusal to ratify the Protocol without developing country participation. An apparent reason for the pressure on developing countries is the fear that emissions from developing countries have grown two times more rapidly than those from the industrialized countries. Between 1900 and 1995, CO_2 emissions from developing countries grew 5.7 per cent per year, while those from the industrialized countries grew 2.3 per cent. If not controlled, emissions from the developing countries will exceed those from the industrialized ones soon after the turn of the millennium, as early as 2010.[10]

Responses from developing countries The call for developing-country participation (mainly made by the US) generates a mixed reaction, especially from developing countries. Collectively under the umbrella of the Group of 77 (G-77), developing countries reject this call on three grounds. First, on a per capita basis, they argue that emissions from developing countries are still very low, and that the industrialized countries' historical emissions far exceed those from the developing countries. Thus, the responsibility lies with the industrialized countries to limit current and future emissions and to remove the build-up from the decades of past emissions. Second, on a legal basis, the Climate Change Convention, the Kyoto Protocol, and the Berlin Mandate already exclude developing countries from any requirement to limit emissions. Thus, under these agreements, it is unlawful to require developing countries to limit emissions. Third, from a factual point of view, developing countries have undertaken, and are still undertaking voluntary domestic actions that limit their current and past emissions. Oftentimes, these actions contribute more to limiting emissions globally than those undertaken by industrialized countries.[11]

At the same time, there are a number of developing countries that have announced their willingness to voluntarily commit to limiting their emissions to internationally binding, quantitative objectives. At COP4, Kazakhstan announced its intention to join the countries listed in Annex I of the Protocol, while Argentina, in a speech by President Carlos Menem, announced its intention to evaluate the possibility of having a voluntary commitment by the next COP. The small island states of Nauru and Niue followed suit. Earlier, South Korea had announced its intention to quantitatively limit its current and future emissions.

Nevertheless, in general, developing countries assert that the call for them to reduce their greenhouse gas emissions is based on two false assumptions. First, it is false to assume that the US is the only country that disproportionately bears the burden of reducing global greenhouse gas emissions. Second, it is false to assume that developing countries are free riders – that is, that they are doing nothing to limit their current and future emissions. In addition, if there is enough incentive, more developing countries will be willing to make voluntary commitments.

Indonesia and Climate Change

The Impact of Global Warming in Indonesia

The increase in global average temperature is expected to lead to severe damages in Indonesia ranging from sea-level rise to other, more frequent natural disasters such as the recent devastating El Niño and La Niña phenomena. Climate change is also expected to lead to an increase in the incidence of various diseases. An increase in the average temperature in Indonesia may lead to an increase in sea level and a change in the precipitation of rainfall, causing serious problems of drought and flooding.[12]

The most devastating impact of climate change on Indonesia is the loss of food security, because unusual patterns of droughts and floods combined with the warming of the Earth will devastate food crops. Impoverished Indonesians will suffer the most from the scarcity of food. While Indonesia is rapidly industrializing, agriculture is still a significant sector in the economy. Traditional farmers whose life and livelihood are dependent on the agricultural sector will suffer, and they are already at the bottom end of the economic ladder.

The combination of an increase in temperature and rainfall may also lead to more incidences of infectious and non-infectious diseases. Some direct public health impacts have already been recorded with regard to global warming, namely climatic stress, heat disorders, skin cancer, alteration of immune response, and cataracts. Indirect public health impacts include changes in agricultural practices that will affect mosquito-borne, snail-borne, and water-borne diseases. Also, overcrowding and malnutrition will likely increase the incidence of tuberculosis, measles, and the bubonic plague. Finally, sea-level rise and resettlement following the construction of dams will lead to inadequate sanitation and the increase of vector-borne and other communicable diseases.[13]

Hosting one of the longest coastlines in the world, Indonesia will suffer significantly from a rise in sea level. Various economically significant places, from beach resorts in Bali to waterfront communities in Jakarta, will be inundated. A sea-level rise will also affect public facilities such as ports, low-lying maritime and other facilities, creating enormous economic losses. About two million people currently live in places less than two meters above sea level, and this number will grow to more than three million by the middle of the 21st century. National parks in Indonesia as well as in other parts of the world will be damaged irreversibly by climate change.

Adapting To Climate Change

Of course, Indonesia may have the option of adapting to global warming. Some streets and railway tracks can be elevated, and flood and control facilities constructed. Coastal communities that depend upon marine and coastal resources will have to overcome the disruption of these ecosystems. Fishing communities, already among the nation's poorest, will need support in making the transition to new livelihoods.

Nevertheless, the cost of adaptation is not trivial. From sea-level rise alone, based on annual rent rates, the cost of the loss of 3.4 million hectares (has) of land due to a half-meter rise in sea level is expected to amount to approximately US$11 billion (in 1990 dollars). Replacing typical housing of people living in the affected rural and urban areas by sea-level rise that are about 3.4 million people would cost approximately US$8 billion. The estimates for national economic loss due to infrastructure damages may amount to approximately US$12 billion. The costs of the increased incidence of malaria, dengue fever, and diarrhea alone would amount to an increase of approximately US$65 billion in the annual cost of health care. These are not even the entire costs associated with global warming adaptation. There are many more indirect costs associated with the disruption of economic development, and there are many more impacts that need to be identified.

Options to Mitigate Global Warming

It is obvious that Indonesia alone can do very little to halt climate change. While Indonesia is considered a 'big emitter' among the ranks of developing countries, it accounts for less than two per cent of the total global emissions of CO_2. In contrast, the US accounts for roughly one-quarter of total global emissions. To put this in perspective, it would require seven average Indonesians to emit the same amount of one average American. If only the emissions from energy-use are taken into account, it would require 32 average Indonesians to emit the same amount of an average American. These disparities in levels of emissions as well as in economic development complicate the intergovernmental negotiation process.

Out of the approximately 700 million tons of CO_2 emitted by Indonesia in 1990, approximately 450 million tons, about four-fifths, came from land-use change, mostly in the forestry sector. As explained above, when forests are cleared, CO_2 is released through the burning of the forests, the burning of wood-waste, and from exposure of the soil by the release of CH_4 from wood decay. Since forests absorb CO_2, clearing forests reduce the capacity of the Earth to absorb the excessive emissions.

The rest of the emissions from Indonesia came from energy production (145 million tons, approximately one-fifth) and industrial processes (five million tons). Emissions from the energy sector are growing very rapidly. Eventually, emissions from the energy sector will surpass those from land-use change and forestry. Thus, it is safe to claim that future emissions will be dominated by the energy sector.

The Forestry Sector

What will be the impacts of reducing deforestation in Indonesia? Will it threaten or actually strengthen security? How much does Indonesia actually gain from the forestry sector? And who gains the most benefits? The most common argument against reducing deforestation is that the forestry industry brings in large amounts of foreign exchange revenues, and that it employs many Indonesians. Thus, a drop in production in this sector may lower state income and create unemployment. This belief merits a second look, however, as it has already been demonstrated that forest management in Indonesia is increasingly more unsustainable, and the rate of deforestation is quite alarming.

The high greenhouse gas emissions from the forestry sector in Indonesia are caused by the rapid rate of deforestation. Until 1990, Indonesia lost more than one million has. of forests every year, and these figures may still be current.[14] The extent of the lack of sustainability of the forestry industry in Indonesia is indicated by the excessive pressure from manufacturers of forest products. In 1990, its existing sawmills and plywood factories required as much as 80 million cubic meters (m^3) of round logs annually. This amount exceeds the capacity of the available forests. The existing concessions could only provide 30 million m^3 while production forests could only provide 22 million m^3. As a result, the choices are to let the sawmills and plywood factories run at less than their optimal load, to supply the required logs from protected forests or stolen woods, or a combination of both. This calculation excludes additional pressures put on the timber industry by pulp and paper factories that claimed to have their own plantations, but whose production capacity far exceeds the possible amount of wood provided by their plantations.[15] Due to the high rate of deforestation, only 90 million has., or 62 per cent, of the total tropical forests remained in Indonesia in 1990. Meanwhile, 12.5 million has. were to be converted for various uses, ranging from transmigration to plantations. From the 77.5 million has. of remaining forests, only 39 million has – or approximately half – still have the potential to be harvested in a sustainable way. In 1990, a government policy to encourage forestry sector development created nearly 600 logging concessions that cover over 60 million has. of production and conversion forests, 296 sawmills, and 119 plywood factories.[16]

The forestry industry in Indonesia is a rent-seeking industry where access to the right people in the bureaucracy is instrumental. It is also largely an oligopolistic and vertically integrated industry, which results in the under-pricing of forest resources and excessive profits enjoyed by the producers or concession holders. More than half of the 65 million has. of forest concessions in Indonesia are held by only 20 Jakarta-based conglomerates.[17] These concession holders are associated in a cartel, the Association of Forest Concession Holders (*Asosiasi Pengusahaan Hutan* Indonesia,

APHI). The chair of the association is the third largest concession holder in Indonesia, and is also a close acquaintance of Soeharto, Indonesia's former President.

The strong lobby by the cartel has left the forestry industry heavily protected. The export of round logs from Indonesia was banned in 1985. This policy completely eliminated foreign industries that use Indonesian logs, but nurtured those within Indonesia. Many of the emerging companies in Indonesia, however, were sister companies of the concession holders. The replacement of the total ban in 1992, with an overwhelmingly high tariff barrier maintained this protection.

As a result of the heavy protection, logs were under-priced because they were sold from one company to another within the same group. While the freight-on-board (FOB) price of logs from Sabah, Malaysia was $145 per m^3, Indonesia's was around $95. Assuming that the logs from Indonesia are similar to those from Malaysia and that the world market price equals the willingness of the world consumers to pay, then the price of Indonesian logs should also have been $145per m^3. Using this willingness to pay as the potential economic rent, the rent obtained in Indonesia by the government was only 17 per cent of the world price in 1990, and had increased from only 8 per cent in 1988. This amount is very low, especially compared with economic rent obtained by the government from the oil sector that could easily reach 75 per cent.[18] In the case of East Kalimantan, only five per cent of the rent actually goes to the local government.[19] Moreover, the presence of forest concessions in West Kalimantan caused a severe reduction, more than 50 per cent, in the local community's incomes.[20]

Indeed, in 1989, the value of exports of forest products contributed $3.5 billion, more than 15 per cent of total export value and comprised more than half of total non-oil export value. Between 1983 and 1989, however, the contribution from the forestry sector to domestic income was a mere one per cent. Within the agriculture sector, forestry only contributed between four to five per cent of the total value added. The forestry sector grew at the low rate of 1.4 per cent per year, much lower than the four per cent growth rate of the entire agriculture sector, and the seven per cent growth rate of the entire economy prior to the current financial crisis.

All of these facts may lead to questioning the claim that the forestry sector is a major contributor to economic development in Indonesia. More so, the facts cast doubt on the sector's actual contribution to local economies. The chip used by Indonesian negotiators in the climate change convention that Indonesia needs to deforest because it needs to alleviate poverty at home may not be as strong as it seems.

The Energy Sector

The energy sector has a double-edged role in the Indonesian economy, namely, to earn foreign exchange and to fuel industrialization. Oil has been the backbone of Indonesian economic development. For a long period, oil dominated Indonesia's exports. As fuel for industrialization, domestic energy has been generated mainly by oil, albeit decreasingly so.

On the energy production side, 90 per cent of crude oil in Indonesia is produced in the provinces of Aceh, East Kalimantan, and Riau. Cumulatively, Riau has been the major producer of exportable crude oil, contributing half of the total. Oil has also been a major industry in Riau that contributes two-thirds of the total regional output. However, Jakarta absorbs the surplus from the oil industry through *Pertamina*, the Indonesian state-owned oil company, and foreign corporations. While these regions contribute significantly to the national economy, their populations remain some of the poorest in the country.[21]

Similar to the production side, national and per capita figures of the growth in energy demand are unable to capture the disparity of energy consumption patterns in different locations. There are highly differentiated household energy consumption patterns between Jakarta, other urban cities, and the rural areas in Indonesia. The use of electricity for cooking in Jakarta is almost three times higher than the national average. While wood dominates fuel for cooking, the fuel of choice in Jakarta is kerosene, chosen by four-fifths of its households in 1990. Similarly, in 1990, 96 per cent of Jakarta's households used electricity for lighting, and the remaining four per cent used kerosene, while kerosene lamps dominated the national total. At the same time, ownership of television sets by Jakarta's households is more than three times the national average. While reportedly 67 per cent of households in Jakarta own a television set, this figure seems to be underestimated.[22] This striking difference between urban and rural areas in Indonesia makes the national average figures practically meaningless.

The Urbanites' Contribution

While all urban dwellers in the capital and largest city of Jakarta enjoy easy access to electricity, only half of those on the island of Java actually have access to electricity. Nationwide, less than one-quarter of Indonesian households actually have access to electricity. These figures suggest that rural households in remote areas of the country are largely without electricity.

Urban areas are also the most industrialized portions of Indonesia. Thus, energy efficiency in the industrial sector can be considered an instrumental way of limiting emissions generated from urban activities. Moreover, energy efficiency makes sense economically. From industrial to household sectors, energy efficiency means reducing overall production costs and increasing competitiveness in the world economy.[23] The potential overall energy savings that could be made between 1995 and 2000 is as much as 160 million Barrels of Oil Equivalent (MBOE), worth more than Rp7 trillion (US$700 million, at the 1998 exchange rate). The most significant saving is expected from the industrial sector, as much as 93 MBOE, while the energy saving target for the commercial and residential sectors is 23 MBOE. These targets will be achieved if all energy conservation tasks for every government agency (including ministries), as specified in the national plan for energy conservation *Rencana Induk Konservasi Energi Nasional* (RIKEN), are undertaken successfully.[24]

In the future, the transportation sector is expected to be the largest emitting sector in Indonesia, especially when the country undergoes major urbanization. This is mainly due to the increased need for greater mobility that leads to an increase in passenger car ownership and an increased need to distribute goods and services throughout the country. Again, Jakarta leads with more than seven times the national average in passenger car ownership since 14 per cent of its households own passenger cars while on average of only 3.5 per cent of all Indonesians do.[25] For each car in Jakarta, a typical commuter emits about one ton of CO_2 per year.[26]

As has already taken place in Singapore, the combination of congestion-pricing – tolling, restricting, and licensing road use – and development of better public transit in Jakarta will reduce the use of private vehicles as the dominant mode of transportation. Cutting fuel subsidies will discourage the use of private vehicles even more. Moreover, switching fuels from gasoline to natural gas in the non-transport sector will reduce urban pollution, whereas urban re-greening will absorb most of the pollution from transportation. Continuing the sound transportation policy already in place in Jakarta will save at least five per cent of the CO_2 emissions from the transportation sector of the entire country.[27]

Options for the Rural Sector

Rural households in remote areas for generations have been utilizing traditional, but renewable sources of energy such as biomass. Indeed, non-commercial energy sources account for more than one-third of the total energy supply in Indonesia. Access for these households to commercial electricity is provided through the rural electrification program that is, in itself ambitious, given the present low rate of electrification in the country. For these areas, providing electricity from renewable energy sources, such as the combination of solar and wind power plants is believed to be economically more attractive than diesel or other fossil fuel-based sources. For some remote areas, the amount of fuel required to transport is more than the amount of fuel actually being transported. The use of renewable energy sources also produce much less local pollution, if any. It is also better for people's health. Already on the drawing board is a plan to install one million solar home systems in rural households in Indonesia under the government's '50 MWp' (Megawatt-peak) program of the Agency for Technology Assessment and Application (BBPT).[28]

The two case studies below illustrate the environmental implications of applying renewable technology in the rural areas of Indonesia. One case study is located in the village of Sukatani on the island of Java. The other is in the more remote villages near the city of Ende in East Nusa Tenggara. These villages were chosen in order to compare whether location is a major factor with respect to the environmental and economic implications of applying renewable technology.

The Sukatani case As the initial pilot project for assessing and experimenting with the solar home system, BPPT picked a hamlet in the Sukatani village, roughly 80 kilometers (km) southwest of Jakarta, and installed a 5.5 kilowatt-peak (KWp) solar panel. Before the solar home system was installed in the village, the nearest power outlet was about 20 km from Sukatani. The cost to extend the grid would have been about US$5,000 per km for low voltage and US$10,000 per km for high voltage.[29]

Without electricity, most of the villagers were unable to conduct activities after dark. At night, they used kerosene-fueled wick lamps, *lampu centir*. These lamps were estimated to consume about a liter of kerosene daily. In addition to being more polluting, greenhouse gas-emitting, dangerous, and expensive sources of lighting, the lamps are only able to produce illuminations that at best create a 'twilight effect'.[30]

Access to electricity implied a seven to ten-fold increase in lighting (*lumens*), mainly because of the increased efficiency of electric lights compared to kerosene lamps.[31]

When the solar home system finally reached the Sukatani villagers, schools have been able to open after dark. Students have been able to learn basic knowledge in the mornings, and learn to read the *Qur'an* – an important aspect of life in that area – in the evenings. When the students go home, they are able to watch news, movies, or the World Cup in their black and white television sets, listen to radios, or for the diligent, study and do their homework in the evenings. School attendance has risen especially for high schools. Every evening, there are about 150 students who come to the *madrasah* to learn to read *Al Qur'an*.

Assuming a 40-year lifetime, the average cost of the solar home system is 17 cents per kilowatt-hour (kwh). The excessive government subsidy for the state-owned electric utility's *Perusahaan Listrik Negara* (PLN), electricity makes it difficult to compare the cost of electricity produced by the solar home system with that produced by PLN. The cost of producing electricity using a small diesel home system ranges between three cents using the subsidized diesel oil price of Rp550 (seven cents) per kwh, and four cents using the unsubsidized price of Rp630 (9 cents) per kwh. In this case, the price of solar power is still very high, roughly twice as much as that of diesel.

The Ende case The district of Ende is located on the island of Flores among the East Nusa Tenggara compound of islands, roughly 1500 km east of Jakarta. There are already 4.5 kw solar home systems installed in Ende. This remote island is inhabited by only 223,000 people, or 110 people per square km. The case study was conducted in the villages of Beramari (about 16 kms outside the city of Ende), Tendambepa (64 km away), and Tomberabu II (roughly 17 km away). In general, all three villages have similar characteristics. Most of the villagers are farmers, with an average income of Rp5000 (67 cents) per day. All live in typical hamlets where the distance between one another is quite far. In Beramari, for instance, the average distance between its four hamlets is around three kms, and the distance from the main road to the nearest hamlet is approximately six kms. The dirt roads separating the hamlets are very slippery when wet and are not suitable for cars.

Given their rough terrain and the low population density, it is easy to understand why the State Electricity Company, PLN, has not provided service for these villages. It would not be cost-effective for PLN to try to build a grid 10 or more kms in length to provide electricity for only 200 villagers whose need for electricity does not exceed 250 kwh daily. Since the distance between villages is far, supplies are provided and sold only irregularly. Villagers can only buy their supplies at a weekly market. When the supply of kerosene is inadequate, then the villagers have to go all the way to the sub-district market. However, there is only one car per 207 heads in Ende,[32] causing most villagers to walk to the market, a distance of about 18 km in order to buy kerosene. A round trip journey of this kind can take one full day.[33]

In the case of Sukatani, diesel is cheaper, costing much less than using a solar home system unit that costs 17 cents per kwh. Meanwhile, in Ende, the best scenario of generating electricity with a four kw diesel generator for 70 households per village is 11.2 cents/kwh, after taking into account the cost of fuel, operation, maintenance, and transportation. In the worst case scenario, say for a village of only 15 households, the generating cost would be around 40 cents per kwh. Thus, for remote villages such as Ende, it is even more economically sound to develop the solar home system.

The Indonesian Villagers' Contribution to Global Environment

These small villages, Sukatani and Ende, have contributed to limiting future emissions of greenhouse gases. The change from the use of kerosene lamp to the solar home system avoids the burning of kerosene that emits both carbon and sulfur dioxide. Assuming that each kerosene wick lamp uses a liter of kerosene daily, the amount of CO_2 emissions that are not made by both the Sukatani and Ende villagers is 3,500,000 liters every year, since 10,000 households obtain their electricity from a solar home system of 50 w. If the villages had used diesel instead of the solar home system, the diesel generator would require about 350,000 liters of diesel fuel. This would amount to approximately three tons of CO_2 emissions annually. While for villages in Java, such as Sukatani, the amount of the CO_2 saved may cost the villagers money, for remote villages such as Ende, the CO_2 savings come with economic benefits. If the 50 MWp campaign is successful, and 50 MWp solar home systems are installed throughout Indonesia's rural households, the amount of CO_2 gas emissions saved will be about 300 tons annually.

While in Sukatani it costs about nine cents more for each kwh for solar power, it may save villagers in Ende up to 31 cents for each kwh. Both Sukatani and Ende, of course, represent extreme cases. Everywhere else in Indonesia will fall between these two extremes. But still, by examining these two cases, one can interpolate the economic benefits of using solar home systems in Indonesia. These two cases show that investing in non-CO_2 emitting energy technologies may actually result in economic benefits. The environmental benefits of avoiding technologies that produce air pollution such as fossil fuel-based technologies, or the ones that require massive resettlements such as large hydropower dams are also significant.

Implications for the Environment-Security Debate and for Policy Development

Policies designed to limit CO_2 emissions might help correct Indonesia's development strategy that is potentially unsustainable. Moreover, the unsustainable development pattern in Indonesia is also aggravated by the inequitable development pattern between Jakarta and the rest of Indonesia. Additionally, while energy efficiency may lead to a net benefit to the whole economy by making the Indonesian economy more competitive in the world market, decentralized renewable energy sources may help poor Indonesian villages in remote areas gain access to commercial energy. In sum, limiting greenhouse gas emissions and joining global efforts to mitigate global warming may lead to an overall strengthening of the Indonesian economy.

If limiting current and future greenhouse gas emissions and contributing to the global efforts to mitigate climate change are good for Indonesia, why are these efforts resisted? The first possible reason might lie in the state's approach to national sovereignty.[34] If the definition of sovereignty is state-centric, then limiting greenhouse gas emissions in Indonesia will be seen as a threat to state sovereignty because of the false perception that limiting emissions disadvantages rather than benefits the economy. But if the definition of sovereignty is to be broadened and made comprehensive to include that of the community, then the entire sovereignty argument is challenged. If the villagers in Sukatani and Ende were to speak of their individual security after they enjoyed the solar home systems, they would argue otherwise.

Second, as is the case with other environmental issues, climate change is a long-term issue. Thus, unless there is a link between it and more short-term issues, there would be no sense of threat, or insecurity felt in Indonesia. In addition to linking long-term with short-term problems, linking global issues such as climate change with more local issues will put it into the context of the daily lives of Indonesians. Thus, the costs and benefits associated with addressing the global issue will have a local context. In turn, the local context – especially the local benefits – will engender a willingness to take action.

Third, since climate change and the reduction of global greenhouse gas emissions are issues dealt with at an inter-governmental level, the smallest unit of analysis at this level is the nation state. This further reinforces the state-centric approach that obscures sub-national interests. Looking at the diversity at the sub-national level would capture the different notions of sovereignty applied in different levels. Oftentimes, state-level interests conflict with the ones at the community level.

The insistence on the 'right to development', while starting from a noble concern, may be misleading. Indeed, dividing the world into a North and a South is a gross simplification of a much more complicated world, many aspects of which cannot be simplified. The north-south divide exists globally, regionally, and domestically. Oftentimes, regional and domestic inequities are more severe than global ones. Contrary to what many developing-country negotiators may argue, policies and measures to combat climate change are, in many cases as beneficial locally and domestically as they are globally. Finally, since addressing climate change may have both economic and environmental benefits, it actually strengthens rather than weakens state-centric security in the long run.

There are lessons to be learned from these cases and their elaboration. Also, the following policy recommendations are indicated by these cases:

1. **Link long-term environmental problems such as climate change with more short-term contexts**.
   As with other environmental problems, climate change is a long-term problem. Few governments – developing and industrialized countries alike – are willing to

invest in abating them. Pointing to parallel benefits that are more short-term (providing rural electricity with half the price, for example), will increase the willingness of governments to take action more immediately.

2. **Link global with local interests**.
    Climate change is one of the most global of environmental problems. Linking this problem with more pressing local problems – for example, linking climate change with local air pollution problems – will engender and likely spur immediate attention from the stakeholders.

3. **Link environmental with developmental interests**.
    For most developing countries, environmental issues take a back seat compared with more pressing developmental issues such as poverty alleviation. Linking long-term environmental issues with developmental issues is crucial in winning stakeholders' attention.

Notes

1   United Nations General Assembly (UNGA) (1992), *United Nations Framework Convention on Climate Change*, United Nations, Rio de Janeiro, Brazil; United Nations Framework Convention on Climate Change (UNFCCC) (1997), *The Kyoto Protocol to the United Nations Framework Convention on Climate Change*, UNFCCC, Kyoto, Japan.

2   Frank, A.G. (1966), 'The Development of Underdevelopment', *Monthly Review*, vol.18, no.4; Gerschenkron, A. (1962), *Economic Backwardness in Historical Perspective*, Belknap, Cambridge.

3   World Commission on Environment and Development (WCED), also known as the Brundtland Commission, *Our Common Future*, 1987, pp.43.

4   Serageldin, I. (1994), *Sustainability and the Wealth of Nations: A Work in Progress*, World Bank, Washington, DC; The World Bank (1997), *Expanding the Measure of Wealth: Indicators of Environmentally Sustainable Development*, Environmentally Sustainable Studies and Monographs Series no.17, The World Bank, Washington, DC.

5   The term 'deforestation' is as contestable as the term 'forest' itself. Depending on the definition of both, the figures may vary. To clarify the confusion, the IPCC is currently undertaking a study towards a Special Report on Land Use, Land Use Change, and Forestry.

6   See Houghton, J.T. *et al.* (eds) (1990), *Climate Change 1990: IPCC Scientific Assessment*, United Nations Environment Program and World Meteorological Organization, Geneva; Houghton, J.T. *et al.* (eds) (1992), *Climate Change 1992: The Supplementary Report to the IPCC Scientific Assessment*, Cambridge University Press, Cambridge; Houghton, J.T. *et al.* (eds) (1995), *Climate Change 1994: Radiative Forcing of Climate Change and An Evaluation of the IPCC IS92 Emission Scenarios*, Cambridge University Press, Cambridge; Watson, R.T. *et al.* (eds) (1996), *Climate Change 1995: Impacts, Adaptations and Mitigation of Climate Change: Scientific-Technical Analyses*, Cambridge University Press, Cambridge.

7   Bolin, 1995. IPCC Statement at the 'First Conference of the Parties to the United Nations Framework Convention on Climate Change' in Berlin, Germany, June 1995 by Prof. Bert Bolin, former Chairman of IPCC.

8   Litfin, K.T. (ed.) (1998), *The Greening of Sovereignty in World Politics*, The MIT Press, Cambridge.
9   *The American University Journal on International Law and Policy*, 1988, pp.515.
10 Sari, A. (1998), 'On Equity and Developing Country Participation', in C.J. Jepma (ed.), *Dealing with Carbon Credits After Kyoto*, Kluwer Academic Publishing, The Netherlands.
11 Reid, W.V., and Goldemberg, J. (1997), *Are Developing Countries Already Doing as Much as Industrialized Countries to Slow Climate Change?*, WRI, Washington, DC., *www.wri.org/cpi/notes/cntrydev.html*.
12 Commonwealth Scientific and Industrial Research Organization (CSIRO) (1992), *Climate Change Scenarios for South and Southeast Asia*, Climate Impact Group, Division of Atmospheric Research, prepared for the Asian Development Bank Regional Study on Global Environmental Issues, CSIRO, Mordialloc, Australia.
13 Asian Development Bank (ADB) (1994), *Climate Change in Asia: Indonesia*, ADB, Manila.
14 Food and Agriculture Organization (FAO) (1991), *Indonesian Tropical Forestry Action Program*, Ministry of Forestry of the Republic of Indonesia, Jakarta.
15 Ramli, R., Ahmad, M., Hafild, E. and Kambai, Y. (1993), *Rente Ekonomi Pengusahaan Hutan di Indonesia (The Economic Rent of Forest Concessions in Indonesia)*, WALHI, Jakarta.
16 *Ibid.*, citing various sources; Hasanuddin, L. (1996), 'Menggugat Keberadaan HPH' (Questioning the Existence of Forest Concessions), *Tanah Air*, no.1, pp.4-7.
17 Hasanuddin (1996), 'Menggugat Keberadaan HPH'.
18 Ramli, R., *et al.*, (1993), *Rente Ekonomi Pengusahaan Hutan di Indonesia*; and Hasanuddin (1996), 'Menggugat Keberadaan HPH'.
19 Triwahyudi, M.A. M. and Farchad, H. (1994), *HPH Dan Ekonomi Regional: Kasus Kalimantan Timur (Forest Concessions and Regional Economy: The East Kalimantan Case)*, WALHI, Jakarta.
20 Hasanuddin (1996), 'Menggugat Keberadaan HPH'; Triwahyudi and Farchad (1994), *HPH Dan Ekonomi Regional: Kasus Kalimantan Timur*.
21 Booth, A. (ed.) (1992), *The Oil Boom and After: Indonesian Economic Policy and Performance in the Soeharto Era*, Oxford University Press, Singapore, Oxford, and New York.
22 BPS (1992), *Population of Indonesia: Results of the 1990 Population Census*, BPS, Jakarta.
23 Transenerg (1988), *Energy Conservation in Indonesia: Final Report*, Directorate General for Electricity and Energy Development, Department of Mines and Energy, Jakarta; Konservasi Energi Abadi (KONEBA) (1989), *Meningkatkan laba Usaha Melalui Manajemen Energi (Increasing Corporate Profits through Energy Management)*, KONEBA, Jakarta; Department of Mines and Energy (DOME) (1991), *Rancangan Kampanye Nasional Konservasi Energi (National Energy Conservation Campaign Plan)*, DOME, Jakarta, Republic of Indonesia; United Nations Economic and Social Commission for Asia and the Pacific (UNESCAP) (1991), *Sectoral Energy Demand Studies: Application of the End-Use Approach to Asian Countries*, ESCAP, Bangkok; United States Agency for International Development (USAID) (1992), *Indonesian Demand-Side Management*, USAID, Washington, DC.; Opheim, K., and P. du Pont (1995), *Indonesia's Emerging Energy-Efficiency Market*, International Institute for Energy Conservation, Washington, DC.
24 DOME (1995), *Rencana Induk Konservasi Energi Nasional, RIKEN (National Master Plan for Energy Conservation)*, DOME, Jakarta.

25 BPS (1992), *Population of Indonesia: Results of the 1990 Population Census*; DOME (1995), *Rencana Induk Konservasi Energi Nasional (RIKEN)*.
26 Sari, A.P., and Susantono, B. (1998), *The Blue Skies Initiatives: Local and National Actions to Reduce Urban and Global Air Pollution in Jakarta, Indonesia*, Pelangi Indonesia, Jakarta.
27 *Ibid.*; See World Bank (1996), *Solar Home Systems Project: Staff Appraisal Report, Indonesia*, Indonesia Policy and Operations Division, Country Department III, East Asia and Pacific Regional Office, The World Bank, Washington, DC.
28 World Bank, *Ibid.*
29 *Ibid.*
30 *Ibid.*
31 *Ibid.*, pp.11. The study provided an example that a 60-watt incandescent light bulb produces the same luminous flux (lumens) as about 60 candles, or 20 kerosene wick lamps or 2 kerosene pressure lamps. Moreover, in quality terms, non-electric lighting is far inferior because of a much lower lumen output level and a more limited spatial distribution.
32 BPS (1995), *NTT Dalam Angka (NTT in Figures)*. The number of cars includes jeeps, sedans, mini and micro buses (usually used for public transportation) and trucks.
33 Benny, an Ende villager (personal communication, March 1999). The absence of electricity also hinders the villagers to listen to their radio, a major entertainment for them. The cost of batteries nowadays is roughly Rp. 5000 (67¢) a pair. A typical radio usually consumes about four pairs of batteries in two weeks. Thus, it requires about Rp. 20,000 a month to keep their radios going.
34 In *Agenda 21*, '... States have, in accordance with the charter of the United Nations and the principles of international law, the sovereign right to exploit their own resources pursuant to their own environmental and developmental policies, and the responsibility to ensure that activities within their jurisdiction or control do not cause damage to the environment of other States or of areas beyond the limits of national jurisdiction.' See United Nations Conference on Environment and Development (UNCED) (1992), *Earth Summit: Agenda 21, The United Nations Programme of Action From Rio*, United Nations Conference on Environment and Development, Rio de Janeiro, Brazil, pp.9.

References

Asian Development Bank (ADB) (1994), *Climate Change in Asia: Indonesia*, ADB, Manila.
Booth, A. (ed.) (1992), *The Oil Boom and After: Indonesian Economic Policy and Performance in the Soeharto Era*, Oxford University Press, Singapore, Oxford, and New York.
BPS (1992), *Population of Indonesia: Results of the 1990 Population Census*, BPS, Jakarta.
Commonwealth Scientific and Industrial Research Organization (CSIRO) (1992), *Climate Change Scenarios for South and Southeast Asia*, Climate Impact Group, Division of Atmospheric Research, prepared for the Asian Development Bank Regional Study on Global Environmental Issues, CSIRO, Mordialloc, Australia.
Department of Mines and Energy (DOME) (1995a), *National Master Plan for Energy Conservation (Rencana Induk Konservasi Energi Nasional, RIKEN)* DOME, Jakarta.
Department of Mines and Energy (DOME) (1991b), *Rancangan Kampanye Nasional Konservasi Energi (National Energy Conservation Campaign Plan)*, DOME, Jakarta, Republic of Indonesia.
Food and Agriculture Organization (FAO) (1991), *Indonesian Tropical Forestry Action*

Program, Ministry of Forestry, Jakarta, Republic of Indonesia.

Frank, A.G. (1966), 'The Development of Underdevelopment', *Monthly Review*, vol. 18, no. 4.

Gerschenkron, A. (1962), *Economic Backwardness in Historical Perspective*, Belknap, Cambridge.

Hasanuddin, L. (1996), 'Menggugat Keberadaan HPH' (Questioning the Existence of Forest Concessions), *Tanah Air*, no. 1, pp. 4-7.

Houghton, J.T. *et al.* (eds) (1995a), *Climate Change 1994: Radiative Forcing of Climate Change and An Evaluation of the IPCC IS92 Emission Scenarios*, Cambridge University Press, Cambridge.

Houghton, J.T. *et al.* (eds) (1992b), *Climate Change 1992: The Supplementary Report to the IPCC Scientific Assessment*, Cambridge University Press, Cambridge.

Houghton, J.T. *et al.* (eds) (1990c), *Climate Change 1990: IPCC Scientific Assessment*, United Nations Environment Program and World Meteorological Organization, Geneva.

Konservasi Energi Abadi (KONEBA) (1989), *Meningkatkan laba Usaha Melalui Manajemen Energi (Increasing Corporate Profits through Energy Management)*, KONEBA, Jakarta.

Litfin, K.T. (ed.) (1998), *The Greening of Sovereignty in World Politics*, The MIT Press, Cambridge.

Opheim, K., and du Pont, P. (1995), *Indonesia's Emerging Energy-Efficiency Market*, International Institute for Energy Conservation, Washington, DC.

Ramli, R., Ahmad, M., Hafild, E. and Kambai, Y. (1993), *Rente Ekonomi Pengusahaan Hutan di Indonesia (The Economic Rent of Forest Concessions in Indonesia)*, WALHI, Jakarta.

Reid, W.V., and Goldemberg, J. (1997), *Are Developing Countries Already Doing as Much as Industrialized Countries to Slow Climate Change?*, WRI, Washington, DC.

Sari, A. (1998), 'On Equity and Developing Country Participation', in C.J. Jepma (ed.), *Dealing with Carbon Credits After Kyoto*, Kluwer Academic Publishing, The Netherlands.

Sari, A. and Susantono, B. (1998), *The Blue Skies Initiatives: Local and National Actions to Reduce Urban and Global Air Pollution in Jakarta, Indonesia*, Pelangi Indonesia, Jakarta.

Serageldin, I. (1997), *Sustainability and the Wealth of Nations: A Work in Progress*, World Bank, Washington, DC.

Transenerg (1988), *Energy Conservation in Indonesia: Final Report*, Directorate General for Electricity and Energy Development, Department of Mines and Energy, Jakarta.

Triwahyudi, Muhshi, M.A. and Farchad, H. (1994), *HPH Dan Ekonomi Regional: Kasus Kalimantan Timur (Forest Concessions and Regional Economy: The East Kalimantan Case)*, WALHI, Jakarta.

United Nations Conference on Environment and Development (UNCED) (1992), *Earth Summit: Agenda 21, The United Nations Programme of Action From Rio*, United Nations Conference on Environment and Development, Rio de Janeiro, Brazil.

United Nations Economic and Social Commission for Asia and the Pacific (UNESCAP) (1991), *Sectoral Energy Demand Studies: Application of the End-Use Approach to Asian Countries*, ESCAP, Bangkok.

United Nations Framework Convention on Climate Change (UNFCCC) (1997), *The Kyoto Protocol to the United Nations Framework Convention on Climate Change*, UNFCCC, Kyoto, Japan.

United Nations General Assembly (UNGA) (1992), *United Nations Framework Convention on Climate Change*, United Nations, Rio de Janeiro, Brazil.

United States Agency for International Development (USAID) (1992), *Indonesian Demand-Side Management*, USAID, Washington, DC.

Watson, R.T. *et al.* (eds) (1996), *Climate Change 1995: Impacts, Adaptations and Mitigation of Climate Change: Scientific-Technical Analyses*, Cambridge University Press, Cambridge.

World Bank (1997), *Expanding the Measure of Wealth: Indicators of Environmentally Sustainable Development*, Environmentally Sustainable Studies and Monographs Series No. 17, The World Bank, Washington, DC.

World Bank (1996), *Solar Home Systems Project: Staff Appraisal Report, Indonesia*, Indonesia Policy and Operations Division, Country Department III, East Asia and Pacific Regional Office, The World Bank, Washington, DC.

Bibliography

Abracosa, R. (1998), *Philippine Urban and Industrial Environment*, Asian Institute of Management, Makati.

Abraham, M. (1988), *The Pesticide Portfolio: Lessons for the Gene Revolution from the Green Revolution*, proceedings of the 'Asian Regional Workshop on Plant Genetic Resources' Conservation and Development and the Impact of Related Technologies' in Malang, East Java, Southeast Asia Regional Institute for Community Education (SEARICE), Manila 6-11 December, pp. 42-3.

Abrahams, P. (1994), 'The Dye is Cast by Growth and Costs', *Financial Times*, 13 May.

Acharya, A. (2001), *Constructing a Security Community in Southeast Asia*, Routledge, London.

Acharya, A., Dewitt, D. B., and Hernandez, C. G. (1995), 'Sustainable Development and Security in Southeast Asia: A Concept Paper', *CANCAPS Papier Number 6*, August.

Alibutud, R. (1993), 'Rough Winds Over Calancan Bay', in E. Gamalinda and S. Coronel (eds), *Saving the Earth: The Philippine Experience*, third edition, Philippine Center for Investigative Journalism, Makati, pp. 69-79.

Almonte, J. T. (2000), *A Human Agenda for ASEAN*, paper presented at the 'Inaugural Meeting of the ASEAN People's Assembly', Batam Island, Indonesia, 24-26 November 2000, distributed as *PacNet 1*, 5 January 2001, CISIS/Pacific Forum, Honolulu.

Amat, S. (1982), 'Promoting National Food Security: The Indonesian Experience', in A. H. Chisholm and R. Tyers (eds), *Food Security: Theory, Policy and Perspectives from Asia and the Pacific Rim*, DC Health and Company, Lexington, Mass., pp. 147.

Anderson, I. (1992), Dangerous Technology Dumped on Third World', *New Scientist*, Vol. 133(7), March, pp. 9.

Anderson, L. (1994), *The Political Ecology of the Modern Peasant: Calculation and Community*, Johns Hopkins University Press, Baltimore, pp. 28.

Asian Development Bank (ADB) (1994), *Climate Change in Asia: Indonesia*, ADB, Manila.

Associated Press (AP) (1998), 'Indonesia to buy rice from Vietnam', *China News*, 6 October, pp. 9.

Awang, K. and Hamzah, M. B. (1996), 'Community Forestry in Malaysia: Overview, Constraints, and Prospects', in Department of Environment and Natural Resources (DENR) and the International Tropical Timber Organization (ITTO), *Community Forestry: As a Strategy for Sustainable Forest Management*, Proceedings of the International Conference, Manila, Philippines, 24-26 May 1996, pp. 175-90.

Baes, A. V. (1991), 'Project CALABARZON and Environmental Degradation', *Midweek*, 25 December.

Baldwin, D. (1997), 'The Concept of Security', *Review of International Studies*, Vol. 23, pp. 5-26.

Barber, C. (1997), 'The Case of Indonesia', *Project on Environmental Scarcities, State Capacity and Civil Violence*, American Academy of Arts and Sciences, Cambridge, MA.

Barr, C. M. (1998), 'Bob Hasan, the Rise of Apkindo, and the Shifting Dynamics of Control in Indonesia's Timber Sector', *Indonesia*, No. 65, April.

Batario, R. (1997), 'The Pillage of Isabela', in C. C.A. Balgos (ed.), *Saving the Earth: The Philippine Experience*, fourth edition, Philippine Center for Investigative Journalism, Pasig City, pp.27-30.

Belcher, M. and Gennino, A. (1993) (eds), *Southeast Asia Rainforests: A Resource Guide & Directory*, Rainforest Action Network, San Francisco, pp. 37.

Bennagen, P. C. (1996), 'NGO and Community Participation in Environmental Programs: A Case Study of the Community Forestry Program', *Philippine Social Sciences Review*, Vol. 53 (1-4), January-December, pp. 53-7.

Bernard, M. and Ravenhill, J. (1995), 'Beyond Product Cycles and Flying Geese: Regionalization, Hierarchy, and the Industrialization of East Asia', *World Politics*, Vol. 47, January.

BHP Engineering Philippines Inc. (1994), *Environmental Impact Statement for the Proposed Sual Coal-Thermal Power Plant*, BHP Engineering Philippines, Inc., Quezon City, pp. 214.

Booth, A. (ed.) (1992), *The Oil Boom and After: Indonesian Economic Policy and Performance in the Soeharto Era*, Oxford University Press, Singapore, Oxford, and New York.

Booth, A. and Baharsyah, S. (1986), 'Indonesia', *Food Trade and Food Security in ASEAN and Australia*, ASEAN-Australia Joint Research Project, Canberra, pp. 21-2.

Booth, K. (1996), '75 Years On: Rewriting the Subject's Past – Reinventing the Future', in S. Smith, K. Booth and M. Zalewski (eds), *International Theory: Positivism and Beyond*, Cambridge University Press, Cambridge, pp. 328-39.

BPS (1992), *Population of Indonesia: Results of the 1990 Population Census*, BPS, Jakarta.

Brandon, C. (1996), 'Reversing Pollution Trends in Asia', *The Environment Industry: The Washington Meeting*, OECD, Paris, pp. 186.

Brandon, C. and Ramankutty, R. (1993), *Toward an Environmental Strategy for Asia*, World Bank Discussion Paper No. 224, World Bank, Washington, DC, pp. 66.

Breimyer, H. F. (1962), 'The Three Economies of Agriculture', *Journal of Farm Economics*, Vol. XLIV (3), August, pp. 680.

Brookfield, H., Potter, L. and Byron, Y. (1995), *In Place of the Forest: Environmental and Socio-economic Transformation in Borneo and the Eastern Malay Peninsula*, United Nations University Press, Tokyo, pp. 101.

Brown, L. D. and Ashman, D. (1996), 'Participation, Social Capital and Intersectoral Problem Solving: African and Asian Cases', *World Development*, Vol. 24(9), pp. 1467-8.

Bruno, K. and Greer, J. (1993), 'Chlorine Chemistry Expansion: The Environmental Mistake of the 21st Century', *Toxic Trade Update*, Vol. 6(2).

Bryant, R. L. (1996), 'The Greening of Burma: Political Rhetoric or Sustainable Development?', *Pacific Affairs*, Vol. 69, Fall, pp. 341-59.

Bryant, R. L. (1997), *The Political Ecology of Forestry in Burma 1824-1994*, Hurst & Company, London.

Buzan, B. (1991), *People, States and Fear: An Agenda for International Studies in the Post-Cold War Era*, second edition, Lynne Rienner, Boulder, pp. 26.

Caballero, E. (1996), *Gold from the Gods: Traditional Small-Scale Miners in the Philippines*, Giraffe Books, Quezon City.

Castleman, E. (1996), 'Workplace Health Standards and Multinational Corporations in Developing Countries', in C. Pearson (ed.), *Multinational Corporations, the Environment, and the Third World*, Duke University Press, Durham, pp. 164.

Center for Strategic and International Studies (CSIS) (1996), *Trade and Environment Linkages: A Case Study from Indonesia*, CSIS, Jakarta.

Clapp, J. (1994), 'The Toxic Waste Trade with Less Industrialized Countries: Economic Linkages and Political Alliances', *Third World Quarterly*, Vol. 15(3).

Clapp, J. (1998), 'The Privatization of Global Environmental Governance: ISO 14000 and the Developing World', *Global Governance*, Vol. 4(3).

Co, E. A. (1996), 'Reinterpreting Civil Society: The Context of the Philippine NGO Movement', in A. G. Alegre (ed.), *Trends and Traditions, Challenges and Choices: A Strategic Study of Philippine NGOs*, Ateneo Center for Social Policy and Public Affairs and Philippines-Canada Human Resource Development Program, Quezon City, pp. 195-6.

Cobbing, M. (1991), *Lead Astray: The Poisonous Lead Battery Waste Trade*, Greenpeace International, Amsterdam.

Colborne, T., Dumanoski, D. and Myers, J.P. (1996), *Our Stolen Future*, Dutton, New York.

Commonwealth Scientific and Industrial Research Organization (CSIRO) (1992), *Climate Change Scenarios for South and Southeast Asia*, Climate Impact Group, Division of Atmospheric Research, prepared for the Asian Development Bank Regional Study on Global Environmental Issues, CSIRO, Mordialloc, Australia.

Coronel, S. S. (1996), 'Unnatural Disasters', in S. S. Coronel (ed.), *Patrimony: 6 Case Studies on Local Politics and the Environment in the Philippines*, Philippine Center for Investigative Journalism, Manila, pp. 13.

Coumans, C. (1995), 'Ideology, Social Movement and Organization, Patronage and Resistance in the Struggle of Marinduquenos Against Marcopper', *Pilipinas*, No. 24, Spring, pp. 37-74.

Coumans, C. (1998), 'Mining Industry Responses to the Debate on Mining in the Philippines', *Intersect*, July, pp. 13-25.

Crovitz, L. G. (1994), *The Asian Manager: Asian Imperatives and Western Perspectives in Sustainable Development*, paper presented at the 'Asian Institute of Management Conference', Manila, Philippines, 17 February 1994.

Cummings, B. (1984), 'The Origins and Development of the Northeast Asian Political Economy: Industrial Sectors, Product Cycles and Political Consequences', *International Organization*, Vol. 38(1).

Dahuri, R. (1996), 'Environmental Impact of One Million Hectare of Swampland and Its Management Strategy', *Farmer Irrigation Newsletter*, No. 11, pp. 6-7.

Dalby, S. (1992), 'Security, Modernity, Ecology: The Dilemmas of Post-Cold War Security Discourse', *Alternatives*, Vol. 17(1), pp. 95-134.

Dauvergne, P. (1997a), 'Japanese Trade and Deforestation in Southeast Asia', in R. De Koninck and C. Veilleux (eds), *Southeast Asia and Globalization: New Domains of Analysis/L'Asie du Sud-East face à la mondialisation: les nouveaux champs d'anlayse*, GÉRAC, Université Laval, Québec, pp. 133-56.

Dauvergne, P. (1997b), *Shadows in the Forest: Japan and the Politics of Timber in Southeast Asia*, The MIT Press, Cambridge.

Dauvergne, P. (1998a), 'Weak States and the Environment in Indonesia and the Solomon Islands', in P. Dauvergne (ed.), *Weak and Strong States in Asia-Pacific Societies*, Allen and Unwin, Sydney, pp. 137.

Dauvergne, P. (1998b), 'Globalisation and Deforestation in the Asia-Pacific', *Environmental Politics*, Vol 7(4), Winter, pp. 113-34.

DENR-Environmental Management Bureau (DENR-EMB) (1992), *A Report on Philippine Environment and Development: Issues and Strategies*, Quezon City, Republic of the Philippines, pp. 2-51.

DENR-Environmental Management Bureau (DENR-EMB) (1994), *Philippine Environmental Impact Statement System Guide: Policies and Procedures*, Quezon City, Republic of the Philippines.

DENR-Environmental Management Bureau (DENR-EMB) (1996), *Philippine Environmental Quality Report (PEQR) 1990-95*, DENR, Quezon City, Republic of the Philippines.

Departemen Kehutanan (Ministry of Forestry) (1992a), *Forestry in Indonesia and Forestry Research and Development*, Ministry of Forestry, Republic of Indonesia, Jakarta.

Departemen Kehutanan (Ministry of Forestry) (1992b), *The Timber Industry in Indonesia*, Ministry of Forestry, Republic of Indonesia, Jakarta.

Department of Energy (DoE) (1996), *Philippine Energy Plan: 1996-2025*, Manila, Republic of the Philippines pp. 30.

Department of Environment and Natural Resources (DENR) (1990), *Philippine Strategy for Sustainable Development: A Conceptual Framework*, Quezon City, Republic of the Philippines pp. 11.

Department of Environment and Natural Resources (DENR) (1993), *Policies, Memoranda and Other Issuances on the National Forestation Program Volume VI*, National Forestation Development Office, Department of Environment and Natural Resources, Quezon City, pp. 88-107.

Department of Mines and Energy (DOME) (1991), *Rancangan Kampanye Nasional Konservasi Energi (National Energy Conservation Campaign Plan)*, DOME, Jakarta, Republic of Indonesia.

Department of Mines and Energy (DOME) (1995), *National Master Plan for Energy Conservation [Rencana Induk Konservasi Energi Nasional, RIKEN]* DOME, Jakarta.

Department of Foreign Affairs and International Trade (1999), *Human Security: Safety for People in a Changing World*, Department of Foreign Affairs and International Trade, Government of Canada, April, pp. 5.

Dewitt, D. B. (1994), 'Common, Comprehensive, and Cooperative Security in Asia Pacific', *The Pacific Review*, Vol. 7(1).

Dixon, C. (1995), 'Origins, Sustainability and Lessons from Thailand's Economic Growth', *Contemporary Southeast Asia*, Vol 17(1), June, pp. 48-9.

Dixon, J. A. and Hamilton, K. (1996), 'Expanding the Measure of Wealth', *Finance & Development*, Vol. 33(4), December, pp. 15.

Djiwandono, J. S. (1996), 'New Concepts of Security After the Cold War', in Center for Strategic and International Studies (CSIS), *The Role of Security and Economic Cooperation Structures in the Asia Pacific Region Indonesian and Australian Views*, CSIS, Jakarta.

Doyo, M.C. P. (1992), 'Postmortem: Calaca', *Sunday Inquirer Magazine*, 12 January.

Dupont, A. (ed.) (1998), *The Environment and Security: What Are The Linkages?*, Strategic and Defence Studies Centre, Research School of Pacific and Asian Studies, The Australian National University, Canberra, pp. 45-64.

Emundson, W. C. and Anderson, S. (1986), 'Geographic Variation and Changing Economic Status in Two Javanese Villages', *Singapore Journal of Tropical Geography*, Vol. 7(1), pp.33-4.

'Environmentalists push for legislation on strict liability for toxic waste importers' (1996), *International Environment Reporter*, Vol. 19(5), March, pp. 179.

ESCAP/UNCTC (1990), *Environmental Aspects of Transnational Corporation Activities in Pollution-Intensive Industries In Selected Asian and Pacific Developing Countries*, UN/ESCAP, Bangkok, pp. 69-70.

ESCAP/UNCTC (1998), *Transnational Corporations and Environmental Management in Selected Asian and Pacific Developing Countries*, UN/ESCAP, Bangkok, pp. 10-1.

Evans, P. (1996), 'Introduction: Development Strategies Across the Public-Private Divide', *World Development*, Vol. 24, pp. 1033.

Falcon, W. P. and Timmer, C. P. (1991), 'Food Security in Indonesia: Defining the Issues', *Indonesian Food Journal*, Vol. 11 (1), pp. 10.

Fellmeth, A. X. (1996), 'Social Capital in the United States and Taiwan: Trust or Rule of Law?', *Development Policy Review*, Vol. 14, pp. 151-71.

Ferry, I. T. (1988), 'Performance of Indonesia's Agriculture: Food Self-Sufficiency and Beyond', *The Indonesian Quarterly*, Vol. XVI(4).

Florentino-Hofileña, C. (1996), 'Searching for Gold in B'laan Country', in S. Coronel (ed.), *Patrimony: 6 Case Studies on Local Politics and the Environment in the Philippines*, Philippine Center for Investigative Journalism, Pasig City, pp. 97-119.

Food and Agriculture Organization (FAO) (1991), *Indonesian Tropical Forestry Action Program*, Ministry of Forestry, Jakarta, Republic of Indonesia.

Fowler, R. (1995), 'International Environmental Standards for Transnational Corporations', *Environmental Law*, Vol. 25(1), pp. 15.

Fox, J. (1996), 'How Does Civil Society Thicken?: The Political Construction of Social Capital in Rural Mexico', *World Development*, Vol. 24, pp. 1089-103.

Frank, A. G. (1966), 'The Development of Underdevelopment', *Monthly Review*, Vol. 18(4).

Fukuyama, F. (1995), *Trust: The Social Virtues and the Creation of Prosperity*, The Free Press, New York, pp. 26.

Gerschenkron, A. (1962), *Economic Backwardness in Historical Perspective*, Belknap, Cambridge.

Gibbs, C. and Bromley, D. (1989), 'Institutional Arrangements for Management of Rural Resources: Common Property Regimes', in F. Berkes (ed.), *Common Property Resources: Ecology and Community-Based Sustainable Development*, Belhaven Press, London, pp. 22-4.

Goldberg, E. (1996), 'Thinking About How Democracy Works', *Politics and Society*, Vol. 24, pp. 7-18.

Gonzales, L. A., Kasryno, F., Perez, F. and Rosegrant, M. W. (1993), *Economic Incentives and Comparative Advantage in Indonesian Food Corp Production*, International Food Policy Research Institute, Washington, DC, pp. 13-4.

Graeger, N. (1996), 'Environmental Security?', *Journal of Peace Research*, Vol. 33(1), pp. 109-16.

GRAIN (1996a), 'IRRI's 15-Ton Super Rice', *Seedling*, Vol. 13(3), pp. 12.

GRAIN (1996b), 'Free Trade Versus Food Security', *Seedling*, Vol. 13(3), October, pp. 8.

GRAIN (1997c), 'The Year of Agricultural Biodiversity Revisited', *Seedling*, Vol. 14(1), March, pp. 6-7.

Greenpeace (1994a), *Database of Known Hazardous Waste Exports from OECD to non-OECD Countries 1989-March 1994*, Greenpeace International, Amsterdam, pp. II-4.

Greenpeace (1994b), *The Waste Invasion of Asia*, Greenpeace, Sydney, Australia, pp. 20-2.

Greenpeace (1996), 'Philippines Fails to Halt Toxic Waste Imports', *International Toxics Investigator*, Vol. 8(4), pp. 12.

Grindle, M. S. (1996), *Challenging the State: Crisis and Innovation in Latin America and Africa*, Cambridge University Press, Cambridge.

Habib, A. H. (1996), 'Regional Security: Trends and Prospects', in Center for Strategic and International Studies (CSIS), *Regional Security Arrangements-Indonesian and Canadian Views*, CSIS, Jakarta.

Handoko, S. B. (1995), 'Beras, Antara Harapan dan Kenyataan', *Business News*, 12 August, pp. 1C.

Harris, S. (1994), 'Enhancing Security: Non-Military Means and Measures II', in B. Nagara and K.S. Balakrishnan (eds), *The Making of A Security Community in the Asia-Pacific*, ISIS Malaysia, Kuala Lumpur, pp. 191.

Hasanuddin, L. (1996), 'Menggugat Keberadaan HPH' (Questioning the Existence of Forest Concessions), *Tanah Air*, No. 1, pp. 4-7.

Heller, P. (1996), 'Social Capital as a Product of Class Mobilization and State Intervention: Industrial Workers in Kerala, India', *World Development*, Vol. 24, pp. 1055-71.

Hernandez, C. G. (1995), *ASEAN Perspectives on Human Rights and Democracy in International Relations: Divergencies, Commonalities, Problems, and Prospects*, Center for Integrative and Development Studies, University of the Philippines, Quezon City.

Hettige, H., Huq, M., Pargal, S. and Wheeler, D. (1996), 'Determinants of Pollution Abatement in Developing Countries: Evidence from South and Southeast Asia', *World Development*, Vol. 24(12).

Hill, H. (1992), *Indonesia's Textile and Garment Industries Development in an Asian Perspective*, ASEAN Economic Research Unit, Institute of South East Asian Studies, Singapore.

Hisahiko, O. (1993), 'Southeast Asia in Japan's National Strategy', *Japan Echo*, Vol. 20.

Holmberg, J., Bass, S., and Timberlake, L. (1991), *Defending the Future: A Guide to Sustainable Development*, International Institute for Environment and Development, London.

Homer-Dixon, T. F. (1991e), 'On the Threshold: Environmental Changes as Causes of Acute Conflict', *International Security*, Vol. 16(2), Fall.

Homer-Dixon, T. F. (1994a), 'Across the Threshold: Empirical Evidence on Environmental Scarcities as Causes of Violent Conflict', *International Security*, Summer.

Homer-Dixon, T. F. (1994b), *The Ingenuity Gap: Can Poor Countries Adapt to Resource Scarcity?*, University of Toronto ms., April.

Homer-Dixon, T. F. (1994c), 'Environmental Scarcities and Violent Conflict: Evidence from Cases', *International Security*, Vol. 19(1).

Homer-Dixon, T. F. (1999), *Environment, Scarcity, and Violence*, Princeton University Press, Princeton.

Homer-Dixon, T. F., Boutwell, J. H. and Rathjens, G. W. (1993), 'Environmental Change and Violent Conflict', *Scientific American*, February.

Hong, E. (1987), *Natives of Sarawak: Survival in Borneo's Vanishing Forest*, Institut Masyarakat, Pulau Pinang, Malaysia pp. 128-9.

Houghton, J. T. *et al.* (eds) (1990), *Climate Change 1990: IPCC Scientific Assessment*, United Nations Environment Program and World Meteorological Organization, Geneva.

Houghton, J. T. *et al.* (eds) (1992), *Climate Change 1992: The Supplementary Report to the IPCC Scientific Assessment*, Cambridge University Press, Cambridge.

Houghton, J.T. *et al.* (eds) (1995), *Climate Change 1994: Radiative Forcing of Climate Change and An Evaluation of the IPCC IS92 Emission Scenarios*, Cambridge University Press, Cambridge.

Hüsken, F. and White, B. (1989), 'Java: Social Differentiation, Food Production and Agrarian Control', in G. Hart, A. Turton and B. White (eds), *Agrarian Transformations: Local Processes and the State in Southeast Asia*, University of California Press, Berkeley, pp. 249.

Hyden, G. (1997), 'Civil Society, Social Capital, and Development: Dissection of a Complex Discourse', *Studies in Comparative International Development*, Vol. 32(1), Spring, pp. 4.

Ichihara, M. and Harding, A. (1995), 'Human Rights, the Environment and Radioactive Waste: A Study of the Asian Rare Earth Case in Malaysia', *Review of European Community and International Environmental Law*, Vol. 4(1), pp. 1-14.

International Tropical Timber Organization (ITTO) (1999), *Annual Review and Assessment of the World Timber Situation: 1998*, ITTO, Yokohama, pp. 98.

Institut Analisa Sosial (INSAN) (1989), *Logging Against the Natives of Sarawak*, INSAN, Selangor, Malaysia, pp. 73-4.

Jatayna, E. A. (1995), 'The Sual Coal-Fired Power Plant: Lessons From the Past', *Politik*, Vol. 2(1), August, pp. 29.

Jayasankaran, S. (1995), 'Waste Not, Want Not: Malaysia needs a waste-treatment facility fast', *Far Eastern Economic Review*, 13 April, pp. 61.

Jemadu, A. (1996), *Sustainable Forest Management in the Context of Multi-Level and Multi-Actor Policy Processes: Case Studies of the Incorporation of the Environmental into Sustainable Forest Management in East Kalimantan-Indonesia*, Katholieke Universiteit Leuven, Leuven, Belgium, pp. 146.

Jones, S. (1994), 'Promoting Human Rights', in B. Nagara and K.S. Balakrishnan (eds), *The Making of A Security Community in the Asia-Pacific*, ISIS Malaysia, Kuala Lumpur, pp. 344-46.

Kaji, G. (1994), 'Challenges to the East Asian Environment', *The Pacific Review*, Vol. 7(2), pp. 212.

Kalmirah, J. (1998), 'Global Dumping Lays Waste to Scavengers' Livelihood', *Basel Action News*, Vol. 1(1).

Karliner, J. (1994), 'The Environmental Industry', *The Ecologist*, Vol. 24(2), pp. 61.

Kasryno, F. (1990), *Diversification as Future Policy Instrument: In Agricultural Development for Indonesia*, paper presented to the World Bank and at 'Regional Workshop on Diversification' in Bogor, Indonesia, 20-22 March 1990. Reprinted in *Indonesian Food Journal*, Vol. 1(2), 1990, pp. 31.

Kelompok Penelitian Agro-Ekosistem (KEPAS) (1985), *The Critical Uplands of East Java: An Agroecosystems Analysis*, KEPAS/ Brawijaya University Research Center, Malang.

Kent, L. (1991), *The Relationship Between Small Enterprises and Environmental Degradation in the Developing World (With Special Emphasis on Asia)*, Development Alternatives, Inc., Washington, DC, pp. 10.

Kircher-Lumbao, L. (1997), 'Laguna Lake Development Authority: Tackling Water Pollution', *Competitive Advantage*, Vol. 1(1), pp.18.

Konservasi Energi Abadi (KONEBA) (1989), *Meningkatkan laba Usaha Melalui Manajemen Energi (Increasing Corporate Profits through Energy Management)*, KONEBA, Jakarta.

Korten, F. F. (1994), 'Questioning the Call for Environmental Loans: A Critical Examination of Forestry Lending in the Philippines', *World Development*, Vol. 22(7), pp. 971-81.

Kummer, D. M. (1991), *Deforestation in the Postwar Philippines*, The University of Chicago Press, Chicago.

Kummer, K. (1992), 'The International Regulation of Transboundary Traffic in Hazardous Wastes: The 1989 Basel Convention', *International and Comparative Law Quarterly*, Vol. 41(3), July.

Kusnadi and Riza, V.T. (1997), 'Rice Mega-Project Pressing to Local People', *Terompet*, Vol. IV(10).

Lindsay, J. (1993), 'Overlaps and Tradeoffs: Coordinating Policies for Sustainable Development in Asia and the Pacific', *The Journal of Developing Areas*, Vol. 28, October, pp. 28.

Litfin, K. T. (ed.) (1998), *The Greening of Sovereignty in World Politics*, The MIT Press, Cambridge.

Lodgaard, S. and af Ornas, A. (eds) (1992), *The Environment and International Security*, PRIO Report No. 3, International Peace Research Institute, Oslo.

Lonergan, S. (1994), *Environmental Change and Regional Security in Southeast Asia*, Project Report No. PR 659, Directorate of Strategic Analysis, Ottawa, March.

Louis Berger International Inc. (1995), 'Preparation of a Master Plan for the Northwestern Luzon Growth Quadrangle', *PAPSP Studies*, February.

Loury, G. (1977), A Dynamic Theory of Racial Income Differences', in P. Wallace and A. LaMond (eds), *Women, Minorities, and Employment Discrimination*, Lexington Books, Lexington, pp. 153-86.

Lucus, A. (1995), 'Chemical Companies Play the Environmental Market', *Chemical Week*, 18 January, pp. 32.

MacNeill, J., Winsemius, P., and Yakushiji, T. (1991), *Beyond Interdependence: The Meshing of the World's Economy and the Earth's Ecology*, Oxford University Press, New York.

Maddock, R.T. (1995), 'Environmental Security in East Asia', *Contemporary Southeast Asia*, Vol. 17(1), June.

Magdalena, F. V. (1996), 'Population Growth and the Changing Ecosystem in Mindanao', *Sojourn*, Vol. 11(1), pp. 120.

Magno, F. A. (1993), 'The Growth of Philippine Environmentalism', *Kasarinlan: A Philippine Quarterly of Third World Studies*, Vol. 9(1), 3rd Quarter, pp. 7-18.

Magno, F. A. (1997), *Crafting Conservation: Forestry, Social Capital, and Tenurial Security in the northern Philippines*, University of Hawai'I, Hawai'I, pp. 163.

Margolis, H. (1982), *Selfishness, Altruism, and Rationality: A Theory of Social Choice*, Cambridge University Press, Cambridge, pp. 11.

Massey, R. I. (1994), 'Impediments to Collective Action in a Small Community', *Politics and Society*, Vol. 22, pp. 421-34.

Matthews, J. T. (1989), 'Redefining Security', *Foreign Affairs*, Vol. 68(2), Spring, pp. 162-77.

McBeth, J. (1998), 'Monopoly of Virtue', *Far Eastern Economic Review*, 30 July, pp. 49-50.

McDowell, M. (1989), 'Development and the Environment in ASEAN', *Pacific Affairs*, Vol. 62(3), pp. 326-7.

McMichael, P. (1994), 'Global Restructuring: Some Lines of Inquiry', *The Global Restructuring of Agrofood Systems*, Cornell University Press, Ithaca, N.Y., pp. 285.

Migdal, J. S., Kohli, A. and Shue, V. (1994) (eds), *State Power and Social Forces: Domination and Transformation in the Third World*, Cambridge University Press, New York.

Migdal, J. S. (1988), *Strong Societies and Weak States: State-Society Relations and State Capabilities in the Third World*, Princeton University Press, Princeton, New Jersey.

Miller, M. A.L. (1995), *The Third World In Global Environmental Politics*, Lynne Rienner Publishers, Boulder.

Ministry of Forestry Directorate General of Reforestation and Land Rehabilitation (1993), *Overview: The Strategy of Reforestation and Land Rehabilitation*, Ministry of Forestry, Republic of Indonesia, Jakarta, February.

Montiflor, M. and Alano, M. L. (1998), 'Mining in Mindanao: Issues and Prospects', *Mindanao Focus*, No. 1.

Moyers, B. and the Center for Investigative Reporting (1991), *Global Dumping Ground*, Lutterworth Press, Cambridge, pp. 14-27.

Myers, N. (1989b), 'Environment and Security', *Foreign Policy*, No. 74, Spring, pp. 23-41.

National Mines and Allied Workers Union (1997), *Case Study on the Mine-Related Environmental Disaster in Marinduque*, National Mines and Allied Workers Union.

National Power Corporation (NAPOCOR) (1998a), *Power Development Program*, National Power Corporation, Manila, pp. 1.

National Power Corporation (NAPOCOR) (1994b), *Resettlement Program: Sual Coal-Fired Thermal Power Plant*, Social Engineering Department, National Power Corporation, Manila, May.

Nelson, D. (1997), 'Toxic Waste: Hazardous to Asia's Health', *Asia Pacific Issues: Analysis from the East-West Center*, No. 34, pp. 3.

Ng Weng Hoong (1995), 'Singapore's Catchphrase: Add Value', *Chemical Week*, 15 February, pp. 40.

Nishikawa, J. (1982), 'The Strategy of Japanese Multinationals and Southeast Asia', in Consumer's Association of Penang (ed.), *Development and the Environmental Crisis: A Malaysian Case*, CAP, Penang, pp. 252.

North, D. (1991), 'Institutions', *Journal of Economic Perspectives*, Vol. 5, pp. 97-112.

Northwestern Luzon Growth Quadrangle Commission Program (1997), *The Northwestern Luzon Growth Quadrangle*, CPPAP Reports.

O'Connor, David (1994), *Managing the Environment with Rapid Industrialization: Lessons from the East Asian Experience*, OECD, Paris, pp. 167-72.

Ofreneo, Rene (1993), 'Japan and the Environmental Degradation of the Philippines', in M. Howard (ed.), *Asia's Environmental Crisis*, Westview, Boulder, pp. 214-6.

Olson, M. (1965), *The Logic of Collective Action: Public Goods and the Theory of Goods*, Harvard University Press, Cambridge, pp. 34.

Opheim, K., and du Pont, P. (1995), *Indonesia's Emerging Energy-Efficiency Market*, International Institute for Energy Conservation, Washington, DC.

Pangestu, M. and Feridhanusetyawan, T. (1996), *Liberalization of the Agricultural Sector in Indonesia: External Pressures and Domestic Needs*, paper presented at the 'Conference on Food and Agricultural Policy: Challenges for the Asia-Pacific', Manila, 1-3 October 1996.

Pargal, S. and Wheeler, D. (1996), 'Informal Regulation of Industrial Pollution in Developing Countries: Evidence from Indonesia', *Journal of Political Economy*, Vol. 104(6).

Peluso, N. L. (1993), 'Coercing Conservation? The politics of state resource control', *Global Environmental Change: Human and Policy Dimensions*, Vol. 3(2), June, pp. 199-217.

'Philippines Changes Position on Waste Imports', *Toxic Trade Update*, Vol. 7(1), 1994, pp. 18.

Poffenberger, M. (1997), 'Rethinking Indonesian Forest Policy: Beyond the Timber Barons', *Asian Survey*, Vol. XXXVII(5), May, pp. 456.

Poffenberger, M. and Stone, R. D. (1996), 'Hidden Faces in the Forest: A 21st Century Challenge for Tropical Asia', *Sais Review*, Vol. 16(1), Winter-Spring, pp. 204.

Porter, G. and Brown, J. W. (1996), *Global Environmental Politics*, second edition, Westview Press, Boulder.

Pura, R. (1993), 'Timber Companies Blossom On Malaysian Stock Market', *Asian Wall Street Journal*, 30 November, pp. 12.

Pura, R. (1994), 'Timber Baron Emerges From the Woods', *Asian Wall Street Journal*, 15 February, pp. 1 and 4.

Pura, R. (1995), 'Bob Hasan Builds an Empire in the Forest', *Asian Wall Street Journal*, 25 January, pp. 4.

Putnam, R. (1993), *Making Democracy Work: Civic Traditions in Modern Italy*, Princeton University Press, Princeton, New Jersey, pp. 167 and 183.

Putnam, R. (1995), 'Bowling Alone: America's Declining Social Capital', *Journal of Democracy*, Vol. 6(1), pp. 67.

Ragragio, C. M. (1993), 'Sustainable Development, Environmental Planning and People's Initiatives', *Kasarinlan: A Philippine Quarterly of Third World Studies*, Vol. 9(1), 3rd Quarter, pp. 35-53.

Ramli, R., Ahmad, M., Hafild, E. and Kambai, Y. (1993), *Rente Ekonomi Pengusahaan Hutan di Indonesia (The Economic Rent of Forest Concessions in Indonesia)*, WALHI, Jakarta.

Ramos, H. (1998), *The Mining Regulatory Framework*, Chamber of Mines of the Philippines, Pasig City, 25 June.

Redclift, M. and Sage, C. (eds) (1994), *Strategies for Sustainable Development: Local Agendas for the Southern Hemisphere*, John Wiley and Sons, Chichester.

Reid, W. V., and Goldemberg, J. (1997), *Are Developing Countries Already Doing as Much as Industrialized Countries to Slow Climate Change?*, WRI, Washington, DC.

Renner, M. (1997), 'Transforming Security', in *State of the World 1997*, W.W. Norton and Company, New York, pp. 115-31.

Rice, D. (1992), 'Living seed banks: a resource for the entire community', *Inside Indonesia*, December, pp. 31-2.

Robison, R. (1978), 'Toward A Class Analysis of the Indonesian Military Bureaucratic State', *Indonesia*, No. 25, April, pp. 28.

Robles, A. (1997), 'Logging and Political Power', in C. C.A. Balgos (ed.), *Saving the Earth: The Philippine Experience*, fourth edition, Philippine Center for Investigative Journalism, Pasig City, pp. 22-6.

Robles, A. and Severino, H. G. (1997), 'Way to a Crisis', in C. C.A. Balgos (ed.), *Saving the Earth: The Philippine Experience*, fourth edition, Philippine Center for Investigative Journalism, Pasig City, pp. 21.

Roht-Arriaza, N. (1997), 'Environmental Management Systems and Environmental Protection: Can ISO 14001 be Useful Within the Context of APEC?', *Journal of Environment and Development*, Vol. 6(3).

Romm, J. (1993), *Defining National Security: The Non-Military Aspects*, Council on Foreign Relations Press, New York.

Royo, A. and Gatmaytan, D. (1991), 'The Philippine Mining Policy: A Case of Obscured Environmental and Social Impacts', *Philippine Natural Resources Law Journal*, Vol. 4(2), pp. 24-38.

Ruckelshaus, W. D. (1989), 'Toward a Sustainable World', *Scientific American*, No. 261, September.

Sandique, R. (1996), 'Rating System for 2000 Industries in Manila Set', *Manila Standard*, 9 December.

Sands, P. (1993), 'Enforcing Environmental Security: The Challenges of Compliance with International Obligations', *Journal of International Affairs*, Vol. 46(2), Winter.

Sari, A. (1998), 'On Equity and Developing Country Participation', in C.J. Jepma (ed.), *Dealing with Carbon Credits After Kyoto*, Kluwer Academic Publishing, The Netherlands.

Sari, A. and Susantono, B. (1998), *The Blue Skies Initiatives: Local and National Actions to Reduce Urban and Global Air Pollution in Jakarta, Indonesia*, Pelangi Indonesia, Jakarta.

Sarido, M. A. (1996), 'Social/Community Forestry Development in Indonesia', in Department of Environment and Natural Resources (DENR) and the International Tropical Timber Organization (ITTO), *Community Forestry: As a Strategy for Sustainable Forest Management*, proceedings of the International Conference, Manila, Philippines, 24-26 May 1996, pp. 111-21.

Schneider, M., Teske, P., Marschall, M., Mintrom, M. and Roch, C. (1997), 'Institutional Arrangements and the Creation of Social Capital: The Effects of Public School Choice', *American Political Science Review*, Vol. 91, pp. 82-93.

Schwarz, A. (1994), *A Nation in Waiting: Indonesia in the 1990s*, Allen and Unwin, St. Leonards, NSW, Australia.

Scott, James C. (1985), *Weapons of the Weak: Everyday Forms of Peasant Resistance*, Yale University Press, New Haven.

Sen, A. (1999), *Development as Freedom*, Alfred A. Knopf, New York, pp. 3.

Serageldin, I. (1997), *Sustainability and the Wealth of Nations: A Work in Progress*, World Bank, Washington, DC.

Severino, H. G. (1997a), 'Fraud in the Forests', in C. C.A. Balgos (ed.), *Saving the Earth: The Philippine Experience*, fourth edition, Philippine Center for Investigative Journalism, Pasig City, pp. 36-42.

Soroos, M. (1994), 'Global Change, Environmental Security, and the Prisoner's Dilemma', *Journal of Peace Research*, Vol. 31(3), pp. 317-32.

'Southeast Asian Activists Call for a Regional Waste Trade Ban', *Toxic Trade Update*, Vol. 6(3), 1993, pp. 5.

'South Pacific Forum to Negotiate a Regional Waste Trade Ban', *Toxic Trade Update*, Vol. 6(3), 1993, pp. 4.

Spitalnik, E. (1992), *Hazardous Waste Management Legislation in Asia*, (mimeo) paper presented at 'International Chemical Regulation Briefing', Washington, DC, 12-13 November 1992, pp. 15.

Sugiartoto, A.D. (1996), 'The Loss of Agricultural Biodiversity: Do Farmers Have the Right to Conserve It?', *Ecosounder*, No. 16, October, pp. 8.

Talaue-McManus, L., Yambao, A. C., Salmo, S. III, and Altilde, P. (1998), *Participatory Coastal Development Planning in Bolinao, Northern Philippines: A Potent Tool for Conflict Resolution*, Conflict Management Case Study, IDRC.

Tarrow, S. (1996), 'Making Social Science Work Across Space and Time: A Critical Reflection on Robert Putnam's Making Democracy Work', *American Political Science Review*, Vol. 90, pp. 389-397.

Taylor, A. (1996), 'Third World looks to First World Cast-offs', *Financial Times*, 16 January, pp. 5.

Taylor, M. (1982), *Community, Anarchy, and Liberty*, Cambridge University Press, Cambridge, pp. 34.

Teehankee, J. C. (1993), 'The State, Illegal Logging, and Environmental NGOs in the Philippines', *Kasarinlan: A Philippine Quarterly of Third World Studies*, Vol. 9(1), 3rd Quarter, pp. 19-34.

Townsend-Gault, I. (1994a), 'Testing the Waters: Making Progress in the South China Sea', *Harvard International Review*, Spring.

Townsend-Gault, I. (1994b), *Ocean Diplomacy, International Law, and the South China Sea*, preliminary draft paper presented at the 'Eighth Asia Pacific Roundtable', Kuala Lumpur, June 1994.

Townsend-Gault, I. (1994c), 'Part IV: SLOCs and Maritime Security', in B. Nagara and K.S. Balakrishnan (eds), *The Making of A Security Community in the Asia-Pacific*, ISIS Malaysia, Kuala Lumpur.

'The Philippines: Human Rights and Forest Management in the 1990s', *Human Rights Watch/Asia*, Vol. 8(3), April 1996.

The World Commission on Environment and Development (1987), *Our Common Future*, Oxford University Press, Oxford.

'Three Regions Move to Ban Waste Trade' (1993), *Toxic Trade Update*, Vol. 6(4), pp. 4-6.

Timmer, C. P. (1989), 'Indonesia's Experience with Rice Market Interventions', *Indonesian Food Journal*, Vol. 1(1), pp. 14.

Timmer, C. P. (1990), Crop Diversification in Rice-Based Agricultural Economies' *Indonesian Food Journal*, Vol. 1(2), pp. 16.

Timmer, C. P. (1991), 'Institutional Development: Indonesia's Experience in Stabilizing Rice Market', *Indonesian Food Journal*, Vol. 11(1), pp. 56.

Transenerg (1988), *Energy Conservation in Indonesia: Final Report*, Directorate General for Electricity and Energy Development, Department of Mines and Energy, Jakarta.

Triwahyudi, Muhshi, M. A. and Farchad, H. (1994), *HPH Dan Ekonomi Regional: Kasus Kalimantan Timur (Forest Concessions and Regional Economy: The East Kalimantan Case)*, WALHI, Jakarta.

Trood, R. (1996), 'The Asia Pacific Region, Economics and New Concepts of Security', in Center for Strategic and International Studies (CSIS), *The Role of Security and Economic Cooperation Structures in the Asia Pacific Region Indonesian and Australian Views*, CSIS, Jakarta.

Ullman, R. H. (1983), 'Redefining Security', *World Politics*, Vol. 8(1).

UNCTAD Division on TNCs and Investment (1995), *World Investment Report 1995: Transnational Corporations and Competitiveness*, UN, New York, pp. 58.

UNCTC (1992), *World Investment Directory 1992*, Asia and the Pacific, Vol. 1, UN, New York.

UNEP-Water Branch (1996), *Final Report of the United Nations Expert Assessment Mission to Marinduque Island, Philippines*, United Nations Environment Programme, Nairobi, September.

United Nations Conference on Environment and Development (UNCED) (1992), *Earth Summit: Agenda 21, The United Nations Programme of Action From Rio*, United Nations Conference on Environment and Development, Rio de Janeiro, Brazil.

United Nations Development Programme (UNDP) (1994), *Human Development Report 1994*, Oxford University Press, New York.

United Nations Economic and Social Commission for Asia and the Pacific (UNESCAP) (1991), *Sectoral Energy Demand Studies: Application of the End-Use Approach to Asian Countries*, ESCAP, Bangkok.

United Nations Environmental Program (UNEP) (1980), *Environmental Assessment Statement: A Test Model Presentation*, UNEP Regional Office and United Nations Asian and Pacific Development Institute, Bangkok, March, pp. 217.

United Nations Framework Convention on Climate Change (UNFCCC) (1997), *The Kyoto Protocol to the United Nations Framework Convention on Climate Change*, UNFCCC, Kyoto, Japan.

United Nations General Assembly (UNGA) (1992), *United Nations Framework Convention on Climate Change*, United Nations, Rio de Janeiro, Brazil.

United States Agency for International Development (USAID) (1992), *Indonesian Demand-Side Management*, USAID, Washington, DC.

United States International Development Agency (USAID) (1994), 'Environmental Policy, Regulations and Institutions of the ASEAN Member Countries', *Report of the ASEAN Environmental Improvement Project Submitted to the United States Agency for International Development*, USAID, Washington, DC.

Usher, A. D. (1988), 'Thailand Becomes a Waste Dump', *The Nation*, 26 June, reprinted in Third World Network, *Toxic Terror*, Third World Network, Penang, Malaysia, 1991, pp. 64.

Utrecht, A. and Sayogyo, P. (1992), 'Policies and Interventions', in M. Grijns *et al.* (eds). *Gender, Marginalisation and Rural Industries: Female entrepreneurs, wage workers and family workers in West Java*, Akatiga, Bandung, pp. 49-50.

van de Fliert, E. and Wiyanto (1996), 'A Road to Sustainability', *ILEIA: Newsletter for Ecologically Sound Agriculture*, Vol. 12(2), July, pp. 7.

Vitug, M. D. (1993a), *Power from the Forest: The Politics of Logging*, Philippine Center for Investigative Journalism, Manila, pp. 16-24, 29-32, 44.

Vitug, M. D. (1993b), 'Is There a Logger in the House?' in E. Gamalinda and S. Coronel (eds), *Saving the Earth: The Philippine Experience*, third edition, Philippine Center for Investigative Journalism, Manila, pp. 62-8.

Vitug, M. D. (1996c), 'A Tortuous Trek To Community Forestry', in S. Coronel (ed.), *Patrimony: 6 Case Studies on Local Politics and the Environment in the Philippines*, Philippine Center for Investigative Journalism, Manila, pp. 121-41.

Wahab, R. D. (1989), 'Overview on Food and Nutrition Policy in Indonesia', *Indonesian Food Journal*, Vol. 1(1), pp. 7.

Wallace, C. (1994), 'Asians Vie for Toxic Trade as Danes seek Ban on Waste from West', *Vancouver Sun*, 24 March, pp. A17.

Walters, P. (1997), 'Borneo's Tribal Backlash', *The Australian*, 22-23 February, pp. 28.

Warren, C. and Elston, K. (1994), 'Environmental Regulation in Indonesia', *Asia Paper No. 3*, University of Western Australia Press, Nedlands, pp. 6.

Watson, R.T. *et al.* (eds) (1996), *Climate Change 1995: Impacts, Adaptations and Mitigation of Climate Change: Scientific-Technical Analyses*, Cambridge University Press, Cambridge.

Westing, A.H. (ed.) (1986), *Global Resources and International Conflict: Environmental Factors in Strategic Policy and Action*, Oxford University Press, New York.

White, B. and Wiradi, G. (1989), 'Bases of Inequality in Javanese Villages', *Agrarian Transformations: Local Processes and the State in Southeast Asia*, in G. Hart, A. Turton and B. White (eds), University of California Press, Berkeley, pp. 298-9.

Wie, T. K. (1997), *Pengembangan Kemampuan Teknologi Industri di Indonesia*, University of Indonesia Press, Jakarta.

Wood, A. (1995), 'Asia/Pacific: Rising Star on the Chemical Stage', *Chemical Week*, 15 February, pp. 36.

'World Bank Endorses Disclosure of Emissions Data as Enforcement Technique', *International Environment Reporter*, Vol. 19(18), 4 September 1996, pp. 774-5.

World Bank (1996), *Solar Home Systems Project: Staff Appraisal Report, Indonesia*, Indonesia Policy and Operations Division, Country Department III, East Asia and Pacific Regional Office, The World Bank, Washington, DC.

World Bank (1997a), *New Measures of Wealth: Expanding the Measure of Wealth, Indicators of Environmentally Sustainable Development*, CSD Ed., Draft-for-Discussion, April.

World Bank (1997b), *Expanding the Measure of Wealth: Indicators of Environmentally Sustainable Development*, Environmentally Sustainable Studies and Monographs Series No. 17, The World Bank, Washington, DC.

World Bank (1999), *Indonesia: From Crisis to Opportunity*, World Bank Report, July.

World Wide Fund for Nature International Discussion Paper (1986), *Agriculture in the Uruguay Round: Implications for Sustainable Development in Developing Countries*, WWF, Gland, Switzerland.

Zarili, S., *et. al.*, (eds) (1997), *Eco-Labelling and International Trade*, Macmillan Press, London.

Index